"*City on the Verge* tells the story of the many Atlantans that are coming together through the creation of the Atlanta BeltLine. While this convergence is at times painful and uncomfortable, it is also long-overdue. Thanks to Mark Pendergrast for presenting his insightful observations about our past, our present, and the opportunity before us as we approach the future."

—Michael Halicki, executive director, Park Pride

"Atlanta is indeed a *City on the Verge*, as Mark Pendergrast observes—it aspires to remake itself into a vital, sustainable, livable mecca. Pendergrast weaves together lessons in urban design, local politics, history, and human nature that pull the reader in like a mystery. His book reinforces the famous Margaret Meade quote about the ability of a small group of dedicated people to bring about change."

—Dennis Creech, cofounder, Southface Energy Institute

City on the Verge

Also by Mark Pendergrast

For God, Country and Coca-Cola
Inside the Outbreaks
Uncommon Grounds
Beyond Fair Trade
Mirror Mirror
Victims of Memory
Japan's Tipping Point

Children's books:
Jack and the Bean Soup
Silly Sadie
The Godfool

CITY
ON
THE
VERGE

ATLANTA AND THE FIGHT FOR
AMERICA'S URBAN FUTURE

MARK PENDERGRAST

BASIC BOOKS

NEW YORK

Published by Basic Books, an imprint of Perseus Books, LLC., a subsidiary of Hachette Book Group, Inc.

Books published by Basic Books are available at special discounts for bulk purchases in the United States by corporations, institutions, and other organizations. For more information, please contact the Special Markets Department at Perseus Books, 2300 Chestnut Street, Suite 200, Philadelphia, PA 19103, or call (800) 810-4145, ext. 5000, or e-mail special.markets@ perseusbooks.com.

Designed by Jack Lenzo

Library of Congress Cataloging-in-Publication Data
Names: Pendergrast, Mark, author.
Title: City on the verge : Atlanta and the fight for America's urban future / Mark Pendergrast.
Description: New York : Basic Books, [2017] | Includes index.
Identifiers: LCCN 2016039907| ISBN 9780465054732 (hardcover) | ISBN 9780465094981 (electronic)
Subjects: LCSH: Urban renewal—Georgia—Atlanta. | Community development—Georgia—Atlanta. | City planning—Georgia— Atlanta. |Urban policy—Georgia—Atlanta. | Social stratification—Georgia—Atlanta.
Classification: LCC HT177.A77 P46 2017 | DDC 307.3/41609758231—dc23
LC record available at https://lccn.loc.gov/2016039907

10 9 8 7 6 5 4 3 2 1

To the memory of:
Willie Mae Pughsley (c. 1908–1975),
otherwise known as Nee by the Pendergrast family
and
John Brittain (Britt) Pendergrast Jr. (1917–2016),
my remarkable father, the epitome of a Southern gentleman—
kind, wise, smart, principled, humble, loving, and funny

This book is also dedicated to my equally remarkable mother,
Nan Schwab Pendergrast (1920–),
compassionate, ever-curious nature-lover and environmentalist,
human rights activist, and still my writing mentor
and biggest supporter

These two photos—of traffic on I-75/85 and bikers on the BeltLine—represent two sides of Atlanta.

CONTENTS

INTRODUCTION Atlanta's Livable Future ix

PART I: BUILDING THE BELTLINE

PROLOGUE Walking the BeltLine 3

CHAPTER 1 Ryan Gravel's Epiphany 13

CHAPTER 2 City on the Move 31

CHAPTER 3 First Bumps Along the BeltLine 47

CHAPTER 4 Two Atlantas: The Racial Divide 63

CHAPTER 5 Learning to Fly While Building an Airplane 85

CHAPTER 6 Mansions and Cat Holes 105

CHAPTER 7 A Stake in the Ground 121

CHAPTER 8 The Public's Health 137

CHAPTER 9 Impossible but Inevitable 155

PART II: NEIGHBORS

CHAPTER 10 East BeltLine: Chic, Walkable Neighborhoods 173

CHAPTER 11 South BeltLine: A Slow Dance to Better Communities 189

CHAPTER 12 West BeltLine: Trouble and Promise 203

CHAPTER 13 North BeltLine: Easy Streets 225

CHAPTER 14 Outside and Inside the BeltLine 243

CHAPTER 15 The Future of Atlanta 267

Epilogue: Georgia on My Mind 291

Acknowledgments 295

Glossary 299

Photo Credits 301

Note on Sources 303

Index 311

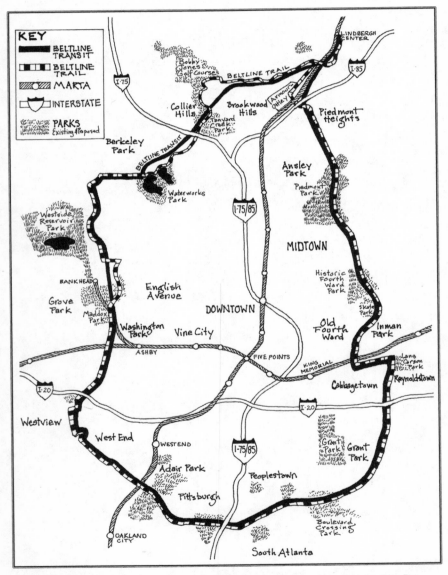

The Atlanta BeltLine. The black line is the twenty-two-mile planned streetcar corridor. The dotted line is the somewhat longer trail, which sometime departs from the corridor.

INTRODUCTION

ATLANTA'S LIVABLE FUTURE

Atlanta is on the brink of either tremendous rebirth or inexorable decline. At the center of a perfect storm of failed American urban policies, Atlanta has the highest income inequality, and its metro area features the longest commutes, in the country; attempts at twentieth-century urban renewal blasted highways through the city center and destroyed neighborhoods; suburban sprawl impaired the environment even as it eroded the urban tax base and exacerbated a long history of racial injustice. Although many cities across America suffer these problems, the issues have collided nowhere so conspicuously as in Atlanta.

Consequently, Atlanta's quest for reinvention maps onto America's broader struggle to renew its cities: to transcend racism, segregation, and gaping economic divides, to transition from cars to public transit and walkable environments, to find new prosperity in the ruins of vanished industries. Having undergone an extraordinary transformation in recent decades, the city is now on the verge of emerging from its adolescence to become a grown-up city, with enough density to support a web of public transit, plenty of parks connected by multiuse trails, bike-friendly streets, and opportunities for people in the most troubled neighborhoods to break the cycle of intergenerational poverty. Yet Atlanta has been on the verge of *something* for most of its relatively brief history, and there is a real danger that the city's leaders will opt, once again, for image over fundamental change. Atlanta cannot afford to wait any longer; nor can the country.

◆ ◆ ◆

The most promising symbol of the city's potential for rebirth is the Atlanta BeltLine. A twenty-two-mile ring of mostly defunct rail lines, running through forty-five neighborhoods girdling Atlanta's downtown,
the BeltLine is currently being transformed into a stunning pedestrian
walkway and potential streetcar line. The project's backers hope that it
will spur redevelopment, urban activism, community organizing, and
environmental awareness. Many see it is a model for the next American
city: walkable and accessible, diverse both economically and racially. Its
success will reflect a remarkable turn of events, since the BeltLine's rail
beds once served to segregate the city by race. Yet, as with all massive
social endeavors, the BeltLine has faced countless obstacles and fierce
critiques, including from those who fear that the project will displace the
city's poorer black residents with wealthier white ones.

City on the Verge dives deep into Atlanta's history but focuses on the
BeltLine's evolving struggles as emblematic of the greater forces sweeping
through the city and country at large. This potential "emerald necklace,"
as architect and city planner Alexander Garvin (who helped plan its new
parks) has called it, could rejuvenate the heart and soul of the city. The
Atlanta BeltLine also provides a wonderful lens for viewing the disparate
areas of the city, north, east, south, and west, rich and poor, white and
black. In literally encircling the city it provides a metaphorical narrative
hoop on which to organize the book, with forays into the inner city as
well as the outlying suburbs.

The success of the Atlanta BeltLine is key to the city's rejuvenation,
helping to reverse the late-twentieth-century "white flight" into the suburbs, which produced some of the worst sprawl in the country. You might
say that the battle over the BeltLine is a matter of life or death: Atlanta
could emerge as a truly great city—or it could fall back into congested
mediocrity.

Because Atlanta combines so many of the nation's urban ills, *City
on the Verge* provides a key to understanding the crises—and potential
renaissance—of American cities generally. "Americans sense that something is wrong with the places where we live and work and go about our
daily business," wrote social critic James Howard Kunstler in 1996. "We
drive up and down the gruesome, tragic suburban boulevards of commerce, and we're overwhelmed at the fantastic, awesome, stupefying ug-
liness of absolutely everything in sight . . . as though the whole thing
had been designed by some diabolical force bent on making human

beings miserable." Atlanta is an extreme case in point. Just a few years after Kunstler wrote, *Time* magazine featured it as the classic exemplar of American urban sprawl: "Once wilderness, [metro Atlanta is] now a 13-county eruption, one that has been called the fastest-spreading human settlement in history. What it leaves behind is tract houses, access roads, strip malls, off ramps, industrial parks and billboards advertising more tract houses where the peach trees used to be."

As a relatively low-density city surrounded by mall-studded suburbs, Atlanta most closely resembles other Sunbelt cities, such as Phoenix, Houston, Dallas, Miami, San Jose, and Los Angeles. The pressure on these urban centers to reinvent themselves through "smart growth" that fosters safe, affordable, dense, mixed-use, transit-friendly neighborhoods will only increase, as nearly 90 percent of US population growth over the next two decades is projected to occur there.

"Atlanta is traffic-obsessed to a degree that, among major American cities, perhaps only Los Angeles can match. And it is the place where traffic and demographic inversion [young adults and affluent retirees moving in to the city, while immigrants and the poor shift to the suburbs] seem . . . to be most closely tied together," wrote Alan Ehrenhalt in *The Great Inversion and the Future of the American City* (2012). Traffic obsessed, yes, because Atlanta is also traffic strangled. This city "has probably been the source of more bad transportation policy than any other in America," wrote David Owen in *Green Metropolis: Why Living Smaller, Living Closer, and Driving Less Are the Keys to Sustainability* (2009).

Unless Atlanta can reposition itself—no longer perceived as a congested, sprawling, auto-dependent area—it risks slowly dissolving into an amorphous urban shell, leaving isolated communities powerless to attract business, fix infrastructure, solve huge health problems, or resolve racial prejudice and income inequity.

Atlanta is not alone in its attempts to adjust to new urban realities. In the era of the automobile, American cities evolved into places that inadvertently made lives more harried and less healthy. Inner cities decayed. People sat in cars rather than biking or walking. Junk food was cheaper and easier to find than fresh fruit and vegetables. The "edge cities" surrounding the urban core, accessible only by automobile, leeched life and business from traditional downtowns. (In metro Atlanta, the oxymoronically named Perimeter Center exemplifies the phenomenon.) Over the past two decades, some US cities have clawed their way back to civility.

Eschewing suburban commuter hell, empty nesters and young professionals have relocated to innovative cities such as Portland, Oregon; Seattle, Washington; and Charlotte, North Carolina, which are far ahead of Atlanta in terms of livable initiatives such as bike lanes, trails, parks, and streetcars.

While not the only such urban project, the BeltLine is the most ambitious and transformative. And with its short, turbulent history, hubris, diversity, creative public-private partnerships, fraught politics, climate, and dramatically contrasting affluence and poverty, Atlanta can serve as a kind of petri dish for the remaking of a city. If it succeeds, it will offer hope and an example for other urban areas; if it fails, it will become a cautionary tale of epic proportions: *this is how to create an unlivable urban area.*

◆ ◆ ◆

So if Atlanta doesn't fail, what will its future look like? What could the BeltLine do for the urban core, for real estate and jobs as well as individuals and families? Here is a hopeful vision:

Atlanta, 2030. John and Susan live in the NuGrape Lofts on Ralph McGill Boulevard, right on the BeltLine. On summer nights, they sit out on the old cement loading dock, enjoying a glass of wine as people stroll by, walking their dogs, romancing, or looking for a bite to eat. Rollerbladers and cyclists zip along in their own lanes. Every few minutes, a streetcar clangs by. On workdays, John walks north on the BeltLine past the Historic Fourth Ward Park, admiring the sunken pond and its amphitheater surrounded by terraces, fountains, and boardwalks, then turns left across a pedestrian bridge to the huge Ponce City Market building, where he works in a café. On his way home, he sometimes ventures a bit farther south on the BeltLine to watch kids perform terrifying maneuvers in the skateboard park. Susan grabs the streetcar, changing at North Avenue to head west toward Georgia Tech, where she is an administrator. On weekends, John and Susan often jump on their bikes to explore the city and the many parks along the twenty-two-mile BeltLine trail that circles it. They can also veer off on spur trails into the city or connect to the Silver Comet trail going toward Alabama. Riding gives them a more holistic feel for Atlanta than driving. The view of the city skyline constantly shifts. They

share the trail and the city with people of all shades and ethnicities—
African Americans, whites, Hispanics, Koreans, Bosnians, Soma-
lis, gays, straights, pensioners, children. They ride past some of the
wealthiest as well as some of the poorest city neighborhoods, though
all property near the BeltLine has gone up in value, as more people
move into the corridor.

Despite many unanticipated setbacks, Atlanta is already realizing
this vision straight out of the "new urbanism" playbook.* The NuGrape
building, headquarters for the soda pop company from 1937 through
1971, has indeed been converted into high-ceilinged lofts, and residents
really do sit out on the former loading dock on summer nights. The Historic Fourth Ward Park, with its nearby skateboard area, was finished in
2011, and the massive old Sears warehouse on Ponce de Leon Avenue is
now the Ponce City Market, a combined retail, residential, and commercial space. The 2.25-mile Eastside Trail section that goes by the NuGrape
Lofts was paved, landscaped, and completed in late 2012. In December
2014, the city inaugurated an east-west streetcar loop—the first in the
city since 1949—through the downtown area, which may eventually link
into the BeltLine system.**

The restoration of the long-empty Sears behemoth and the replacement of a flood-prone area of abandoned warehouses and decaying businesses with a large park are near-miracles in a city that has specialized in
tearing down historic buildings and underfunding even its existing parks.
And the BeltLine itself, its Eastside Trail jammed with pedestrians, bikers, and dog walkers, is perhaps the greatest miracle, repurposing a derelict corridor of mostly abandoned rail lines as a combination of trails,
parks, mixed-income housing, retail and office space, and possible public
transit that may revitalize the city.

Twenty-two percent of Atlanta's population lives along the BeltLine,
which is, according to land use strategist Christopher Leinberger, "the
most important rail-transit project that's been proposed in the country,

---

* "New urbanism," a term that dates from the 1980s, is actually not so new, since it
   seeks to recapture positive elements of preautomobile city life, promoting walkability,
   public transit such as streetcars, mixed-use developments, and peaceful, active parks.
** The streetcar loop, which runs in traffic, has low ridership and has been managed
   poorly. It remains to be seen whether the BeltLine will host streetcars in addition to
   bikers, runners, and walkers.

possibly in the world." *New York Times* reporter Richard Fausset called the BeltLine "a staggeringly ambitious engine of urban revitalization." Kaid Benfield of the Natural Resources Defense Council deemed it "the country's best smart growth project . . . so enormous, so multifaceted, so ambitious and potentially transformative, and so complicated that it is difficult to know where to start."

The story of how the BeltLine began in 1999, as a master's thesis by an unknown architectural grad student named Ryan Gravel, developed a grassroots following, and ultimately gained acceptance from Atlanta's mayors, corporations, and nonprofits, all the while pushing through various obstacles that threatened to derail the project, is complicated and fascinating. And although particular to this city's struggle to create the BeltLine, the convoluted politics, legal issues, and improvisational strategies should inform other urban efforts, which inevitably face their own challenges. The often overlooked but crucial metropolis of Atlanta can inform the future of our cities nationwide, with their own all-too-familiar woes.

But this book goes well beyond the BeltLine project, transformative as it may be. It also analyzes the city and region, looking at such issues as transportation, race, housing, education, religion, the environment, energy, public health, business, politics, and the economy. Mirroring the spur trails off the BeltLine, spur sections discuss related places and subjects.

Still, the BeltLine remains the project that will link disparate areas of the city. Though this massive undertaking will take at least another decade or two to complete, undoubtedly encountering many more bumps along the way, it is well under way, supported with funds stemming from Home Depot, Coca-Cola, Cox Enterprises, and UPS, among others. The city government is squarely behind the effort.

In *Makeshift Metropolis: Ideas About Cities* (2010), Witold Rybcynski noted, "Large cities currently have a number of significant disincentives: faltering school systems, high tax burdens, unwieldy municipal bureaucracies, poor services, and unresponsive governments." Again, God knows, Atlanta has provided ample evidence. But with the BeltLine maintaining the momentum generated by its grassroots origins, the city government has become more responsive; services are improving, and schools are likely to follow in time. Still, this story is far from over and involves failures and looming questions as well as successes.

Although set in the present with a view to the future, *City on the Verge* draws on a rich historical context. A century ago, cities may have been dirty and polluted, but they were dense, vital hubs of industry and commerce. Workers lived in neighborhoods near factories (like Atlanta's Cabbagetown, near the Fulton Bag and Cotton Mill) serviced by railroads. Wealthier people lived further out along the streetcar lines in the first suburbs (like Inman Park). During the 1920s, the automobile began to change that way of life and culture. In the postwar era, desegregation and white flight to the suburbs hollowed out downtowns, a trend ultimately tied to important public health issues such as air pollution, global warming, water availability, affordable housing, and increased obesity.

Still a young city, Atlanta has yet to clearly define itself or its future. After General William Tecumseh Sherman reduced it to ashes in 1864 during the Civil War, it re-created itself as the "Phoenix City," and it has been reinventing itself ever since, boasting about the "Atlanta Spirit," labeling itself "the World's Next Great City," all the while unsure of its real character. "If Atlanta could suck as well as it blows, it would be a sea port," one cynic observed in the 1890s, implying that Atlantans were blowhards. Although never a typical Southern city, it has that patina of gracious living cheek by jowl with hardscrabble poverty. It has precious few historic buildings, having routinely torn down the old and thrown up new skyscrapers (or parking lots, stadiums, and convention centers). Unplanned development has rendered metro Atlanta a mishmash of malls and crowded expressways, with mostly segregated neighborhoods surrounding a hollowed-out downtown core. Its public schools are deeply troubled.

Yet Atlanta remains a tremendously appealing place to live. People who move to the city for their own or a spouse's job usually come to love its diversity, energy, distinctive neighborhoods, restaurants, theater, museums, music, sports, and recreational opportunities. More young people are choosing to live "in-town," helping to rejuvenate troubled neighborhoods. For a major metropolitan area, Atlanta still retains a small-town, intimate feel. Everybody seems to know everyone else, along with the latest gossip. And yes, it does indeed foster a type of Southern hospitality you won't find in New York. Amid accents of all kinds, you'll still hear "How y'all doin' today?" Although the summers can be brutally hot and humid, nothing makes you appreciate a swimming pool or ice-cold Coca-Cola more, and then there are the warm, magical summer nights. Atlanta winters are mild; springtime explodes with daffodils, azaleas, and dogwoods; and the autumn is long and mellow.

Atlanta offers diversity in all senses of the word. It is a troubled, dynamic, appealing, contradictory city, and the BeltLine project has the potential to envelope it with a livable new urbanism where people can walk and bike, enjoy parks, and get around on streetcars (or bus rapid transit) and rapid transit. The BeltLine will link to new urban farms whose fresh food can contribute to better health, along with an active lifestyle.

◆ ◆ ◆

As an Atlanta native with a profound personal involvement with the city, I now live far away in northern Vermont. Yet I have continued to monitor the problems and progress of my birthplace through the years as I have returned to visit family and friends, as well as to research two other Atlanta-related books (*For God, Country, and Coca-Cola* and *Inside the Outbreaks*).

I wrote most of *City on the Verge* in standard journalistic third person, but readers will find me popping up in the first person throughout the book. I grew up in the city, and my family's roots in the region extend back generations. I was born on October 1, 1948, the year before the decommissioning of Atlanta's last streetcars in favor of trackless trolleys (buses with overhead electric lines), themselves soon replaced by diesel-fuming buses. I recall my father giving the finger to Ku Klux Klansmen as we drove past the field where they were burning a cross in Marietta. During my childhood African Americans had separate schools, bathrooms, and drinking fountains. Like most upscale families, we had a black maid, whom I loved deeply, though I knew virtually nothing about the part of town in which she lived.

As a teenager, I worked for a summer as a welder's assistant at Southern Cross Industries (formerly the Southern Spring Bed Company), where my father was an executive. My great grandfather had founded the business in 1884, two years before Coca-Cola was invented in Atlanta, in the same era that produced the BeltLine railroads, which skirted the overburdened central rail junctions and helped to open the outlying area to industry. Today that bedding factory on Martin Luther King Jr. Drive (formerly Hunter Street) has been converted into the Mattress Factory Lofts. Ironically, MLK Jr. also worked there for a summer as an adolescent.

I remember when the "Atlanta Population Now" sign on Peachtree Street, which tracks the growth of metropolitan Atlanta, broke 1 million people in 1959 (it now exceeds 6 million in a thirty-nine-county area, projected to swell to 8 million by 2040). I remember when Interstate 75 plowed through the red clay near my home on West Paces Ferry Road in the 1960s.

That road was named for the man who operated a ferry across the nearby Chattahoochee River. I used to canoe on its muddy waters, colored and polluted by the runoff from eroded developments upstream. I knew that Native Americans once lived there too. I found their arrowheads in the woods. On a school trip, I visited the Etowah Indian Mounds, where ancestors of the Creek Indians lived 1,000 years ago. On a family vacation to the mountains of North Carolina, I watched *Unto These Hills*, a dramatization of the 1838–1839 expulsion of the Cherokees along the "Trail of Tears."

Yet it didn't occur to me that European settlers had killed or driven out the Creek and Cherokee who used to live in what I knew as Atlanta. And despite unearthing musket balls from the Civil War, seeing *Gone with the Wind* (which premiered in Atlanta in 1939), and visiting the Cyclorama near the Grant Park Zoo, it didn't occur to me that this war was fought because those white men had imported and enslaved the Africans whose ancestors provided domestic servants for the wealthy enclave in which I grew up. Like most children, I simply accepted my world as the given order. Only in retrospect did I recognize what a small and privileged bubble that world represented.

So the research for this book has in many ways given me an opportunity to explore my native city for the first time. I have walked the entire BeltLine and stayed overnight with kind hosts in its wildly disparate surrounding neighborhoods. I have interviewed hundreds of people, ranging from the homeless, to Mayor Kasim Reed and former mayors Shirley Franklin and Sam Massell, to BeltLine and neighborhood leaders and activists present and past. I have also spent time in Gwinnett County to the north; Clayton County to the south; Decatur, Clarkston, and Stone Mountain to the east; and Serenbe to the southwest.

All of this has reminded me once again what a marvelous, crazy blend of a city Atlanta is, where a chic, upscale restaurant like Two Urban Licks, housed in a cavernous former warehouse right next to the BeltLine in the Old Fourth Ward, lies only minutes from Bedford Pine, a subsidized housing complex along Boulevard Avenue that is notorious for drug deals, crime, and prostitution. The ultramodern reflective skyscrapers of Buckhead and Peachtree lift out of concrete pads that ooze red clay. With more trees than any other major American urban area, Atlanta looks like a forest from on high, and the whole city thrums on a summer night with the sound of cicadas and the scent of magnolias. Yet it has a paucity of parks compared to most other American metropolises and is one of the least pedestrian-friendly cities in the world.

Walking the BeltLine, interviewing the homeless, the police, the neighbors, the drug dealers, the activists, the developers, the hustlers, the hip-hop artists, the new immigrants, the entrepreneurs, the academics, the students, the nouveau riche, and the old guard, I have sought to connect the dots of past and present, rich and poor, black and white. The BeltLine, in encircling the city, connects areas whose inhabitants hardly know one another now. It has also served for me as a kind of metaphor in a personal journey of reconnection and discovery.

I am opinionated and passionate about my native city. Nonetheless, I won't express many opinions again until the final chapter. I prefer to let the facts and characters speak for themselves so that readers are free to make their own judgments. By the time I offer my own, perhaps those conclusions will dovetail with yours, based on the stories you've read—or perhaps not.

A road map of the book you're about to read is necessary. The contents reflect original research, extensive historical reading, news synthesis, nearly four hundred interviews, and old-fashioned shoe-leather journalism. In Part One, chapter styles trade off with one another. One set of chapters offers an unbroken linear narrative of the BeltLine's evolution and struggle, while alternating chapters offer expansive perspectives on Atlanta's history, transportation and racial issues, housing, public health, urban planning, education, and more. Part Two offers a panoramic view of the city from the ground level, with chapters exploring the neighborhoods adjacent to the BeltLine, towns "outside the Perimeter"— or OTP—of the city proper, and, finally, the troubled downtown "hole" in the BeltLine donut. By the end we've brought the story up to date and look to Atlanta's future.

That future looks hopeful but is by no means etched in stone. There is no guarantee that the entire BeltLine loop and other sustainable development efforts will be completed. The city doesn't even own the entire BeltLine right-of-way—the railroads still own about 40 percent—and the project has really just begun. Its financing remains unclear, as does whether streetcars will (or should) parallel the trail. Yet it is a good and worthy fight, one that has inspired the city in ways I never could have imagined just a few years ago. I hope you will take inspiration from the effort and join me in rooting for my hometown and the rest of America's cities.

BUILDING THE BELTLINE

Part I explains how the BeltLine developed, bringing the story to the end of 2015. Alternating chapters explore relevant Atlanta history and other issues, such as race and health.

WALKING THE BELTLINE

On a mild December day in 2011, I am walking the southern half of the Atlanta BeltLine with Ryan Gravel, whose 1999 thesis inspired this enormous project to lay trail, transit, and parks along a twenty-two-mile loop. Abandoned for decades, the loop had been all but forgotten, even as it encircled the city's downtown and touched dozens of neighborhoods. When we began our walk, the project was five years along, had overcome extraordinary opposition, and was already galvanizing the city.

A tall, lanky man in his late thirties, Gravel speaks calmly, logically, and sparingly, almost in a monotone. His hair turned white a decade ago, giving him a certain gravitas. No one could accuse him of having a dynamic presence; yet his determined advocacy for his vision of a rejuvenated Atlanta, anchored by this loop of former (and current) railroad beds, shines through in everything he says and does.

We met this morning at the Inman Park Metropolitan Atlanta Rapid Transit Authority (MARTA) station on the southeastern side of the city, then walked through the station and over the Hulsey Rail Yard, a large terminal for trains. This is one of three places along the BeltLine that pose major obstacles and discontinuities—where it is unclear how to connect the trail-transit loop seamlessly. Will CSX, the railroad that owns the Hulsey Yard, agree to sell and move? Or will the BeltLine tunnel under it, go around it, or find some other solution? Walking the BeltLine today shows me something I haven't fully grasped before: how very physical the act of renewal is, the necessity of contending with the city as it is to build something better.

Ryan Gravel on the future BeltLine, December 2011

Then we walk west down Wylie Street past the rail yard and turn left, heading south onto the future BeltLine, the beginning of a three-mile stretch where a train brings sand twice a week to a concrete plant, the sole remaining customer on this dead-end stretch.

We walk through Reynoldstown to the left and Cabbagetown to the right, two of the forty-five neighborhoods along the BeltLine. Cabbage-town, where poor white employees of the local cotton mill once lived, has become a trendy enclave in the past few years. Today, however, we will walk through some of the poorer south and west Atlanta neighborhoods, mostly African American, while more affluent, largely white neighbor-hoods lie to the north and east.

Just before we cross Memorial Drive we pass an old railroad depot converted into an upscale restaurant; to the right are the new Lofts at Reynoldstown Crossing, built in an old Triumph motorcycle factory, with a few affordable units subsidized by the BeltLine project.

Now we walk along Bill Kennedy Way, crossing Interstate 20, one of the few places where the planned BeltLine streetcars must run in the street rather than along defunct railroad lines. To the left is Glenwood Park, a new urban community built in 2006 by Mindspring founder

Charles Brewer. With its Drip Coffeehouse, restaurants, and townhouses, it exemplifies the relatively dense, mixed-used development that the Belt-Line should attract.

We walk past a huge pile of sand near the concrete plant, then through a wooded area along the track. To the left is a hill covered with kudzu that Gravel says will one day be a park. A billboard looms above with a message from the Mormons. Two red-tailed hawks fly overhead. To the right through the trees, we can see the towers of downtown Atlanta. If I couldn't see them, I ponder, I might think I was on a country road, even though the BeltLine is usually within a three-mile radius of the heart of the city. Yet I know that the Grant Park neighborhood is on our right, and Ormewood Park is on our left.

As I walk around the southern half of the BeltLine today, I am struck by how the city views shift and shade with different angles and times of day. Because the railroad grade had to remain relatively level, despite Atlanta's location in the rolling foothills of the Appalachian Mountains, the corridor sometimes rises above people's backyards. In some places it runs through old warehouse rows; in others it burrows through beautiful old tunnels and runs in cuts below street level. During long stretches you can see the connected contours of the city and its rolling hills and creeks as you never could from a car.

When Ryan Gravel first walked the BeltLine, in places he had to bushwhack through this kudzu corridor.

We walk past derelict concrete pads where public housing units were razed in the past decade (as were most of the "projects" in Atlanta), past makeshift chicken coops from which we hear crowing. "Fighting cocks," Gravel says. But aren't they illegal? "Of course," he says, deadpan.

Now we reach the Peoplestown neighborhood on the right, where we leave the trail to walk through the adjacent D. H. Stanton Park, one of the newly renovated parks along the BeltLine. Built atop an old landfill, the playground once seeped unremediated methane gas until the day a little girl caught fire as she came down a sliding board and apparently created a spark. She survived, but the park was bulldozed. Now it features solar panels, a splash pad, and a new playground.

Angel Poventud joins us at Stanton Park. A CSX conductor who runs trains through the northwestern section along the future BeltLine (the only truly active rail section), Poventud is among the BeltLine's most enthusiastic devotees. He probably knows the corridor better than Gravel, having walked it dozens of times in the past three years. His answering machine identifies him as "Angel of the BeltLine." Upbeat and friendly, with a bushy head of curly black hair, Poventud is a familiar figure in Atlanta.

We continue to walk along the BeltLine, past a derelict warehouse now serving as a paintball battleground. "Over there is a carpet recycling plant," Poventud says. "In the summer, when they are busiest, everything around here is covered in carpet fiber. It's pretty terrifying. Don't hang out there too long."

We pass a burned hulk, a former city maintenance facility, then swing west under Interstate 75/85. Beyond the bridge on the right is a gigantic, abandoned thirty-one-acre asphalt lot that once served as a truck transfer station. Beyond it lies Pittsburgh, one of the poorest African American neighborhoods in Atlanta. To the left is Capitol View Manor, still troubled but in better shape and, as the name implies, offering a view of the capitol's gold dome. "I live down there," Gravel says, "past those trees."

We now walk on a dirt path, the rails removed. Only a few years ago, this trail was nearly impassable because of the kudzu, and few ventured here other than the homeless, who established makeshift shelters. Some stretches are still overgrown with weeds and strewn with trash, despite repeated cleanup efforts. I am reminded of Ryan Gravel's advice e-mailed before our BeltLine hike: "Sneakers should be fine—it used to be that I would recommend bringing a machete and a snake-bite kit, but fortunately those are no longer necessary."

A little farther along, Poventud leads us to the right through some trash and vines onto Lexington Avenue by Adair Park. "This is my house," he says. We take a tour of this small home in which no one could possibly live, with peeling paint, fallen ceilings, and black mold. Poventud bought it for $14,000 and plans to fix it up. "I'll live here someday, right on the BeltLine!" he asserts. The drug dealers next door recently moved out, he adds hopefully.

We resume our northward trek on the BeltLine, under a three-bay bridge that holds Murphy Avenue, Lee Street, and MARTA and railroad lines. Here Poventud calls out to Abraham, a homeless man who has lived for nine years in a jury-rigged lean-to under the bridge. Water puddles amid the garbage.

We continue past West End to the right and the Westview neighborhood on the left, where a sign says, "Hosea Feed the Homeless." Soon the corridor narrows as we walk down Warehouse Row, as Gravel calls it, a forlorn stretch of mostly abandoned industrial buildings, then through a gulley below street level, past Enota Park on the left (to be expanded as part of the BeltLine project), and under I-20 again, as the interstate runs west out of the city. A branch of Proctor Creek originates near here in the Mozley Park neighborhood, though it is often buried and terribly polluted as it runs north toward the Chattahoochee River.

In the early twentieth century, most of these neighborhoods were upper-class white streetcar suburbs, as was Adair Park. After World War II, when whites fled to the suburbs and poorer African Americans moved in, neighborhood stores and industries failed, and the area fell into decline. Aside from the Kroger and Big Bear supermarkets in West End, the area is a "food desert," with junk food and liquor far easier to find than fruits and vegetables.

We end our day, late in the afternoon, in the Washington Park neighborhood on the west side, halfway around the loop.

◆ ◆ ◆

Four months later, in April 2012, I meet Ryan Gravel and Angel Poventud again at Washington Park to resume our walk clockwise around the northern part of the BeltLine. This time, however, our route is not so straightforward. Because much of the northwestern corridor still hosts active freight trains (with Poventud often driving them), it isn't clear where the BeltLine will go. A map shows two alternate routes, to the east and west, both of which somehow have to traverse Howell Junction, a valley of five converging rail lines.

We walk north through an encampment created by "urban home-steaders," as Poventud describes those who have erected tents and hovels amid the weeds. We then have a choice—we can attempt to follow a kudzu-choked abandoned line (nearly impassable) to the right or follow a CSX line, the easier route, under Joseph E. Boone Boulevard. We take the latter. Then we turn right onto another CSX rail line that goes north through Maddox Park, once a beautiful recreation area, now taken over by drug dealers. The swimming pool lies empty and cracked, and the homeless camp out in the clubhouse. The surrounding Bankhead and Grove Park areas are among the poorest neighborhoods in Atlanta, and we can see boarded up homes as we walk along the train track. Nearby, to the west, is a huge old quarry that will be filled with water, the center-piece of a future Westside Park, which will be the crowning jewel of the new BeltLine parks.

At this point we leave the railroad track to walk along a series of roads. We pass by the King Plow Arts Center, a repurposed industrial site, on West Marietta Street. Gravel says that he would prefer this route, when the BeltLine is eventually built here, but he is philosophical about the outcome. "This isn't the kind of project you can control. You are just lucky to participate in it." We scurry through a hole in a fence and down a hill to Howell Junction, a dense and (to me) terrifying conjunction of railroad lines. "Don't worry," Poventud assures me. "The trains go really slow through here."

We continue north, following another CSX line under Huff Road, past the Atlanta Waterworks on the right, under Howell Mill Road, over Northside Drive, and under I-75, which runs northwest toward Chatta-nooga. Now we have crossed over into stabler, more well-to-do, predom-inantly white areas, with Berkeley Park and Collier Hills to the left and Loring Heights and Atlantic Station to the right.

In most of this northwestern quadrant, the BeltLine trail will proba-bly separate from the planned transit. On the train track, we cross a high wooden trestle (after ascertaining that no trains are coming), below which the Northside BeltLine Trail already runs alongside Tanyard Creek. (I had walked this bucolic path with my brother, who lives nearby.)

We follow the railroad track under Collier Road, named for a pioneering Atlanta resident, and on the right we pass Piedmont Hospital, the largest employer on the potential BeltLine. The CSX rail we're following now curves due east and runs under Peachtree Street, the central spine of Atlanta. On the right lies Brookwood Hills, a neighborhood of lovely homes established in the 1920s. We leave the track briefly to visit Peachtree Creek, which here runs parallel on the left over some riffling rapids.

Now we approach the Armour/Ottley Yard on our right, a light industrial area that is home to MARTA's maintenance facility, various rail lines, and businesses such as SweetWater Brewing Company. At this point, near the northern end of the BeltLine, we scramble up a twenty-foot slope, leaving the CSX line and climbing to the Norfolk Southern track, which we will follow south along the loop's eastern edge. Somehow the BeltLine transit will have to make this vertical climb more gradually.

I am feeling overwhelmed with the enormity of this BeltLine project and how much it's going to cost: at least $4 billion. It has to surmount so many physical challenges, including brownfields remediation, installation of handicap-accessible ramps to adjacent neighborhoods, and earthmoving to create a corridor next to the active railroad line. It has yet to obtain the rights to almost half of the corridor.

When I give vent to my concerns, Ryan Gravel answers calmly. "Sure, there are all these obstacles to be overcome, but this is not rocket science. Look at how they created Spaghetti Junction," he says, referring to the complicated, expensive knot of stacked expressway interchanges north of Atlanta where I-85 and I-285 (the Perimeter) meet.

"Look at the new international terminal at the airport. I mean, they built an entire runway over the interstate there." He is referring to the terminal about to open at Atlanta's airport, which took four years to complete and cost $1.4 billion. "Sure, this is a complex, expensive, long-term project, but it can be done." *He's right*, I think. *We're used to paying insane amounts for other forms of transportation. Why not this streetcar and trail loop?*

The afternoon sun on this spring day slants down on two drunks asleep near the tracks. We step around them on our walk south, leaving the Piedmont Heights neighborhood to our left. A golf course abuts the railroad to the right, and beyond it we can see the beautiful winding, tree-shaded roads of Sherwood Forest and Ansley Park, upscale white suburbs. We pass Ansley Mall on the left, skirting the rear parking lot and businesses that currently face away from the unused rail corridor we're walking on. We enter Piedmont Park and cross Clear Creek several times as we continue south on the dirt path that follows the former rail line. Passing a dog park on the right, we end our walk at the Park Tavern just before the BeltLine trail crosses the busy intersection at Monroe Drive near 10th Street.

◆ ◆ ◆

On a previous day, wearing a hard hat that Ángel Poventud lent me, I had already walked with him along the remaining 2.25 miles of the Belt-Line, from this point down to DeKalb Avenue, where it dead-ends into the Hulsey Rail Yard, near the Inman Park Station, where this walking tour began.

This section, called the Eastside Trail, was under construction, the first segment of the BeltLine to be completed later in 2012. Poventud and I had seen the huge old Sears building looming to the right as we crossed Ponce de Leon Avenue, named for the springs from which Clear Creek sprang—now buried somewhere under pavement near the Sears building, which was being renovated into Ponce City Market.

We walked past the Historic Fourth Ward Park, just nearing completion to our right, past Two Urban Licks, the restaurant in an old warehouse to the left, and the skateboard park on the right. Multistory apartment buildings rose like mushrooms in this new area, quickly becoming one of the hottest in Atlanta. The Old Fourth Ward, birthplace of Martin Luther King Jr. and until recently mostly African American, was gentrifying, with quite a racial mix. Part of the BeltLine mandate is to provide thousands of affordable housing units, but already surging rents were forcing lower-income residents out of this neighborhood. This issue will challenge Atlanta, a city with vast economic inequities, in years to come.

◆ ◆ ◆

I walked the twenty-two-mile BeltLine loop at the beginning of my research for this book, which took another four years to complete. The Eastside Trail, opened in October 2012, was an immediate hit. On weekends, it is jammed with bikes, rollerbladers, baby carriages, strolling couples, and dog walkers. In the fall of 2014, Ponce City Market, still in development, rented its first apartments, as restaurants and other businesses began to move in.

As this book goes to press, the Westside Trail is nearing completion, but it's not clear whether it will jump-start development in the poverty-stricken area. Most of the BeltLine project remains uncompleted. The next step could be acquisition of the defunct southern CSX rail line that will connect the Eastside and Westside Trails. Meanwhile, the city already owns the trail running north through Piedmont Park from the end of the Eastside Trail, and construction could proceed there. The huge acreage around the former quarry remains undeveloped, with the nearby northwestern stretch of the BeltLine left as the last challenge in an area with active rail. Not one streetcar has yet rolled along the corridor.

The Atlanta BeltLine has been a long time coming and may miss its 2030 deadline for completion, but it is happening, and what began as a master's thesis and grassroots movement may indeed help to transform Atlanta into one of the most desirable cities in the country. If its progress thus far is any indication, however, the path will be full of unanticipated challenges.

CHAPTER 1
RYAN GRAVEL'S EPIPHANY

···

When the design of public infrastructure directs private action, architecture and planning become political.

—Ryan Gravel, *Belt Line—Atlanta*, December 1999 master's thesis

Most summer mornings in 1995, Ryan Gravel, then twenty-two, sat behind his steering wheel in the I-285 Perimeter gridlock as he drove from his suburban home in north Chamblee, Georgia, to work as an intern at Fowler Design Associates, an Atlanta architecture firm. He hated the commute. "There are a lot of great things about Atlanta, but this wasn't one of them, and I was quite miserable," he recalled. He daydreamed about the spring when, as a college senior at the Georgia Institute of Technology (Georgia Tech), he had studied in Paris at the École Nationale Supérieure d'Architecture de Paris–La Villette. What a contrast! Taking the metro or walking everywhere, he hadn't needed a car. "I was in the best shape of my life. I lost twenty pounds in a month and felt great." Pedestrian-friendly neighborhoods, all with their own markets offering fresh food, dotted the city. Life was more civilized and healthy. Why couldn't Atlanta be like that?

Nor was Gravel happy with his job at Fowler, where he designed suburban malls. "I felt I was part of the problem." In the fall of 1996, after the Atlanta Summer Olympics, Gravel returned to Georgia Tech to earn a joint master's degree in architecture and city planning. As he searched for a thesis topic, he thought about the old Atlanta rail lines he had explored as an undergrad. Also, as part of his graduate work, he had compiled a facilities inventory for the Atlanta Public Schools, which took him into every city neighborhood. "My experience touring around, combined with knowledge of the old rail lines, got me interested in how connected these communities could be." He realized that four of those lines—originally the Atlanta & Richmond Air-Line Railway, Seaboard Air Line Railway, Atlanta & West Point Belt Line, and Louisville & Nashville Railroad Belt Line—encircled the city, within two or three miles of the downtown area, and ran through dozens of diverse neighborhoods.

By the late 1800s, a spiderweb of rail lines had converged in Atlanta's congested downtown area. These four freight lines had been built to bypass the central train terminal. In response, industries sprang up along the new rails, then in surrounding neighborhoods. After World War II, however, with the domination of trucks, cars, and national businesses, most rail service dwindled or died, as did the associated industries.

When Gravel explored the area on foot, he found barren stretches of track made virtually impassable by kudzu, the ubiquitous Japanese vine widely planted in Georgia in the 1940s to control erosion. Abandoned warehouses and factories lined the tracks, where the homeless had thrown up encampments. On only one stretch of track in the northwestern sector did CSX still have a busy rail line. In another dead-end section to the southeast, trains ran sporadically to deliver sand to a concrete manufacturer. Why not turn this corridor into public transit? Gravel envisioned a Southern version of Paris, a revitalized city with local markets and connected neighborhoods. He would call it the Belt Line, named for a couple of the old rail segments.*

Not Entirely a New Idea

On hearing his idea for the BeltLine, Gravel's Georgia Tech advisor, Randal Roark, was immediately supportive. In fact, he told Gravel that his epiphany wasn't entirely new. "It's similar to the Cultural Ring project I worked on before the 1996 Olympics." Roark had served as the planning director for the Corporation for Olympic Development in Atlanta (CODA), when Starling Sutton, a real estate developer and community

---

* The term would later be contracted to BeltLine. To avoid confusion, I have used the latter term in this book, other than in direct quotes with other usage.

activist, approached him with a novel idea—which he called the Cultural Ring—that he had been working on since the 1980s. He wanted to use eighteen miles of the abandoned rail corridor as a venue for tourists, connecting unique cultural and artistic sites in Atlanta.

In the early 1990s, Sutton was helping to convert two vacant industrial buildings, the old King Plow factory on Marietta Street and the abandoned Candler cotton compress factory on Auburn Avenue, into artists' studios and lofts (the current King Plow Arts Center and Studioplex). Both would be part of the Cultural Ring. In the end, nothing came of the project, other than interesting academic projects for Roark's Georgia Tech architecture students. Now, Roark showed some of them to Gravel.

Intrigued, Gravel studied the Cultural Ring concept, but it seemed unworkable to him as described, and it ignored the southern route he had identified. He wasn't interested in a project to shuttle tourists around Atlanta. "I thought if we reused the corridor for real transit and combined it with appropriate changes to zoning and subdivision regulations, then it would also bring economic benefits and growth. The design of public infrastructure could ensure that the project accomplished more than just moving people around. It could change the city's growth patterns"—that is, suburban sprawl, downtown desertion, automobile addiction, racial divisions, and inequitable development.

As he conducted more research, Gravel found that the idea of repurposing the abandoned or underused rail corridors went back even further. He discovered that the initial 1960 plans for MARTA, the city's rapid transit line, followed the northeastern and northwestern sections of the BeltLine. He found an artist's mockup, showing a MARTA train running past the Sears building on Ponce de Leon Avenue along the northeastern stretch of his proposed BeltLine—eerily similar to Gravel's vision of a streetcar running along the same rail corridor.

In November 1989, the Rails to Trails Conservancy, then a three-year-old nonprofit based in Washington, DC, sponsored a study of abandoned rail corridors in the metropolitan Atlanta area. The subsequent report, completed in 1991, noted that 2,500 miles of Georgia railroad track had been abandoned, 340 miles of it in the previous five years, with 70 miles approaching the "chopping block." Yet Georgia had only a single, 1.5-mile rail-trail, in the city of Rome. "Atlanta has the opportunity to be pro-active instead of reactive to abandonment trends in the rail industry," the report stated. "Now is the time to begin converting the railroad's intricate pathway through city and county into a long curving park of beauty, resource and recreation for all the people of Atlanta."

The report detailed the ten rail lines entering Atlanta, along with their rail-trail potential, but it was most enthusiastic about the BeltLine idea, here called the Circle Line:

> As Atlanta surveys its sobering lack of open space and its diminishing prospects for linear greenways, the 20 miles of rail line circling downtown gain significance. Established at a time when the city's only concern was facilitating rail transportation, it presents an unexpected potential legacy for recreational development and community connection. To encircle a major American city with a combined 20-mile rail rotary and rail-trail park would be a feat of extraordinary vision and brilliant engineering. . . . The Circle Line is a living, albeit hidden, community corridor that connects Atlanta to Atlanta.
>
> Political leadership and community commitment will determine the Atlanta metropolitan area's rail-trail future. . . . It can only succeed if there is political will and public determination behind its mission.

The Rails to Trails Conservancy report was never made public. On the front of the copy I obtained from a former Georgia state director of the Trust for Public Land, someone had scrawled, "Not released due to political reasons. Excellent report." When I asked the report's author, Marianne Fowler, about it, she recalled that the report had been printed and she had already booked her ticket from Washington, DC, to Atlanta, when she learned that the publication's release had been cancelled. An anonymous source told her, "Your Circle Line would connect white and black Atlanta, and they don't want that."

It isn't clear which political entity squashed publication, but a little later in 1991 the idea resurfaced when Ed McBrayer created the PATH Foundation to plan, capitalize, and build a hard-surface trail system in and around Atlanta. McBrayer, a native of Gainesville, Georgia, had become a biking enthusiast during the fifteen years he lived in Colorado, where he switched from aerospace engineer to home builder. In 1986, he moved back to Atlanta, where he put his bike in the basement. "There was no safe place to ride, so there was very little cycling in Atlanta," he recalled. But in 1990, when the city was chosen to host the 1996

Olympics, all the talk about Atlanta's becoming a truly cosmopolitan, international city inspired McBrayer and a couple of friends to start biking again, and they pondered how to develop a bike trail system in time for the games. "We started with a tiny grassroots organization, selling T-shirts and fund-raising with spaghetti dinners."

An article about McBrayer's efforts in a Buckhead neighborhood newspaper caught the eye of Jim Kennedy, scion of the Cox Enterprises media empire, which owned, among many other businesses, the *Atlanta Journal-Constitution*. Kennedy, an avid bike racer, was part of a four-man team that would win the Race Across America the following year, setting a world's record. With his and other influential people's support, McBrayer's new foundation launched successfully. On Saturday mornings during the spring of 1991, his group of "Trailblazers" explored potential greenway trail segments.

In 1992, the PATH Foundation drafted its "Greenway Trail Corridor Plan," outlining immediate and future plans. "Imagine cycling or walking for hours on wide, beautifully landscaped paths within a string of parks," the report urged, that "are filled with pedestrians, cyclists and joggers from all over Atlanta." Cast as linear parks, the new trails would provide "new threads to knit together neighbors, neighborhoods and communities throughout Atlanta."

And they would improve security. "Homes and businesses adjacent to trails in other urban areas experience less crime due to the level of activity on the trail." Unfortunately, few Atlantans believed this assertion. At the time, they feared that new urban paths would just attract vagabonds and criminals. Over his decades-long leadership of the PATH Foundation, McBrayer would become used to such attitudes. "I fight a blood battle every time I build a trail," he sighed.

The report noted that PATH was negotiating with jazz vibraphonist Lionel Hampton to buy land in southwestern Atlanta that eventually became a trail named after the famed performer. The foundation's early successes also included the Freedom Trail, which parallels the Freedom Parkway going by the Carter Center in east Atlanta, and a trail out to Stone Mountain that follows an old trolley line. The PATH Foundation report proposed putting trails in several parts of what would become the BeltLine, including a section on the west side between Washington and Maddox Parks and another on the east side's Norfolk Southern line. Neither of those went forward in the 1990s. Instead, after the Olympics,

PATH worked on the Silver Comet Trail, a 61.5-mile rails-to-trail project that took ten years to complete and runs from just outside Atlanta to the Alabama border.

One behind-the-scenes person provided a common thread to all of these projects. Alycen Whiddon, a landscape architect, had been an urban planner for the city of Atlanta since 1985 and chaired the Mayors Green Ribbon Committee, which had aimed to double Atlanta's public acreage by 1996. "I dreamed big," she recalled. "Why not?" She had worked on the censored Rails to Trails Conservancy report with Marianne Fowler and helped to draft the 1992 PATH Foundation document. In 1993, she authored a "Parks, Open Space and Greenways Plan" for Atlanta in which she coined the term "Cultural Ring" and first proposed the loop. "Yes, I gave Starling Sutton my Cultural Ring idea. I thought it was important to involve as many people as possible," Whiddon said. "It didn't matter who got the credit for it." Whiddon had revised her concept from bike trail to Olympic tourism venue, but still no one had risen to the challenge of implementing her original vision.

A Master's Thesis

Thus, by the time Ryan Gravel completed his paper in December 1999, various people had proposed using all or part of the old railroads encircling Atlanta, but nothing had come of their plans. Gravel's master's thesis, titled *Belt Line—Atlanta: Design of Infrastructure as a Reflection of Public Policy*, laid out a detailed blueprint for his much broader vision. In just over a hundred pages, he provided a philosophical justification that included historical background and comparisons to other cities. Atlanta was, he observed, "the poster child of the contemporary city, [suffering] from traffic congestion and the ecological consequences of unmitigated sprawl." He noted that, although architect Rem Koolhaas had called Atlanta a "centerless city," people were starting to move back to the core. "The [surrounding] Atlanta [metro] region is beginning to choke on its own success," Gravel asserted.

Indeed, people might literally be choking on its air pollution. "Since 1997, the metro area has been non-compliant with Federal clean air standards and has been cut off from Federal dollars for road building until a plan is developed to bring its air quality back into compliance." Gravel proposed that a "Belt Line" loop of streetcars—modeled on those

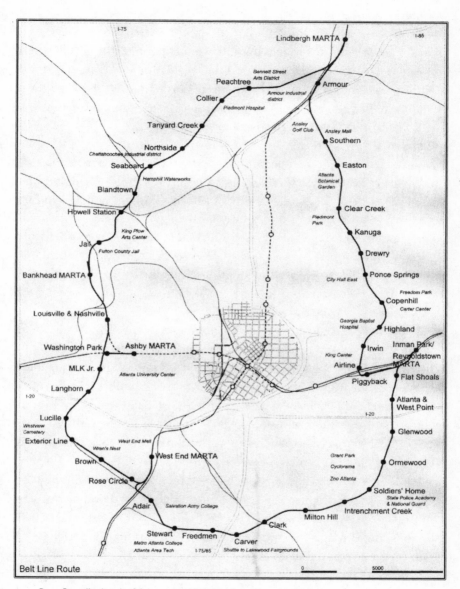

Ryan Gravel's sketch of the proposed Belt Line from his 1999 thesis

of Portland, Oregon—form part of a public transit solution to Atlanta's woes. He hoped that Atlanta would follow the "Paris model," which had layers of public transit for different needs: the metro and buses served central Paris, the RER brought in suburban commuters, the SNCF trains connected to other French cities, and the TGV provided high-speed rail to larger cities in France and elsewhere in Europe. "The Belt Line must be connected to new rail lines, new bus routes, and a broader dedication to public transportation and urban ecology."

He then provided detailed plans for the BeltLine loop, including forty-five streetcar stops spaced about a third of a mile apart. Parallel tracks would enable streetcars to run in both directions. A ride around the whole route, at an average speed of fifteen miles per hour (including stops), would take an hour and a half. Gravel, who had clearly done his homework, provided numerous photos he had taken of potential BeltLine segments from each of the four quadrants. He included architectural line drawings of streetcars poised at stops, complete with overhead electric lines, a man and woman about to board, and a man in a wheelchair waiting at the opposite track.

Many areas would require redevelopment so that the front would face the streetcars and trails, with new streets built to connect to the Belt-Line. But, Gravel emphasized, there should be minimal parking, since the whole point was to encourage public transit. Changes to city codes and zoning should "prioritize pedestrians, cyclists, and transit over automobiles" and ban suburban-style cul-de-sacs. New residential buildings should offer relatively high density; at the same time, their height and bulk should "not overpower pedestrians, but actually define a coherent space." Photos showed the sort of older Atlanta apartment buildings he preferred as models: generally three stories high with densities ranging from thirty to sixty units per acre. "The Belt Line winds between neighborhoods, not through the middle of them. This positions it perfectly for small, walkable commercial nodes where it crosses main thoroughfares."

Gravel acknowledged the need to overcome many obstacles. He envisioned his BeltLine intersecting with five MARTA stations, requiring "awkward diversions" in each case. The former rail lines, running by old industrial sites, suffered from "serious soil contamination and other environmental problems," necessitating remediation. There were differences in topography and major discontinuities where the route would have to "deviate from those [old rail] lines to make necessary connections," including a proposed tunnel under the Hulsey Rail Yard north of Cabbagetown. Gravel estimated that the BeltLine would cost around $1 billion, about the same as Portland's eighteen miles of streetcar lines.

The logical place to start construction would be the northeastern section, he noted, but it ran primarily past "gentrified, middleclass eastside neighborhoods, and construction priority for this line might exacerbate historical discrimination in public transportation against African American neighborhoods." He therefore suggested beginning with the southern part of the BeltLine because it had a "tremendous amount of redevelopable territory." The challenges of running alongside active railroads would probably render the northwestern segment "least viable," thus the last developed. Still, he hoped that this section might serve "as a tool for industrial redevelopment . . . to reinvigorate Atlanta's industrial base."

Oddly, Gravel made no effort to justify the BeltLine's viability as a streetcar line, an issue that would haunt the project in the coming years. "This is not a transportation study," he claimed. "It does not justify light rail transit according to current ridership projections." The southwestern segment, he wrote, "alone solves few transportation problems." Perhaps, however, "if the redevelopable territory associated with the Belt Line is handled appropriately, future population and employment growth on those sites will support it."

That growth would be equitable, he hoped. Elsewhere in Atlanta, he acknowledged, "the gentrification of neighborhoods by the middle class is homogenizing older communities, pushing out the resident poor." He hoped the BeltLine would somehow mitigate such trends but suggested no methodology. At least Gravel raised the issue of affordable housing, but efforts to resolve it satisfactorily through the BeltLine would be frustrating.

While confident that much development would occur along the new streetcar route, Gravel emphasized that "the Belt Line should accomplish more than just an improved system of public transportation. It has the potential to change the way we look at Atlanta." Instead of dividing neighborhoods, the old railroad tracks could reconnect "home and destination, rich and poor, black and white." Perhaps the city's problems could lead to its salvation. "Troubled by pollution and congestion, Atlanta can seize this chance to redefine itself."

Gravel summarized his grand plan for the BeltLine's streetcar project: "Much the same way an infrastructure of highways led to suburban expansion and inner city depopulation in the second half of this century, an expansion of mass transit infrastructure will lead to both the revival of the inner city and the protection of our natural ecology and agricultural resources." His vision was revolutionary in scope. Other cities had converted abandoned railroad corridors into streetcar lines or trails, but none proposed to connect disparate rails in a loop within two or three miles of a major urban center. In 1999, Friends of the High Line was just forming, though construction on this mile-and-a-half elevated length in New York City would not begin until 2006, and the High Line would offer no transportation benefit, just an unusual, relaxing tourist attraction. The Atlanta BeltLine that Gravel envisioned would knit the city together again.

Randal Roark was so impressed with his advisee's thesis that he assembled key Atlanta figures to hear Gravel present it, just before Christmas in 1999, on the cusp of a new millennium. In the audience, acting as a kind of jury, were Mike Dobbins, Atlanta's planning commissioner; Tom Weyandt, head of the Atlanta Regional Commission's Comprehensive Planning Department; and several others. Gravel, then twenty-seven, was terrified. "He was a kind of shy guy," Roark recalled. "I almost had to prop him up there to make his presentation." Gravel's girlfriend, Karen (later his wife), recalled that his hands shook so badly she feared he might drop the papers. Once he got started, though, Gravel explained the project in his low-key, articulate way. "They were all quite wowed," Roark said. "They saw the opportunity right away."

Mike Dobbins, who would later teach planning at Georgia Tech and became a major critic of BeltLine transit plans, didn't remember it quite that way. "Ryan did a fine student project—creative, elegantly presented, and well developed within its own architecture/urban design premises, but it did not include any transportation analysis. I gently pointed this out at the time, but my attitude toward student projects is to accentuate the positive." It never occurred to Dobbins that anything would come of the pie-in-the-sky thesis.

A Grassroots Movement

Nor did it occur to Ryan Gravel. He graduated, got a job with a local architectural firm, and shelved his utopian scheme. A couple of years later, he was eating lunch around a conference table with two colleagues, Mark Arnold and Sarah Edgens, and the conversation turned to master's thesis projects. Arnold had designed a synagogue in Berlin that incorporated a

Holocaust memorial. Edgens had planned a New Orleans music school. Then Gravel explained his BeltLine concept. "It was an *aha* moment," Arnold recalled. "It was such a great idea." Edgens, who had lived without a car in Boston, Massachusetts, and Portland, Oregon, was equally enthusiastic and told Gravel, who seemed painfully shy, that she would help to promote his plan.

With support from Arnold and Edgens, Gravel put together a twenty-one-page synopsis of his thesis, including a map of the BeltLine and its projected stations. In a cover letter, dated July 30, 2001, Gravel, Arnold, and Edgens wrote that their proposal aimed to "protect and revive historic neighborhoods, facilitate access to affordable housing, accommodate an influx of new residents, redevelop available land, and provide alternative and desperately needed means of transportation."

While the 1999 thesis had promoted only streetcars, the three colleagues decided to incorporate bike trails and park connections: "Light rail transit can coexist with bicycle and pedestrian paths, creating a thin necklace of green that connects several major city parks." They added that the project would be "comparatively easy and quick to implement," an assertion belied by future developments. They mailed the package to fifty people, including the mayor, governor, and various transportation and planning agencies. The polite brush-offs they received in response essentially said, "Good luck with that."

All but one, that is. Cathy Woolard, the city council member from District Six, which contained the northeastern segment of the BeltLine, had received a copy of the letter as chair of the Transportation Committee. Woolard, who had served in the Peace Corps and was originally drawn to politics as a gay activist, was open to radical new ideas. Her constituents had been complaining about the kudzu-ridden desolation of the abandoned rail tracks with its homeless encampments, demanding to know when this eyesore would be cleaned up. Others expressed alarm at rumors that a high-speed train would run by their homes. She had also attended a PATH presentation by Ed McBrayer in which he proposed building a trail there as part of an expanded, rehabilitated Cultural Ring concept.*

---

* Indeed, the new version of the Cultural Ring, adapted by Alycen Whiddon of the Atlanta Bureau of Planning in September 2000 and now called a Transit and Recreational Greenway, appeared to have been influenced by Gravel's thesis, published less than a year before. It proposed "quiet, non-polluting [i.e., electric] buses" to run initially, "but in the long term options exist for trolleys or light rail transit."

When Woolard became chair of the Transportation Committee, its primary emphasis had been a fifth runway for Atlanta's airport. *OK*, she thought, *but what else should we focus on? Improved roads? Public transit?* So she called a meeting of every relevant transportation-related agency—MARTA, Georgia Department of Transportation, Atlanta Regional Commission, Georgia Regional Transportation Authority (GRTA), City of Atlanta Department of Planning—and asked what plans they had for the city. The state and regional outfits concerned themselves primarily with getting commuters in and out of Atlanta efficiently. "But the city people had no clue or plan," Woolard recalled. She thought, *Oh my God, we're about to have transportation done to us.* She was concerned that the primary focus was on the suburban commuters outside the Perimeter Expressway (I-285) rather than the city residents. Angry and frustrated that no one seemed concerned about transit options within the city limits, she walked back to her office, put her feet up, and opened a fat manila envelope that had just landed on her desk.

She pulled out Ryan Gravel's map of the BeltLine and was mesmerized. "I instantly got it." This solved the problem of the garbage-strewn rail corridor and gave her transportation plans for the city. "I had lived in Washington, DC, and I had watched their rapid transit expand while Atlanta's stagnated," she said. "I saw the BeltLine as a way to connect to MARTA and expand its system."

Woolard called Ryan Gravel, who immediately came to see her, bringing Sarah Edgens and Mark Arnold. "They were really nervous," Woolard observed. "Ryan was soft-spoken and not real talkative, but he walked me through it, and I understood that it was a way to install a loop of permanent transportation infrastructure in place to encourage development." She had no idea how to proceed, but she told them, "Together, we'll do this. It's a great vision."

Two weeks later, in a basement of the Virginia Highlands Baptist Church, not far from the abandoned rail corridor, Woolard called a town meeting where Gravel presented his idea, using a beat-up carousel projector. At the same event, Ed McBrayer of the PATH Foundation pitched his idea for a trail. The following day, he sent an e-mail suggesting that they join forces, and when the BeltLine finally began to lay down trail, it would use PATH's concrete.

Over the next three years, Woolard and Gravel held neighborhood meetings, first in District Six, then, when she became city council president in January 2002, in all the BeltLine communities.* In April 2002, Maria Saporta, longtime reporter for the *Atlanta Journal-Constitution*, gave the BeltLine its first press coverage. The MARTA system was "woefully inadequate," Saporta noted. "By using existing railroad rights of way, Atlanta could build on its hub-and-spoke transit system. Perhaps more importantly, it could open thousands of acres to urban redevelopment." She quoted Woolard: "For the inside-the-Perimeter gang, we need a vision," and the BeltLine was it. Besides, what else could you do with the corridor? "People can have either kudzu and vagrants, or a very big train, or this." Saporta gave her enthusiastic support: "At long last, Atlanta leaders are beginning to think creatively about real solutions for its transportation problems."

Those problems were glaringly obvious, as one letter to the editor noted later in 2002: "Atlanta has sold its soul to the automobile, which produced a city built on sprawl." Other solutions also being bandied about included a streetcar to run north-south on Peachtree Street, the main thoroughfare of the city; a "C-Loop" streetcar that would begin in the southeast, run up around the west side, and curve over to Emory University in the northeast, forming a rough letter *C*; and a commuter passenger rail to connect to other cities, ending at a "multimodal station" in the downtown "Gulch."**

But none could compete with the BeltLine idea, which caught fire, giving people a vision for a future they wanted to be a part of. The Belt-Line took on a life of its own. National Public Radio covered it. In March 2003, Council President Woolard took developers and public officials on a bus tour, tracing the rail corridor loop.*** Mindspring founder Charles Brewer, a developer who had just broken ground for Glenwood Park, a mixed-use, walkable community in southeastern Atlanta adjacent to the

---

* Sarah Edgens and Mark Arnold also went to the community meetings for a while.
** The Gulch is the original ground-level area where trains intersected in downtown Atlanta. Because of the congestion, viaduct streets were built atop much of the area in the 1920s, with the remaining open area called the Gulch. Plans called for multiple modes of transportation—bus, rail, and perhaps streetcar—to converge there.
*** That same month, another "tour" of the BeltLine took place as part of an attempted census of the homeless in Atlanta. A reporter followed members of a team who tramped the old eastern rail corridor: "The path was sometimes muddy and sometimes tricky. The trestle over Ponce was so full of holes that the only safe place for feet was on the rails. . . . The group passed makeshift tents [and] a double or triple occupancy cardboard box home."

planned transit path, was aboard for the two-hour ride. "We would love the BeltLine," he said. "Just bring it on down."

In May 2003 GRTA included the BeltLine in a transit plan for regional bus service, and by July the Atlanta media noted that it was "picking up momentum," being considered, along with the C-Loop, by a newly launched MARTA feasibility study. "The BeltLine has more constituencies behind it than any project I've ever done," Woolard said. "This project has really captured the imagination of the city." For once, here was an idea that people could be *for* rather than *against*. Developers, community organizers, environmentalists, transit advocates, green space seekers, biking/hiking enthusiasts, public health physicians, historic preservationists, affordable housing advocates—all took ownership of the project and contributed ideas. Letters to the editor, usually a way for disgruntled citizens to vent, were all favorable. One called the BeltLine "the single most exciting idea for the city of Atlanta I have ever heard."

Despite all of the enthusiasm, though, how would it get done? Where would funding come from?

The BeltLine's Early Friends

By this time, Alycen Whiddon, who for nearly two decades had advocated for Atlanta rails-to-trails programs and parks from her position at the Atlanta Department of Planning, had finally decided to leave the city bureaucracy. "I was ready for something new. The thing about planning is, you make a lot of plans, but they seldom get implemented." In 2001 she took a job at a small, innovative Atlanta architectural firm focusing on new urbanism projects. Of course, she lent her full support to Gravel and Woolard's BeltLine project. "Thank God they resurrected the idea. I felt like I was beating a dead horse by then, that people would see me coming and roll their eyes."

Whiddon suggested funding the BeltLine through a tax allocation district (TAD), a relatively new mechanism used to pay for the conversion of the derelict Atlantic Steel property into Atlantic Station in Midtown, with a $77 million bond floated in October 2001. The TAD would freeze the amount of property tax that the city received from a defined area over a set span of years. As the project (whatever it might be) brought new businesses and higher property assessments to the area, the additional tax increment would go toward funding the project, producing a kind of snowball effect: the more taxes the improved district produced, the more money it would generate to pay for further improvements, which would augment tax revenue, and so on.

TADs worked best in decaying, impoverished areas slated for improvements. Touted as win-wins, they did have potential downsides: foregone revenue for the city, county, or participating school district for the TAD's duration and unanticipated economic snags. Still, they seemed to provide a relatively painless way to target funding for troubled areas.

Whiddon suggested creation of a circular BeltLine TAD that included the train corridor, along with adjacent abandoned warehouses and undeveloped property, but avoided established, thriving neighborhoods. Over twenty-five years—about the time Gravel and Woolard thought the BeltLine would take to implement—increasing property values ought to provide substantial funding. (Whiddon did not point out that, without some kind of subsidy program, such swelling values would inevitably push out low-income residents.) City Council President Woolard thought a TAD was a great idea and asked Whiddon to come up with a rough estimate of its area and how much money it might raise.

In a white paper dated September 10, 2003, titled "The BeltLine Transit Greenway: Economic Opportunities," Whiddon estimated that 2,854 acres of undeveloped or underdeveloped land within a quarter mile of the future BeltLine corridor yielded $18.5 million in taxes annually. Building out just 30 percent of this acreage, she figured, would generate an extra $210 million per year in incremental taxes. Even if these revenues materialized only in the final ten years of the project, the TAD would produce over $2 billion. That, along with federal, state, and city grants and philanthropic donations, ought to pay for the entire project. Whiddon admitted that this back-of-the-envelope estimate needed further study, but it gave the project credibility and momentum.

As president of the city council, Woolard managed to get the BeltLine included in the City of Atlanta's 2003 Comprehensive Development Plan, which provided no money but gave it the legitimacy needed to take further steps. In the meantime, Woolard pestered Atlanta mayor Shirley Franklin. "For almost two years we met weekly to discuss city matters," Franklin remembered, "and in each meeting Cathy [Woolard] had news about the BeltLine and ideas about what the city should do." But

Franklin was mostly occupied with budget deficits, potholes, and sewers. On taking office in January 2002, she found that the city was nearly $100 million in arrears. She'd had to slash jobs, cut her own salary, and raise taxes.

A few weeks later, an Environmental Protection Agency administrator told Mayor Franklin that Atlanta was out of compliance with the US Clean Water Act and would owe $80 million in fines if she didn't take immediate action. Atlanta's aging combined sewage and storm water system frequently flooded. Franklin had earned her political stripes by serving under Maynard Jackson, the first black mayor of Atlanta, and Mayor Andrew Young, who had been out of the country so frequently that she'd really run the city. Now she dubbed herself "the Sewer Mayor" and tripled water taxes while campaigning for clean water. Once she had gotten on top of the issue (which was never truly fixed), she was ready to consider the BeltLine. In her January 5, 2004, State of the City speech, Franklin called the BeltLine a "great vision," though she went no further.

Franklin now asked the Atlanta Regional Commission to include the BeltLine in *Mobility 2030*, the forthcoming Regional Transportation Plan (RTP), which included a list of potential federally funded projects for the next twenty-five years. But the mayor couldn't simply demand its inclusion, so Cathy Woolard and her staff rushed to figure out how to get the BeltLine into the RTP document. They sought initial funding for a bike path on the northeastern corridor as a foot in the door. Just two hours before the deadline, they got the application in, and the BeltLine appeared in *Mobility 2030*, slotted for $150 million over multiple years. The money was completely hypothetical, but now the BeltLine had at least made it into the requisite official document.

In February 2004, Cathy Woolard and Ryan Gravel incorporated a nonprofit called Friends of the Belt Line, modeled after a similar grassroots organization in New York City that was promoting the High Line. Actress Jane Fonda, who lived in a loft condo near the defunct Atlanta rail corridor, narrated a promotional video for the BeltLine. Shortly before Gravel issued the first newsletter for the new organization, dated April 26, 2004, Woolard resigned from the city council in order to run for the US Congress, hoping to find more funding for the Atlanta transit loop in Washington. "At that point, the BeltLine had moved past what a city council president could possibly do," Woolard recognized. "We had done what we could as a grassroots movement. It needed the mayor to be the champion, with the feds and state. Shirley needed to own it."

Mayor Shirley Franklin agreed. "Once Cathy left office to run for Congress, I took a serious look at the project." As part of a survey of unsheltered homeless people (the mayor spearheaded efforts to help Atlanta's large homeless population), Franklin had recently walked an eastern section of the BeltLine in the dead of night, which gave her an eerie familiarity with the possibilities. Here was a long-term endeavor that could form part of her legacy. Though it would barely have gotten under way during her term in office, she saw the BeltLine as a project that could help the city define itself. Franklin pondered the haphazard way Atlanta had grown. "Historically, great cities have been planned by founders with a long-term vision. I saw the BeltLine project as a way to superimpose a twenty-first-century plan on an existing city."

At that point, in the spring of 2004, Mayor Franklin turned the analysis and review of the BeltLine project over to Greg Giornelli, president of the Atlanta Development Authority (ADA), the city's development arm, later to be called Invest Atlanta. Giornelli had worked with Franklin in the 1990s on the redevelopment and revitalization of the city's East Lake community, a groundbreaking project that replaced drug-infested public housing with a desirable mixed-income development, along with a trailblazing charter school, providing a regional and national model for other troubled neighborhoods.

Now Franklin asked Giornelli to figure out how to make the BeltLine work. The first priority was funding. How could Atlanta possibly pay for it? A tax allocation district might help, but Giornelli was skeptical of Alycen Whiddon's $2 billion estimated yield over twenty-five years. He decided to fund a serious study of a BeltLine TAD's feasibility and formed a twelve-person committee. Symbolically, to announce the committee's formation on May 13, 2004, Shirley Franklin stood in front of a boarded-up brick Atlanta & Western Railroad station on Memorial Drive, smack on the future BeltLine. "Imagine," she said. "Right here we are laying the vision for the next hundred years for the city."

In June, ADA president Greg Giornelli called the BeltLine a "huge priority." The same month, Ryan Gravel, with his wife expecting their first child, quit his job in order to devote more time to Friends of the Belt Line, hoping to cobble together a living as a consultant. A fellow architect offered him free office space and a computer at his Community Housing Resource Center, a nonprofit that helped fix up homes for the elderly.

With the BeltLine gaining political traction and garnering media attention, hungry developers began to circle, smelling money. Giornelli promised to work with them, offering to help companies get needed information "as fast as possible." Everything appeared to be moving forward at warp speed.

At that point, in the summer of 2004, if its proponents had known what challenges and obstacles the BeltLine would face in the coming years, they may well have given up. But before we journey further down that bumpy road, for historical context it's important to look back at how Atlanta first came to be and evolved, with transportation as a major cause, curse, and possible cure.

CHAPTER 2
CITY ON THE MOVE

•••

*Atlanta has forgotten its founding principle, the very reason
Terminus was founded: Transportation. Transportation
drives economic and real estate development. It has been
the case for the 6,000 years we have been building cities,
and your ancestors knew it, but you have forgotten it!*

—Christopher Leinberger of the Brookings Institution
in a speech to the Atlanta Rotary Club, April 2012

After months of hiking through rolling hills, in November 1836 Stephen
Harriman Long, a topographical engineer, informed the Georgia state
legislature that he had located a suitable spot on a flattened ridge, seven
miles east of the Chattahoochee River, where a railroad line running
northwest to Tennessee should begin, or end, depending on the perspective. In his report, Long called this spot Terminus, the name it retained
in 1837 when he drove the first stake, designated as the Zero Mile Post,
into the ground there.

Until recently only Native Americans had occupied the area—the
Cherokee to the northwest of the Chattahoochee and the Creek to the
southeast of the river. Both tribes were driven out, despite an 1832 US
Supreme Court ruling in favor of the Cherokee. In 1838, the year after
Terminus was established, soldiers rounded up virtually all of the Cherokee in Georgia for a forced march west on the "Trail of Tears," during
which a quarter of them died.

The engineer, Stephen Long, saw no future in the location he had identified. In refusing an offer of cheap land there, he wrote, "Terminus will be a good location for one tavern, a blacksmith shop, a grocery store and nothing else." He was mistaken. By 1854 four railroads met at the original Terminus—the Western & Atlantic running northwest to Tennessee, the Macon & Western going south to Macon, the Georgia Railroad east to Augusta, with a connection to Savannah on the coast, and the Atlanta & LaGrange headed southwest.

After a three-year stint as Marthasville (named after the governor's daughter), in 1845 the makeshift railroad junction was renamed Atlanta, the feminine form of the final word of the Western & Atlantic railroad line. Atlanta was officially incorporated as a city in 1847, when a circle with a one-mile radius was drawn from the Zero Mile Post to define its boundaries. By 1854, this collection of whorehouses, shanties, and saloons had grown to host cotton warehouses, stores, banks, insurance companies, a hotel, a flour mill, a gun shop, a shoemaker, carriage shops, tanneries, and metal-working factories, such as the Atlanta Rolling Mill, that produced railroad tracks. The burgeoning city had a medical school, a hospital, churches, newspapers, and other businesses, as well as one small park and a cemetery. The Moral and Reform Party mayoral candidate had beat the Free and Rowdy Party nominee, and the denizens of the infamous Snake Nation and Murrel's Row, home to thieves, gamblers, prostitutes, cock fights, and drunken brawls, had been dispersed.

By 1859, when the first city directory was published, Atlanta comprised nearly 10,000 people and had become a vital transportation hub for the entire South. Its leading citizens were merchants, businessmen, real estate speculators, and railroad managers, not the plantation owners of rural areas. "Atlanta is rapidly overcoming the obstacles to its growth and prosperity and making the surrounding country, and neighborhood villages, all tributary to its prosperity, permanency, and celebrity," the directory asserted. Mayor Luther Glenn bragged, "Atlanta lies embosomed . . . diamond-like, in the very center of Georgia, yea, of the South," even though it was as yet a bit "rough and unpolished."

This kind of Atlanta braggadocio would become familiar over the next century and a half, but Atlanta really was a cosmopolitan place in comparison with the rest of the South, due primarily to its location as the nexus of a railroad network.

The Phoenix City

During the Civil War, because of Atlanta's strategic location and importance, General William Tecumseh Sherman laid siege to the city in 1864, cut its railroad supply lines, and forced its capitulation. Sherman left the burned city in ruins, making a mockery of the "permanency" claimed just five years earlier. "All that remained to attest to the former existence of great mills and factories were a few battered brick walls, and an occasional chimney looking grim and gaunt," wrote an 1865 visitor, soon after the Confederate surrender.

But by the end of that year, 150 Atlanta stores were back in business, and all of the railroads were running again within two years of the war's end. Atlanta, calling itself the Phoenix City, rose from its ashes in a flurry of activity, doing $4.5 million in business in 1866, and two years later it became the state capital. "Atlanta is a devil of a place," wrote a visitor that year. "The men rush about like mad, and keep up such a bustle, worry and chatter, that it runs me crazy." A Northern reporter described the "never-ending throng of pushing and crowding and scrambling and eager and excited and enterprising men, all bent on building and trading and swift fortune-making," with most of that frenetic activity linked to the rails. "The four railroads entering here groan with the freight and passenger traffic and yet are unable to meet the demand of the nervous and palpitating city."

Atlantans were eager to prove their renewed loyalty to the Union, as long as it attracted Yankee investment. In 1867, prominent leaders proposed erecting a 145-foot Lincoln Monument in Atlanta in memory of the recently assassinated president, though it was never built. The city hosted increasingly elaborate expositions in 1881, 1887, and 1895. For the first event, General Sherman returned to the city he had destroyed seventeen years earlier and declared, to great applause, "We are now in a position to say, every one of us, great and small, thank God we are American citizens."

Henry Grady, the dynamic young editor of the *Atlanta Constitution*, became the most vocal advocate of the "New South," in 1886 assuring a New York audience that the South had "new ideas and aspirations" and that its "diversified industry . . . meets the complex needs of this complex age." It had put "business above politics." The New South was "thrilling with the consciousness of growing power and prosperity." Grady told the

Yankees, "We have smoothed the path to southward, wiped out the place where Mason and Dixon's line used to be, and hung our latch-string out to you and yours." From the ashes of Civil War Atlanta, he said, "we have raised a brave and beautiful city . . . and have builded therein not one ignoble prejudice or memory."

Railroads and their associated industries remained the city's biggest employers and drove the economy throughout the last half of the nineteenth century, serving new businesses such as the Chattahoochee Brick Company, founded by James English in 1878, or the Fulton Bag and Cotton Mill, founded in 1889 in the Cabbagetown neighborhood. The curving lines of the tracks even influenced the city streets, as still reflected by some of the twists and turns of today's downtown avenues.

But Atlanta was bursting with entrepreneurial enterprises of all sorts, including patent medicines to treat neurasthenia, a mythical disease that afflicted high-powered businessmen and refined ladies whose depleted nervous energy supposedly needed replenishing. One of these "nerve tonics," created in Atlanta in 1886, contained mostly sugar water but also featured essential flavoring oils and extract of coca leaf and kola nut: it went by the name Coca-Cola. The combination medicine/soft drink would fund many Atlanta fortunes and philanthropies.

Streetcar Suburbs

In the late nineteenth and early twentieth centuries, trolley lines contributed mightily to the municipal expansion. In 1871 Richard Peters and George Adair inaugurated the first venture, the Atlanta Street Railway Company, a short stretch running west by Peters's house and ending at Adair's back door. Both owners had come to Atlanta in the 1840s to work on the Georgia Railroad and seized the opportunity to buy cheap land (around $5 an acre). They realized that providing trolley access to their lots might improve real estate sales. At first horses pulled the trolleys along the rails, but mules proved more reliable. In an effort to improve the dirt roads, the city insisted that all trolley companies pave their rights-of-way.

In 1874 the company extended its initial line to West End, a town that predated Atlanta but was later annexed by the city. The same year, the company laid tracks east on Decatur Street to Oakland Cemetery and northwest along Marietta Street to the Atlanta Rolling Mill, thus encouraging working-class neighborhoods along that route. The company also sent mule-drawn trolleys north along Peachtree Street, where wealthy Atlantans began to build large homes.

For the long warm season, April to September, they extended the Peachtree line in a ninety-degree turn to the east to Ponce de Leon Springs, in the watershed that produced Clear Creek. There, like the legendary Florida "Fountain of Youth" of Spanish explorer Juan Ponce de Leon, the waters supposedly possessed curative powers. Railroad workers building the Atlanta & Richmond Air-Line Railway, the first rail constructed on what is now the BeltLine loop, had discovered two springs in 1868. The rail line was completed in 1871 and renamed the Southern Belt Line by 1894. The water tasted of sulfur, but the crew credited it with helping to cure their various afflictions. This health spa eventually became an amusement park, with a four-acre lake on the north side of the tracks.

Until the coming of the trolleys, Atlanta had grown primarily along the railroad tracks in lines radiating for a mile outward from the inner city. In 1889, the city limits were expanded to a 3.5-mile diameter and now included new neighborhoods such as those on the streets surrounding Grant Park, developed by Lemuel Grant, the same engineer who designed Atlanta's Confederate fortifications during the Civil War. It featured trails, a lake, and a few display animals purchased from a bankrupt circus—lions, three monkeys, a camel, a hyena, a black bear, a raccoon—that eventually became Zoo Atlanta. In 1893, Grant Park became home to the Cyclorama, a gigantic circular oil painting of the Battle of Atlanta.

Grant was an officer of the Metropolitan Street Railroad Company, which provided trolley service to Grant Park, at first by horse and then by coal-fired steam engines called "dummies" because their similarity to streetcars would supposedly prevent their scaring the horses and mules. To encourage ridership, in 1886 the company began offering free Sunday afternoon concerts in the park. Like many other Atlantans, Lemuel Grant grew up elsewhere—Frankfurt, Maine, in his case—just as Richard Peters had come from Philadelphia. Grant, too, had come to Atlanta in the 1840s to work for Georgia Railroad.

In 1889, developer Joel Hurt, an Alabama native, first ran an electric streetcar east along Edgewood Avenue, a straight east-west road he had constructed to reach his newly developed Inman Park, Atlanta's first planned suburb. Influenced by famed landscape architect Frederick Law

Olmsted, Hurt created gently curving streets that followed the natural terrain, in addition to parks, and planted over seven hundred trees. The handsome, quiet electric trolley of the Atlanta and Edgewood Street Railway featured polished brass handles and a finished oak interior with comfortable cane seats. A small wheel atop a pole kept the trolley connected to an overhead electric line.

By the turn of the century the large Victorian homes of Inman Park held, in addition to Joel Hurt's family, many of Atlanta's prominent citizens, including a cotton dealer, hardware store owner, stove manufacturer, minister, physician, and insurance agent, as well as bankers, attorneys, real estate developers, trolley and railroad managers, and other high-powered businessmen, such as Asa Candler, the Coca-Cola tycoon who built his Callan Castle home there.

Electric streetcars proliferated quickly, putting the horses and "dummies" out of business. For a few years, a Nine-Mile Circle line ran in a loop through the wooded northeastern section of the city, a kind of predecessor to today's BeltLine. In 1891, Joel Hurt bought out five other streetcar lines to form the Atlanta Consolidated Street Railway Company, with 80 percent of the funding coming from New England and New York investors. For the next ten years his firm dominated streetcar growth in the city, although many other competing companies sprang up, failed, merged, or survived. One ran a line southwest through the in-town working-class Pittsburgh neighborhood—so named because its polluted air was similar to the famed steel town's—to Capitol View, a new suburb offering a nice vista of downtown. All of the streetcars allowed development along their lines, as people sought to escape the soot, grime, and noise of the downtown train junction.

Atlanta had one hundred miles of trolley lines serving over 100,000 people by 1894, when the American Street Railway Association held its annual convention there. That year the *Street Railway Journal* described how various Atlanta trolley lines were spurring growth: "Already the road [with trolley] has developed the territory through which it passes, new houses having gone up all the way from Atlanta to the terminals [in Grant Park, East Lake, Decatur, and Camp McPherson]." Another line to the northwest went "through a woody, wild, romantic region, with many curves and grades, but which is rapidly building up with new homes."

Coal-fired power stations—later augmented by hydroelectric dams—provided electricity for the streetcars; one was even located on the Southern Belt Line railroad to enable delivery of coal directly to the boiler. Because the railroad crossings in downtown Atlanta had become so crowded, these "belt lines"—this one to the northeast of the city—were being built to circumvent the congestion. The Seaboard Air-Line Belt Railway ran through northwestern Atlanta starting in 1893, the Atlanta & West Point Belt Line to the southeast starting in 1899, and the Louisville & Nashville Railroad Belt to the southwest, beginning in 1902.*

Henry Atkinson, a Boston native who had moved to Atlanta in 1886, owned the Georgia Electric Light Company, which featured "one of the largest and most complete lighting plants in the entire south," according to the 1894 *Street Railway Journal* article. "Current is not only furnished for arc and incandescent light, but also for power purposes," sold to streetcar lines, printing shops, and factories.

Throughout most of the 1890s, Henry Atkinson and Joel Hurt remained friendly competitors and colleagues. Both men had incorporated their own banks—Atkinson's Southern Banking and Trust Company and Hurt's Trust Company of Georgia—to help finance their multiple ventures. In April 1899, Hurt announced that his bank, with the help of the Mercantile Trust & Deposit Company of Baltimore, was buying out several other streetcar lines and that he also planned to establish "a new power and lighting plant." He subsequently renamed Atlanta Consolidated as the Atlanta Railway & Power Company.

Infuriated that Hurt was challenging his electric company, Atkinson found backing from the Old Colony Trust Company of Boston to buy a competing streetcar line, renaming it the Atlanta Rapid Transit Company. The subsequent business fracas between Hurt and Atkinson, which spilled into the courts and newspapers, was dubbed the "Second Battle of Atlanta." In 1901, Atkinson emerged as the winner. The two major streetcar lines and electric utilities merged as the Georgia Railway & Electric Company, later known as the Georgia Power Company, today one of the most powerful corporations in the state.

Atlanta was expanding both outward and upward. Joel Hurt built the eight-story Equitable Building in 1892, topped by the eleven-story Flatiron Building in 1897, the fourteen-story Empire Building in 1901,

---

* The history of the railroads that would eventually become the Atlanta BeltLine project is more complex than this simple chronology, since dynamic competition and railroad mergers and failures of the late nineteenth and early twentieth centuries produced a confusion of names and owners.

the sixteen-story Fourth National Bank in 1905, and finally the ornate seventeen-story Candler Building, built in 1906 with Coca-Cola money, which reigned as Atlanta's tallest skyscraper for the next two decades. Businesses continued to grow, including the Atlanta Hoop Company, founded in 1901, which later became Atlantic Steel.

In 1907, a novel portrayed Atlanta as a Southern cosmopolitan mecca for a newcomer: "The lights of the great city gleamed below him, and the elevators in the skyscrapers around winked at him as they passed from floor to floor. 'O, mighty city!' he murmured, softly, 'I love you, love you! We will run the race together. Breathe thou the spirit of thy glorious haste into my nostrils!'" Another character scoffed on being asked if she were a native. "Born here!" she laughed. "Have you ever heard of any one who was born in Atlanta?"

Elegant mansions for Atlanta's wealthy elite sprouted north along Peachtree Street and down Ponce de Leon Avenue, including Druid Hills, a suburb with linear greenways designed by Frederick Law Olmsted. Asa Candler moved from Inman Park to a huge home there. Further down Ponce, opposite the amusement park and next to the BeltLine, the Atlanta Crackers baseball team began playing in 1901. In 1904, real estate developer Edwin Ansley bought land for Ansley Park off Peachtree, where winding roads led to future upscale homes.

In 1907, the streetcar line pushed farther north along Peachtree, outside the city limits, to Buckhead, a rural outpost named after a deer's head mounted over a tavern door. Originally the site of several gristmills and sawmills, as well as pottery businesses that used its abundant red clay, Buckhead was destined to become a wealthy enclave in the coming decades.

By 1912, Atlanta had 195 miles of streetcar tracks, a maze of public transit that allowed its citizens to go virtually anywhere. The roads on which the trolleys traveled were relatively comfortable because by law the transit companies had to pay 40 percent of the paving cost, but as cars came to predominate, that funding source would dry up.

The Triumph of the Internal Combustion Engine

Automobiles were just beginning to compete for space on those roads, along with horse-drawn buggies and pedestrians. In 1901, the first car, a

Locomobile, drove into Atlanta. Within eight years, thirty-five car deal-erships had sprung up, and in 1915 Ford built a manufacturing plant on Ponce de Leon Avenue, next to the railroad tracks.

A 1914 photo of downtown Five Points in Atlanta shows a metropolis where people could still walk safely among the trolleys, autos, horses, and pushcarts. Just ten years later, smelly, gas-powered automobiles had taken over the streets and slowed streetcars, as a 1924 photo taken at Marietta and Broad Street demonstrates.

Atlanta had a traffic problem, despite construction of a few viaducts over the railroad tracks that converged in the city center and blocked auto travel. In 1922, the newly formed city planning commission recom-mended street widening as a solution, an approach that has never worked in the long term. Already trucks were competing with rails. "The cost of trucking is a much larger factor in the cost of most goods than is the railroad freight," noted the commission's report. Trucks were beginning to take more goods to their final destination, albeit inefficiently. "Many products are transferred by vehicles in city streets a half dozen times be-fore they reach the consumer."

1914 Atlanta street scene

1924 Atlanta street scene

Impeded by traffic congestion, streetcar service slowed. Private un-
licensed autos called "jitneys" sped in front of streetcars, offering somewhat cheaper rides and greater flexibility. Many people began to consider
the streetcars a nuisance, blaming them rather than automobiles for the
congestion.

In 1923, Atkinson's transit company presented a "Constructive Plan
for Solving Present and Future Transportation Problems of Atlanta" to
the mayor, suggesting improvements to the trolley system along with sup-
plementary bus service. The following year, a New York consulting firm
headed by John Beeler submitted a scathing report. "The city's tardiness in
evolving a definite city plan, coupled with the rapid and noteworthy growth
in all phases of its life, is the underlying cause of the present acute situation."

The Beeler report recommended banning jitneys, building more viaducts over the rail lines, and adding motor coach service (buses) to extend streetcar lines. Some of these suggestions were implemented, though
they actually hastened the switch from rail and streetcar to motorized
vehicles. "The evermore massive invasion of the city by the automobile
actually negated the benefits of many of the Beeler recommendations,"
noted historian O. E. Carson, "including the Pryor Street and Central
Avenue viaducts, which by the time of their completion in 1929 allevi-
ated the bumper-to-bumper traffic to a lesser degree than anticipated."

In 1925 city leaders mounted a vigorous advertising campaign called
"Forward Atlanta," which succeeded in luring 762 new businesses to the

area in the next four years, including Sears, Roebuck and Co., which built a huge retail and mail-order headquarters on Ponce de Leon Avenue, replacing the former amusement park and permanently burying the springs. Although the railroads continued to carry freight and passengers, ever-greater reliance on gasoline-powered vehicles eroded their dominance. To the south, Atlanta, pioneering in another transportation mode, opened America's first air-passenger terminal in 1931; it would eventually become the world's busiest airport.

Atlanta's leaders began to see streetcars as old-fashioned anachronisms. Newer suburbs such as Morningside, Brookwood Hills, Home Park, Virginia-Highland, Candler Park, Ansley Park, and Sylvan Hills relied increasingly on auto transport. As early as 1905, an Atlanta newspaper had praised Ansley Park as the first suburb built with cars in mind for "everybody who rides, drives, or 'motors' an automobile, for all roads must lead to these, the only driveways in Atlanta." Atlanta's first city bus began operation in 1925, further adding to pollution from exhaust and foreshadowing the end of the less agile streetcar.

The Depression and World War II rationing of gasoline and rubber gave the trolleys a reprieve, but even during the war, in 1943, the city council called for the elimination of all electric streetcars: "The complete substitution of trackless trolleys and gasoline motor buses for street railway lines . . . would be a long step forward in the modernization of Atlanta's transportation facilities and the solution of its congested traffic problems." The call to "modernize" was heeded. The last Atlanta streetcar ran in April 1949, a few months after I was born.* Until 1963, some rubber-tired electric buses (trackless trolleys) continued to run soundlessly by connecting to overhead wires, but then smelly, polluting diesel buses took over completely.

The Downtown Disconnectors

By 1949, Atlanta was already ahead of the rest of the nation in constructing a limited-access north-south expressway, called the Downtown Connector, that eventually split into Interstates 75 and 85, though they still merge to plow through downtown Atlanta, crossed by the east-west

---

* The decommissioned Atlanta streetcars were sent to Korea, where they had a second life.

Interstate 20. Attempts to relieve traffic congestion by increasing capacity (adding multiple lanes) or by adding the Perimeter Expressway (I-285) just made matters worse, as the metro Atlanta population expanded along with the roads.

In 1946, Atlanta commissioned a comprehensive highway and transportation study by national traffic consultant H. W. Lochner of Chicago. Noting that "Atlanta is approaching a period of great growth and prosperity," he proposed four-lane expressways (with room to expand to six lanes) to cut through the heart of the city, along with one-way downtown streets and off-street parking in lots or garages. Lochner urged replacing the streetcars and suggested using express motor buses on the new interstate highways. His report envisioned new parks and children's playgrounds abutting the expressways that would raze "substandard areas."

Atlanta's population had reached 300,000 by 1946, and already people were spreading into surrounding farmland. "The automotive age . . . has led many companies in Atlanta . . . to locate sizeable plants in semi-rural areas," wrote Lochner. "This policy generates a great deal of highway traffic, and in time will cause dispersal of population."

That year, Atlanta responded to the Lochner report by voting for a $16.6 million bond issue to begin constructing a new six-lane north-south expressway. By 1952, two segments had been completed on the north and south ends of town, when the newly created Metropolitan Planning Commission issued *Up Ahead: A Regional Land Use Plan for Metropolitan Atlanta*, which included recommendations for a future in which "suburban sprawl"—a phrase used in the report—would result in an expanding metropolitan area. Atlanta's city boundaries had just extended to engulf 118 square miles, adding 100,000 new citizens, but the real growth would occur in the greater metropolitan area. "American genius will make better automobiles and highways. Suburbs will then push farther and farther out." Unlike many other cities, Atlanta had no natural boundaries. "No physical barriers stand in the way of outward expansion—no ocean or lake or mountain or large river."

While *Up Ahead* recognized that these developments could sow the seeds of new problems and that the downtown area was already beset with slums and the flight of business, it expressed general pleasure with future prospects. "Crowded, congested cities could be on their way out. In their place we could have a new type of city in the future—wide, green, open and well-planned. Its people would be on wheels and wings, moving swiftly from suburb to suburb, from rim to core and back again." The key to all of this was a "vast web of coordinated arterial trunk highways," starting with the completion of the Downtown Connector. The report included a layout for the ideal new suburb, featuring single homes built in nested cul-de-sacs, accessed by a single entrance and exit to a highway, with an industrial park on the other side.

"Population density can be low," the authors wrote. "Green ridges and creek valleys can provide open park areas." Such trends pointed to "a future Metropolitan Atlanta of great comfort, beauty and efficiency. . . . The future pattern can include 30 or more large 'communities' separated by free-flowing arterial highways." The report included a proposal to convert the BeltLine railroads into an "Inner Belt Highway" loop for trucks.

Thankfully, that plan for the BeltLine wasn't implemented, but the future envisioned in *Up Ahead* mostly came true, albeit with unintended results: massive sprawl, gridlock, air pollution, white flight, and central city deterioration replete with surface parking lots where buildings had once stood. The "free-flowing arterial highways" got a big boost in 1956 with the passage of the Federal Aid Highway Act, which authorized construction of the Interstate Highway System, with the federal government footing 90 percent of the bill.

Meanwhile, the once mighty railroads largely fell into disuse. Over three hundred passenger trains had passed through Atlanta in the 1920s, disgorging at the magnificent Terminal Station, built in 1905. Union

Atlanta's Terminal Station, soon after its completion in 1905. It was razed in 1972.

Station, with its plantation-style columns, was added in 1930. Now people drove cars; they didn't ride trains. Fewer freight trains pulled into the downtown Gulch, and the BeltLine trains skirting the central city faltered as the industries they served failed or moved further out, where trucks served them. In 1972, both Terminal and Union Stations were destroyed. Only a moribund Underground Atlanta (the former street-level covered by viaducts) and rarely used Gulch remained of the former railroad glory.

The development of a subway system provided some hope that Atlanta might, as one writer of the time put it, have a "return to reason," but MARTA failed to garner enough votes to pass in the first referendum in 1968. It squeaked by in 1971 but passed only in Fulton and DeKalb Counties, which agreed to pay a 1 percent sales tax, while Gwinnett and Cobb to the north and Clayton to the south voted it down, mostly because of racist fears that inner-city blacks would ride the subway out to the lily-white suburbs.

The state legislation authorizing MARTA provided no state support, making it unique in the country in that respect. It also forced the transit authority to spend half of its funds on operating costs and the remainder on capital improvements, giving management no flexibility in building and maintaining the system. Some insiders opined that the fifty-fifty split was a poison pill inserted into the legislation by segregationist governor Lester Maddox to hamstring the agency.

The federal government supported simultaneously funded subway systems in Atlanta, San Francisco, and Washington, DC. In the latter two cities, the systems grew over time with sufficient support, whereas the Atlanta system repeatedly cut service and raised fares to survive. Most riders, other than those going to the airport, were lower-income residents with no other options.

MARTA stations—mostly overbuilt concrete monstrosities set amid acres of parking lots—did not engage pedestrians or encourage vibrant surrounding communities. Assuming that commuters would drive to the stations, planners didn't bother to place them in convenient locations. Instead, to save money, the MARTA lines generally followed railroad right-of-ways, which often did not intersect with desirable pedestrian destinations. As criminal activities increased in these concrete islands, MARTA police closed many pedestrian entrances in order to maintain better surveillance, thereby lessening the transit system's attractiveness and connection to surrounding neighborhoods.

Various attempts to solve the greater metro Atlanta region's traffic snarls stumbled. In 1997, when metro Atlanta failed to meet a deadline for developing a transportation plan that would bring the area into Clean Air Act compliance, the federal government cut off funding for new road projects. In response, in 1999 Georgia governor Roy Barnes created the Georgia Regional Transportation Authority (GRTA), with strong statewide regulatory powers and a mission to "improve Georgia's mobility, air quality, and land use practices." As a transportation writer observed, "The creation of GRTA was a remarkably progressive and forward-thinking act, giving Atlanta the opportunity to begin to escape its reputation as 'Sprawlanta,' air, water, and land offender of the first magnitude." Following a legal settlement with the Georgia Department of Transportation and the Atlanta Regional Commission, the federal government lifted the ban on road construction in 2000.

After Barnes failed in his reelection bid, however, GRTA wound up becoming a glorified bus company, running daily express buses from the suburbs into downtown Atlanta without connecting with MARTA. No effective umbrella organization existed to coordinate transportation issues in the Atlanta region. While the Atlanta Regional Commission, an intergovernmental coordination agency for the metro Atlanta area, was charged with developing the region's long-range transportation plan, the agency lacked the authority to require compliance.

This was the situation that spawned Ryan Gravel's master's thesis and confronted Mayor Shirley Franklin and Greg Giornelli, head of the Atlanta Development Authority, as they tried to figure out how to fund the BeltLine.

CHAPTER 3
FIRST BUMPS ALONG THE BELTLINE

···

*Many people and regimes have come and gone during the
short life of the BeltLine, and many have tried to take credit
or otherwise leave their mark—some selfishly and some
not. I think this means that the BeltLine has brought out
the best and the worst in people and organizations. And it
has attracted some really good talent to the project.*

—Jim Langford, former Georgia state
director of the Trust for Public Land

In early March 2004, the vision for the future BeltLine expanded after
the Trust for Public Land (TPL) acquired a new Georgia state director,
Jim Langford, an environmentalist, businessman, and former Coca-Cola
executive. Founded in 1972, the nonprofit trust buys land for parks or
other protected areas with the intention of reselling them to governmen-
tal entities. On March 31, Langford attended a lunchtime meeting with
Mayor Shirley Franklin in a city hall conference room, where Tim Committe, a wealthy developer who had built a few Atlanta high-rises, invited
an impressive group of people to support what would ultimately become
the BeltLine. He intended to purchase and develop the northeastern portion of the corridor.

Alycen Whiddon, one of the original BeltLine pioneers, was there
with her report on how a tax allocation district (TAD) could help fund
the BeltLine. Ed McBrayer from the PATH Foundation came to express
interest in building the trail. And Alexander Garvin, a Yale professor,

architect, city planner, and author of *Urban Parks and Open Space* as well as *The American City: What Works, What Doesn't*, flew down to endorse the concept.

Committe's plans came to naught, and today few know he was ever involved in the early BeltLine development, but the unpublicized meeting had a profound impact. "Everyone went into high gear," Langford recalled. "We thought, *The developers are circling; we'd better get on top of this thing.*" The lunchtime presentation helped solidify Mayor Franklin's support for the transit loop, and within two weeks, Ed McBrayer had secured half of a $3 million pledge to begin building bike trails along the future BeltLine. On April 12, 2004, the *Atlanta Journal-Constitution* reported on the pledge under a banner headline, "BeltLine Gathers Support," noting that MARTA was including it in an ongoing study of transit alternatives and that "[Shirley] Franklin is taking a lead role with the BeltLine now that Cathy Woolard has announced plans to resign from the city council to run for Congress."

The Emerald Necklace

The following week, neighborhood activists for the Old Fourth Ward in eastern Atlanta came to Langford's office, seeking help for a new park they wanted to create south of the huge old Sears building. Could Langford help them by getting the Trust for Public Land to buy land as an interim step? As TPL specialized in buying and conserving property that might otherwise be commercialized, Langford took a serious look at the idea. He was amazed by what he saw.

That same week, Atlanta was buzzing with talk about the BeltLine concept. "I looked at the map," Langford recalled, "and oh my gosh, the BeltLine ran right next to this park they wanted us to help with. And I saw that the BeltLine ran through Piedmont Park a little further north." Intrigued, he decided to look at the entire loop and noted other parks already adjacent or close to that corridor—Grant, Washington, Maddox, Adair, and Stanton, among others. Perhaps the BeltLine could serve not only as public transit but as a circular, linear greenspace connecting new and old parks around Atlanta. Plenty of vacant or underused properties stretched along the old railroad tracks.

In June 2004, Langford called city planner Alexander Garvin, whom he had met at the lunch presentation, and asked him to investigate the idea of using the BeltLine to connect parks. Langford secured funding from the Arthur Blank Foundation (Blank cofounded the Atlanta-based Home Depot) to pay for Garvin's study. This was the first of many crucial private donations, without which the BeltLine would never have gotten under way.

Garvin—with former student and associate Jim Schroder—flew down to reconnoiter. They met with Ryan Gravel to discuss the Belt-Line. "To my amazement, I found that Ryan had never walked all of it," Garvin recalled. "I discovered frighteningly large gaps. It wasn't continuous, a railroad was running on it in parts, and sometimes on one side of the BeltLine, the land was forty feet higher than the other side." Waiting for their flight back at the Atlanta airport, Garvin turned to Schroder and said, "I don't know if we can do this."

But in an incredibly short time, they did. Garvin hired Ryan Gravel as a consultant, providing the now unemployed head of Friends of the Belt Line with valuable income, along with two other young Atlantans. On one memorable hot July day, Jim Schroder and Ryan Gravel walked the entire BeltLine. "We were young and in good shape," Schroder recalled. "We started at 6:30 a.m. and finished after 8 p.m." In some places, the kudzu was so lush that they had to crawl through it. Schroder was nervous about trespassing on active rail right-of-ways, but Gravel reassured him, recalling how he and a friend used to hop the freights for fun as Georgia Tech students.

The biggest *aha* moment came on a sunny September day, when Garvin, Schroder, Gravel, and Langford flew over the future BeltLine corridor in a helicopter. "What's that?" Garvin cried, pointing at a huge hole in the ground. It was the Bellwood Quarry, less than a mile from the western edge of the BeltLine. Together with adjacent property, it represented a potential new park of nearly six hundred acres, dwarfing Piedmont Park.

In late December 2004, the Trust for Public Land published Garvin's glossy 141-page report, *The BeltLine Emerald Necklace: Atlanta's New Public Realm*. Dedicating the book to Frederick Law Olmsted, the dean of American landscape architects, Garvin appropriated the phrase "emerald necklace" from Olmsted's description of his nineteenth-century chain of parks and waterways through the Boston Fens, forming a kind of inverted *U* shape. But in Atlanta's case, the Beltline would truly be a necklace around the entire city center.

In the report, Garvin included a chart of American cities and the percentage of parkland they possessed. At the top was San Francisco, with 19.8 percent. Atlanta lay near the bottom with 3.8 percent. Garvin's team identified 1,401 acres of potential new parkland and trails (an increase of 43 percent), enlarging Atlanta's parkland to 5.5 percent of the city—not a gigantic statistical improvement, but one that would provide access to parks and trails in previously neglected areas around the Belt-Line loop.

"After decades of explosive development," Garvin wrote in the report, "Atlanta is primed to become the quintessential American city of the 21st century. . . . Almost miraculously, a vacancy exists in Atlanta: a belt of railroad rights-of-way that circle the city's inner neighborhoods, two miles from downtown." The BeltLine would give Atlanta "an opportunity which far exceeds that of any major American city: to create a city-wide system of parks and transit, to create stronger, more attractive communities, and to actively shape a new and improved public realm framework that will positively impact residents' quality of life for generations to come."

Garvin's enthusiasm was contagious, but his report made some rosy, questionable assumptions that would haunt the BeltLine project in the years to come. For instance, he posited that the Atlanta Waterworks, fenced off since 1996 due to concerns about bioterrorism, would be opened to the public as a park and that CSX would relocate to allow the BeltLine to cross the Hulsey Rail Yard, opening another forty acres of open space. He also assumed the creation of three new MARTA stations in places where the BeltLine intersected with the rapid transit line, even though each would cost over $100 million. Garvin acknowledged that there were major discontinuities and that in places the corridor was too narrow to accommodate two tracks and a trail. But he assured readers, "Every potential obstacle can be overcome by a coordinated, ambitious plan."

Garvin recognized that putting both trail and transit in a loop around downtown Atlanta would take decades and that maintaining momentum (and funding) for the project might be difficult. He estimated that acquiring the right-of-way and building the transit would cost over $1 billion. Consequently, he recommended that the trail be completed first, since it would require "a fraction of that cost." Because tax allocation district funds couldn't kick in for at least two years—assuming a TAD secured all necessary agreements and jumped legislative hurdles—Garvin suggested, "Atlanta's major foundations and philanthropic organizations can fund the multi-use trail as the Beltline's first step." Land for the transit portion should be reserved for later use. Ryan Gravel accepted this pragmatic approach but continued to believe that streetcars should grace the BeltLine as soon as possible. The following year, a team of experts, including several Georgia Tech professors, would look at the feasibility of transit on the BeltLine in addition to a multiuse trail.

On the back of the report, Garvin placed a photo of Bellwood Quarry that he had taken from the police helicopter. The massive new proposed park was a stretch, since Vulcan Material Company held a lease on it that expired only in 2034. But it stirred the imagination. Garvin envisioned the quarry filled with water from the nearby Chattahoochee River, with a dam creating a waterfall paid for by corporate sponsors (maybe Coca-Cola could name it Dasani Falls after its bottled water), with whitewater kayaking, a pool below for sailboats, and a swimming area with a beach.

Garvin's report made national headlines in a *Christian Science Monitor* story in January 2005, which called the plan for connected parks a "bold urban experiment." The report quoted Garvin, who extolled Atlanta's trees but lamented its lack of public space: "Atlanta is green all right, but it's green in people's backyards." That month, the Trust for Public Land announced that it had received a $2.5 million grant from the Blank

Bellwood Quarry (back cover of *The Beltline Emerald Necklace*)

Foundation to begin purchasing future parkland along the BeltLine. Because of Atlanta's limited population and tax base, donations from major philanthropies funded directly or indirectly by city-based corporations—Home Depot, Coca-Cola, Cox Enterprises, and others—would prove essential to jump-starting the project.

Wayne Mason Buys a Chunk of the BeltLine

As Garvin was writing his report, he, along with everyone else involved with the BeltLine, was startled to learn that Gwinnett County developer Wayne Mason had succeeded where Tim Committe had failed. News broke in mid-October 2004 that Mason had negotiated the purchase of a 4.6-mile-long rail corridor from Norfolk Southern for $25 million.* This was the northeastern section of the BeltLine, running from Interstate 85 down to DeKalb Avenue, nearly a quarter of the entire loop.

Cathy Woolard, who had lost her bid for a congressional seat and was back working with Friends of the Belt Line while setting up as a lobbyist and consultant, was delighted that the developer had snatched the property away from the Georgia Department of Transportation, which had wanted it for a possible commuter rail line. "Wayne Mason is a great guy," Woolard said, "and clearly he understands the value of what he's got."

Indeed he did, as subsequent events would prove. Mason, then a sixty-four-year-old native of Snellville, Georgia, had become a legendary figure in nearby Gwinnett County, which he had helped remake from a sleepy rural agricultural backwater into the fastest-growing region in the Southeast. As a child with dyslexia, Wayne Mason hadn't done well in school, but for money he plowed gardens behind a one-eyed mule and peddled eggs in Atlanta. When he was fifteen, he served as general contractor for his parents' new house. In his twenties, he sold tires for Goodyear.

Initially as a sideline, he and his brother built and sold houses, then land, in the process becoming millionaires. They also invested in funeral homes, banks, and liquor stores. Mason, who called himself a "dealaholic," loved the whole process. "It's like marbles, where you have a special one, a cat's eye, and you play it and you win. It's fun." He asserted,

---

* Because Norfolk Southern insisted on closing the deal by year's end, the railroad reduced the price to $24.5 million.

"I'm going to die doing my last deal." As a county commissioner in the 1970s, Mason was in a position to approve roads and water and sewer lines that happened to enhance his property values. "No matter where I pave a road, I'm going to catch the devil," he said, "for I own property all over the county, and about any paving project will help me in some way."

It seemed ironic that Mason, who had been a driving force behind the sprawling suburbs of metro Atlanta, should now be leading the movement back into the city to promote density, walkability, and public transit. Landscape architect Alycen Whiddon, who signed onto his team, was skeptical at first, but she became convinced that he was truly excited about the BeltLine project. "This area represents an incredible revitalization opportunity for the city," Mason said. He wanted to promote "a live-work-play environment, including the feasibility of greenways and park spaces, transit possibilities, and housing choices." He planned to promote substantial development. "You have to have some vision," he said.

At first, Atlanta Development Authority (ADA) president Greg Giornelli, who had commissioned a feasibility study for the BeltLine tax allocation district, welcomed Mason's intervention as a "positive development." Mayor Shirley Franklin, who knew Mason through their mutual involvement in Democratic Party politics (he had contributed to her campaign), also welcomed the purchase, which meant, she said, that "the area can be redeveloped." Alexander Garvin was cautiously supportive as well, though a month later, in his December 2004 report, he wrote, "The rights-of-way must be purchased immediately, before Atlanta's booming real estate market snatches them away. Already, a private developer who supports the Beltline project has placed the northeast quadrant under contract. Future purchasers may not be as sympathetic."

Wayne Mason, working with his son Keith, a lawyer who had served in the Bill Clinton administration, wanted to move forward quickly with plans to develop the property. "We'll talk to everybody who's got an interest," the elder Mason said. "We'll get it all on the table, see what makes sense, and make a decision." He was particularly entranced with Piedmont Park, which he said was "as vital to Atlanta as Central Park is to New York." Not having to answer to a board of directors, he could act decisively and told a reporter, "Development and the formation of transit and parks on his portion of the corridor will be easy."

At an early-morning meeting about the BeltLine, held on January 18, 2005, more than two hundred big-money developers, consultants, lawyers, and supporters gathered to hear Wayne Mason as he took the podium for the first time since his purchase. He declared an end to the days of the "half-acre [lot], swing set and a dog" suburban dream. "Every developer from Nashville to Jacksonville was there," said Ed McBrayer of the PATH Foundation. A reporter observed that they "appeared eager to line up behind Mason."

All the pieces seemed to be coming together for the BeltLine. The long-awaited MARTA "inner core" study offered four possible transit options, including the BeltLine. A MARTA official said, "From what we've heard in the community, yes, we should build it." As a reporter noted, the project had produced "an epidemic of civic hope."

March 2005 brought completion of the feasibility study for the tax allocation district. Over a twenty-five-year time frame, the report estimated, a BeltLine TAD would add more than $20 billion to the combined tax bases of the city, Fulton County, and the Atlanta Public Schools, supporting between $1.3 billion and $1.7 billion in TAD bonds, issued on the basis of the incremental tax revenue, above and beyond any tax receipts when the TAD was formed. The total cost of the BeltLine, including a bidirectional trolley line and multiuse trail, would be from $2 billion to $3 billion. "Given the likelihood of attracting matching federal grants for transit, philanthropic funding for parks, and creative public-private partnerships for certain development opportunities," the report concluded, the TAD bonds should suffice to make the project a reality. The report's independent cover letter called the analysis "rigorous, thorough, and conservative" and predicted, "A completed BeltLine will vault Atlanta into the top tier of the world's great places to live."

Creation of a BeltLine TAD required drafting an official "redevelopment plan" approved not only by the city council but by Fulton County commissioners and the Atlanta school board, since those three entities would all have to agree to relinquish the additional TAD tax revenue for twenty-five years. Shirley Franklin and Greg Giornelli said they hoped to complete the process by year's end.

Letters to the editor about the BeltLine were enthusiastic. "In an era when politics is utterly divisive, it is refreshing to find an issue about which there is something approaching consensus," one man wrote. Even a cautious critic said in wonder, "I've never seen such a massive force of people in this city united around a concept like the BeltLine. I just hope it isn't blind allegiance."

The Twin Towers

In mid-April 2005, Mayor Franklin announced her appointment of businessman Ray Weeks to head a new organization, soon christened the Atlanta BeltLine Partnership, to move the project forward. The name signaled that it would supervise others involved in BeltLine development, such as the Trust for Public Land and the PATH Foundation, and would also partner with philanthropies and corporations by seeking their financial support. Gravel's Friends of the Belt Line was an earnest grassroots effort to engage everyday citizens, but Franklin thought that the ambitious Belt-Line project needed professional management with official city sanction and would have to engage ongoing support from the business community.

Ray Weeks had made his fortune by developing industrial parks, first in Gwinnett County, then throughout the Southeast.* With a master's degree in urban studies and a long history of civic service—advancing progressive public policies on land use, regional planning, and environmental protection—and as a former CEO focused on execution and the bottom line, Weeks seemed a good choice to tackle such a complex project.

Over the next four years, the BeltLine job would occupy Weeks seventy hours a week, without pay, and he eventually donated $1.3 million to the project. "It was incredibly stressful in the first year," he recalled. "I just couldn't see how it could happen. I was operating with so few resources." He hired a small initial team that included a public policy consultant and two recent college grads. Weeks also knew he would need a strong board and chose its members carefully for the specific expertise and influence they could bring to the project. Phil Kent, CEO of Turner Broadcasting, contributed a $300,000 video that was essential in communicating the vision. The Reverend Gerald Durley, Clara Axam, and Mtamanika Youngblood, all African Americans, had community organizing skills and important neighborhood ties. Others brought legal talents to the board. All agreed to serve at Mayor Franklin's request and because of Weeks's reputation for getting things done.

From the beginning, Weeks and Mayor Franklin had to cobble together the resources they needed. Because there was no money to pay for consultants, the two leaders called on their contacts. Ultimately a

---

* Weeks's father, a high school dropout, founded the family fortune by selling Pecan Twirls, then established the Weeks Corporation to develop industrial sites. His son took over the company and dramatically expanded it.

confluence of ad hoc resources got the project off the ground. Atlanta's
Robert W. Woodruff, Arthur Blank, and James M. Cox Foundations
would prove indispensable.

Wayne Mason considered himself a former Gwinnett mentor to the
younger Weeks and was pleased that his friend was taking over as the
city leader of the project. At a meeting with Keith Mason and others on
May 5, Weeks stated that the Masons' involvement was a terrific opportunity and said, "The BeltLine will sink or swim based on the success of
this [Mason's northeastern corridor development] project." Because the
developers needed to make a profit and the city needed density near the
BeltLine, in his view, it could be a win-win situation. But the two men's
relationship would soon fracture.

Two weeks later, an *Atlanta Journal-Constitution* headline read, "Beltline High-Rise Proposed; Residential Units Would Border Piedmont
Park." At a Midtown Neighbors' Association meeting, one of Mason's
lawyers let slip that the developer planned to put two residential towers,
at least twenty stories each, just north of the intersection of 10th Street
and Monroe Drive. Keith Mason wouldn't confirm the report, saying,
"We're considering a number of options for the property we own along
the corridor." The reporter predicted, "The local neighborhoods could
protest buildings of that size bordering the city's central park. A proposed
parking deck [in the park] has run into organized and angry resistance."

On May 20, the day after the article appeared, Ray Weeks was
scheduled for a conference call with Keith Mason and Jane Langley, the
Masons' public relations representative. While waiting for Mason to get
on the line, Weeks told Langley that the proposed towers would never
succeed and that if they proceeded, he could not support the Mason
team. During the long subsequent phone conversation, Keith Mason
refused to back off, saying that failure to go forward with the proposal
would suggest that they weren't serious about developing the property.
Indeed, many cynical observers would later accuse the Masons of never
intending to build anything, which was not the case.

On Thursday, June 2, 2005, the Masons filed requests to rezone their
property with the city, revealing their detailed plans for the first time.
The inches-thick package included projections for low-, medium-, and
high-rise residential and retail units strung along the 4.6-mile corridor.
But they would only develop a third of the land, and Wayne Mason offered to donate half of the acreage for green space, trails, and a planned

transit line. "Mason delivered on his promise to propose a project that would make it more fun to live, work, and play in the Midtown area," wrote an Atlanta reporter.

Despite the complex plans, however, most readers focused on the two towers proposed to border Piedmont Park. They would be thirty-eight and thirty-nine stories high, nearly twice the height previously reported, with the bottom seven levels reserved for parking. The transit line would run through the buildings. "You want density where you have open space," Wayne Mason explained. "A lot of Sun Belt cities have proven they can grow out. This project will prove if Atlanta can grow up."

Several newspaper editorials praised Mason's plans, but neighborhood activists reacted swiftly and negatively. Without immediately installed public transit, the development would spew too many cars onto the already crowded streets, they said. The towers would cast shadows on the surrounding homes and block their view of the park. A letter to the editor from an Atlanta resident complained that Mason's plan "eliminates the greenway, replacing it with a narrow strip that runs under his parking decks." On Saturday night, June 11, the Atlanta Development Authority, which oversaw the new BeltLine Partnership, held its first public workshop for the northeastern neighborhoods. "This is not going to be a gripe session about the Mason plan," ADA president Greg Giornelli said in opening the four-hour meeting, but over two hundred angry residents griped anyway. Giornelli assured them that the city would not consider any rezoning requests before establishment of the full BeltLine plan.

Over the next few months, the furor over Wayne Mason's plans only intensified, with neighborhood activists distributing fliers that asserted, "The BeltLine Can Be Better Than This." Another bitter resident called the towers "twin monoliths to corporate greed and unbridled development right in Atlanta's residential heart." When the developers offered to downsize the buildings, using a stair-step design to reduce their long shadows, one activist leader responded by saying that *nothing* should be built next to the park. "The area should remain open space."

Ray Weeks, Greg Giornelli, and Shirley Franklin distanced themselves from the Masons—failing to include them on committees, not responding to requests in a timely manner, and generally turning a cold bureaucratic shoulder. Franklin felt betrayed because she thought Wayne Mason had agreed not to file for rezoning until after her reelection that fall. Mason and his team held a series of neighborhood meetings in an attempt to allay fears, but with his pinstripe suits, gold cufflinks, and rapid-fire South-in-the-mouth patter, he seemed to fit the stereotype of the suburban developer in *A Man in Full*, Tom Wolfe's 1998 novel about Atlanta: "That was what a real estate developer was, a one-man band!" thought Wolfe's protagonist, Charlie Croker. "They had to think you were some kind of omnipotent, flaw-free genius." In the novel, Croker even builds a mixed-use development crowned with a forty-story tower in an eerie foreshadowing of Mason's plans.

In August 2005, to advise the tax allocation district committee, Ray Weeks established a Land Use Task Force with twenty-two members, mostly metro Atlanta developers with experience in mixed-use, residential, retail, office, and industrial projects. In what seemed a deliberate slap in the face, he did not invite Wayne Mason, the developer who owned nearly a quarter of the BeltLine, to serve on the task force.

Release the following month of the eighty-eight-page "Atlanta Belt-Line Redevelopment Plan" provided detailed boundaries and justification for the 6,100-acre TAD. The report cited community opposition to the towers and suggested "the retention of this site as greenspace." In preparing the report over the previous months, the planning team had consulted with "various stakeholder interests, including local government officials, residents, non-profit groups, and developers"—but no one from the Mason team.

Yet Wayne Mason didn't give up. He hired a team of transit experts, including the firm that had planned the Portland, Oregon, streetcars, to explore the best options for his portion of the BeltLine. He implied that he could indeed be a speedy one-man band. "I think transit on my part of the BeltLine will work as a stand-alone," he said. "It makes a lot of sense for the guys who are developing it to put the transit in. This doesn't have to be government-sanctioned or federally funded."

In late November 2005, Mason sweetened his proffered deal. Now, instead of half the corridor, he would donate two-thirds of the property for public transit, trails, and green space. The transit study he had commissioned advised him to expand the width for transit to forty-six feet in most places. But the deal was off the table if he couldn't build some version of his towers. "We can only do that if we're successful with a zoning that makes economic sense." The city could always buy his land, he said, "and then they can do whatever they want with it. But it defies logic to do that."

Rushing to Get the TAD Approved

As the tumult over Mason's proposed development continued, Ray Weeks and Greg Giornelli mounted a full-court press to get the BeltLine tax allocation district approved before year's end—a daunting task that required convincing the Atlanta City Council, Fulton County Commission, and the Atlanta Public Schools board to forego incremental tax revenue increases for the next twenty-five years.

And before they could even get started, on September 29, 2005, a panel of transportation experts, commissioned by the Atlanta Development Authority to study the BeltLine transit component, issued a white paper that cast serious doubt on its feasibility. Three of the five authors were Georgia Tech professors. "Of all the information generated in support of the BeltLine concept," they wrote, "ridership appears to be the least studied or understood. This is perplexing." They questioned whether enough people would ride BeltLine streetcars to get to work since "there are few locations along the BeltLine where large and dense concentrations of jobs are expected." And transfers to rapid transit were problematic since "the BeltLine crosses the MARTA line between stations typically at least one half mile away." The old circumferential rail lines, built long before MARTA, did not intersect at any rapid transit stations. Nor were plans in place to pay for ongoing operating costs.

The white paper gave lukewarm support to BeltLine transit, saying that it should remain an ultimate goal, but for these reasons, as well as the discontinuity challenges, the authors questioned the wisdom of immediate pursuit of the transit component. "It is the most expensive, the most technically challenging, the longest to get going and build out, and the furthest from identifying how it might actually get done." After the report came out, one of the Georgia Tech profs quipped, "Some people are going to kill me for that, but I have tenure."

Mike Dobbins, the former Atlanta planning commissioner who had heard Ryan Gravel's thesis presentation in 1999, was another of those Georgia Tech authors, and he soon emerged as BeltLine transit's most vocal gadfly. A few weeks later, as votes on the TAD loomed, Dobbins wrote an open letter to Mayor Franklin about the "flaws and unaddressed issues" of the TAD proposal. He praised the BeltLine's trails and linked parks but slammed streetcars. "This clear boon to the future city is dragged down by a transit concept . . . that is unproven and . . . highly problematic." To work, he asserted, transit had to connect homes to destinations such as work, shopping, or events. "The problem with the BeltLine is that it's all origins and no destinations."

Mayor Franklin responded with an adamant defense. "The BeltLine is Atlanta's future. Transit is critical to the BeltLine, and it will work, and it will provide the framework for a higher quality of life for every resident of our great city."

Few paid attention to Dobbins the naysayer. Ray Weeks and Greg Giornelli were too busy organizing a massive lobbying effort in favor of the TAD votes, starting with the city council. "For any major plan or project, there comes a time for action," Giornelli said. "For the BeltLine, that time is now." Mayor Franklin asked for a "leap of faith" to pass the TAD. "Despite the sense of unreadiness, the opportunity to create the Beltline will slip away if we don't act now," she emphasized, stressing that passage must happen soon. Seize the moment so that Atlanta could sell over $100 million in bonds and funnel taxes collected on new development in 2006 toward the project. If the TAD were delayed, land prices would go up, and someone like Wayne Mason might buy key parcels. TAD money was also needed to leverage federal funding with matching dollars. The *Atlanta Journal-Constitution* urged passage in an editorial, wryly observing, "The BeltLine cannot single-handedly erase blight in poor neighborhoods, cure traffic congestion or, for that matter, the common cold." But it was an important project, and TAD passage was the key next step.

Ray Weeks and his BeltLine Partnership set up a war room with files about every official whose vote they would need to secure the TAD. The biggest challenge was getting Fulton County commissioners, Atlanta Public Schools board members, and city officials to agree on the terms of the deal. Leaders for each entity had their own agendas, which made the negotiations extremely challenging. The team identified who among the BeltLine volunteers was best suited to contact each official.

The BeltLine Partnership launched a website; distributed fliers, brochures, and newsletters; and held a flurry of neighborhood meetings, many at churches. Mayor Franklin and Ray Weeks held a breakfast for neighborhood planning unit (NPU) leaders from around the city.* Eight

---

* In 1974 Atlanta was divided into twenty-five neighborhood planning units, labeled alphabetically (NPU A, NPU B, and so forth), with each containing several distinct neighborhoods. NPUs can advise on but not dictate policy.

bus tours took city council members and other influential people to see strategic parts of the future BeltLine, including an impressive overlook of the Bellwood Quarry. In a prepared Q&A session, the BeltLine Partnership reassured skeptics. "We are absolutely committed to the BeltLine transit," and the critical white paper wouldn't change that. "The fact that some parts of the BeltLine do not show large potential ridership today is not surprising—this is a plan for the future, not reacting to the past."

Because the BeltLine bordered so many Atlanta neighborhoods, city council members were, in general, favorably inclined. The carefully drawn TAD boundaries excluded areas with single-family homes so that potential developments would not threaten to encroach on established residential neighborhoods, including affluent Buckhead properties. According to Georgia law, the whole TAD rationale was to improve areas that were "economically and socially depressed" when viewed as a whole. That designation certainly applied to poverty-stricken, mostly black neighborhoods to the south and west. As those areas attracted growth, however, gentrification might very well push out poor residents. Deborah Scott, the African American executive director of the Georgia Strategic Alliance for New Directions and Unified Policies (STAND-UP), a new nonprofit promoting community benefits, pushed for the hiring of locals in building the BeltLine and to set aside 25 percent of the TAD bond money for "workforce" housing.* In the end, that figure dropped to 15 percent, which was supposed to pay for 5,600 affordable housing units over a twenty-five-year time frame. After considerable debate, the city council approved the TAD by 12–3 in early November.

The negotiation with the Atlanta Board of Education was more difficult. Getting to an agreement was essential, because Atlanta schools grabbed about a half of all property taxes. City negotiators suggested that the schools should receive 5.5 percent of all TAD bonds sold, which would come to an estimated $95 million over twenty-five years, to help pay for improved and new schools to serve a projected inflow of students. The board members insisted on a fixed amount rather than a percentage, agreeing in mid-December to a hefty $150 million in total payments. This concession, made hastily in order to secure a contract, seemed doable at the time, given the income projections for the TAD, but would create huge

---

* As the BeltLine was built, few locals got hired, ostensibly because they were not qualified.

problems down the line. No payments would be due for the first five years, but for the next twenty years, the city agreed to pay the schools $7.5 million annually. Above and beyond that, it agreed to donate a suitable piece of land and to pay an additional $10 million to construct recreational facilities and/or athletic fields on it. The contract included another provision requiring that all developers who received TAD money pay $25,000 to the school system. Finally, up to 840 low-cost housing units would be reserved for teachers and other staff members.

That left only the Fulton County Commission, whose buy-in had at first seemed a sure thing, but three commissioners repeatedly demanded more information about plans for affordable housing, deferring the vote. Finally, on December 22, 2005, they passed the TAD by 5–1, after the city agreed to pay $27 million in TAD dollars to the Atlanta-Fulton Public Library System. TAD bonds could now be floated, offering Atlanta the opportunity, as one pundit said, to "dream big and in hyper-speed."

Not So Fast

Well, not quite. The Wayne Mason affair remained unresolved, a maverick Buckhead lawyer was about to cause trouble, and other unforeseen crises would arise. But before continuing the BeltLine saga, in which racial issues loomed large, let us look back to see how two separate but unequal Atlantas developed.

CHAPTER 4
TWO ATLANTAS: THE RACIAL DIVIDE

···

Again we have a city that struts before the world as the
liberal gateway of a great section, but is really the same
old Atlanta steeped in the foul odors of ante-bellum
traditions and held firmly in the remorseless clutch of a
vile and unreasonable race prejudice.

—Jesse Max Barber, "The Atlanta Tragedy," 1906

Atlanta is an interesting case for investigating the causes
of urban inequality. It is a city that presents a paradox of
phenomenal growth in contrast to the unexpected high
level of inner-city poverty and economic stagnation, and
of a black mecca in contrast to the unexpected high level
of segregation.

—David Sjoquist, *The Atlanta Paradox*, 2000

There are really two Atlantas, black and white, and despite native son
Martin Luther King Jr. and Atlanta's central place in the civil rights
movement, the racial divide remains an often unspoken aspect of every
other issue facing the city, including transportation, housing, food, education, religion, health, and the environment. Today, African Americans
live primarily in the southern and western parts of the city and whites to
the north and east. The BeltLine will connect them all and promises, at
long last, to promote mixed-race neighborhoods and equal enjoyment of

its trails, transit, and parks, if sufficient affordable housing and jobs accompany the project.

Yet historical roots influence contemporary behavior and decisions for a city just as childhood experiences remain crucial to adult attitudes for an individual. Not that long ago—about a century and a half—most African Americans living in Atlanta were slaves, the property of white owners who could sell or mistreat them at will. Many of their grandparents or great grandparents had been abducted and shipped from Africa, enduring unspeakable conditions that they barely survived.

The state of Georgia, founded by James Oglethorpe as a colony for the "worthy poor" of England as an alternative to debtors' prison, banned slavery until 1750. By 1775, however, it had 18,000 slaves, mostly put to work cultivating rice in the coastal region. In 1793 in Savannah, Eli Whitney invented the cotton gin, which made cotton king and created a huge demand for slave labor. When still called Terminus, Atlanta was home to only fifty African Americans, all but two of them slaves; by the time of the Civil War, 460,000 Georgia residents lived in bondage.

During the war, some Atlanta slaves thrived. For instance, Prince Ponder ran a grocery store, selling provisions, tobacco, and whiskey, and managed to purchase his freedom. Others, not so fortunate, were forced into press gangs to build fortifications against the Yankees. "The black'uns they have got," said runaway slaves, "are dying up like any thing, for they work 'em so hard, and half starves 'em besides."

After the War

While white Southerners soon embraced a romantic version of the Civil War as the "Lost Cause," ex-slaves celebrated their freedom, even as they struggled to survive. Freedmen from rural areas converged on Atlanta, swelling the black population from 1,900 to 10,000 out of a total 22,000. A Yankee soldier observed that ex-slaves were "huddled together, where any thing can be found to shelter them, while many sleep without shelter [other] than the sky."

Among the occupying forces were black soldiers, whom a reporter for the *Atlanta Daily Intelligencer* called "a great outrage," asserting that Negroes lived in "idleness, vice, and profligacy," all in-born racial traits. "Freedman he may be, but he will still retain the characteristics of the African race. What God has implanted in his *nature*, man may not, cannot remove." A white diarist in Gwinnett County, to Atlanta's northeast, predicted blacks' extermination. "They are now of little profit to their [former] owners and they cannot make out by themselves. Work they will not. . . . The whites will kill them in self-defense." A Northern official reported that he had heard similar false assertions: "They are killing their children. They are guilty of inebriation. The whole population is diseased and degraded."

Many of the Union soldiers, stationed at the McPherson Barracks (later Fort McPherson), just to the southwest of Atlanta, also mistreated freed slaves, but at least they provided protection from wanton white violence. The federal government created the Freedmen's Bureau in 1865, and before the organization's demise seven years later, the Atlanta field office helped reunite slave families, started schools, and founded a rudimentary hospital for African Americans. The American Missionary Association also founded black schools, including the elementary-level Storrs School and Atlanta University. When the commissioner of the Freedmen's Bureau visited the Storrs School in 1868, he asked, "What shall I tell the children in the North about you?" Twelve-year-old Richard R. Wright said proudly, "Tell them, General, we're rising."* Wright was later valedictorian of his Atlanta University class and started a Philadelphia bank. "We Are Rising" became Atlanta University's school anthem.

For a few years, Georgia black men could vote and hold office, and on July 21, 1870, several hundred African Americans marched down Peachtree Street to celebrate their enfranchisement by the recently ratified Fifteenth Amendment. Henry McNeal Turner, a black minister and Republican state representative, gave a fiery speech. He was there, he declared, "to demand my rights and to hurl thunderbolts at the men who would dare to cross the threshold of my manhood. Am I not a man, because I happen to be of a darker hue than honorable gentlemen around me?" A few months later, in a fraudulent election, he lost his seat, but Turner went on to become a bishop of the African Methodist Episcopal (AME) church.

The Reconstruction period lasted officially until 1877, when the federal government withdrew its troops from the South, but poll taxes, white-only primaries, and literacy requirements had effectively disenfranchised Georgia blacks long before that. The Ku Klux Klan (KKK),

---

* No relation to Richard Wright, author of *Black Boy*.

founded in Tennessee in 1865 by six Confederate veterans, sought to maintain white supremacy through intimidation, violence, and murder. Grand Wizard Nathan Bedford Forrest came to Atlanta in 1868 and established a Georgia Klan, headquartered in the city. KKK activity waxed and waned over the years, but the racist outlook it represented didn't vanish. "Atlanta thus became, paradoxically, a bastion of both white supremacy and black autonomy, a locale in which competing visions of the post-emancipation world emerged," wrote historian William Link in *Atlanta, Cradle of the New South: Race and Remembering in the Civil War's Aftermath*. Once established, that two-sided nature would endure, in various guises, into the twenty-first century.

The Gilded Cage

By 1886, the year that John Pemberton invented Coca-Cola, Atlanta was a boomtown at the height of the Gilded Age. The following year, the city adopted a new seal featuring a phoenix rising from the flames, along with the Latin word *Resurgens*, meaning "rising again." As white Atlantans strove to make their fortunes in the bustling city, boosters talked about the "Atlanta spirit," which helped make it the "Gate City" to the South. It featured several grand hotels, an opera house, a governor's mansion, and numerous factories and shops. For rural black sharecroppers, Atlanta represented hope for steady wages and independence from plantation life. They worked in the city's slaughterhouses, hotels, factories, rail shops, and cotton mills. Others became waiters, barbers, bootblacks, porters, draymen, hack drivers, and teamsters. Black women worked in some factories and as domestic servants and laundresses. Carrie Steele, a former slave who worked for Central of Georgia Railroad as a stewardess in Union Station, started an orphanage for homeless black children in an abandoned boxcar and then opened the Carrie Steele Orphan Home in 1888.

The city also had some black skilled laborers, particularly bricklayers and carpenters, and professionals, such as businessmen, lawyers, dentists, doctors, undertakers, journalists, teachers, professors, and ministers, who dressed in the same elegant Victorian garb as their white counterparts. Some African Americans succeeded in making their fortunes. For instance, former slave Alonzo Herndon opened a barbershop, serving an exclusively white clientele, in the elegant Markham House in 1886. He eventually owned six barbershops, invested extensively in real estate, and created the Atlanta Life Insurance Company, in the process becoming a millionaire. In addition to Atlanta University, five other black colleges were founded in the city—Clark College (1869), Morehouse College (originally Atlanta Baptist Seminary, 1879), Spelman College (originally Spelman Baptist Female Seminary, 1881), Gammon Theological Seminary (1883), and Morris Brown College (1885). Impressive black churches were also established in Atlanta: Friendship Baptist (1862), Big Bethel AME (1865), First Congregational (1867), Wheat Street Baptist (1870), and Ebenezer Baptist (1886).

In his "New South" speech of 1886, Henry Grady assured New Yorkers that "the South of slavery and secession" was dead. "We have caught the sunshine in the bricks and mortar of our homes, and have builded therein not one ignoble prejudice or memory," he asserted, adding, "The free Negro counts more than he did as a slave. . . . No section shows a more prosperous laboring population than the Negroes of the South; none in fuller sympathy with the employing and land-owning class. He shares our school fund, has the fullest protection of our laws and the friendship of our people."

Despite this rosy picture, Grady and other white Atlantans continued to regard African Americans as innately inferior. Black citizens did not enjoy the full protection of the law: mobs could lynch them with impunity. Their elementary schools were inadequate, their teachers underpaid, and there was no black high school. African Americans tended to live in flood-prone valleys or next to railroad lines, cemeteries, dumps, or slaughterhouses in homes often not serviced by electricity, running water, or paved roads. In the 1880s, in building Edgewood Avenue to carry his electric streetcars to Inman Park, Joel Hurt tore down black housing on Foster Street.

The Georgia convict-lease system, instituted in 1876, enabled the use of black prisoners as virtual slave labor, subject to brutal treatment by businesses such as Joel Hurt's Tennessee coal mines, which he bought in 1895. Hurt urged his guards to shoot workers who tried to escape and to flog them frequently. "He wanted men whipped for singing and laughing," a former chief warden said. The imprisoned men often died from punishment or disease.

Conditions were equally dire at the Chattahoochee Brick Company near Atlanta, owned by wealthy white James English, a bank founder and former Atlanta mayor. In *Slavery by Another Name: The Re-enslavement of Black Americans from the Civil War to World War II*, historian Douglas

A black prisoner tied around a pick-ax in an early twentieth century Georgia labor camp

Blackmon documents in horrific detail how English's overseer whipped
and murdered his workers with impunity. Grady's claim to "have caught
the sunshine in the bricks and mortar of our homes" was thus horribly
inaccurate—rather, the bricks absorbed the groans of tortured black
laborers.

Henry Grady revealed his own racial prejudice in several venues.
In 1881, after viewing a performance of *Uncle Tom's Cabin*, he called the
"plantation darkey" "the happiest laborer on all the earth." In a Texas
speech in 1887, he said that "the hope and assurance of the South" was
the "clear and unmistakable domination of the white race." The following year, Grady warned of the "menace of negro domination" posed
by allowing African Americans to vote, an attitude shared by most of
his white associates. In December 1889, less than two weeks before his
death at age forty-nine from pneumonia, Grady asserted that the white

plantation owner had elevated the black slave to "heights of which he had not dreamed in his savage [African] home."

Despite their exclusion from city parks and relegation to overcrowded, filthy "Jim Crow" railroad cars, many black Atlantans remained proud and hopeful. In 1894, Edward Randolph Carter, minister of Friendship Baptist Church, published *The Black Side: A Partial History of the Business, Religious, and Educational Side of the Negro in Atlanta, Ga.* Atlanta's African Americans had "leaped over impediments, gone ahead, purchased the soil, erected houses of business and reared dwellings," he wrote. Given an equal chance, blacks could "accomplish what any other race has accomplished." In the book's introduction, Henry McNeal Turner wrote of black people's "genius, skill, bravery, adventure and enterprise." God was color-blind, and there was "no such place as a white heaven, where every angel, cherub and seraph is white."

In 1895, in what would become Piedmont Park, Atlanta hosted the Cotton States and International Exposition, a world's fair meant to tout Southern achievement, entice Northern capital, and encourage international trade. Partially funded by federal dollars, the exposition featured a 25,000-square-foot Negro Building that was, to the amazement of the *Atlanta Constitution*, "built by negroes, under the supervision of negroes, and filled with exhibits showing the progress of the colored race."

At the opening ceremony for the Negro Building, Adrienne Herndon, an elocution instructor at Atlanta University and the wife of Alonzo Herndon, read a poem by a black Virginia professor that included the lines "Disfranchisement, injustice and prejudices gone, / We'll rejoice together at the coming of the dawn." Then keynote speaker J. W. E. Bowen of Gammon Theological Seminary asserted, "All men are natively and equally endowed with the essentials of humanity and divinity." An African American must be "a man among men, not so much a black man, but a man though black." Richard Wright, who as a boy had proclaimed, "We are rising," gave a speech saying that solving the South's racial problems required "exact and untrammeled justice to all its citizens." Near the entrance of the Negro Building stood a large sculpture titled "A Negro with Chains Broken but Not Off," a visual representation of incomplete freedom.

Despite such assertions of black dignity, however, placards on some exposition buildings admonished, "Dogs and Negroes not admitted."

African Americans sat in separate sections for programs and performances and used separate restrooms and eating facilities. Black women
were excluded from the Woman's Building, planned by Rebecca Latimer
Felton, who proclaimed two years later, "If it needs lynching to protect
woman's dearest possession from ravening human beasts, then I say lynch
a thousand a week, if necessary."

In the midway near the Negro Building was the popular Old Plantation exhibit, one of President Grover Cleveland's favorites when he visited the exposition. On the front porch sat a "great fat old negro aunty,"
according to the *Atlanta Constitution*, who assured visitors that the dancers
inside were authentic: "Dis here am sho 'nough 'possum-eatin' black nigger in here; 'tain't no black-faced white trash." A white member of the
audience reviewed the show: "Real negroes on the platform before us,
dancing wildly, and singing in that queer crooning animal way."

Today we remember the exposition primarily for the opening-day
speech of black educator Booker T. Washington, head of the Tuskegee
Normal and Industrial Institute in Alabama and the nation's most influential (and careful) black spokesman. He reassured nervous whites,
"The wisest among my race understand that the agitation of questions of
social equality is the extremest folly." Rather, he counseled, "in all things
purely social we can be as separate as the fingers, yet one as the hand in
all things essential to mutual progress." Washington advocated for blacks
to focus on learning useful trades. In his view, "ignorant and inexpe-
rienced" freed slaves had foolishly tried to enter politics, but they were
better off "in agriculture, mechanics, in commerce, in domestic service,
and in the professions. . . . There is as much dignity in tilling a field as in
writing a poem. It is at the bottom of life we must begin, and not at the
top." Besides, he said, black workers wouldn't join unions or go on strike.
They were "the most patient, faithful, law-abiding, and unresentful people that the world has seen." Washington emphasized "the importance of
cultivating friendly relations with the Southern white man, who is their
next-door neighbor."

Washington's message met with wild cheering from the white audience and the approval of President Cleveland and the *Atlanta Constitution*.
This "Atlanta Compromise" speech came to haunt the uneasy relations
between the races in the city for decades to come. The black orator had utterly ignored the lynching epidemic; there were 8 in Georgia that year, and
the state led the nation with 386 lynchings between 1889 and 1918. The

year after his speech, the US Supreme Court's *Plessy v. Ferguson* decision, upholding the "separate but equal" concept, legalized Jim Crow segregation. Until the 1960s, black Atlantans would attend separate-but-unequal schools. Theaters, hotels, restaurants, water fountains, swimming pools, and parks were segregated. Black court witnesses swore on a separate Bible, lest white hands touch the same holy book. For African Americans in the late nineteenth century, the Gilded Age was more of a cage.

The 1906 Race Riot

Some black Atlanta leaders severely criticized Booker T. Washington's conciliatory attitude. By the turn of the century, very few whites were their "next-door neighbors," unless Washington meant the domestic servants who lived in shacks in back alleys behind wealthy white homes. Most blacks lived in neighborhoods in west, east, and south Atlanta called Darktown, Niggertown, Shermantown, Pittsburgh, Summerhill, or Brownsville. "The colored man who . . . say[s] that the Negroid race does not want social equality . . . is either an ignoramus or is an advocate of the perpetual servility and degradation of his race variety," wrote Bishop Henry McNeal Turner, who ultimately concluded that America held no viable future for blacks and advocated their return to Africa.

W. E. B. Du Bois, who moved to Atlanta in 1897 as a professor of history and economics at Atlanta University, became the most prominent critic of Booker T. Washington. In his 1903 book, *The Souls of Black Folk*, Du Bois explored "the strange meaning of being black here at the dawning of the Twentieth Century." In dealing with the white majority, he wrote, there was always an unspoken question: *How does it feel to be a problem?* "It is a peculiar sensation," he wrote, "this double-consciousness, this sense of always looking at one's self through the eyes of others, of measuring one's soul by the tape of a world that looks on in amused contempt and pity." Black men longed "to attain self-conscious manhood," but they were continually thwarted.

Raised in Massachusetts and educated at Harvard, Du Bois espoused an elitist philosophy in which the African American "Talented Tenth" would lead their people to true freedom. Du Bois lambasted Washington's "old attitude of adjustment and submission," which urged African Americans not to pursue political power, civil rights, or higher education. "Is it possible," he asked, for blacks to "make effective progress in economic lines if they are deprived of political rights, made a servile caste, and allowed only the most meagre chance for developing their exceptional men?"

In his book, Du Bois credited Atlanta with being "south of the North, yet north of the South . . . peering out from the shadows of the past into the promise of the future." The city had "crowned her hundred hills with factories and stored her shops with cunning handiwork." Yet Du Bois worried that the "Gospel of Pay" had become all-important. "It is replacing the finer type of Southerner with vulgar money-getters," among African Americans as well as whites. "The well-paid porters and artisans, the business-men—all those with property and money" were the rising black middle class. Still, African Americans in Atlanta were "unthought of, half forgotten" by the white world.

Except when it came to rape allegations. Rumors spread that black men, tanked up on alcohol and cocaine, were attacking white women. "Use of the drugs among negroes is growing to an alarming extent," wrote an *Atlanta Constitution* reporter in 1901. "Quite a number of soft drinks . . . contain cocaine." Coca-Cola did contain a small amount, quietly removed in 1903, but the rumors continued. Decatur Street, which ran southeast from the Five Points center of Atlanta, was notorious for its dives, burlesques, and dance halls, where black couples sensuously danced the Itch, the Grind, and the Slow Drag. Whites feared what might emerge from this den of iniquity.

In 1905, Thomas Dixon published *The Clansman: An Historical Romance of the Ku Klux Klan*, adapted for the stage and performed that year in Atlanta. In one scene a freed slave attempted to ravish a white teenaged girl, who leaped off a cliff to her death. "Lynch him!" the Atlanta audience screamed, and on stage the KKK obliged as the crowd cheered. The following year, during a bitter gubernatorial campaign, candidates Hoke Smith and Clark Howell both stoked the racist flames. Smith wanted to legally disenfranchise blacks. Not to be outdone, Howell countered, "This is a white man's country, and it must be governed by white men." Beginning in July 1906, the newspapers began to highlight black attacks on white women, a few accounts apparently true, most false.

"If the negro were no longer a part of our population," wrote the *Atlanta Georgian* on September 5, 1906, "the women of the South would be freed from their state of siege. . . . But under the black shadow of the fiendish passion of these ebony devils our women are . . . completely slaves." Sheriff John Nelms vowed, "We will suppress these great indignities upon our fair wives and daughters if we have to kill every negro within a thousand miles of this place." On September 21, the *Atlanta News* portrayed the "terrifying spectacle" of a partially dressed black man, "his yellow lips forming insulting phrases," as his "hand brushed against her [a white woman's] clothing." The paper's evening edition printed an editorial headlined, "It Is Time to Act, Men; Will You Do Your Duty Now?"

The next day, Saturday, September 22, 1906, this powder keg exploded, as newsboys hawked extra editions throughout the day alleging four new attempted assaults, one of which involved a white woman simply seeing a black man outside her window and calling the police. By 8:30 p.m., thousands of whites had massed at Five Points, egging one another on into minor skirmishes and assaults. At 10:30 p.m., the crowd attacked a streetcar carrying white women and black men. At least three black men were beaten and stabbed to death in the back of the trolley. The mob stopped nineteen other streetcars that night, assaulting and killing several other black passengers. Elsewhere, they shot bootblacks even as they

Illustration depicting the 1906 Atlanta Race Riot

polished white men's shoes, killed a black woman shopper, chased and murdered railroad porters outside Union Depot, and marched east toward Darktown, where black residents fired into and drove back the mob.

Over the next few days, sporadic violence continued. On Monday night, after hearing rumors of a planned retaliation, seven policemen and three deputized citizens mounted an offensive against the Brownsville neighborhood in south Atlanta, whose citizens defended themselves. In the gunfight, a white policeman and black grocer were killed, and a mob then murdered two escaped blacks. Soon afterward, Northern white journalist Ray Stannard Baker investigated.

> When I went out to Brownsville, knowing of its bloody part in the riot, I expected to find a typical Negro slum. . . . I was surprised to find a large settlement of Negroes practically every one of whom owned his own [attractive] home. Near at hand, surrounded by beautiful grounds, were two Negro colleges—Clark University and Gammon Theological Seminary.

President Bowen of the seminary, who had spoken eloquently at the 1895 exposition and had no part in the violence, was beaten over the head by a policeman and arrested during a Tuesday morning raid, along with 256 other black Brownsville residents.

Mortality data vary, with estimates ranging from 25 to 250 African American and 2 to 6 Caucasian deaths during the riot. Contrary to widespread reports that only lower-class whites made up the mob, the assailants included a doctor, dentist, clerk, business college student, carpenter, butcher, and railroad employee.

The Atlanta Race Riot of 1906 made international news and had a profound impact on race relations in the city over the following century. Some black families hastily departed. One such refugee asked Baker, "How would you feel if you saw a governor, a mayor, a sheriff, whom you could not oppose at the polls, encourage by deed or word or both, a mob of 'best' and worst citizens to slaughter your people in the streets and in their own homes and in their places of business?" W. E. B. Du Bois reacted by writing "A Litany of Atlanta": "Bewildered we are, and passion-tost, mad with the madness of a mobbed and mocked and murdered people. . . . Sit no longer blind, Lord God, deaf to our prayer and dumb to our dumb suffering. Surely Thou art not white, O Lord, a pale, bloodless, heartless thing?" Du Bois also bought a shotgun. He left Atlanta in 1910, shortly after helping to found the National Association for the Advancement of Colored People (NAACP).

For the majority of African Americans who remained in Atlanta, the omnipresent threat of violence hung heavy. Led by black elite leaders such as Reverend Henry Hugh Proctor of the First Congregational Church, they sought cautious alliances with powerful white leaders who hated the bad publicity and business disruption the riot had brought Atlanta and wanted to avoid another embarrassing outbreak of violence—not unlike Atlanta's twenty-first-century business leaders, who are exceedingly conscious of the city's image. But blacks remained in the inferior position of having to push politely for change while enduring subtle or overt prejudice, condescension, and broken promises. Proctor asked that Atlanta appoint black police officers, for instance, and white lawyer and chamber member Charles Hopkins agreed to do so, but the city had no black police for four decades.

The riot generally reinforced rather than lessened Southern white prejudices. In 1908, even stronger Georgia disenfranchisement legislation was passed. Yet, because elite blacks and whites now at least met to discuss their problems, in 1911 Booker T. Washington declared the race riot "a blessed visitation." In his comprehensive *Veiled Visions: The 1906 Atlanta Race Riot and the Reshaping of American Race Relations*, David Godshalk summarized the riot's long-term impact: "Atlanta's unbroken tradition of biracial compromises—rooted in long-standing interracial relationships dating back to 1906—primarily benefitted their white and black negotiators while only cosmetically addressing the city's glaring racial and class inequities."

Leo Frank and the Rebirth of the Ku Klux Klan

Atlanta's Jews experienced a similar terror when Leo Frank, the Jewish superintendent of an Atlanta pencil factory, was falsely convicted of the 1913 rape and murder of thirteen-year-old Mary Phagan, a child laborer in his employ. Although many German Jews had become wealthy business owners in Atlanta—including Jacob Elsas, who owned the Fulton Bag and Cotton Mill, and my maternal great grandfather, Otto Schwab, who cofounded the Atlanta Furniture Company, which transmuted into the Southern Spring Bed Company—anti-Semitism was widespread, and Jews were excluded from the upper-crust white Capital City Club and Piedmont Driving Club. When Georgia's outgoing governor commuted Leo Frank's death sentence, a white mob stormed the prison and lynched him in August 1915. Postcards featuring his body hanging from a tree sold briskly in country stores.

In the wake of Frank's lynching, nearly half of Georgia's Jews fled the state, and those who remained tried to assimilate. Many, including my maternal grandparents, hid their Jewish ethnicity. In November 1915, three months after the lynching, fifteen white men climbed Stone Mountain, a granite dome outcrop east of Atlanta, burned a giant cross, and revived the moribund Ku Klux Klan, targeting Jews, Catholics, and African Americans. A few weeks later, D. W. Griffith's recently released film *The Birth of a Nation*—based on Dixon's *The Clansman* and glorifying the original Klan—elicited rebel yells in Atlanta movie theaters. On December 6, 1915, wearing hooded sheets, new KKK members rode down Peachtree Street on horseback, firing guns into the air and urging whites to "save, reform, and protect" the South.

Headquartered in Atlanta, the new KKK became wildly successful in the 1920s, with 6 million members nationwide. In 1921 the Klan bought an elegant home in Buckhead on Peachtree and renamed it the Imperial Palace. Local membership crested 15,000 and included leading white Atlanta businessmen, educators, clergy, police, judges, and politicians. Coca-Cola advertised in the Klan's official newspaper.

During this same period, Atlanta's residential segregation became more pronounced. A 1915 promotional brochure for the elegant Ansley Park in north Atlanta promised that the neighborhood would never admit black residents. That same year, a black chain gang built Judge Howard Palmer's new home in Inman Park. Grant Park's swimming pool, built in 1917, was for whites only. Brookwood Hills, established in 1922 adjacent to Ansley Park, prohibited "selling, renting, or otherwise disposing of . . . property to persons of African descent."

In the Old Fourth Ward, to the east of downtown, from 1910 onward, whites in the exclusive Jackson Heights area objected to African Americans living nearby. They attempted to move black Morris Brown College out of their neighborhood (in 1929 it did shift to join Atlanta University on the west side). After the Great Fire of 1917 swept through the Old Fourth Ward up to Ponce de Leon, white residents tried to ensure segregated rebuilding. In the wake of the fire, the Atlanta Real Estate Board pushed for the establishment of a city planning commission, "mainly for the purpose of taking steps towards converting a portion of the fire-swept area into an esplanade to separate the two races," as the commission's first annual report in 1922 stated. "Property damage, encroachment of the races, [and] the building of narrow roadways" were all "harmful to the best interest of the city."

The proposed esplanade was never built, but Ponce de Leon Avenue became the unofficial boundary line between white neighborhoods to the north and black ones to the south. To this day, several streets change names there, with Briarcliff becoming Moreland and Monroe turning into Boulevard.

As a consequence, the black community of Atlanta focused on its own segments of the city, with Auburn Avenue, running east off Peachtree near downtown, becoming known among blacks as "Sweet Auburn." The street had 121 African American businesses and 39 professional offices by 1930. Blacks had their own stores, banks, nightclubs, hotels, restaurants, beauty schools, funeral homes, churches, and newspapers. "Atlanta became, in effect, two separate cities—one white, one black," wrote Andy Ambrose in his history of Atlanta.

Black entrepreneur Heman Perry, who arrived in Atlanta with nothing in 1908 and started an insurance company, bank, real estate firm, and other enterprises, built a middle-class black enclave in the early 1920s on Atlanta's west side, near Atlanta University. Until then, as a contemporary noted, "if a Negro wanted a decent home to live in, he waited until some white person wanted to sell his." Perry put up pretty little bungalows on three hundred acres, erected Booker T. Washington High School (1924), and helped secure nearby Washington Park, which had its own swimming pool and dancing pavilion—the first Atlanta high school and park for African Americans. Perry overextended and went bankrupt, but despite KKK bombings and intimidation, this first planned black community established a major black presence on Atlanta's west side.

Racial discrimination became federal policy during the New Deal era, with the Home Owners' Loan Corporation and Federal Housing Administration (FHA) assuming that black residences would adversely affect neighborhood home values. The FHA recommended that subdivisions adopt exclusive covenants and suggested the following phrasing: "No person of any race other than the _____ shall use or occupy any building or any lot."

At the same time, Atlanta built the nation's first public housing—segregated, of course—in 1936 and continued to throw up public housing units for impoverished black residents (in poor black neighborhoods or fringe areas) for the next five decades. Initially desirable places to live, over time the decaying buildings, with their concentration of poor, underemployed African Americans, became notorious drug and crime havens. "In the 1930s and 1940s," wrote one historian, "[Atlanta's white] civic elites and agencies used slum clearance and public housing to eliminate mixed-race neighborhoods, raze small concentrations of black housing that still punctuated the predominantly white north side, establish buffers between black and white neighborhoods, and concentrate black families in the city's core and west side."

In 1936, Margaret Mitchell's *Gone with the Wind* reinforced racial stereotypes. A five-year-old during the Atlanta Race Riot of 1906, Mitchell never forgot the terrifying but unfounded rumors that blacks from nearby Darktown were going to invade her neighborhood of Jackson Hill and burn her home. In the novel, Scarlett O'Hara ventures to "Shantytown," "filled with outcast negroes [and] black prostitutes," where a black robber rips her corset and puts his hands between her breasts.

The movie version of *Gone with the Wind* premiered in Atlanta in December 1939 at Loew's Grand on Peachtree Street for whites only. Blacks had to wait four months to view it at a theater in the Odd Fellows Hall on Auburn Avenue. At a costume ball celebrating the film's release, however, Reverend Martin Luther King Sr. and his ten-year-old namesake dressed up as slaves to sing with the Ebenezer Baptist Church choir for the all-white audience.

White and Black Flight

Black soldiers who fought fascism during World War II (in segregated units) came back home to the same Jim Crow situation. In late 1945, the Ku Klux Klan surged into the spotlight (or firelight) yet again with a rally atop Stone Mountain, featuring a three-hundred-foot-wide cross lit by fuel oil, visible from sixty miles away, "to let the niggers know the war is over and that the Klan is back," as one attendee said. Dozens of Atlanta policemen joined.

In *White Flight: Atlanta and the Making of Modern Conservatism*, historian Kevin Kruse documents Atlanta's postwar battle over housing. "The end of World War II brought a severe housing crisis to Atlanta, as thousands of veterans returned home to discover the city had not only failed to build new homes during their absence but actually started to destroy old ones." In 1946, as more African Americans began to move west of Ashby Street (now renamed Joseph E. Lowery Boulevard), a neo-Nazi group, the Columbians, posted signs reading, "Zoned as a White Community," featuring their lightning insignia. That same year, two white Atlanta streetcar conductors shot and killed two black veterans; neither was prosecuted.*

But times were finally changing. In 1946, the US Supreme Court declared Georgia's all-white primary unconstitutional, and a massive registration campaign added 18,000 new black Atlanta voters in less than two months. African Americans suddenly accounted for a quarter of Atlanta's electorate. Longtime mayor William B. Hartsfield, formerly a staunch segregationist, subsequently became a political pragmatist, working with black leaders to promote incremental, slow change. For instance, he hired the city's first African American police officers in 1948, though they could not arrest white people and had their own segregated precinct in the Butler Street YMCA on Auburn Avenue.

That same year, businessman Ivan Allen Sr., who had led the 1925 Forward Atlanta ad campaign, published *The Atlanta Spirit* (1948), a slim volume extolling the virtues of the city and complacently accepting *status quo* inequities: "Here is a city of slums and skyscrapers; of crowded wooden Negro cabins and palatial homes that are the equal of any to be found in the great cities of the North."

Nonetheless Hartsfield worked behind the scenes with older black leaders, such as William Holmes Borders and John Wesley Dobbs, and with the white business elite, most notably Robert Woodruff, known as "The Boss" at Coca-Cola, whom Hartsfield called "my number one friend on earth." In his 1953 book, *Community Power Structure: A Study of Decision Makers*, sociologist Floyd Hunter documented this uneasy alliance, observing that there existed a separate-but-unequal black power structure.

During the 1950s and 1960s, African Americans moved further west into white neighborhoods, such as Mozley Park, West End, Adair Park, and

---

* Unarmed Madison Harris had just stepped off a streetcar when the conductor yelled, "Boy, give me that gun," and shot him. In the other incident, Walter Lee Johnson stood on a sidewalk and shouted, "Straighten up and fly right!" (a popular Nat King Cole song), to a passing friend. A streetcar conductor, thinking he was mocking him, shot Johnson.

Grove Park, and elsewhere to the east and south, despite threats, bombings, and repeated attempts to draw various racial boundaries. In *Up Ahead*, the 1952 Atlanta planning document, white leaders worried about "a serious concentration of Negroes in unhealthy and inadequate downtown neighborhoods" that led to their moving into white communities. "The present tension between races in several areas within the city is unhealthy and dangerous. It also hurts property values." The report consequently proposed "Negro Expansion Areas" in decentralized communities. "New housing will be needed for other thousands who might be displaced from crowded downtown areas by expressway construction and redevelopment."

Meanwhile, Mayor Hartsfield introduced his "Plan of Improvement," which led to the January 1, 1952, expansion of Atlanta's city limits, primarily to incorporate Buckhead, the wealthy community to the north, thereby ensuring a white majority for the next two decades, as Atlanta's black population dropped instantaneously from 41 to 33 percent. (The annexation included my parents' house, so as a three-year-old, I became a citizen of Atlanta.)

In 1955, the year after the *Brown v. Board of Education* decision mandated eventual school desegregation, Hartsfield declared Atlanta "the city too busy to hate," and it did indeed avoid most of the racial violence that occurred in places like Little Rock and New Orleans. Still, it was unclear whether Georgia public schools would survive. For several years, it appeared that Atlanta public schools might be shuttered. In 1958, white supremacists bombed the Temple, Atlanta's oldest synagogue, because Rabbi Jacob Rothschild had publicly supported integration. That same year, my mother, Nan Pendergrast, cofounded Help Our Public Education (HOPE) to lobby for the schools to remain open and integrated. In December 1960, a dynamite blast destroyed the west side English Avenue School after its transition from white to black students.

Also in late 1960, young black activists, along with Martin Luther King Jr., tried to eat at the Magnolia Room restaurant at Rich's Department Store, a prominent downtown landmark, and were arrested. Owner Richard Rich, who didn't want to offend his white customers, held out until the following year but was then forced to integrate. Despite Ku Klux Klan street protests, most other Atlanta stores and restaurants allowed African American customers by 1964, when white supremacist Lester Maddox (later Georgia's governor) famously closed his Pickrick Restaurant rather than integrate.

In the fall of 1961, Mayor Hartsfield carefully orchestrated the official integration of Atlanta's public schools, with nine black seniors uneventfully entering four high schools. The city reaped positive national publicity, with the *New York Times* praising it as a "new and shining example" for the New South. "The reality," observed historian Kevin Kruse, "was that the city had enacted a minimalist program of tokenism that amounted to the smallest commitment to desegregation imaginable." The new black students were ostracized, harassed, pushed, tripped, spat on, and cursed. White teachers tacitly encouraged such behavior by ignoring it. One girl found a note in her locker: "Go back to Africa, Jungle Bunny." As the rate of school, park, swimming pool, restaurant, and department store desegregation increased in the early 1960s, white flight snowballed. In 1962, for instance, after a local elementary school switched from white to black, Grant Park homes sold to blacks within weeks.

"As they fled from the schools in record numbers and at record speeds," wrote Kruse, "yet another desegregated public space passed from segregation to resegregation, with barely any time spent on true 'integration' at all." Wealthy whites sent their children to private north-side schools such as Westminster and Lovett, which in 1963 denied admission to Martin Luther King Jr.'s son, remaining all white. (Westminster stayed segregated until 1967, the year after I graduated from its high school.) Some less affluent whites still sent their children to public schools, but many others fled to the northern suburbs of Cobb and Gwinnett Counties. By 1973, 84 percent of Atlanta's public school students were black; ten years later, it was 95 percent.

Moderate Ivan Allen Jr. replaced Hartsfield as mayor in 1962, continuing to rely on the informal power coalition headed by Coca-Cola's Robert Woodruff. In January 1965, when white business leaders planned to boycott an Atlanta dinner to honor Martin Luther King Jr. for his receipt of the Nobel Peace Prize, Woodruff let it be known that they *would* attend, and they did. Woodruff shared some of his generation's racist attitudes, having privately likened extending the vote to blacks to giving ballots to chimpanzees, but he wanted to protect Atlanta's image. When King was assassinated in 1968, Woodruff provided the Coca-Cola jet to fly his body back to Atlanta for the funeral, and while other cities were torn by riots, Atlanta was not.

That same year, black Atlantans voted down a referendum to establish the Metropolitan Atlanta Rapid Transit Authority (MARTA) because plans called for limited service to black areas, particularly outly-ing public housing projects such as Perry Homes on the west side. In 1971, with promises of improved rail and bus connections to black neighbor-hoods, the referendum passed in Atlanta, Fulton, and DeKalb Counties, instituting a 1 percent sales tax to fund it, but it failed in Gwinnett and Cobb Counties to the north and Clayton County to the south due to fears that African Americans would ride the rails out to the white suburbs. In Atlanta a MARTA branch line eventually reached the Bankhead Station to the west, but the promise to link further out to Perry Homes was never fulfilled. The MARTA system, plagued by underfunding and limited service, was nonetheless so vital to impoverished blacks without automo-biles that racist whites joked that it stood for "Moving African Americans Rapidly Through Atlanta."

During the 1960s, Atlanta's white population declined by 60,000, while its black population increased by 70,000, and in 1974 a black ma-jority finally elected young Maynard Jackson Jr.—the grandson of vet-eran black leader John Wesley Dobbs—as mayor. Jackson shook things up, awarding city contracts to black-owned businesses and instituting the ongoing Neighborhood Planning Unit system, to give local groups more of a voice. Still, he ultimately realized that he needed the white business community's support, and the informal ruling coalition was renewed. Yet Jackson presided over an extremely troubled city, where the white minority held 95 percent of the wealth. In 1978, when Atlanta had the highest crime rate in the country, one acerbic commentator called it "a 60 percent black city that floats in a sea of white suburbia whose inhabi-tants desperately avoid contact with the untouchables."

By 1980, another 100,000 whites had fled the city, and Atlanta was actually more segregated than it had been in 1940. The city's popula-tion had peaked at nearly 500,000 in 1970, but by 1990 it had declined to 394,000. After that, the city population slowly began to grow again, with more whites moving back in the twenty-first century, narrowing the black majority.

Still a Tale of Two Cities

When Andrew Young, a former civil rights activist and UN ambassador, followed Jackson as mayor from 1982 to 1990, he embraced the white business community and approved a record 20,000 building projects in his first three years. But downtown Atlanta still suffered, replete with structures in disrepair and surface parking lots. There was also a growing class divide between poverty-stricken and well-to-do African Americans. Symbolically, Rich's Department Store closed in 1992; since then, the coalition of white and black leaders running two essentially separate cities has persisted.

In the decades following the 1996 Atlanta Olympics, the crime-ridden, decaying public housing projects were demolished, replaced by mixed-income developments, with many former inhabitants receiving Section 8 vouchers and dispersing to suburbs. The Olympics helped transform Atlanta in a variety of ways, including the creation of Centennial Olympic Park, north of downtown, which has provided a home at its edges for businesses, the World of Coca-Cola, the Atlanta Aquarium, the College Football Hall of Fame, and the Center for Human and Civil Rights.

Though more liberal than many Southern cities, Atlanta continues to maintain fundamentally unequal schools, jobs, parks, and medical care for blacks versus whites. From the 1960s onward, stadiums, civic centers, expressways, and other developments displaced impoverished black neighborhoods, and the surrounding communities usually did not benefit. That trend continued into the twenty-first century, as Home Depot cofounder Arthur Blank paid for the building of a new, $1.5 billion retractable-roof stadium, right next to the 1992 Georgia Dome (which would be torn down) on Atlanta's west side, to house his Atlanta Falcons football team. Two venerable black churches—including Friendship Baptist Church, whose minister wrote *The Black Side* in 1894—had to be demolished to make room, and the huge construction project loomed over me in 2014 and 2015 as I conducted research for this book in my hometown.

Today it is not unusual to see a mixed-race couple in Atlanta, and social and business integration is advancing, but this city remains one of the most racially segregated in America in terms of neighborhoods, social events, churches, and civic organizations, and racial concerns still help shape virtually every Atlanta issue.

CHAPTER 5

LEARNING TO FLY WHILE BUILDING AN AIRPLANE

· ·

> *The Beltline is a bundle of solutions to the very challenges that threaten to limit Atlanta's health and prosperity: traffic; deficient greenspace and recreation; and uneven economic development—benefitting some neighborhoods while leaving others behind.*
>
> —Ray Weeks, chair, Atlanta BeltLine Partnership, 2008

In the four years (2006–2009) following the rushed passage of the tax allocation district (TAD) funding mechanism, the enticing BeltLine vision clashed repeatedly with the reality of racial tensions, politics, bureaucracy, egos, and economic turmoil. Yet, almost miraculously, the project continued to advance during this troubled period.

When the CEO of Vulcan Material Company saw his Bellwood Quarry on the back cover of Alexander Garvin's *The BeltLine Emerald Necklace* report, he initiated negotiations to sell. The huge gravel pit was nearly played out anyway. Once the TAD money was authorized at the end of 2005, he struck a tentative deal with the city. On Tuesday, January 10, 2006, just days after beginning her second mayoral term, Shirley Franklin stood near the edge of the quarry to announce the impending purchase. The largest jewel on the necklace, still a diamond in the rough, would indeed grace the BeltLine. The city would pay Vulcan $25 million to buy out its lease and would purchase the land from Fulton County* for another $11 million.

The Atlanta city attorney negotiated the deal, along with Ray Weeks. "The BeltLine as a project really snuck up on the city," Weeks recalled. "When I got started there were no resources—no board, no money, no staff." Things weren't that much better two years later when Vulcan decided to sell the quarry. The tax allocation bonds had not been issued, so other funds had to be found. The head of watershed management for the city was lukewarm about the BeltLine, but he, like other city department heads, understood that it was Mayor Franklin's top priority. So the city council authorized the purchase of the quarry and additional acreage, using park improvement and watershed management funds, reserves they hoped the TAD bond funds would reimburse.

The new African American city council member for District 2, Kwanza Hall, was delighted. The focus on Wayne Mason's corridor in the largely white, affluent northeastern quadrant had alarmed neighborhood leaders in poor black areas of Atlanta. They feared that city history would repeat itself, with poorer African Americans treated as second-class citizens. The quarry lay to the northwest, near the demolished Perry Homes public housing complex (partially replaced by the mixed-income West Highlands development), Grove Park, English Avenue/Bankhead (known as "The Bluff"), and other impoverished black areas. The siting of this huge BeltLine park nearby showed a real sign of progress. "We've hit the bulls-eye," Hall crowed. "Northwest Atlanta was a less desirable neighborhood for so many years in so many eyes. Locating it here means something."

The quarry had been operating for over a century, begun as a Fulton County work camp using black chain gang labor to break the granite into gravel. In 2006, despite an average age of only thirty-three, the area had a 40 percent unemployment rate, so any kind of nearby development might be an improvement. Longtime residents—most of them renters—were also happy that they would no longer have to endure the loud blasts from the quarry, the rumbling trucks, and the dust that settled over clotheslines and cars.

---

* The majority of Atlanta lies in Fulton County, but part of the eastern side lies in DeKalb County.

The pending purchase hit a three-month snag when Fulton County, which owned the 137-acre chunk of land leased to Vulcan, demanded as part of the deal that Atlanta provide five hundred jail beds for the over-flowing inmate population at the Fulton County Jail—mostly African Americans convicted of drug charges in what some have called a "new Jim Crow" era of mass incarceration of black men. Ironically, sale of this quarry originally dug by leased black convicts was being held up because the nearby Fulton County Jail was overflowing with black prisoners. In the end, Fulton got only 175 Atlanta jail beds, while the agreed-upon payment to Fulton County went up to $15.2 million.

The city's plan for the big hole in the ground and the surround-ing land wasn't clear, and Vulcan had two years to clear and clean the grounds, so nothing would happen for a while. Mayor Franklin talked up Alexander Garvin's suggested waterfall, which would spill over a dam dividing a reservoir from a recreational area. Garvin himself grew vi-sionary upon hearing news of the sale. Kayakers could play below the waterfall, as rock climbers scaled the cliffs. The surrounding fields would provide spaces for soccer, baseball, horseback riding, and perhaps an ice skating rink.

The city had no budget for the new park, but the Atlanta Department of Watershed Management, which helped finance the purchase, planned to use the quarry as a thirty-day backup water supply for the city, which endured increasingly frequent droughts and was engaged in a protracted, unresolved lawsuit with neighboring Alabama and Florida over water rights to Lake Lanier, formed by damming the Chattahoochee to the north. The department's commissioner soon made clear that he intended to put a fence around the quarry. "You don't want recreation on your reservoir," he said. Besides, it had to be protected against "terrorist acts." He added, "The sheer walls, the height of the bluffs and the depth of 300 feet would make it a fairly dangerous recreation facility." Clearly, the mayor and watershed commissioner had conflicting agendas, but for the moment, the area remained undeveloped anyway.

Some were skeptical of the ballyhoo over what would eventually be called the Westside Park. "Its impact on the surrounding African-American communities could be devastating," wrote one worried critic. "While the BeltLine promises to bring hope and renewal to them, the opposite is bound to happen. Developers will no doubt seize upon inexpensive and abundant land and build mixed-use developments with price tags that will far exceed the median income of these communities. . . . Atlanta's new 'emerald necklace' will seem more like a noose to [poor black] city residents."

These understandable concerns about gentrification would arise repeatedly over the coming years, as the BeltLine leadership struggled with how to fund affordable housing. But the commissioner needn't have worried about overhasty development of the Westside Park. Nothing much would happen there for the next decade.

Turf Battles

Elsewhere around the BeltLine, however, speculators were snatching up land with decaying or abandoned buildings and parking lots. "The price of land along portions of Atlanta's planned Beltline is skyrocketing," a local reporter noted early in 2006. Over the previous five years, Atlanta's population had grown by 35,000 people, a kind of reverse white flight, as older empty nesters and young singles moved back from the suburbs to avoid long commutes and partake of a hip urban experience that the BeltLine plans exemplified.

Jim Langford, the Georgia director of the Trust for Public Land (TPL), raced to grab key acreage before the developers got there first. "We felt tension every day—and that tension would go up or down based on what new headline or new land deal we were pursuing," Langford recalled. In 2005 Georgia TPL had bought its first piece of land for what would eventually become the Historic Fourth Ward Park, then an area of old warehouses and vacant lots adjacent to the future eastern BeltLine. In the spring of that year, Langford began offering weekly BeltLine bus tours for potential donors and supporters. "Jim was a real missionary for the project," recalled Will Rogers, national CEO of the Trust for Public Land. "He's a force of nature."

Langford and his team moved quickly to acquire property around the future BeltLine. "We divided up our target parcels among four TPL project managers, each negotiating deals as fast as possible and staying just ahead of the developers," Langford said. They also found a few civic-minded owners who sold their parcels at 60 percent of what they could have made.

Following the authorization of the BeltLine TAD, the city's ability to repurchase property from the Trust for Public Land seemed assured, so the national TPL office opened up larger lines of credit for this unusual project. Consequently, Langford ramped up land purchases in 2006. But in his rush to acquire property, he also ran into conflict with BeltLine Partnership head Ray Weeks. It was probably inevitable that the two strong personalities would clash, especially once the Partnership exerted its authority. Weeks was planning a $60 million capital campaign and insisted that TPL cease approaching major foundations directly for money. Instead, Langford's group would get a portion of the Partnership's donations.

After a tense conference call in February 2006, Langford sent an e-mail to his team: "TPL does not want to surrender its donor base to the BeltLine Partnership for solicitation for a capital campaign." But Langford lost that battle.

For his part, Weeks was concerned about what seemed to him the unnecessarily high prices TPL was paying for future parkland. Weeks was a hardcharging businessman used to commanding his troops. "I am a CEO type," Weeks recalled, "and I wasn't used to having so many constituencies. I'm not an expert politician."

Publicly, however, the BeltLine Partnership presented a united front. Langford and his team continued to buy land frantically over the next year. By June 2007, TPL had spent $43 million and purchased virtually all of the parkland envisioned in Garvin's *BeltLine Emerald Necklace* report. That was TPL's mission, which did not include the connecting trail/transit corridor. In that month, satisfied and exhausted, Jim Langford resigned from the Trust for Public Land and founded the Million-Mile Greenway organization to encourage other communities to pursue similar projects. Under a new director, the Trust for Public Land would continue to play a BeltLine role, but it had accomplished its major task.

The Park That Sewage Funds Paid For

Much of the land that TPL purchased lay in what would become the Historic Fourth Ward Park, which had first sparked Langford's interest in a connected ring of BeltLine parks after neighborhood activists paid him a visit early in 2004. Getting the park built would help to catalyze the successful developments near the eastern BeltLine. Ironically, the future park really owed its success to Atlanta's antiquated, inadequate combined sewage/storm water system, which meant that overflow from a summer thunderstorm could turn the city's streams into virtual toilets. To resolve the issue, in response to a federal consent decree, Atlanta's Department of Watershed Management was building hugely expensive underground retention tunnels to moderate future flooding.

Bill Eisenhauer, an Atlanta engineer and environmental activist, was the behind-the-scenes force behind the new park. For years, he had been a thorn in the side of Atlanta water officials. In 2001, when the city announced plans to spend $1.9 billion (which turned into $4 billion) to dig gigantic tunnels to contain combined sewage/storm water overflow, Eisenhauer loudly protested that the plans were ridiculously expensive, risky, and impractical. Instead, he urged that Atlanta build detention ponds to hold storm water above ground, then release it slowly and harm-lessly into the drainage system.

City officials ignored Eisenhauer, whom they considered a gadfly. So in 2003, the engineer convinced nearby residents to promote the park idea south of North Avenue in the Old Fourth Ward, while he remained in the background. Three years later, as TPL was assembling the land, the De-partment of Watershed Management finally signed on to the plan, but only because the city wanted to sell the former Sears warehouse, then called City Hall East. Its basement and parking lot tended to flood, and a park featuring a detention pond would solve that problem. Watershed Manage-ment ultimately agreed to pay $30 million for the land and pond, shaving $15 million from what the underground tunnel option would have cost.

Watershed Management's ample budget was crucial to the park's development, yet the department remained a kind of "silo" in the city bureaucracy instead of working closely with Parks and Recreation and other departments. Nonetheless, this first attractive detention pond pro-vided the prototype for solving flooding issues in southern and western neighborhoods around the BeltLine.

Throwing Sand in the Gears

The Watershed Management money came at a particularly crucial time. In 2006, as the city of Atlanta was preparing to issue its first TAD bonds to pay for the BeltLine, a lawsuit filed in Fulton Superior Court claimed the city couldn't do so. Buckhead lawyer John Woodham, a maverick sole practitioner, challenged the public schools' authority to forego taxes intended to pay for children's education and instead divert the money to a TAD.* In January 2007, the Fulton Superior Court judge ruled against him, but Woodham filed an appeal with the Georgia Supreme Court.

The legal victory for the future TAD money was encouraging. Mayor Franklin said, "We feel confident that with the validation of the bonds, we can move this Beltline project forward, especially now that we have the Beltline Inc. up and running." She was referring to Atlanta BeltLine, Inc. (ABI), which Ray Weeks had created as the implementation arm that would actually plan and build the BeltLine trails, parks, and street-cars, leaving the Partnership as a fund- and consciousness-raising non-profit that also focused on affordable housing and jobs. Weeks insisted on folding Ryan Gravel's Friends of the Belt Line into the Partnership.**

The structure of the BeltLine organizations would be critical to the ambitious project's success. Because the BeltLine used public funds, the Atlanta City Council would never agree to turn over money to a private, nonprofit organization, so a public entity, under the umbrella of the Atlanta Development Authority, had to execute the project. Still, even though technically a part of the development authority, ABI had to be perceived as a semiautonomous, effective organization that could deliver on the huge project. "We wanted it to have a big presence," Weeks commented, "and be seen as entrepreneurial." The top staff person became its "CEO."

This chief executive officer was Terri Montague, selected in September 2006 after a national search by a headhunting firm. A graduate of the Massachusetts Institute of Technology with master's degrees in city planning and real estate development, Montague had worked on community development and affordable housing issues for a national organization. "I am also a person of color," she noted, "which is important when you

---

* Some people considered Woodham an annoying crank who enjoyed gumming up the works. He had, for instance, gone to court to fight a traffic ticket for his alleged failure to use his turn signal, and when he lost, he appealed.

** The mushrooming Atlanta bureaucracies and acronyms can be confusing, so I have put a glossary in the back of this book. The Atlanta Development Authority (later renamed Invest Atlanta just to be more confusing) oversaw the BeltLine Partnership, originally headed by semiretired developer Ray Weeks. Then, amoeba-like, it split off Atlanta BeltLine, Inc., which would be the large organization to plan and build the BeltLine. The BeltLine Partnership, with a skeleton crew, would continue to raise private money to support the project, and it also came to focus on affordable housing issues in BeltLine neighborhoods.

are leveraging development, which historically means displacement and gentrification." She seemed perfect for the job and promised to reach out to national foundations for money.

But that money never materialized, and Montague, promised a staff of nineteen people, found herself in a temporary office with three co-workers and no photocopier. She felt overwhelmed, working fourteen-hour days, six days a week. "We had to create everything from nothing and still be visible in the community, dealing with neighborhoods, elected leaders, the Atlanta Public Schools board, the mayor, the BeltLine Partnership, advisory boards, developers," Montague recalled. "It was like building a plane while you learn to fly it."

When Montague arrived, she inherited a five-year strategic BeltLine plan released in July 2006 as a pro bono effort by the local office of the Boston Consulting Group (BCG), which had contributed staff time valued at roughly $5 million over the course of a year to develop it. No blueprint or template existed for BCG to borrow from or adapt. No city had ever undertaken anything like this before, so the planning started with broad concepts and diverse views of what the BeltLine should or could be.

The BCG plan provided the blueprint for the BeltLine's first five years, though no one knew what curveballs the economy might throw during that period. Conditional statements filled the carefully worded document. "Plan is based on limited and conceptual engineering studies. Budgets may be adjusted. . . . Critical opportunities or circumstances may arise." It envisioned a $427 million budget for the next five years, with $280 million coming from TAD bonds and the balance from phil-anthropic donations, local/city opportunity bonds, and federal funds. The plan called for completing at least two sections of the BeltLine trail, with directions to "secure and develop as much Right-of-Way [to the rail corridor] as possible" and to "do everything possible to ensure transit at earliest opportunity." There would also be public art on the BeltLine and $42 million for new affordable housing units over the next five years.

But the city couldn't float the TAD bonds with Woodham's appeal pending. The Buckhead lawyer presented his case to the Georgia Supreme Court in September 2007. Montague complained publicly that he was "throwing sand in the gears" and that she still had just a nine-member staff. But it appeared only a matter of time before this nuisance lawsuit was finally laid to rest and TAD bonds could be issued.

In February 2008, the judges returned a surprising, unanimous verdict in Woodham's favor, ruling that the Georgia constitution did not allow the use of school taxes for tax allocation districts. The decision caused consternation and dismay among TAD supporters statewide. For the BeltLine, it would mean the loss of an estimated $850 million over the twenty-five-year TAD life span.

Ray Weeks, now chairman of the BeltLine Partnership—Valarie Wilson, an African American with a background in human services administration, had come aboard in 2006 as its director—wrote an editorial calling the Supreme Court ruling a "bump in the road," and the heads of the Robert W. Woodruff and Arthur Blank Foundations reiterated their support. The capital campaign had already raised $28.7 million, almost half of the $60 million goal.

The only way around the Supreme Court decision was to amend the Georgia constitution, which required the approval not only of the Georgia Senate and House but the majority of the state's voters. Led by Kasim Reed, a charismatic black senator from Atlanta whose political star was clearing rising, the bill passed in the legislature. Georgians for Community Redevelopment, a well-funded business lobbying group, campaigned vigorously for the measure, while critics called the school-related TAD "an insidious form of corporate welfare at the expense of our children's education." On November 4, 2008, as the nation elected Barack Obama the country's first black president, Georgia voters narrowly approved the referendum, allowing school taxes to help fund TADs.

The BeltLine funding had been saved, it appeared, although the legislation permitted school boards to opt out of the TAD agreements. The Atlanta Public Schools board promised to stay in the BeltLine TAD but amended the contract, with a first payment due on January 1, 2013. By the year 2030, the city promised to pay the schools a total of $163 million out of TAD bond proceeds, in addition to $10 million for a new recreational center—an agreement that would lead to bitter controversy.

Wayne Mason Plays Hardball

Terri Montague and ABI also had to contend with Wayne Mason's ownership of the northeastern corridor of the BeltLine, where plans for thirty-eight- and thirty-nine-story towers adjacent to Piedmont Park had sparked protests. For most of 2006, Mason and his son had continued to lobby for the right to rezone and develop the narrow 4.6-mile corridor.

The Masons pointed out that if implemented, their development plans would generate an estimated $100 million in TAD bond proceeds, which could then fund other portions of the BeltLine project. In addition, they were donating forty-three acres of land. Otherwise, ABI would have to buy the entire sixty-five acres that the Masons owned. In a "Myths/Facts" document, they dismissed the "myth" that they were "unwilling to compromise and work with neighborhoods." On the contrary, the Masons had held sixty neighborhood meetings, agreeing to "significant revisions and modifications" and widening plans for both the transit corridor and the trail. Those who insisted on no development were misguided. "Open space without development does not support transit. Open space generates $0.00 in TAD revenue."

Nor would their developments generate too much traffic if streetcars ran through them. They debunked one final myth: "The BeltLine can succeed without the Mason property." There was no way that the twenty-two-mile circuit could succeed without a section equaling nearly a quarter of the loop.

The Mason argument was compelling, and its facts were not in dispute. But complaints that the towers would overshadow adjacent residences and that the planned streetcar would have to run under the new buildings were also valid. Ryan Gravel's original plans did not foresee huge towers with streetcars crammed beneath them. Still, not all neighborhoods along the Mason corridor objected. Those in the poorer, blacker southern section of the Old Fourth Ward, adjacent to Inman Park, went on record as supporting the Mason plans. But opponents from the wealthy, white Virginia-Highland neighborhood, site of the two proposed towers, dominated a packed public hearing held in mid-September 2006. At that meeting, the planning commissioner promised to release within ten days an innovative plan, a "unique application that's never been seen before. . . . We think this could be a 'win-win' for the BeltLine and everyone involved in the application."

On Tuesday, September 19, 2006, the planning commissioner revealed his "win-win" plan to the Masons. He wanted them to trade their land for the right to develop housing units in unspecified locations elsewhere around the city. Understandably enraged by this seemingly ridiculous offer, Wayne Mason asked to see Mayor Shirley Franklin face-to-face, but she couldn't find the time. On Thursday, Mason walked away. He withdrew his zoning application. Roy Barnes, the Georgia ex-governor who pioneered the Georgia Regional Transportation Authority and whom Mason had hired as an advisor, lamented that city and BeltLine officials had "decided to be very hostile to this developer" and made the process impossible. Mason said he wasn't sure what he would do with the property. Maybe he would sell it to another developer. Maybe he'd just hold on to it and "let [his] grandchildren worry about it." The majority of the land was zoned industrial, he pointed out, which would allow "everything from hotels to salvage yards."

Most letters to the editor following Mason's abandonment of negotiations were hostile. "Greed has a new face: Wayne Mason, the one-time Beltline baron," wrote one Atlantan. "Mason screamed like a petulant child and withdrew his so-called 'offer' for developing the northeast Beltline track." But one writer supported Mason's thwarted plans, complaining that "small-minded homeowners" were threatening the future of the city. He noted that Piedmont Park was underused. "Every young person I talk to about the BeltLine wants high-density buildings, cafes, shops and more street life. But the conversation is being controlled by a wealthy, powerful and loud minority."

Although others besides affluent activists objected to Mason's plans, this letter writer made a valid observation. Perhaps the BeltLine wasn't ready for that much density and height in one location, but the power struggles, politics, and dueling egos may have squandered an early opportunity to jump-start BeltLine development and funding.

In the following months, Mason threatened to sue the city, challenging its right to rezone BeltLine property it didn't own. He then put up chain-link fencing to punctuate his private ownership of the corridor. Behind closed doors, Jim Langford of the Trust for Public Land negotiated a tentative deal, offering $39 million for the land. But the agreement never went anywhere because ABI president Terri Montague told Langford to back off—she would negotiate the purchase.

In November 2007, after complex negotiations, Montague ended up getting the city to sign a contract to buy the Mason corridor for an overpriced $66 million, with Mason providing a $45 million short-term loan to facilitate the deal, since ABI didn't have the cash. Interest and principal payments would be deferred for the first six months. The city of Atlanta borrowed $23 million from three banks, while Barry Real Estate, a private Atlanta developer that saw a possible opportunity, contributed only $1.5 million. The deal was "an important sign of momentum," said Terri Montague.

At that point, she and other city officials were confident that the Georgia Supreme Court would soon dismiss the Woodham lawsuit challenging the TAD, enabling the city to float bonds to pay off Mason. But that didn't happen. As of May 31, 2008, the city began to make $450,000 monthly interest payments to Mason, with the entire loan due on October 31, 2008, a few days before the vote to amend the constitution to allow the inclusion of school taxes in TAD funding.

Meanwhile, the credit market was tightening as the inflated real estate bubble collapsed and foreclosures on homes increased. Interest rates for municipal bonds rose in response to the burgeoning subprime mortgage crisis in early 2008.* "We have never seen this kind of chaos in the municipal bond market," said the BeltLine's financial advisor, urging the city to delay any attempt to issue bonds.

In mid-September 2008, Lehman Brothers declared bankruptcy, triggering the onset of the Great Recession. A month later, an Atlanta reporter noted, "Bond rates have increased sharply in the past three weeks," and "The BeltLine sits on the sidelines for now, waiting for the market to improve. But a deadline is looming." If the city defaulted on the Mason loan, the developer had the right to call off the deal and retain ownership of the land, along with the money he had already received.

On Wednesday, October 29, 2008, two days before the loan deadline, the Atlanta City Council voted to issue $64.5 million in bonds to support the BeltLine, with $45 million going to pay off Wayne Mason's short-term loan. Montague then negotiated to buy out Barry Real Estate for $3.5 million—$1.2 million more than Barry had put into the deal, including interest payments. Montague was clearly under immense pressure to gain sole control of the property for ABI.

Eugene Bowens, the black activist head of the Tax Allocation District Advisory Committee (TADAC), a citizens' group created to advise ABI, lambasted the expensive deal with Wayne Mason and Barry Real Estate. Having complained repeatedly about TADAC's exclusion from the decision-making process, he now wrote that spending the majority of

---

* A local government or one of its agencies issues municipal bonds. Federally tax exempt, they were generally considered safer than corporate bonds, but that began to change with the Great Recession of 2008.

the bond proceeds for the northeastern quadrant was "not equitable or appropriate."

Wayne and Keith Mason had bought the land four years before for $24.5 million. Including interest payments, they sold it for $71 million. Many believed, erroneously, that they never really intended to develop the property. They had spent some $5 million on lawyers, engineers, consultants, and permits. In the end, Wayne Mason did not personally make a huge profit, since he had given most of the ownership of the Belt-Line corridor to his children, retaining only 7 percent for himself. And as the Great Recession hit, he lost virtually everything. "I had $100 million in cash," he recalled, "but I was on the hook for $267 million," and the failing banks called in his loans.

A flamboyant self-made man straight from the pages of a Southern gothic novel, Wayne Mason saw himself as the white knight of the Belt-Line, charging in to lead a sustainable, profitable venture in new urbanism. Instead, he ended up watching the project from the sidelines as his overextended real estate empire crumbled.

Mortgage Fraud in 30310

The economic collapse could not have come at a worse time for the Belt-Line. The TAD bonds, finally authorized, were nearly impossible to float. The city managed to issue $78 million in bonds to nine investors only in December 2009, and those proceeds mostly just refinanced the privately issued bonds for $64.5 million that had allowed ABI to buy out Mason the previous year. This amount was far less than the $200 million originally forecast for the first full TAD bonds, and these would be the only such bonds issued for many years to come.

In the meantime, speculators had continued to drive up the price of land around the corridor. In September 2007, Georgia Tech professor Dan Immergluck published a study showing that land values and property taxes in BeltLine neighborhoods, particularly in the poorer southwestern quadrant, were rising faster than in other parts of the city. "The BeltLine is a great idea," Immergluck told a reporter, "unless we're going to build it on the backs of poor folks." He feared that rich people in "shiny new homes" would predominate.

Immergluck didn't point out that many of the shiny new homes built in these poor neighborhoods were never occupied. They were part of

the mortgage fraud epidemic spawned by easy credit during the real estate boom. Area code 30310, covering West End, Westview, Pittsburgh,
and Adair Park, had the second-highest number of foreclosures in the
country. Beginning in 2001, Kevin Wiggins demonstrated how the scam
worked in West End, where he contracted to purchase dozens of homes
in poor condition for as little as $24,000; before the sales went through,
he deeded the properties to unqualified straw buyers, such as college students or relatives, falsified their information, and obtained financing for
them, and then paid them a percentage of the inflated mortgages taken
out on the allegedly renovated, fraudulently appraised properties. Wiggins would flip the homes, reselling them for ever-increasing amounts,
sometimes $100,000 more than the original price. Virtually everyone
in the chain of fraud took a profit through commissions, kickbacks, or
inflated home values. The American taxpayer ultimately footed the bill.

Many banks, which also made money on each transaction, were
happy to fund what amounted to a mortgage pyramid scheme. Atlanta-
based Omni National Bank, for instance, specialized in fraudulent house
flipping. "Atlanta's downtrodden neighborhoods proved a gold mine for
Omni and its founders, who amassed tens of millions of dollars' worth of
mansions, company stock and a private jet," wrote reporters in the back-
wash of the bank's collapse. As a result, "hundreds of homes that should
have been improved instead sit vacant and crumbling." Georgia had the
dubious distinction of leading the nation in bank failures.

Kevin Wiggins, who made $7 million from his scheme, was caught
and convicted, but many others, including those who built brand-new
homes and flipped them to straw buyers for ever-higher sums, remained
anonymous, just as the houses remained foreclosed and empty. On the
desolate battlefield left in the wake of the Great Recession, entire blocks
of houses sat vacant, when not occupied by drug dealers or prostitutes.
The "Dirty Truth Campaign," a 2007–2009 southwestern Atlanta initiative, photographed tires strewn on front lawns and burned-out homes
rank with weeds and garbage. "This vacant property issue is an assault
on the family," said an exhibit organizer. "It's tearing our city apart."
One mother in the Pittsburgh neighborhood said that her teenage daughter had been raped on the front porch of an abandoned home. It is little
wonder that a contemporary article on the Next American City website
called Atlanta "a portrait of dysfunction."

The vacant homes in the southern part of the city stood in stark contrast to the gigantic "McMansions" thrown up in wealthy northern Atlanta neighborhoods. These had become so numerous by 2006 that Shirley Franklin issued a temporary moratorium on such massive home building on lots where older, smaller homes once stood.

Sometimes the good intentions of white liberals who supported the BeltLine failed to connect with black residents on the southern and western sides of town. In 2007, for instance, Danielle Roney and Diana Mulhall published *BeltLine Cultural Impact Study*, a lushly-illustrated call for the inclusion of the arts along the BeltLine: "Imagine a city where arts and culture draw visitors from around the world, year-round." They envisioned theater, dance performances, studios, and cultural centers—all fine ideas, but with little connection to the immediate needs of devastated neighborhoods. Richard Bright, a West End minister and health educator, instead noted that the BeltLine "could be a marvelous opportunity to develop comprehensive planning" to address local concerns about housing, health, and jobs.

By 2009, there was no need for a moratorium on building McMansions or anything else. Many ambitious projects faltered and failed because of the credit collapse, including several around the BeltLine. The Georgia office of the Trust for Public Land was stuck, to the tune of $25 million, with property not yet acquired by the city that Jim Langford had purchased near the top of the real estate market. With inadequate TAD income, the city had no way to buy it anytime soon, so the trust had to resell it in the private sector, beginning in 2008, though it would take years to unload all of it. "It broke our hearts, because it would have been fabulous for the BeltLine," recalled Helen Tapp, who took over as Georgia TPL director from Langford. The city never acquired the sold land. In retrospect, Langford's acquisition strategy may have been somewhat overaggressive, but he could not have foreseen the Great Recession and its impacts.

NIMBYs and WIMBYs

Nonetheless, there was some demonstrable progress along the BeltLine. The Trust for Public Land had, in fact, secured the most vital potential parkland adjacent to the corridor. The PATH Foundation, under Ed McBrayer's leadership, was building two segments of bicycle-cum-walking trails on the western side of the project, along Tanyard Creek to the northwest and White Street to the southwest. Both trails had actually been planned independently of the BeltLine and then included in the loop, though neither lay in the rail corridor itself. The planned streetcar path along the corridor would be twenty-two miles long, but in several places, where there wasn't room for the bike trail to parallel the rails, it would bend away from the corridor. There would also be "spur" trails off the BeltLine, so that the entire BeltLine trail system would be thirty-three miles long.

The contrasting reactions of the two neighborhoods next to these two projects—Collier Hills in the far northwest and West End to the southwest—illustrate glaringly how socioeconomic and racial issues have affected the BeltLine. Tanyard Creek is a lovely little tributary of Peachtree Creek, which empties into the Chattahoochee River. The site of one of the bloodiest conflicts during the Battle of Atlanta during the Civil War, most of the low-lying, flood-prone land along the creek already belonged to the city, and the civic-minded Howard family donated more adjacent land. It would seem a no-brainer to put in a one-mile-long, twelve-foot-wide concrete trail that would eventually provide a link in the northwestern quadrant of the BeltLine trail system.

But when announced in 2007, the planned trail ran into immediate, vociferous opposition from residents of Collier Hills just south of the Bobby Jones Golf Course in a classic NIMBY (not in my backyard) protest. The primary focus of the conflict was ostensibly a meadow that people used for picnics, Frisbee games, and an unofficial dog park. The PATH Foundation wanted to run the new trail through the meadow, since going on the other side of the stream would force it too close to the creek. After much back-and-forth, in early 2008, Terri Montague announced that the trail would indeed run through the meadow because the alternative would cost too much and require removal of too many trees. "The community came forward with great energy," she said, "but we would be remiss to ignore these other considerations as we go forward."

Following a firestorm of further outrage, Montague reversed herself three months later, agreeing to run the trail on the other side, which required a variance from the Georgia Environmental Protection Division permitting the trail to run within twenty-five feet of the stream.

McBrayer and his team devised new methods to protect trees and filter water runoff from the trail before it ran into the creek.

It didn't matter what McBrayer did—Collier Hills activists spat out his name with a contempt usually reserved for the devil. Race was an unspoken issue. This upscale white neighborhood lay only a few miles from the African American Bankhead area, with its unemployment, poverty, drugs, and violence. Once the BeltLine trail connected the two neighborhoods, would all of these issues filter into their community?

In contrast, the mostly African American West End neighborhood in southwestern Atlanta welcomed the 1.7-mile trail that would run along White Street, viewing it as a WIMBY (wanted in my backyard) project. The effort "promises to transform weedy patches, trash-strewn lots and kudzu-choked thickets into a linear park," a reporter predicted. A resident said he hoped the new trail would help revitalize his neighborhood, hit hard by foreclosures. Ed McBrayer said that the trail, the first to be completed on the BeltLine, would give the entire endeavor credibility. "This will make it real. All of this work isn't just a pipe dream."

In October 2008, the West End BeltLine trail officially opened with a five-kilometer race followed by a community celebration. As the first official piece of the BeltLine, it was an important accomplishment, but it didn't amount to much more than a widened sidewalk. At the same time, construction crews broke ground for the new Historic Fourth Ward Park and its detention pond.

A Near Rerailment

Early in 2009, ABI chief Terri Montague faced yet another unexpected challenge that could have destroyed plans for the BeltLine. Following the expensive purchase of the Masons' northeastern corridor, the city had asked former owner Norfolk Southern Railway to formally abandon the railroad rights for that section of unused track, a process to be completed on January 22, 2009. The day before that deadline, the Georgia Department of Transportation (GDOT) and Amtrak jointly filed a request with the US Surface Transportation Board to block the abandonment process, citing its need to preserve the corridor for a possible high-speed commuter rail that would hopefully run into a to-be-constructed Multi-Modal Passenger Terminal (MMPT) in the derelict downtown Gulch.

The long-planned but unfunded MMPT would link buses, MARTA, rail travel, and (hopefully) future streetcars.

Mayor Shirley Franklin wrote an urgent letter to Congressman John Lewis, seeking help to counter what she called "GDOT's boorish behavior and Amtrak's willingness to play along." The outraged mayor complained, "For a state agency to now flip-flop and at the last minute attempt to derail a well-thought-out and partially implemented plan is truly appalling." A 250-person crowd protested at the edge of Piedmont Park. "I would like to see high-speed commuter rail," said one participant, "but not through Piedmont Park."

Weeks and Franklin worked frantically to derail the GDOT proposal. The city's most influential lobbyists, who all worked for major Atlanta corporations, swung into action. Weeks, working behind the scenes to persuade GDOT to abandon the proposal, called on his friend Rudy Bowen, chair of the GDOT board. "That's the kind of alchemy that got the Beltline to happen," Weeks observed.

Though on the books for years, plans for a commuter rail connecting Atlanta to other cities in Georgia (e.g., Athens, Macon, or Columbus) or outside the state (e.g., Chattanooga, Tennessee; Birmingham, Alabama; or Charlotte, North Carolina) had never gone anywhere. At that point, an $87 million federal grant to fund rail between Atlanta and Lovejoy, twenty-five miles to the south, had sat untouched for five years, awaiting matching state funds. "We have invested far too much in the BeltLine and have seen too much growth and investment for it to be stymied by the actions of a state agency that does not have a viable plan or funding for commuter rail," wrote Shirley Franklin.

But GDOT and Amtrak were understandably concerned about losing the corridor. Amtrak's *Crescent* line from New York City to New Orleans was the only passenger train that still went through Atlanta, and it stopped only in northern Atlanta, off Peachtree Road at Brookwood Station, a small, inadequate terminal near the Brookwood Hills neighborhood. "This station is a joke," wrote one typical reviewer, "and, as a native to Atlanta," he found it an embarrassment. "MARTA does not have a train station nearby and Amtrak does not offer long-term parking. So if you're taking a trip, you may have to get creative." The train merely skirted northern Atlanta. There was no simple way for a passenger train to go through the city to the south.

The restoration of extensive commuter rail to Atlanta should unquestionably occur, but Mayor Franklin was right to question the incredibly bad timing of this last-minute attempt to block an essential portion of the BeltLine. Neither GDOT nor Amtrak had any viable plans or funding mechanism to make their proposal happen, and alternative routes existed.

After two anxious months, GDOT finally caved to political pressure, reversing itself and agreeing to pursue a hypothetical commuter rail path through lines in western Atlanta to get to the Gulch and its hoped-for MMPT. The BeltLine was saved.

Following that victory, Ray Weeks announced he was stepping down as chair of the BeltLine Partnership. He'd worked sixty- to seventy-hour weeks for four years. "I had to get out, that was enough," he recalled, but he needed to find a good replacement. At the top of a long list was John Somerhalder, CEO of AGL (Atlanta Gas Light) Resources, who was relatively new to Atlanta. Nonetheless, he led a well-respected company and, as an avid cyclist, was interested in trails. Even more importantly, he had a collaborative leadership style. As vice chair of the important Funds Allocation Committee, Weeks appointed Charlie Shufeldt, a retired SunTrust banker.*

Exit Terri Montague

In May 2009, Terri Montague announced that as of September 1, she would resign as ABI president after a rocky three-year tenure. As a non-Atlantan taking over an underfunded, challenging project, she was, in retrospect, perhaps the wrong choice. Yet she had faced a daunting task. "I knew it was going to be hard," she observed, "but I didn't know that it was going to take two years for us to get our primary funding source. And when we were finally ready to sell the bonds I didn't expect that the financial and capital real estate markets would have collapsed." Nor had she anticipated having to pay so much for the Masons' northeastern corridor, the subsequent sniping from Eugene Bowens of TADAC, the bitter battle over the Tanyard Creek trail, or the last-minute GDOT intervention. "I didn't get a whole lot of sleep," she said. No one was

---

* Four years later Somerhalder was chosen to chair the board of Atlanta BeltLine, Inc., while remaining on the Partnership board. Charlie Shufeldt took over as the Partnership board chair.

forcing her out, she said, but "three years of working under-resourced has a way of feeling much longer."

Though Montague had left, the battered BeltLine project would continue under new leadership, and the vision of a loop of trails, parks, and transit still attracted most Atlantans, whether they lived in Buckhead mansions or Bankhead slums. For the city's large homeless population, however, the BeltLine meant very little other than further displacement.

CHAPTER 6
MANSIONS AND CAT HOLES

··

It is our utopias that make the world tolerable to us: the cities and mansions that people dream of are those in which they finally live.

—Lewis Mumford, *The Story of Utopias*, 1922

Poor naked wretches, whereso'er you are,
That bide the pelting of this pitiless storm,
How shall your houseless heads and unfed sides,
Your looped and windowed raggedness, defend you
From seasons such as these? Oh, I have ta'en
Too little care of this!

—William Shakespeare, *King Lear*

It's difficult for most of us to conceive of what it's like to be homeless, to have no safe place to call our own. As part of my quest to understand my native city, I found my visits in homeless encampments and shelters both profoundly disturbing and inspiring because of the tragic stories I heard and the resilience of the human spirit I encountered. It would take a book in itself to deal adequately with this topic in Atlanta, which is among the worst American cities in terms of the wealth gap between haves and have-nots, but it certainly deserves a chapter. First, though, you need to know something about Buckhead, the affluent community where I grew up, to appreciate that gaping divide. And that means telling you something about my childhood home.

In the 1950s and 1960s, I lived with my family on a hilltop on West Paces Ferry Road, near the intersection with Nancy Creek Road. Our near-vertical driveway gave me plenty of exercise on my way home from Margaret Mitchell Elementary School, named for the author of *Gone with the Wind*. Once I arrived at the top, I was surrounded by forest, other than the lawn, swimming pool, paved turnaround with basketball hoop and badminton court, two-car garage, and two-story brick colonial home with four upstairs bedrooms, quite useful for a family with seven children.

I didn't feel privileged to live in this Buckhead neighborhood, with its large houses (some with columns) set far back from the road, green expanses of lawn, lush flower gardens, azalea bushes, magnolias, pines, oaks, and pink-flowered mimosas. Here lived Atlanta's wealthy doctors, lawyers, business executives, and other professionals. The father of one of my best friends was CEO of the Georgia Power Company. My father was vice president of the Southern Spring Bed Company (later renamed Southern Cross Industries), the company my mother's grandfather had cofounded.

I took this world for granted. On my way home from school, I waved at the black yardmen who maintained neighbors' grounds, though my father mowed his own small lawn and my mother took great pleasure in tending her flower gardens, including wildflowers she collected. Our black maid, Willie Mae Pughsley, always made the family dinner before my mother drove her to catch the bus back to her home, which I never saw.

In the eighth grade, I entered the Westminster School for Boys, whose bucolic campus lay just down the road. Separated from the girls' school by the administration building, it prepared the children of Atlanta's wealthy elite for college, with many going on to Ivy League schools. We were all white, although Westminster's cooks and maintenance men were black. Upon graduation in 1966, I went to Harvard, along with several classmates.

I did not know much about the rest of Atlanta. Mostly, I stayed safely and naively inside what is sometimes called the Buckhead Bubble. Now, some fifty years later, the area remains unchanged in many ways. The same streets feature some familiar homes, set back behind sweeping lawns, though Latinos rather than African Americans mostly maintain the yards. As this book went to press, my elderly mother still lived in that big brick colonial on the hill, but its next-door twin, built by the same developer in the early 1950s, had been torn down a few years before to make way for a monstrous McMansion.

Other gigantic homes have replaced various domiciles throughout Buckhead. In recent years when I accompanied my parents on their morning dog walk, we sometimes went to Garraux Road, an exclusive dead-end street off Ridgewood that is quiet and wooded, with only a rare vehicle. As we walked down the road, we could see a fortress-like home behind a wrought-iron fence with guard dogs. It belonged to Tyler Perry, the black filmmaker, actor, and television producer, who bought the seventeen-acre spread in 2007.* Perry, who arrived in Atlanta with nothing in 1990 at age twenty-two, is not the only affluent African American who has moved to Buckhead, but the area remains overwhelmingly white.

The heart of Buckhead, however, has changed beyond recognition. When I was growing up, the area near the intersection of West Paces Ferry (which becomes East Paces on the other side), Peachtree, and Roswell Road had a sleepy, small-town feel. Now business and residential skyscrapers thrust skyward in a thriving, traffic-jammed center of commerce, as businesses have marched north along Peachtree.

Homeless on the BeltLine

I never thought of my childhood home as a mansion; nor would most people. It's an aging, rectangular brick colonial on nearly three acres, and some awful day new owners will probably tear it down to build a McMansion. But to those who cannot afford a roof over their heads, who live on the streets, in vacant lots, or in Atlanta's shelters, the house where I grew up certainly would qualify as a mansion.

Take the story of Michael, forty-six, a homeless white man I met when I volunteered one December morning in 2011 at the Open Door Community at 910 Ponce de Leon Avenue. Over his free lunch, he told me that he lived with his dog, Tippy, somewhere on or near the Belt-Line in a "cat hole," slang for a hidden abode whose exact whereabouts he would not reveal for fear someone might take it from him. He told me how he got stabbed there one night but was saved by an anonymous black man who stayed all night to protect him and then left. "I believe he was an angel," he said, wide-eyed.

---

* Perry later sold it and moved to an estate in Johns Creek, a northern Atlanta suburb.

Homelessness remains a huge problem in Atlanta, where the climate makes it possible to live outside most of the year, despite hot, humid summer days and occasional subfreezing (even snowy) winter nights. Until the administration of Shirley Franklin, the city of Atlanta largely ignored the issue, since Fulton and DeKalb Counties were supposed to take care of it but didn't.

That's not to say there weren't temporary shelters and efforts to feed the homeless. The Salvation Army developed its first Atlanta home for working men in 1900. The faith-based Atlanta Union Mission, started during the Depression in 1938 as a soup kitchen, began providing housing in the 1960s. The Atlanta Community Food Bank was formed in 1979. The Open Door Community opened its doors in 1981, and the Metro Atlanta Task Force for the Homeless purchased a large building on Peachtree Street in 1997. Under Mayor Franklin, the Gateway Center, providing temporary housing and referrals, opened in 2005.

Despite the city's 2003 publication of *A Blueprint to End Homelessness in Atlanta in Ten Years*, over a decade later at least 4,300 people lived without their own shelter every month within the Atlanta city limits, though a firm census figure is impossible. Various shelters and organizations serve and feed some. Others remain, by choice or happenstance, outside the system set up to help them. Most of Atlanta's homeless are African American men, though the number of single mothers and children has risen, especially since the Great Recession, which commenced in 2008.

People become homeless—unable to rent or own a normal roof over their heads—for a variety of reasons, including illness, bad decisions, criminal records, posttraumatic stress disorder (particularly among veterans), unemployment, drug or alcohol addiction, domestic violence, physical disability, or simply insufficient income. An alarming number of people spend far more than the suggested 30 percent of their earnings on rent, and a whole predatory industry has arisen to take advantage of those who are repeatedly evicted and lose most of their possessions in the process. Since the start of the deinstitutionalization movement in the 1960s and the eventual closure of the state mental hospital in Milledgeville, Georgia, more of the mentally ill have become homeless or been imprisoned. Some critics now call Fulton County Jail the largest mental institution in Georgia.

The homeless set up kudzu-shrouded encampments on the BeltLine corridor, among other places. In 2011, as cleanup efforts for the future pedestrian/streetcar loop intensified, a reporter visited several people who lived under bridges or in makeshift huts along the BeltLine. He met Sammy, a Cambodian man in his thirties, who lived under the Freedom Parkway bridge and earned a living of sorts by cleaning parking lots and emptying trash for bars in Little Five Points, a hip area not far from the eastern section of the BeltLine. The police had already asked several of his homeless neighbors to leave, and he knew he would have to depart soon. "I don't know where to go," he said.

"It's not a good place for them to be," observed a homeowner near Piedmont Park and the BeltLine. That was undoubtedly true, but she didn't seem worried about where a better place might be. "They can't mix with regular people," she complained. "They want to destroy everything the BeltLine is putting in."

Further north on the BeltLine, the reporter met Roger, who lived with his cat, Cleopatra, under the Piedmont Road bridge near Ansley Mall. On the west side of the loop, he encountered Tony, who wore long johns, despite the heat, to fend off mosquitoes, under a bridge near Washington Park. Further south, near the West End neighborhood, Isaac had lived for nine years in a tree house hidden among the kudzu. By day, he studied auto mechanics at Atlanta Technical College.

A few months later, as I walked the BeltLine on the west side, I spoke to John, a middle-aged black man with a missing front tooth who clung to a hanging vine as he told me that he was a "lone ranger." I asked what he meant, and he said, "Well, when you get into the English language and the theory of different things, everybody has different perceptions, and it would be hard again for you to really understand me." He was friendly, but I didn't press him further about his background.

Mad Housers

It's a good bet that none of these men still lives on the BeltLine, where two sections of trail would have been near completion by the time this book was published. One woman, who camped out in an abandoned home near the BeltLine in the Old Fourth Ward, doesn't live there anymore because she is dead. After neighbors on the street complained repeatedly that a decaying house on Daniel Street—once owned by Coca-Cola magnate Asa Candler—had become a crack den, in May 2011 a demolition crew hired by the city knocked it down without checking inside. Janice Durham, fifty-one, was living there. Ironically, the funeral home that posted her obituary gave notice of her "homegoing service" and interment.

Gone, too, are several BeltLine encampments that Mad Housers, a volunteer organization started in 1987 by Georgia Tech students, helped to build on or near the BeltLine. Atlanta BeltLine, Inc., staff partnered with HOPE Atlanta, originally a traveler's aid organization, to find apartments (rent-free for a year) for the displaced, but many were located far from job sites, and some men ended up back on the streets.

One spring afternoon in 2015, I visited three of the still-extant homeless encampments supported by Mad Housers, which built small huts out of plywood for the homeless, partly to do good but in equal measure to protest the smug status quo. "In the beginning, we put them any damn place, in people's faces, knowing they would be torn down," recalled President Nick Hess, who began volunteering in 1989. They built one, for instance, near Freedom Parkway in front of the Jimmy Carter Library.

"Now our philosophy is that our clients have enough problems already; they don't need to become political symbols. So we focus on trying to help folks get stabilized with the shelters." They offer two standard designs—a Hi Hat version, twelve feet high at the peak, six by eight feet on the ground, with a six-by-six-foot loft, or a Low Rider, designed to avoid detection in more visible places, which is four feet at the peak and four by eight feet on the ground. A woodstove made from four stacked five-gallon paint cans heats the Hi Hats. All homes are insulated and feature locks, which are highly valued.

Mad Housers serves the chronically homeless, those you see pushing shopping carts along the streets. "We help people with really big problems," Hess says. "Sometimes they just had amazingly bad luck, but often there is a mental health or substance abuse problem." For my tour, Hess, an architectural software designer in his professional life, referred me to his wife, Tracy Woodard, who does "client outreach" for Mad Housers when she is not freelancing as a violinist. She estimated that three-quarters of their clients had mental health or addiction issues, alcoholism being the most prevalent. That most shelters do not allow people to drink explains their preference to remain outdoors.

Woodard and I drove to southwestern Atlanta to visit the Stewart Encampment off Connell Avenue, named for nearby Stewart Avenue, now renamed Metropolitan Parkway. There I met Rick, fifty-nine, who complained of arthritis. "My health ain't too good." A black navy veteran with white hair and mustache, he lived with his fiancée, Robbie, in a Hi Hat hut with a kind of attached tarp-covered porch. Lettuce grew in milk crates. Rick had worked in asbestos abatement for ten years, then labored for independent contractors doing home improvements, but with his health issues and the recession, that work disappeared.

Nearby I found a fetid, mosquito-breeding body of water that turned out to be the old swimming pool of Funtown, a defunct amusement park that once featured rides, a miniature golf course, and a model rocket showing a film of an imaginary trip to the moon. In 1964, Martin Luther King Jr. complained that his daughter couldn't go there because it was for whites only. Two years later, it closed because its owners refused to integrate. Now black and white homeless men live there.

Further along the path, I met Joe, a native of Ghana, who had a heart attack the year before and walked with a cane. He kept a minilibrary of books in a storage shed and showed Woodard that his two-paint-can cookstove was rusting out and needed replacement. He got his mail at a U-Haul location on Metropolitan Avenue, where he could charge his cell phone and fill a container with drinking water.

Sarge, a white Korean War veteran with severe posttraumatic stress disorder, lived next door, but Woodard advised against talking to him. "He's kind of paranoid." We left to pick up her six-year-old son, Karl, at a charter school in the Old Fourth Ward, before visiting two more home-less camps. Then we drove back to their house in Oakland City, not far from the future BeltLine.

I wondered whether the well-intentioned Mad Housers might just be enabling dependent behavior, so I asked Nick Hess about the issue. "Look," he said, "our clients are exactly like you and me, but with bigger problems that they can't get past. Regardless of your issue, once you be-come homeless, that becomes your biggest immediate problem." Yes, he encouraged the homeless to take advantage of any program that could help them back on their feet. "But a homeless person in a hut is better than one not in a hut. Don't lose track of that."

A Gateway Toward Home

While Mayor Franklin's homelessness initiative didn't eliminate the problem in ten years, it did have major impacts, helping to halve the number of unsheltered homeless in Atlanta. The city built and filled over

3,000 supportive housing units for homeless people with mental or physical disabilities, and in 2005 it opened the four-story Gateway Center on Pryor Street in the southern part of downtown Atlanta, in a former city jail. It provides a total of 330 beds and eight residential programs for homeless men, including veterans, addicts in recovery, resident assistants who mentor others, resident interns who are learning job skills by working in the kitchen, a Life Changers program, and many other services. Residents are encouraged to find full- or part-time employment and save money during their stay.

In a program called Street-to-Home, once a month in the early morning hours social workers seek out men living under bridges or in homeless encampments and encourage them to board a bus for Gateway, where the first-floor Client Engagement Center acts as a kind of triage, offering help with family reunification, health care, and housing. And there are showers, a clothing closet, and toilets. (One of the many battles Atlanta homeless advocates lost was an effort to fund sufficient public toilets.) Working with social workers, members of Peers Reaching Out are formerly homeless men who try to help others facing the same struggle.

The organization is called Gateway because it is intended to serve as a portal to a continuum of care and a transitional reentry to self-sufficiency in some kind of affordable housing. Veterans are allowed to stay at the center for up to two years, but other programs range from ninety days to a year. There are also beds for men recuperating after a hospital stay.

Georgia Works!, a program within the center, finds minimum-wage jobs for homeless men who remain drug and alcohol free, while providing life-skill training. It lasts up to a year and ends with a formal graduation ceremony. The typical client is a middle-aged, black, male felon who has child support obligations, has not held a steady job for two years, has been homeless at least a year, and has a history of substance abuse.

So far, most of the graduates have not slipped back into addiction, crime, or homelessness. "There is a perception that the homeless don't really want to work," said Executive Director Phil Hunter, an African American who grew up in south Atlanta and, although a Morehouse graduate, was himself once a homeless cocaine addict. But treated with dignity and given a chance to start a new life, Hunter's clients can become regular employees and begin to honor renegotiated back child support payments.

The Gateway Center's core partner is the United Way Regional Commission on Homelessness, but it also works with the Georgia

Two Georgia Works! graduates

Department of Labor, Grady Hospital, and a total of sixty different organizations. Mercy Care offers a medical clinic there. Though designed to help only men, who constitute the majority of the homeless, for a while Gateway gave emergency shelter to women and children as well.

At Gateway, I met Damon, fifty-three, who made a living laying tile until three men robbed him, broke his ankle, and landed him in Grady Hospital for a week. Then he slept behind the Sweet Auburn Market below the I-75 overpass and ate food thrown out there. "I been here two months," he told me. "They fixed my teeth, I got new glasses, and I found me some peace." He had worked two days for a caterer the previous week.

I also talked to Russell, fifty-five, once a crack addict living in abandoned houses. He did occasional electric work but would also steal copper out of vacant homes. He had gotten clean through the Gateway program and was now a resident advisor, wearing a "Back on My Feet" T-shirt, part of a running program to encourage homeless men to feel proud, fit, and independent. He helped prep food in the Gateway kitchen, worked at the front desk, and said that he had tapped into a "spiritual base that keeps [him] balanced."

A Refuge in the City

Another full-service Atlanta shelter grew out of a Church of God min-
istry effort in the English Avenue neighborhood known as "The Bluff,"
a poverty-stricken black area on the west side, not far from where the
gleaming new stadium funded by Arthur Blank was rising from the
ground. Pastor Bruce Deel, then thirty-seven, opened a small shelter
there on Christmas Day in 1997 when the temperature dropped to seventeen degrees Fahrenheit. In 2003, he persuaded the Mimms family to
donate a 210,000-square-foot warehouse on Joseph E. Boone Boulevard,
and the Regional Council on Homelessness invested over $2 million of
the $10 million needed to refurbish it. Deel named the gigantic edifice
the City of Refuge, after the Old Testament towns where those who
committed manslaughter could seek asylum. Set in one of the roughest,
poorest areas of Atlanta, it offers 325 beds for homeless women and their
children—mostly African American—plus an impressive array of programs for both men and women. It has become the primary entry point
for services to homeless women in Atlanta.

Deel, a white native Virginian raised in the Pentecostal Church,
feels that God called him to this service, and he has persevered, with his
wife, in raising his five daughters in the neighborhood, despite thirty-four
break-ins, three stolen vehicles, and several death threats. "Yes, there
were times when we considered leaving," he told me, "but God has a plan
for our lives. This was our destiny, and whatever happens, happens."

Single women and mothers with children can stay at the shelter up
to six months, receiving a full range of medical, mental, dental, and vision services, plus vocational training and help finding a job and home,
and there is a "safe house" for victims of sexual trafficking. The City of
Refuge offers full day care, parenting classes, financial management, and
addiction recovery. "There is a spiritual component for those who want
it," Deel said. "I pastor a church on campus, with Bible studies and religious support groups. But it isn't required." What *is* required, however, is
that residents have no weapons or drugs and don't steal or curse at staff.
"They also have to be in a case management program while they are
here," Deel said. "We are not just a shelter."

The organization's 180 Degree Kitchen—named because it fosters
a complete change of attitude—cooks 12,000 meals a month for residents, after-school programs, and Wednesday night dinners and Sunday

morning breakfasts for the homeless on the streets, while training culinary arts students and placing them in jobs with many Atlanta restaurants. The kitchen also cooks for the shelter's food truck and catering service. The greenhouse, using a hydroponic system, grows greens and raises crawfish and tilapia. There is a gym, an auto-skills training center, and the Bright Futures Academy (grades six through twelve), most of whose graduates go to college.

"I didn't believe that I would ever have to come to a shelter," a young resident mother said. "But the door was open at the right time in my life, because I need stability for the children and for me to be able to get myself together where I can go back to work." Another young mother explained, "I was a typical soccer Mom for about five years. I thought I had a good life, but then things started changing between me and my husband. He got more abusive, especially with my oldest son." She ended up at the City of Refuge, where she and her children were thriving. "There's so much that's offered that's uplifting. I've never been made to feel ashamed, and my kids totally are made to feel, *We're going to focus on you and your problems.*"

"Our success is pretty dramatic," Deel observed. In the Mothers with Children program, 92 percent of participants have moved on to independent living after their six-month stay. Proud of and somewhat astonished by the rapid growth of his shelter and its programs, Deel also serves as a consultant for affiliate shelters using the same model in California, Ohio, Virginia, Tennessee, Jamaica, and the Dominican Republic.

Yet on the block adjacent to his own Atlanta shelter, only half the homes are occupied. Drugs and violence reign. "A gang shooting took place on our property three weeks ago," Deel told me. Directly across the street, the corner food mart sells junk food, lottery tickets, and cigarettes, but "at 3 a.m. you can buy any drug you want in their parking lot."

The Battle Lines at Peachtree and Pine

Other Atlanta homeless shelters and services for both men and women include the Atlanta Mission, which dropped the word "Union" from its name a few years ago. A nonprofit that "transforms, through Christ, the lives of those facing homelessness," it operates My Sister's House, with beds for 264 women and children, as well as a daytime shelter that offers homeless mothers counseling, medical care, and educational stipends.

The Shepherd's Inn has room for 450 homeless men, and Atlanta Mission also operates Fuqua Hall, transitional housing for 92 men. And there are Solomon's Temple, the Salvation Army's Red Shield facility, Covenant House, Serenity House, and Mary Hall Freedom House for female veterans, as well as many church-based programs such as a women's transitional shelter run by the First Presbyterian Church. Together all of these efforts reduced the number of unsheltered Atlanta homeless people by an estimated 51 percent from 2011 to 2015.

But the largest homeless shelter in Atlanta, officially called the Metro Atlanta Task Force for the Homeless, is also the most controversial, in large part because of its location right on Peachtree Street on the northern cusp of the downtown area, at the intersection with Pine Street, a few blocks south of the Fox Theater. All day, homeless people hang out across Pine Street and behind the building, on Courtland, giving the area a reputation for drugs and crime.

Anita Beaty, a soft-spoken white woman in her early seventies, has run the center since it opened in 1997. Raised in Columbia, South Carolina, in a family with aristocratic Southern roots but little money, Beaty was once a debutante. She came to Atlanta in 1983 to be a theatrical costume designer. Two years later, she volunteered at the Open Door Community, where she encountered a black woman who was abusing her infant son. Beaty ended up adopting him, which inspired her and her husband, Jim, to become involved in homeless issues.

The Task Force for the Homeless got its start in 1981, after seventeen homeless men died during a cold snap. In 1985, Anita Beaty took over the organization. In the run-up to the 1996 Atlanta Summer Olympics, she became a vocal advocate for homeless rights, as the city offered free bus tickets to any homeless people who would leave town. The Task Force sued the city over sweeps to clear the streets in which police carried blank arrest papers preprinted with "African American male" and "homeless."

In 1997, the year after the Olympics, a Coca-Cola heir named B. Wardlaw, a family black sheep who wrote a book called *Coca-Cola Anarchist*, paid $1.3 million for three adjoining vacant buildings on the northeastern corner of Peachtree and Pine, originally built for the automotive industry. He donated the 95,000 square feet of space to the Task Force.

Many early supporters became critics of Beaty, and she does not have a good working relationship with the Gateway Center or the Atlanta business community. She and her lawyers have claimed in legal actions that the city and Central Atlanta Progress (CAP), the organization lobbying to improve the downtown area, engaged in a deliberate effort to close down Peachtree and Pine. First they allegedly arranged to cut off funding; then, when the Beatys had to get a $900,000 mortgage to keep running, according to Beaty's lawyers, CAP found someone to buy it and foreclose on the property. When the huge shelter failed to pay its water bill, the city cut off its water until the shelter's lawyer pointed out that the Fulton County Jail owed much more, nearly $2 million in uncollected water bills, and no one was trying to close it.

The lawsuits over the shelter dragged on as I was researching this book. Local media coverage, even in *Creative Loafing*, the alternative Atlanta weekly, was generally negative toward Anita Beaty and her homeless shelter, portraying Peachtree and Pine as a warehouse for the homeless that did them more harm than good by fostering dependence and allowing people to live there too long, sometimes for years. In 2015, the Atlanta mayor declared his intention to seize the building through eminent domain as a public health hazard that fostered tuberculosis outbreaks. Yet several other shelters also had tuberculosis problems, and Peachtree and Pine followed public health guidelines from the Centers for Disease Control and Prevention.

I spent two afternoons there, taking a tour and interviewing Anita Beaty and some of her resident advisors (former homeless occupants) whose lives the shelter had helped to transform. For a place with a budget slashed from $2 million a year to a pittance, it appeared to be in pretty good shape. True, the 464 bunk beds for men on the second floor looked like an army barrack, but the room was clean. In the evening, the floors and administrative offices were covered with mats, where women and children slept. Because of the crowded conditions, single women had to sleep on chairs in the waiting room. On a cold winter night, over 1,000 people sometimes stayed at Peachtree and Pine. "We're the only place in Atlanta that will always take people no matter what," Beaty said. They may exclude themselves after the intake process, however, by refusing to obey the rules (no drugs or alcohol, no violence, no theft).

Despite drastic budget cuts, the shelter offered general equivalency diploma classes, a computer lab, MARTA tickets, and job referrals. The raised-bed gardens on the roof had just produced seventy pounds of vegetables for the kitchen, and someone kept bees and a pet rabbit up there as well. A retired art teacher had set up a gallery on the main floor off Peachtree, where she painted portraits of the homeless occupants.

Beaty's e-mails all end with a quotation: "Apathy in the face of relievable human misery is radical evil." So I was not surprised by her eloquence in defending her shelter. "I like to ask people, when they first come here, 'What would make your heart sing? What are your dreams? Let's make this experience change everything for you.'" When I asked how difficult she found dealing with homeless people, she corrected me. "Homelessness is an experience, not a blood type or a kind of personality. It's an experience of being extremely poor and not having a place to go that you can depend on. So it's temporary."

She claimed that the ragtag homeless who camped out on the other side of Pine Street were not staying at her shelter, since they refused to obey the rules. The police in the precinct across the street wouldn't ask them to move along, she said, because they wanted to make the shelter look bad. I hung out across the street for a while, talking to "Alabama," fifty-nine, a black man who sold for a dollar small bottles of vodka that

Anita Beaty at Peachtree and Pine, hugging a child who gave her a donation of change from her purse

he bought for sixty-eight cents. He confirmed that he didn't stay in the shelter, though he had done so in the past, "the very first night that door swung open." He said that police from surrounding areas came and dropped homeless people here on the street.

In response to an article on the shelter's controversial battle to survive, a former tenant named Chuck wrote, "In 2006 I found myself homeless, addicted, jobless, broke, with only the clothes on my back." He went to Peachtree and Pine, got referred to a detox program, then lived at the shelter for two and a half years. "I worked every day and saved $15,000." When he left, he was able to purchase his own home.

I asked Anita Beaty if she would be willing to convert the huge Peachtree and Pine facility into a mixed-income, mixed-use facility that could be profitable in this Midtown location. Sure, she said—if, and only if, so many people didn't need the facility as a place of last resort, even when it meant sleeping on a hallway mat or chair.

Shortly before this book went to press, I asked Beaty for an update. Had the eminent domain threat subsided? "That threat has lain quiet, but not dead," she responded. "Now the pressure from the 'streets' and the drugs and weapons is escalating, with little to NO help from the police." There had been a recent drive-by drug-related shooting at 2:30 a.m.

Critics of the shelter say the homeless should be housed elsewhere in smaller facilities with more services. If the shelter were not located on Peachtree, or not so large, or did not attract drugs and violence to the streets outside, it may not have encountered such bitter opposition. It is unfortunate that all of those concerned with the homeless in Atlanta cannot work together.*

Winston's Search for Dignity

At the Open Door Community, ordained Presbyterian ministers Ed Loring and Murphy Davis, who are married, have provided free meals, vitamins, clothing, showers, and a passionate, angry kind of liberation theology since 1981. The second time I volunteered there, the Open

---

* Atlanta parodist Ben Palmer's City of Atlanta Facebook page offered this faux regulation: "We take being poor very seriously. If you are caught being poor anywhere near or around Atlanta, our cameras will take a picture of you and you will receive a ticket in the mail. If you do not have a postal address, you will be collected in a paddy wagon and taken off to jail. Your ticket will then be mailed to jail."

Door was serving a full turkey dinner with stuffing and soup for lunch. As staff distributed tickets to those waiting outside, I tried to conduct some interviews, but only Winston, a trim black man in his forties, would talk to me. He said he was staying at Peachtree and Pine. No, it wasn't too bad there as long as you kept to yourself. When he declined a lunch ticket, I asked why, since it was really going to be a great meal, and hey, it was free.

"I don't need no free lunch," he said. "I can buy my own. I just come here for a shower." Angry, he got up, shouldered three huge garbage bags bulging with cans, and walked west toward downtown. I rushed to apologize, saying I hadn't meant to offend him, and offered him a ride. He declined. Hours later, I saw him miles away on the west side of town, still carrying his bags to a metal recycling center.

CHAPTER 7
A STAKE IN THE GROUND

To say, "Transit may never happen," is a defeatist view.
The idea of a loop of trails, parks, and streetcars circling
the city is beautiful in its simplicity, but it couldn't possibly
be built all at once. It needs to be done in segments, which
will each have to perform on Day One.

—Brian Leary, CEO, Atlanta BeltLine, Inc., December 2011

The plight of the homeless was not at the top of the BeltLine agenda as the challenging project struggled in the wake of a collapsed economy and the resignation of its frustrated first director. The next few years would be crucial in establishing the long-term viability of the BeltLine, especially since, at this point, almost no physical progress had been made. People loved the idea, but the potential loop remained just that—potential.

In September 2009, Brian Leary, thirty-five, was chosen to head Atlanta BeltLine, Inc. (ABI), replacing the departing Terri Montague. Leary took a substantial salary cut in leaving his previous position, but the job seemed made for him. Like Ryan Gravel, he had attended Georgia Tech for his undergraduate and master's degrees in city planning, with a focus on transportation and land development. After writing his thesis on the redevelopment of the defunct Atlantic Steel plant, he joined a local developer in transforming it into Atlantic Station, a mixed-use project in the heart of Midtown. Before the BeltLine, it was Atlanta's flagship redevelopment project.

Leary was white, male, intimate with the Atlanta scene, and an articulate proponent of the BeltLine vision, which he called "our next Olympic moment." Full of energy and enthusiasm, he observed, "There's something in the water in Atlanta that makes it such a special place, that allows a grad student from Georgia Tech to have this crazy idea to redo Atlantic Steel and then help do it. And Ryan was a year behind me, with his BeltLine thesis. This just doesn't happen other places in the country."

Leary wanted a streetcar to run on the BeltLine, asserting, "The goal of transportation isn't moving people, it is economic development." The promise of green space, amenities, and mobility would attract new homes and businesses. "That's true even in a place like Bankhead," he said, "with its Third World conditions." He anticipated that as the Belt-Line catalyzed growth, land and housing costs would go up, so he also promised to pursue affordable housing options.

On the Skids?

Yet Leary couldn't have taken over the BeltLine project at a more diffi-cult time. Just four days after he got the job, the *Atlanta Journal-Constitution* published an article asking, "Is the BeltLine headed for the skids?" The reporter pointed out that the strategic plan for the project hadn't been revised since 2006, before the financial crash rendered its projected $1.7 billion in income over the twenty-five-year lifetime of its tax allocation district (TAD) unrealistically rosy. The city's deputy chief operating of-ficer, quoted in the article, tried to remain upbeat: "If anything might have changed, perhaps it will require a little bit more reliance upon other funding sources than we originally thought."

Although a 2008 constitutional amendment had made it possible to use school taxes to support the project through the TAD, a new John Woodham lawsuit challenging the retroactive nature of the constitu-tional amendment had again frozen the use of those funds to float bonds. The suit was just beginning its lengthy trek through the legal system.* Recognizing the urgency, Leary hired an in-house lawyer during his first month on the job.

Leary also moved quickly on other financial fronts. The city had ne-gotiated the first TAD bonds for $64.5 million under the worst possible

---

* Woodham finally lost the suit in October 2012.

conditions in the fall of 2008, as the recession hit. In December 2009 Leary persuaded the city to refinance the bonds, now at more favorable rates, and secured $78 million with the same payment schedule, netting $13.5 million in extra funding for the BeltLine. Still, the total amount was far less than the $200 million originally forecast for the first full TAD bonds.

Before Leary's time, under Terri Montague, ABI had signed an agreement with the Georgia Department of Transportation (GDOT) to lease the southwestern section of abandoned rail required for the BeltLine, but the price tag of $18 million seemed exorbitant to Leary. "I knew the GDOT people from my negotiations to build the 17th Street bridge over the interstate for the Atlantic Station development," he recalled, so he invited its key officials to take a special BeltLine bus tour with him. At one point, Rudy Bowen, the GDOT chair, called out, "Stop the bus!" His grandfather had owned a sawmill nearby, he said, and as a boy he had jumped in the sawdust piles. "A light bulb went on for him," Leary observed. "He was thinking, *Hey, I guess Atlantans are Georgians, too.*" Bowen agreed to abide by an independent appraisal of what that southwestern corridor was really worth, and the price came down to $1.6 million, though Leary found the years-long delay in the actual closing to be frustrating.*

From his experience as a private developer, Leary understood the importance of personal relationships, especially in Atlanta. So he continued his special bus tours for important decision makers, including CEOs and executives of potential corporate donors such as Coca-Cola and Home Depot; real estate developers; officials with the Atlanta Regional Commission, MARTA, and the Georgia Regional Transportation Authority; and even Georgia Supreme Court justices. "I knew Mark Toro, who owns North American Properties in Atlanta, from an Atlantic Station project, so I invited him and his wife on the tour," Leary said. "He was blown away by it and ended up building apartments on the BeltLine."

Leary's bottom-line philosophy: "Nothing will happen unless people open up their wallets." That included philanthropists, developers, and other businesspeople, with whom Leary practiced the fine art of schmoozing and gift giving he had learned while working on the Atlantic Station project. He regarded Atlanta BeltLine, Inc., as a private nonprofit organization that just happened to be funded by the city of Atlanta, so that

---

* The closing on the lease option agreement with GDOT finally took place in 2014.

he could act on his own, with entrepreneurial instincts, which included sending flowers to the wife of a prominent builder who was hospitalized, along with a get-well card. "The $50 for those flowers was a lot cheaper than millions of dollars that might be lost otherwise," said Leary.

The new BeltLine chief also spent a good deal of time speaking about the innovative project, accepting invitations to conferences or events in other cities. "I thought it was the most important urban project in the country," he said, "and the chances of attracting money from the likes of the Gates or Ford Foundation or the federal government would improve if I spoke at a Smart Growth conference in Louisiana or testified before Congress in favor of a transportation bill." He spoke at or attended transportation-related conferences in Los Angeles, Seattle, Jacksonville, Baton Rouge, New Orleans, Charlotte, Charleston, Detroit, Salt Lake City, Chicago, and Savannah, as well as making repeated trips to Washington, DC.

A Brash, Charismatic New Mayor

Shortly after the BeltLine hired Leary, Democrat Kasim Reed, forty, became Atlanta's new mayor in a very close contest with Mary Norwood, a white city council member, winning by just 715 votes. Reed had served as Shirley Franklin's campaign manager during her first mayoral campaign, and as a state senator, he had led the fight to amend the state constitution to allow the use of school taxes for TAD funding. Now the former entertainment lawyer, who lived in the upscale black suburb of Cascade Heights in the far southwest of Atlanta, vowed to work closely with Republican governor Sonny Perdue (and later with his successor, Nathan Deal). Relations between Atlanta and the state of Georgia had hitherto been notoriously tense; conservative state politicians regarded the big-city liberals as enemies, with more than a tinge of racial prejudice in the mix. Thus, the collaboration between the white governor and black mayor was unusual and encouraging.

Reed inherited a troubled city budget from outgoing Mayor Shirley Franklin, but in his first term, he managed to reform the ailing city pension fund, hire more police to combat street gangs, and reopen recreation centers in poor sections of the city, calling them Centers of Hope. He also championed the BeltLine, vowing that he would get it finished within eight to twelve years instead of the originally envisioned twenty-five. "It's hard for the public to remain engaged in it," Reed said. "You are already seeing BeltLine fatigue." As with a number of the mayor's pronouncements, however, he didn't explain how he was going to pull off this miracle.

Reed, who had campaigned hard for Barack Obama's presidential bid, also promised to seek federal funds for the Peachtree Streetcar project—involving a north-south stretch up Atlanta's spine as well as a shorter east-west downtown loop (none connecting to the BeltLine)—estimated to cost $300 million. Instead, in 2010 he managed to secure a $47.6 million TIGER (Transportation Investment Generating Economic Recovery) grant in the second round of federal stimulus funding, intended to jump-start the economy via public transportation projects. In typical opportunistic Atlanta planning fashion, Reed dropped the main thrust of the streetcar plan, which was to run the line up Peachtree Street, connecting residents and businesses from downtown through Buckhead. Instead, for an estimated total of $72 million, the city would put a streetcar only on the ancillary east-west loop, running from Centennial Park on the east side to the Martin Luther King Center in the west.

In an editorial headlined "Streetcar Will Lead Atlanta Toward Future," Reed boasted that the city had received the largest TIGER II in the country. In fact, the "Atlanta Streetcar" loop, which would travel one way down Edgewood and return a block away on Auburn Avenue, wouldn't head anywhere most Atlantans needed to go. It would primarily serve tourists visiting the World of Coca-Cola, the Georgia Aquarium, the Center for Civil and Human Rights, and the Martin Luther King Center. Nonetheless, Reed envisioned a streetcar network extending onto and within the BeltLine to "enable residents and visitors to navigate the city without relying on an automobile." If this costly vision ever became reality, it would be a case of "back to the future," recreating a part of the extensive streetcar system that Atlanta had destroyed in its quest for modernity in the postwar era.

In his chauffeur-driven black Ford Taurus, Kasim Reed zoomed around Atlanta, routinely putting in fourteen-hour days as he cut ribbons, met with neighborhood groups, chatted with CEOs, or talked to Tyler Perry's agent, who had been Reed's college classmate. Flashing his Hollywood smile, he traded on his charm, energy, youth, and what he termed "a really strong will." As he saw it, he had a "mandate to execute," and he was determined to move as quickly as possible to encourage deals that would bring more business and growth to Atlanta. In college, Reed's favorite book was Michael Korda's *Power*, and he clearly enjoyed wielding it. It remained to be seen whether he would do so effectively.

The Eastside Trail and Ponce City Market

On first meeting Brian Leary, Reed told him that every time he mentioned the BeltLine, he needed to call it "the *Atlanta* BeltLine." Impressed, Leary subsequently changed the logo to include the city's name. "Kasim Reed is a force of nature," Leary said. "He focuses like a laser on where he wants the city to go."

Leary himself focused on getting actual parts of the BeltLine built. "The right structure had been set up," Leary recalled, "with the Belt-Line Partnership raising money and ABI to design and execute, but no real physical progress had been made." True, some tangible projects were under way, with the Northside Trail along Tanyard Creek nearing completion, despite loud neighborhood protest. The PATH Foundation was about to break ground for the West End Trail, mostly along streets leading to Westview Cemetery. Crews were working on the first phase of the Historic Fourth Ward Park, while D. H. Stanton Park in Peoplestown and part of Boulevard Crossing Park near Grant Park would be finished in the next two years. "The question of if the BeltLine will happen should be put to rest," Leary told a reporter, "because we are under construction."

In fact, however, no section in the actual BeltLine corridor had been built, even though ABI owned the northeastern section that the city had purchased for an exorbitant price from Wayne Mason. ABI officials had told Jim Kennedy, the Cox Enterprises chairman who provided essential funding for the PATH Foundation, that it would cost $5 million to lay down a trail on a prime section of that corridor, starting at 10th Street and Monroe and heading south 2.25 miles to Irwin Street. Taking that route would avoid dealing with the controversial parcel just to the north where Mason had planned to build his two towers. But when Kennedy offered to donate $2.5 million, half of the money for the trail, Leary's predecessor, Terri Montague, had objected to building the first section of trail on the east side, with its upscale and gentrifying neighborhoods. That would appear racially and economically inequitable.

Kennedy insisted, "We have got to build something to show people what it will be. Once we build it, people will say, 'Now you've got to finish it.'" He persuaded insurance provider Kaiser Permanente to pony up another $2.5 million because of the potential public health benefits of the trail. By the time Brian Leary arrived, the money had been pledged, but the trail had not been designed, since Montague had decided not to build anything before the design and approval of the entire twenty-two-mile loop.

Leary decided to move ahead anyway, recalling the words of visionary New York builder Robert Moses: "Once you sink that first stake, they'll never make you pull it up." But Leary had to deal with Fred Yalouris, then sixty-one. Before the BeltLine brought him on as the design director in 2008, he had spent a decade as director of architecture and urban design for Boston's "Big Dig" project to bury a downtown highway. Yalouris, who had a PhD in classical archaeology, had previously served as a Harvard dean. Although he had no design training, he noted that he knew "how to handle smart people with big egos."

Yet Yalouris had his own ego and insisted on what many considered an overdesign of the future Eastside Trail. An inherent conflict arose between the pragmatic, get-it-done approach of the PATH Foundation's Ed McBrayer and the ABI's insistence on long-term planning and implementing a world-class, exemplary project. Although sometimes frustrated by Yalouris, Leary too wanted the Eastside Trail built ready for an eventual streetcar. McBrayer preferred to throw down a pedestrian and bike trail in the middle of the corridor. If and when there was funding for a streetcar, you could always rip it up and redo it.

McBrayer lost that battle, and the trail was shoved over to the side of the corridor, requiring expensive granite retaining walls at various points. Yalouris and his design team didn't want a line painted down the middle of the path, insisting that one side of the concrete have a rougher, sandblasted, somewhat darker surface than the other to differentiate it. To prepare for eventual streetlights and a streetcar, concrete-encased PVC conduits were run under the trail, accessed by manhole covers every five hundred feet. Astra Group, a construction company based in Woodstock, Georgia, that was building the Historic Fourth Ward Park, won the Eastside Trail contract, breaking ground late in 2010.

The trail took two years to complete, since, in addition to the retaining walls, bridge repair and construction, and landscaping, it required substantial environmental cleanup. The Astra crew ran into unanticipated problems: a slope that collapsed into a parking lot, unmapped storm sewers under the former rail line, eroded pipes that leaked water into the right-of-way. "The abandoned rail corridor was everyone's back door, so industrial users and tenants just dumped stuff there," the Astra CEO said. Where Freedom Parkway crossed the trail, the construction crew ran into a buried trash pit of broken concrete, wood, and asphalt shingles—probably from homes destroyed in anticipation of a raised expressway that neighborhood activists ultimately stopped.

The total cost, which included $750,000 from Trees Atlanta for the BeltLine arboretum plantings, topped $12 million—far more than the original $5 million estimate—over half of which had to come out of the TAD bond money, since there were no matching federal funds. Even at the price of $6 million per mile, the Eastside Trail incorporated very few access points. For instance, even though it ran next to the Historic Fourth Ward Park, then under construction on the trail's western side, there was no official connector. Nor was there any lighting for night use.

As the Eastside Trail construction began in October 2010, Mayor Reed was finally able to sell the huge old Sears building for $27 million to Jamestown Properties, a German-owned private equity group.* Jamestown, which had redeveloped the hugely successful Chelsea Market in a former Manhattan Nabisco factory, now partnered with Atlanta-based developer Green Street Properties and pledged to spend another $180 million to turn the 2.1-million-square-foot building into a mixed-use development with retail, business, and residential sections to be called Ponce City Market.

The deal provided an enormous boost to the BeltLine running next to the old Sears, which still had a rail spur diving directly into the building. Jamestown planned eventually to use it as a bike ramp to connect with the trail. "It [the Ponce City Market project] is fundamentally important to the BeltLine," Leary said, since the deal was happening in the middle of "the worst real estate market in the last 80 years." Demonstrable BeltLine progress was finally under way, at least on the east side.

---

* Before the Great Recession, the Sears building had been under contract for $36 million to a real estate consortium headed by Emory Morseberger, who envisioned it as a mixed-use "Medici Center" that would connect expertise from Emory University, Georgia Tech, the Atlanta University Center, the Carter Center, and the Centers for Disease Control and Prevention, among others. He planned a substantial affordable housing component, focusing on those with disabilities who could use wheelchairs to navigate the BeltLine to get to the Shepherd Spinal Center to the north. But the recession disabled the deal.

Peaceful, Skating Along, but Affordable?

In June 2011, while the Eastside Trail was being built and the mammoth old Sears began its four-year transformation into Ponce City Market, the first phase of the Historic Fourth Ward Park was completed along the trail's inner flank. An early visitor reveled in the unexpected quiet of the seventeen-acre plot of land, with its graceful curving paths, splash pad, and small outdoor amphitheater next to a 2.4-acre pond with a fountain and water cascade. "I don't hear any noise here, except for the water," she said. "There are no cars. No commotion. It is very calming." The land had until recently featured a trucking company, contaminated soil, ramshackle buildings, and homeless encampments. Brian Leary called it the "first jewel in the Atlanta BeltLine's emerald necklace," adding, "This is one of the most under-parked neighborhoods in an under-parked city."

Rob Brawner, deputy executive director of the BeltLine Partnership, echoed Leary. In addition to raising funds to support the project, the Partnership was responsible for community outreach and grassroots support, which included running weekend bus tours around the future Belt-Line. Since 2007, some 10,000 people had taken the tour, which stopped at the gigantic quarry that would one day be a reservoir. "Now when they see this park," Brawner said, "it is breathtaking."

A bit to the south, tour participants could also see young people carving, grinding, and kickflipping in a new BeltLine skate park next to a field and playground. Skateboarding legend Tony Hawk helped design the ramps and quarter pipes and attended the opening ceremonies after his foundation donated $25,000 toward its completion. Kids and young adults, along with a smattering of more mature skateboarders, instantly swamped the venue. Councilman Kwanza Hall, who represented that district, was ecstatic about the new park. "Children love it. Dogs love it. Birds love it." The park would "raise the brand of the Old Fourth Ward," he said.

Indeed it did. By the summer of 2012, new apartments and loft buildings were popping up near the Eastside Trail and the park. Many of the residents were hip, young, and single, attracted by the walkable lifestyle. The arrival of the so-called Millennials (young people born from the 1980s on), mostly white, was elevating property values and rents in the traditionally black Old Fourth Ward neighborhood. Though well aware that gentrification could displace poorer African Americans, BeltLine staffers could do little to prevent the process. True, 15 percent of the TAD funds—$8.8 million from the first bonds—was set aside to support affordable housing, but even with an extra stipend, most developers were loath to commit the hot new units to such purposes. And unless forced to do so by mandatory inclusionary zoning or other such legislation, they likely never would.

Instead, next to the future BeltLine on Memorial Drive, ABI took advantage of a former Triumph motorcycle factory, now a nearly completed condo building that had gone into foreclosure in the recession. In September 2011, the BeltLine organization bought it for $3.7 million and prepared the units for sale. The two-bedroom units in the Lofts at Reynoldstown Crossing, named for the neighborhood, sold quickly to police, firefighters, teachers, and other qualifying individuals—people who earned no more than 80 percent of the area median income (AMI). They were able to buy the condos for $90,000 to $150,000 instead of paying market prices, which ran to over $200,000.

ABI slowly doled out other affordable housing money for down-payment assistance to families earning no more than $68,300, with good credit and $1,500 to contribute to the closing. Although ABI didn't buy any more condo buildings, it offered help to qualified buyers at the lower-end Sky Lofts condos, which opened in late 2011 in the West End neighborhood.

Such assistance reached only a small number of middle-income rather than poor people, however, and the housing was not guaranteed to remain affordable forever. Atlanta BeltLine Partnership chair Valarie Wilson spearheaded efforts that had, thus far, raised nearly $40 million for the BeltLine—pretty good, given the recession, but still short of the original goal of $60 million. Wilson was also particularly interested in the concept of community land trusts, a mechanism to keep homes permanently affordable. The idea, pioneered in Vermont and elsewhere, was for the trust to own the land, so that new owners bought only the housing component, promising to part with it for an affordable price should they sell it in the future. The purchase price and taxes were substantially lower than for traditional housing.*

---

* The pioneering effort to build community land trust homes actually took place in southwest Georgia in 1969 as an outgrowth of the civil rights movement. Charles and Shirley Sherrod founded New Communities, Inc., a land trust and collective farm, but they could not finance residential homes.

Wilson sponsored the Atlanta Land Trust Collaborative as an umbrella organization for what she hoped would be a group of neighborhood community land trusts. But the idea proved a hard sell. "In the South, you have arrived when you own land," Wilson observed in 2012. "It's the American dream. People have to understand that this isn't a trick to take their homes from them. I wish I could tell you that we have homes we have been able to put into the land trust, but we still need to get it up and going."

Getting People onto the BeltLine

To keep people focused on the BeltLine vision, in 2010 Fred Yalouris came up with Art on the BeltLine, an annual event to put temporary sculpture, mosaics, paintings, and other art onto the future corridor. To kick off the event, New Orleans transplant Chantelle Rytter proposed a lantern parade, drawing five hundred people with homemade lanterns onto the muddy, weedy trail at night in a glorious, ghostly procession. "Atlanta needed to believe that the creepy place behind the dumpsters would become our country's best urban renewal project," she recalled. The BeltLine Lantern Parade would become an annual tradition, with thousands more participating each year.

Art on the BeltLine was a hit, luring people onto the trails, with young artists vying to win space in each year's exhibits. By the third year the program received nearly two hundred submissions from graffiti artists, sculptors, painters, performers, and dancers. Despite the lack of an official paved path, people walked their dogs, did yoga, and spread picnics near the art installations. Still, the program annoyed some residents. "The painted junk cars are completely vandalized and homeless live in them," complained one Atlanta resident months after the first exhibits. "Get rid of them."

To encourage community involvement and ownership of the trail, the BeltLine Partnership, in conjunction with Park Pride, an Atlanta nonprofit lobbying for more and better park space, asked local businesses and residents to "adopt" a portion of the corridor and take responsibility for removing kudzu and trash, mowing grass, and reporting suspicious activities. The BeltLine also sponsored five-kilometer and longer runs along the West End, Tanyard Park, and Piedmont Park trails, with prizes, gift certificates, and other activities, though the events focused on community over competition.

The T-SPLOST Splat

Meanwhile, plans for a new regional 1 percent sales tax to fund badly needed transportation projects finally came to fruition. The Georgia governor and legislature had been talking about the idea since 2007, but it took until April 2010 for the politicians to agree to put it to a public referendum. Kasim Reed got a great deal of the credit, since he had lobbied heavily for the bill. The new mayor "has spent more time at the Capitol than some of the lawmakers he had gone there to see last week," a reporter observed.

The proposed penny tax, the Transportation Special-Purpose Local-Option Sales Tax, had an unfortunate acronym, T-SPLOST, which sounded something like regurgitation. The bill divided the state of Georgia into twelve regions. A "roundtable" of local elected officials from each would draw up a list of projects to submit to voters for approval. If the bill passed, the tax would fund projects for ten years. "The vote could represent the region's biggest single infrastructure investment in 40 years or more, changing the way residents work, live, and move," observed one reporter.

A prolonged debate ensued over potential transportation projects in the ten-county metro Atlanta region. Kasim Reed served on that roundtable, along with other mayors and county commissioners, and pushed hard for inclusion of the BeltLine in the smorgasbord of projects to receive funding. He insisted that the "anti-Atlanta tone that has been pervasive for years" in the surrounding suburbs was now changing. By August 2011, when the list was eventually whittled down to a realistic goal of $6.1 billion (plus another 15 percent to be spent on local discretionary projects), the BeltLine was on it, with promised funding of $602 million, which would include ten miles of streetcar lines along the east and west flanks of the corridor as well as connecting lines to downtown and Midtown.

The BeltLine became a lightning rod for criticism by the OTP ("outside the Perimeter") crowd, led by the mayor of Sandy Spring, just to Atlanta's north. The T-SPLOST, she said, was intended to relieve congestion and improve the regional transportation system. But the BeltLine website itself "makes it abundantly clear that its objective is economic development, not traffic congestion relief." She cited the Mike Dobbins panel that questioned whether there would be sufficient ridership to support streetcars on the corridor. Mayor Reed defended the BeltLine, which, combined with direct routes into the heart of the city, he said, would provide "critical last-mile connectivity." He dismissed critics: "They are running the same tired play of pitting the suburbs against the city."

Indeed, letters to the editor indicated just such a split. Forget mass transit options, advised a frustrated suburban commuter. "Start widening every major road and highway at warp speed. Consider double decking roads. If it's already six lanes wide, make it eight." The proposed list of projects—a political compromise that directed a little over half of funding to forms of mass transit, with the balance going to road projects—came under immediate assault from all sides. Tea Party activists hated mass transit. The local Sierra Club wanted members to vote against the new tax because it didn't sponsor *enough* transit. "Every new track-mile of light rail built would be matched by 16 lane-miles of road expansion," complained the Sierra Club state director. Even the local chapter of the National Association for the Advancement of Colored People objected that the proposed tax wouldn't fund mass transit to African American neighborhoods.

At the polls on July 31, 2012, the T-SPLOST suffered resounding defeat in the ten-county area, although the majority of Atlantans voted for it. Even though commuters more than doubled the city's population daily, the split between the urban and suburban perceived interests proved intractable. As one observer noted prior to the vote, victory for the bill would not have been a cure-all anyway: "Even if the tax is approved, and even if every project on the list is completed as planned, come 2023 metro Atlanta will still lack a real regional transit system, with no rail-based transit linking the core to suburban counties, and no rail links among the suburbs."

True, but now the gridlock and lack of mass transit options would persist, and the BeltLine would not receive the huge funding boost that would have put streetcars on parts of the corridor. Indeed, it appeared that BeltLine transit would not materialize for years, if ever.

BeltLine Spending Scandal

But the BeltLine project itself was by no means defeated. It would, as one reporter observed, "continue taking shape as a scattering of redevelopments, parks and trails that planners hope to eventually link into a continuous loop." Brian Leary tried to put the best face on the disappointing vote.

"When [the BeltLine] was conceived, T-SPLOST wasn't part of our plan. So now we're back to Plan A," he said. "We're a wily and creative bunch. We're going to look behind every tree and every rock" for transit funding.

Eleven days later, Leary and his twenty-three-member staff came under fire when an investigative reporter for the *Atlanta Journal-Constitution* broke a story about questionable BeltLine expenditures—not current ones but from April 2010 until May 2011. "The wine bottle holder sent by BeltLine staffers to their boss's fiancée last year came with a congratulatory note on her upcoming wedding," the article began. "What it did not say was who picked up the tab for the $106.22 gift: Atlanta taxpayers." The reporter went on to complain about "elaborate staff retreats, stays at pricey hotels, and expensive meals at some of the city's finest restaurants."

The expenses in question included $489.22 for beer kegs to launch an Art on the BeltLine event, a $27.95 parking ticket Leary got while attending a downtown meeting with the mayor, and his $7 dry cleaning bill (a waiter spilled food on him before a speaking engagement). When thirty-two BeltLine staff and guests attended a Braves game, they spent $2,100 on soft drinks, chicken wings, pretzels, and popcorn—at $65 a person, an indication of just how overpriced stadium junk food can be. In all, BeltLine staffers charged around $5,000 for food and beverage expenses in a little over a year and another $5,000 on trips around the nation to conferences and networking events.

In the business world from which Leary had come, such expenses were routine and penny-ante, but the newspaper coverage, which hammered away for the next week, made them sound extravagant and nearly criminal. Readers responded, suggesting a spurious connection between the transportation tax defeat and the spending scandal. "Read about the BeltLine spending and then, with a straight face, tell me again how I'm an uneducated buffoon for voting against T-SPLOST." "Now we know what the BeltLine folks meant by 'We're a wily and creative bunch.'" "The BeltLine Boozing incident is just another example of the type of behavior that got T-SPLOST voted down." Fulton County commissioner Emma Darnell, a black member of the BeltLine board, complained, "There's no way we can support that kind of waste and extravagance." She wanted money to go toward revitalizing blighted areas, not "$2,000 trips to Braves games." An editorial pontificated, "The BeltLine now faces the task of living down its staff's high living."

Leary, whose first child had been born in July, publicly apologized for the expenditures, even though the board had approved all of them, and he paid back $3,000 with a personal check. The whole affair seemed particularly strange in light of the estimated $14 billion that Georgia Power was planning to spend on two new nuclear reactors or the $1.2 billion estimate for a potential new stadium for the Atlanta Falcons football team.

But the furor clearly wasn't dying down, and the board forced Leary to resign at the end of August 2012. "In hindsight, I would have done things differently," he recalled. "The BeltLine is too special of a project for any one person to be a distraction, and that was happening." Some anonymous insiders did not lament Leary's departure, despite the pettiness of the spending scandal. "He was just a showboat," claimed one. "He never raised any money. He never came up with a new strategic plan."

Yet BeltLine lawyer Patrise Perkins-Hooker, who remained at her job until 2016, strongly defended Leary, calling him "an exceptional visionary and marketing genius" whose national promotion of the BeltLine laid the groundwork for future recognition and funding. The spending scandal was "craziness," she said; it had focused on petty expenses while ignoring the millions Leary had saved the project.

The first five-year BeltLine plan had expired in 2011. Leary hadn't seen the point in creating a second one, when few of the goals of the first had been achieved. Nonetheless, that year he set the wheels in motion for a new *Strategic Implementation Plan* that would lay out phased goals for the entire life of the project. The following spring he chose a consultation team led by Perkins + Will.

On Leary's departure, Lisa Gordon, the BeltLine's African American chief operating officer, stepped in as interim director until a national search came up with a suitable new CEO. In the meantime, the BeltLine project was actually progressing remarkably well, with thriving bus tours, art and activities on the trails, several new parks, and the Eastside Trail nearing completion, along with sprouting apartment high-rises nearby. As Leary had observed, "Our parks and trails are concrete and steel and granite. It's a real investment. And it's a permanent one."

Ironically, Leary's ouster occurred just before the Eastside Trail finally opened to the public in October 2012. It was instantly mobbed by bikers, joggers, rollerbladers, skateboarders, strollers, dog walkers, and just plain gawkers. On Mother's Day, May 12, 2013, over 18,000 people hit the trail to enjoy the sunny spring weather, and more than 1 million people traversed it over the following year.

As a developer, Leary had focused on the BeltLine primarily for its potential to lure new businesses to the loop. But it also had important implications for some of the overwhelming public health issues facing Atlanta, along with other American cities. Before continuing the BeltLine story, we need to explore those concerns.

CHAPTER 8

THE PUBLIC'S HEALTH

....

Many people and organizations now recognize how the existing built environment is harming public health and needs to be redesigned or retrofitted. . . . Toxic, contaminated air is a factor in asthma; having insufficient sidewalks, bike paths, and parks is a factor in obesity; a lack of access to fresh food and farmers' markets is a factor in diabetes; and so forth.

—Dr. Richard J. Jackson, *Designing Healthy Communities*, 2012

On a scorching, humid Atlanta summer day in 1999, Dick Jackson, a doctor and epidemiologist at the Centers for Disease Control and Prevention (CDC), was driving from his office in Chamblee to the main CDC campus on Clifton Road for a meeting on the leading causes of death in the United States in the twenty-first century. They would likely be, in descending order of prevalence, heart disease, cancer, chronic lower respiratory diseases, accident, stroke, Alzheimer's, diabetes, influenza and pneumonia, kidney disease (nephritis), and suicide.

Jackson, who had begun his career as a CDC Epidemic Intelligence Service officer, tracking down the sources of infectious disease epidemics, then pesticide exposure and other environmental hazards, pondered how the obesity epidemic was at least partially responsible for many of those leading causes of death, including heart disease, cancer, stroke, and diabetes.* And lifestyle stressors, including too much time in automobiles, contributed to accidents and suicides. *Add smoking and air pollution for respiratory diseases*, he thought.

He was driving down Buford Highway, a seven-lane road with little traffic. It had once served as the main thoroughfare running northeast out of Atlanta into Gwinnett County, but now Interstate 85, which paralleled it, took most of the traffic. This stretch of the road had become a mecca for cheap, multiethnic restaurants—Vietnamese, Korean, Thai, Malaysian, Cuban, Mexican, Bangladeshi, and others—and apartment buildings, but it had no sidewalks, and traffic lights where pedestrians could safely cross were sometimes spaced a mile apart.

As he drove, Jackson saw a stooped older woman, clearly suffering from osteoporosis, walking along the side of the road with heavy plastic shopping bags in each hand. She paused and looked across the road, searching for a good time to cross. "She had red hair and looked like my mother," Jackson recalled. At his meeting, Jackson's thoughts kept returning to the woman. "If she were to collapse," he thought, "the cause of death would be listed as heat stroke, and there would be no mention of the upstream causes—the absence of trees, a black tar road, too many cars, too much air pollution, and lack of public transport." And if she were hit by a truck, the cause of death would be motor vehicle trauma, not lack of sidewalks and insufficient pedestrian crossings.

That incident served as an epiphany for Jackson, who subsequently became an ardent proponent for rethinking and restructuring the "built environment," recognizing that how we build our cities, transportation systems, and infrastructure has a profound public health impact. In his 2012 four-part public television documentary and accompanying book, *Designing Healthy Communities*, he preached a New Urbanist health mantra. Children should be able to walk or ride bikes to school. A public park (as opposed to impervious blacktop) "captures rainwater, reduces pollution, raises property values, and improves physical, mental, and social well-being." In his program, he singled out the BeltLine as the "largest redevelopment project in the United States," a visionary effort that would "forever change the face of Atlanta."

---

* I interviewed Dick Jackson for my 2010 book, *Inside the Outbreaks*, a history of the Epidemic Intelligence Service.

Jackson sounded a near-apocalyptic alarm about the importance of such transformative projects. "Sixty-eight percent of Americans over age twenty are overweight or obese," he wrote, "and obesity in U.S. children and adolescents has tripled in just over a generation. One in three American children is overweight." Many develop type 2 diabetes. "If current trends are not reversed," Jackson prophesied, "this could be the first generation of American children to have shorter life spans than their parents."

In 2012 I drove down Buford Highway with Sally Flocks, founder of PEDS, which originally stood for Pedestrians Educating Drivers on Safety, though its focus quickly expanded beyond merely instructing drivers to lobbying for better crosswalks, sidewalks, and street design. A California native, Flocks had moved to Atlanta at age twenty-five in 1977, shortly after getting married. Six months later, an epilepsy diagnosis meant she could no longer drive. Fortunately, she lived in Ansley Park, just off Peachtree, and could walk to the grocery store, dentist, and doctor, and a bus stopped a block from her house. When MARTA opened, she could walk to the Arts Center MARTA station. In 1996, a car turning left almost knocked her off the curb, inspiring her to write an editorial in the local paper. She got such a response from other frustrated pedestrians that she founded PEDS.

I videotaped our drive down Buford Highway, with Sally Flocks providing commentary. You can watch it and other appalling footage on YouTube by searching there for "Buford Highway pedestrians." Flocks noted that there were no sidewalks, but people had created a dirt trail, mostly from walking to a bus stop. "It's hilly, so the drivers can't see who might be crossing the street," she said as we drove. "No crosswalks and a forty-five-mile-per-hour speed limit. If you hit somebody at that impact, they're gonna be dead." Indeed, between 2004 and 2014, 154 people died while attempting to cross Buford Highway, making it the second most dangerous road in the metro Atlanta area.

Belatedly, in 2014 the Georgia Department of Transportation (GDOT) put sidewalks along a stretch of the highway, along with some median islands and flashing pedestrian lights. Instead of imposing a "road diet" and getting rid of the unneeded outside lanes on each side to create sidewalks and bike lanes, GDOT left the seven-lane drag strip in place, spending over $10 million to buy the right-of-way for sidewalks and retaining walls.

Still, thanks to PEDS and other organizations, GDOT finally endorsed the concept of "Complete Streets," in which automobiles, public transportation, bicycles, and pedestrians maintain some kind of safe equilibrium. A $250 million infrastructure bond, approved by city voters in March 2015 for fixing roads, bridges, and sidewalks, should bring substantial improvements, though retrofitting multilane Atlanta streets such as Peachtree, Northside Drive, Piedmont, Boulevard, Lee Street, or Ponce de Leon Avenue will be difficult and controversial, necessitating various forms of road diet. Part of the bond funds was allocated to fix dangerous, broken city sidewalks, for years the responsibility of home owners and businesses along their stretch of road. Mayor Reed refused to change the old ordinance's wording, however, for fear of creating an "unfunded mandate" to fix all city sidewalks forever. Meanwhile, only 40 percent of Atlanta's streets had any sidewalks at all.

Bicycling the Atlanta Way

In 2008, an irate driver wrote a letter to the Atlanta paper complaining about bikers: "Traffic is bad enough without people taking a recreational ride down a major road while productive members of society are trying to get to actual destinations." Such attitudes showed just how far the city still had to go to become bike friendly, despite the PATH Foundation's sustained efforts on its network of recreational trails (nearing three hundred miles in Georgia), including the BeltLine. Rebecca Serna, the young executive director of the Atlanta Bicycle Campaign (later renamed the Atlanta Bicycle Coalition), commuted to work by bicycle and felt called upon to respond to this letter. Since she'd started riding her bike to work, Serna wrote, she had lost fifteen pounds, and she saved $8,500 a year by ditching her car and sharing her husband's when necessary. She felt energized and alert after her twenty-minute ride each way. She pointed out that bike commuters save the public thirteen cents a mile in congestion and pollution costs. Finally, she noted, "We're not clogging up traffic, we *are* traffic."

Yet Atlanta lagged far behind many other cities in almost every aspect of bicycling. In 2006, *Bicycling Magazine* ranked it as one of the three worst cities in the country for cyclists. A 2008 survey found that over a third of Atlanta's bike riders didn't wear helmets, and a quarter rode on the sidewalk—somewhat understandably, since there were few bike lanes on the crowded streets. The surveyors even saw an SUV swerve into a rare bike lane on Edgewood Avenue, nearly running down two bikers. The Department of Public Works posted "Share the Road" signs, a lame response. To protest the dominance of the automobile, on the last Friday of every month, hundreds of Critical Mass bicyclists gathered defiantly to block intersections. Such behavior only exacerbated antagonisms on both sides. "There is a war going on between Atlanta's motorists and bicyclists," a local reporter observed.

Over the next few years, however, Atlanta experienced a sea change in attitudes toward cycling. In 2010, Rebecca Serna launched "Atlanta Streets Alive," securing permission to temporarily block off two miles along Auburn and Edgewood Avenues, so that people could walk, bike, dance, and socialize where cars usually ruled. The program was a hit, and the renamed Atlanta Bicycle Coalition continued to sponsor such road parties in different neighborhoods, even blocking off Peachtree Street for one festival featuring music and a bicycle parade.

Georgia Tech students started a bike-sharing program in 2012, inspiring the city to plan a similar effort to begin in 2016, though Atlanta was far behind Boston, Chattanooga, Portland, Washington, DC, and other cities. Serna noted that biking on city streets was good not only for riders' health but for business. Cyclists could more easily stop to shop with the money they were saving on gas, maintenance, and parking. "Welcome to the new Atlanta," wrote a journalist late in 2013, as a short section of Ponce de Leon got bike lanes and a road diet, "where streets already hemmed in by development are being reconfigured to allow bicyclists to safely share the road."

It was not happening fast enough for Serna, however, who observed the following year, "We have more lanes than we need for traffic to flow. Often, we have the wrong lanes—dangerous, poorly marked reversible lanes, also known as 'suicide lanes.' Four lanes work like just two when you don't create turn lanes to handle cars stopped, waiting to turn left." Though it seemed counterintuitive, traffic could actually flow more quickly with just two lanes and a middle turn-only lane.

In 2014, the first weeklong annual Atlanta Cycling Festival featured bike polo, bicycle scavenger hunts, bike camping, and much partying, with over 2,000 cyclists in attendance. *Atlanta VeloCity Magazine*, a new publication devoted to bikes, declared that the city was "hooked on cycling."

Late in 2015, the city appointed twenty-nine-year-old Becky Katz, a New York native, as its first "chief bicycle officer," with the goal of achieving 120 miles of Atlanta bike paths or lanes.* In hiring her, Mayor Kasim Reed said he wanted to make Atlanta "the most bikeable, walkable, livable city in the Southeast."

Atlanta's Troubled Waters

Insufficient sidewalks and bicycle facilities were not Atlanta's only shortcomings in terms of residents' health. Its rivers and streams were polluted. Toilet paper used to festoon the vegetation along Peachtree Creek and its tributaries.

The basic layout of the city's overwhelmed water treatment and disposal system dates from 1892. Water, pumped out of the Chattahoochee River just upstream from where Peachtree Creek flows into it, gets treated at the waterworks site off Howell Mill Road on the city's west side, then distributed to homes and businesses. Wastewater is collected in sewer pipes that frequently run parallel to streams, because gravity flow makes those routes the path of least resistance. That water gets treated and returned to the Chattahoochee just downstream of the Peachtree tributary.

Because Atlanta is so hilly, its boundaries actually include five distinct watersheds. Since their headwaters are all relatively close by, they don't generate sufficient water for the city, and the granite underlay hinders underground sourcing, making the broad Chattahoochee an essential water source.

The largest watershed is Peachtree Creek, fed by the North Fork; South Fork; and Clear, Tanyard, and Nancy Creeks. David Kaufman tells their story in riveting detail in his 2007 book, *Peachtree Creek: A Natural and Unnatural History of Atlanta's Watershed.* An avid canoeist from childhood, Kaufman became fascinated with the polluted waters that had once served as pristine waterways for the Creek Indians and as power sources for the gristmills and sawmills of early Atlanta. When he canoed

---

* Becky Katz was brave to take the new job, since she had been hit by a car while biking earlier that year, totaling her bike and breaking her wrist and shoulder socket.

the creeks, he encountered junk, sewer lines, and water so foul that he feared tipping over into it.

During the twentieth century, streets, parking lots, and buildings covered the city, so that the rain hitting these impervious surfaces flowed more swiftly down drains. Summer thunderstorms routinely blew sewage out of manhole covers and into the creeks. As the sewage pipes aged and cracked, they also leaked into the waterways they followed.

By 1925, the upper reaches of Tanyard Creek were buried and re-named the Orme Street trunk sewer. In 1971, part of it collapsed near Midtown's 14th Street, washing away two buildings in the middle of the night. The city simply filled the hole with dirt and rebuilt. Then in June 1993, a storm dumped 3.6 inches of rain in forty minutes, and the trunk sewer failed under a Marriott Courtyard hotel parking lot on Techwood Drive, killing two people, who were "siphoned into the sewer like ants down a bathtub drain," as Kaufman put it. The city finally overhauled that sewer line for $10 million.

The Upper Chattahoochee Riverkeeper, a watchdog environmental organization, sued the city over its dysfunctional water system and won.* In a 1998 consent decree, the city agreed to a massive infrastructure overhaul, begun under Mayor Shirley Franklin, although the final compliance deadline has been delayed until 2027. In most parts of the system, sanitary and storm sewers were separated. In others, giant tunnels were cut into bedrock to hold combined sewage/rainwater overflow. And as we have seen, the cheaper, better solution was to build attractive detention ponds, as was done in the Historic Fourth Ward Park.

In 2015, I met with Jo Ann Macrina, commissioner of the Atlanta Department of Watershed Management, and some of her staff to discuss current plans. They were pursuing a hybrid solution. In July 2012, a torrential downpour had resulted in raw sewage flooding homes and yards in Peoplestown, which led to the Southeast Atlanta Green Infrastructure Initiative, an attempt to reduce storm water runoff by installing permeable pavers along selected streets and "rain gardens," planted depressions with raised curbs, to absorb extra water. That's reasonable, but they also set out to destroy an entire block of homes in Peoplestown, to which the home owners objected strenuously. There was still not enough room to

---

* The group later shortened its name to Chattahoochee Riverkeeper.

handle all the extra storm water, so they built a 5-million-gallon storage vault underneath a parking lot next to Turner Field and planned another 7.8-million-gallon underground vault nearby.

The Proctor Creek watershed, which includes most of west Atlanta, remained a flood-prone disaster area. Watershed Management had just begun to look at solutions. Long-term plans include more parks and re-tention ponds, many of them proposed in a 2010 study by Park Pride.

In addition, with help from the Trust for Public Land, a group of Atlanta businesspeople created Emerald Corridor LLC, planning to re-mediate Proctor Creek and, through a "mitigation banking" system, sell credits for it to other developers who create environmental problems with streams. In late 2015, the US Corp of Engineers rejected their mitigation plans, so they had to pursue alternate strategies. The related nonprofit Emerald Corridor Foundation planned to build a 9.2-acre park along Proctor Creek near the future Westside Park, the BeltLine's property around the old quarry, which the Department of Watershed Manage-ment would fill with Chattahoochee River water in the next few years to serve as a thirty-day emergency supply for the city.

Going Green

Despite its infamous traffic and water woes, Atlanta was trying to go green. In 2010, Mayor Kasim Reed announced his intention to make the city one of the top ten in the country for sustainability. He launched a "Power to Change" initiative and created a new Office of Sustainabil-ity. By 2015, that office was producing results, working with more than three hundred other Atlanta stakeholders representing neighborhoods, schools, businesses, community organizations, and government agen-cies. The permitting process for electric vehicle charging equipment was streamlined. That year, the city passed an ordinance forcing buildings over 50,000 square feet to submit annual energy and water usage data, establishing a baseline for improvements.

One Atlanta institution had already been pushing for energy and water efficiency for nearly four decades. In 1978, Dennis Creech and a small group of volunteers established the nonprofit Southface Energy In-stitute, subsequently creating the EarthCraft certification for green build-ings. On Pine Street, the three-story Southface Eco Office, topped by a green roof and solar panels, features two cisterns for catching rainwater and uses 84 percent less water and 90 percent less energy than comparable 10,000-square-foot office buildings.

Creech recalled that as a young environmental zealot, he was out to "stop the bad guys," but he soon realized that a carrot worked better than a stick. Energy efficiency is practical and profitable for builders as well as occupants. "It's much cheaper to save energy than produce it," Creech observed. Working with Southface, area foundations, and the business community, the city of Atlanta adopted the "Better Buildings Challenge," committing more than 100 million square feet of commercial building space, including seventy-three city facilities, to reducing energy and water consumption by 20 percent by 2020.

In what Creech called "the stupidest law in Georgia," it was illegal for any home owners or businesses to allow third parties to lease solar panels for their roofs. The state finally changed that law in 2015, letting people sign leases with solar companies, which often required little or no money down and saved on monthly electricity bills. The city of Atlanta pledged to install solar panels atop twenty-eight city buildings.

Almost as remarkable as the change in solar power law was the fact that Mayor Reed was talking about climate change—a topic traditionally ignored or denied by Georgia politicians and businesspeople. The Atlanta Office of Sustainability announced its Climate Action Plan at a 2015 Sustainable Atlanta Roundtable, providing an overview of best practices to reduce greenhouse gas emissions while requesting the assistance of some fifty sustainability experts across the city. Over the next several years, the city planned to convert its outdoor lighting to LEDs, saving millions of dollars over the lifetime of the project. The city approved the opening of a new nonprofit Center for Hard to Recycle Materials (CHaRM, get it?) to recycle household hazardous waste, bulky trash, and other items might otherwise get dumped in landfills or streams. In November 2015, Mayor Reed and Stephanie Stuckey Benfield, his director of sustainability, flew to Paris to attend the United Nations Climate Change Conference.*

The green building industry had become a profitable, high-profile enterprise, adding $16.35 billion to Georgia's gross domestic product from 2011 through 2014 while generating 191,000 jobs, and the US Green

---

* In late 2016, Benfield was promoted as Atlanta's "chief resilience officer" (with funding from the Rockefeller Foundation) to tackle issues such as transportation, food resiliency, and economic opportunity. John R. Seydel III, Ted Turner's grandson, was appointed as the new sustainability director.

Building Council predicted that the next four years would double those figures. Even Georgia Power, previously lukewarm on renewables, agreed to add 1,200 megawatts of solar, wind, and biomass statewide by 2021.

Atlanta is also blessed with a leafy green canopy, partly due to Trees Atlanta, begun in 1985 with the limited purpose of planting a few trees around downtown developments. Marcia Bansley, previously an environmentalist and lawyer, took over Trees Atlanta that year and steadily grew it for the next twenty-six years, with a strong push during the preparations for the 1996 Olympics. After the Games, she and Greg Levine, a landscape architect who coordinated volunteers and is now codirector, branched out into neighborhood plantings of native trees such as oak, black gum, magnolia, pecan, elm, maple, and long-leaf pines, while ripping out invasive kudzu, privet, and English ivy and identifying venerable "Champion Trees," some dating back to Revolutionary times.

Trees Atlanta has now planted over 100,000 trees, including the beginnings of the BeltLine Arboretum, which will stretch the entire length of the twenty-two-mile corridor. Volunteer docents lead educational tours of the Eastside Trail, and in 2015 the organization, which then boasted twenty-six full-time employees, opened its Trees Atlanta TreeHouse facility, opposite the Krog Street Market, near the Eastside Trail, to further educate visitors. "Tree planting is helpful," said Levine, "but education is the key to preserving our urban forest, and the BeltLine Arboretum may be our best tool to reach more of the public."

Metro Atlanta's air quality has also been improving, despite a growing population. As late as 1999, only 41 percent of summer days had good or moderate air quality. By 2014, 95 percent featured decent air quality. Although power generation had gone steadily up, greenhouse gas emissions were declining, due in large part to Georgia Power's switching from coal to natural gas—not necessarily great news for the environment, since the cheaper gas came from fracking (underground hydraulic fracturing). Tougher standards had also reduced automobile emissions.

Michael Chang, a Georgia Tech professor who has served on a team monitoring Atlanta air quality since 1996, told me that they recorded the last Code Purple day ("very unhealthy") in 2002. "We reached a turning point in 2004, when most coal plants and industrial boilers finally complied with the Clean Air Act." He believes that as the metro area swells to a predicted 8 million people in thirty years, tighter standards will result in lower emissions. "We've cut the low-hanging fruit," he said, "but there are still things to be done. With the BeltLine and other public transit improvements, we should see families with one instead of two cars, and there will be more pedestrians and cyclists, as well as electric and hybrid cars."

Health Inequities

Despite such good news, Atlanta still has startling health disparities. Not surprisingly, the wealthier, whiter north and east sides have better health outcomes in virtually every category, while more environmental pollution, inadequate nutrition, and shorter life expectancies afflict the poorer, blacker south and west sides. For instance, despite better air quality overall, air pollution from particulates is worse in Atlanta neighborhoods near the interstates, particularly where I-75 and I-85 join as the Downtown Connector, as well as near rail yards, where diesel locomotives spew black carbon particles, and industrial areas, where truck travel is heaviest—all concentrated in south and west Atlanta.

Examining health outcomes for Fulton County is illuminating, since its southern district includes much of south and west Atlanta. The death rate from asthma is five times higher there than in the wealthiest northern district of the county. Why? The answer has only partly to do with less access to health insurance and quality medical care or air pollution from the nearby interstates. The real culprit is residential air quality. In these impoverished neighborhoods, most people rent, often in substandard housing with water leaks and mold. A landlord might slap a coat of paint over a water-stained wall just before a new tenant moves in, and many do not install high-quality air filters; some provide no air filtration at all.

The infant mortality data for Fulton County is equally revealing. In 2014, for every 1,000 live births, 4.4 white babies died, while 13.8 black infants perished. In other words, if you were born to African American parents in that county—almost certainly meaning in the southern part— you were more than three times as likely to die at birth as a white child, and you were twice as likely to have a low birth weight. For every white mother in Fulton County who didn't survive childbirth in 2014, four black mothers died.

The death rate from all causes in the county is a third higher for blacks than whites. Twice as many Fulton County blacks die in car crashes as whites. Violence is far worse in the impoverished neighborhoods: in

2014 thirteen times more African Americans there were murdered than whites. For years Atlanta has lingered at or near the top in central city rankings of violent crime rates in the ten largest American metro areas.

Yet three times as many whites committed suicide in 2014 in Fulton County, which seems counterintuitive, given the much more difficult lives of African Americans. When faced with a daily struggle for existence, perhaps people have less time to ponder whether that life is worth living, though clinical depression does not discriminate by race. But the stresses of being poor and black, and the lack of stable marriages and relationships, also generated a rate of sexually transmitted infection one hundred times greater for blacks than whites.

Other alarming statistics for 2014 in Fulton County: 8.5 times more deaths from AIDS for blacks than whites; 6.5 times more tuberculosis cases for African Americans; over three times more deaths from diabetes; over twice the mental illness rate (and these numbers reflect individuals seen at a clinic, so incidences are severely undercounted).

When I unearthed these statistics from the Georgia Department of Public Health OASIS website, they reminded me of ninety-year-old Lula Bailey, whom I had met in a troubled southern Atlanta neighborhood. She had lost five of her six children—one had died soon after birth; she lost four others to AIDS, murder, high blood pressure, and a car crash.* Her story made these statistics all too real.

An African American surgeon, Charles Moore, is trying to do something about these overwhelming health issues in Atlanta's west side at his HEALing Community Center. The New York native, educated at Harvard Medical School, specializes in ear, nose, and throat cancers. Practicing at Grady Hospital, he kept seeing poor black patients with huge, fatal tumors. They had no insurance, no transportation, and no money. He kept thinking, *Someone should do something about this*, and ultimately realized it would have to be him. After providing care out of the back of his Subaru, he founded the health clinic on Martin Luther King Jr. Drive, offering a broad range of care on a sliding scale. It also has a mobile unit.

In 2015, Robert Putnam's *Our Kids: The American Dream in Crisis* made it alarmingly clear that the situation in inner-city Atlanta is not unique. "Whether we are rich or poor, our kids are increasingly growing up with kids like them who have parents like us," he wrote. "Rich Americans and

---

* See Chapter 11.

poor Americans are living, learning, and raising children in increasingly separate and unequal worlds, removing the stepping-stones to upward mobility." He documented that the collapse of the traditional family "hit the black community earliest and hardest," largely because of stress and poverty. De facto class and racial segregation led to unequal educational, health, and job opportunities. And many more fathers were in prison, thus absent, or, as ex-cons, could not secure jobs or pay child support. "More than half of all black children born to less educated parents in 1990 experienced parental imprisonment."

Atlanta was among the cities Putnam featured in his book. "By the early twenty-first century, Atlanta had the largest, most rapidly growing gap between rich and poor of any major American city," he observed. "That gap is heavily racial, of course, but within the black community itself, class and income differences have also grown." He made an important point that I want to emphasize. In this book, I have focused on inner-city neighborhoods where many (but by no means all) African Americans are poor, often high school dropouts, un- or underemployed, resorting to drugs or crime because there is little alternative. But the metro Atlanta area has a burgeoning black middle and upper class, mostly living in the suburbs or wealthier city neighborhoods, whose parenting, education, lifestyle, and values resemble those of their white counterparts. Class distinctions in Atlanta increasingly mean more than race.

The Atlanta University Center on the west side is a beacon of black higher education in the midst of this poverty. Donald Speaks, an African American physician who works there at the Morehouse School of Medicine, summarized the problems surrounding that oasis: "Poverty is endemic on the west side of Atlanta. Children are chronically malnourished. Caregivers have an extremely high incidence of mental illness of one level or another, with a high rate of illiteracy or intergenerational educational failure. There are terrible housing conditions, public transportation is woefully inadequate, and many can't afford cars." All of these issues, coupled with a dearth of health-care facilities, help explain why there are such glaring health disparities in Atlanta.

Vacant or Abandoned

Nothing can be worse for public health than insecure, stressful communities. Anyone who drives through the southern and western parts of Atlanta can't miss the fact that in some neighborhoods, many homes have been boarded up, abandoned, or taken over by squatters or drug dealers; in some instances only weedy vacant lots remain where houses once stood. A 2012 citywide Atlanta survey revealed that 12.3 percent of all city properties featured vacant lots or homes, mostly concentrated in the south and west, where helpful interventions were desperately needed.

The Georgia Tech website for Atlanta's Neighborhood Quality of Life and Health Project, which contains a wealth of information on individual communities, includes a dramatic color-coded Atlanta map with a bright red swath (the darkest in this black-and-white rendition) of Atlanta's poorest neighborhoods slashing from the northwest to the southeast, while the richest neighborhoods lie just north of that line.

In an effort to help an overwhelmed city Housing Code Enforcement Bureau, in 2014 the city initiated a program for inmates of Atlanta jails to "clean and close" abandoned homes. One day in May 2015, I drove to the Atlanta Detention Center to meet a group of young men on work release.* A police sergeant brought us in a van to 232 Laurel Avenue in Mozley Park, just north of I-20. On a previous day, the men had removed kudzu and boarded up the house, so today they picked up trash, fixed a gutter, and cut down shrubs and small trees in the yard. The inside plumbing and copper wiring had been stripped out and the house vandalized.

The attending Code Enforcement officer said that his department had cleaned and closed fifty-seven homes in the previous year, but that hardly put a dent in the problem. A supervising corrections officer said that it was hard to keep out people who really wanted to break in. He had thrown the same man out of a vacant house three times. The last time the man had broken in through the roof. "His mother lived near there," the officer explained.

Food Deserts

In addition to containing blighted residential neighborhoods, the southern and western areas of Atlanta are also notorious "food deserts," where grocery store chains such as Publix and Kroger are few and far between,

---

* I used a GPS device while driving to the Detention Center and was surprised that it was just north of downtown, apparently in a nice building. It turned out to be the upscale Capital City Club. I had driven to 254 Peachtree *Northeast* rather than to the correct address at 254 Peachtree *Southwest*, a little over a mile to the south, and a world away.

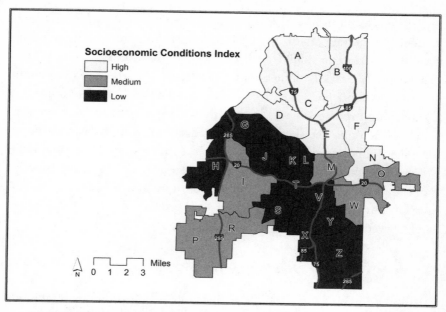

Atlanta's Neighborhood Quality of Life & Health Project map

while corner stores proffer fatty junk food and sodas. Ironically the American poor are generally more overweight than the rich, and obesity is 51 percent more prevalent among African Americans than among whites.

Yet farmers' markets and urban vegetable gardens are also on the rise in Atlanta, which now has a city director of urban agriculture. The Sweet Auburn Curb Market on Edgewood Avenue offers organic vegetables and meat (including whole hogs) to a mostly African American customer base. A few blocks away (until it moved to Ashview Heights in west Atlanta in 2016) the six-acre Truly Living Well Wheat Street Gardens in the Old Fourth Ward held raised-bed gardens that grew abundant vegetables on the site of a former public housing project.

Truly Living Well grows produce in several other Atlanta locations, educates gardeners and consumers, and sells vegetables through a CSA (community-supported agriculture) partnership. It also runs summer camps for children, combining farming with swimming, arts and nature crafts, skits, music, and games—directly fighting childhood obesity through education, nutritious foods, and activities.*

---

* Rashid Nuri, founder and CEO of Truly Living Well, brought his agricultural expertise to Atlanta after a career with Cargill took him around the world. It turns out we were in the same Harvard class as undergraduates.

Other neighborhood gardening initiatives in south and west Atlanta connect people directly to their food sources while making these devastated areas more attractive and secure. The Atlanta Community Food Bank collects and distributes some 60 million pounds of food annually to organizations that serve over 80,000 people per week, in addition to establishing urban gardens through the Georgia Food Oasis collaborative. Bill Bolling, who founded the food bank in 1979 and built it into a thriving nonprofit with over one hundred employees and 20,000 annual volunteers, noted, "Half of the people who come for food have jobs but can't make it." The majority of clients must choose between paying for transportation, medical care, rent, or food, and 40 percent of the households served include a member with diabetes.

Healthy on the BeltLine

Bill Bolling is an advocate for the BeltLine, which promises to connect people, making Atlanta a "more efficient and equitable city," while building community and providing a new way to walk or bike to get to the grocery store or to work. Michael Eriksen, dean of the School of Public Health at Georgia State, similarly praised the BeltLine's "social capital benefits," which might provide the biggest long-term public health impact by strengthening "the web of relationships in a community—the goodwill and sense of shared purpose." In other words, simply getting people out on the trail, where they could get to know one another, might improve health. A health-impact assessment of the potential BeltLine, conducted between 2005 and 2007, came to the same conclusion, noting that "large health disparities were detected" along the loop. That report inspired health insurer Kaiser Permanente to contribute millions to the BeltLine.

There's no question that exercise is one key to good health, so walking and biking the BeltLine helped, as did the various running races along the path, along with the free yoga, aerobics, bike instruction, sunrise and sunset walks, play days for kids, group jogs, and other classes.

Anyone could sign up to "Walk with a Doc" along the BeltLine or other Atlanta trails, where they could talk (for free) about health issues and seek advice in an informal setting. "I had about thirty people, from twenty-somethings to one grandma, men and women," said one physician. "We walked about two miles and talked about heart health, diet, and exercise." People could also choose a nutrition walk with a certified dietician to learn about healthy eating.

The Eastside Trail might look like a mere fourteen-foot-wide, two-mile-long piece of concrete, but there were other, less obvious public health benefits. For one thing, the project runs through restored, cleaned-up brownfields. And when athenahealth, which sells electronic health records, moved into Ponce City Market, the company requested direct access to the BeltLine for its employees.

The incoming CEO of Atlanta BeltLine, Inc., Paul Morris, laid out an idealistic vision. "If you really believe in the anatomy of a community, then you have to have healthy people. They have to be able to live and work and play and shop and learn in places that are within the community. It needs the infrastructure to support all those activities. That's what the BeltLine seeks to do, making it possible for people who live there to stay there."

In the face of the blight, poverty, abandoned homes, and poor health of residents on the south and west sides, through which the BeltLine would pass, Morris's promise seemed unattainable. Would the trail really catalyze dramatic improvements? And if it did, would the impoverished, undereducated, unemployed residents really be able to stay there?

CHAPTER 9

IMPOSSIBLE BUT INEVITABLE

···

> *Many in my generation want communities in which we*
> *can walk, rather than drive, to get around. . . . We want*
> *pedestrian access to our jobs, friends, and communities.*
> *We yearn for this access not because we desire*
> *modernization or innovation but because we are nostalgic*
> *for a simpler past.*
>
> —Jessica Estep, twenty-seven, explaining in 2014
> why she moved to Atlanta from the suburbs

By the end of 2015, as the BeltLine's tax allocation district (TAD) approached its tenth anniversary, the biggest, most innovative combined trail/transit/park urban project in the country continued to progress toward its uncertain completion, despite road blocks, disappointments, harsh critiques, and a contract that would have virtually killed the project if it were enforced. As the second major paved section of the corridor neared completion, despite unforeseen obstacles, the seemingly impossible loop nonetheless began to assume an aura of inevitability to most Atlantans. And a new leader was overseeing the project.

On July 1, 2013, Paul Morris moved to Atlanta as the new CEO of Atlanta BeltLine, Inc. (ABI). He took over from Lisa Gordon, the chief operating officer who had kept the organization afloat for several months, following the departure of Brian Leary in the wake of a spending scandal blown out of proportion by the media.

Morris, fifty-three, arrived from North Carolina, where he had been deputy secretary for transit in that state's Department of Transportation. An Oregon native trained as a landscape architect, he brought thirty years of varied experience in transportation, urban redevelopment, and public parks. Several years back, his friend Alex Garvin had told him excitedly about working on the BeltLine plans, and Morris had followed the project from afar. "I admired its ambition and holistic thinking," he said. Now he took over the potentially transformative loop at a crucial time, when the Eastside Trail's success had raised expectations and hopes but future funding remained problematic.

In 2005, BeltLine plans envisioned that the newly created TAD would produce about $3 billion for the project over its twenty-five-year life span. But until 2011, John Woodham's lawsuit prevented ABI from receiving its portion from school taxes, and in the meantime the Great Recession had severely affected redevelopment around the BeltLine corridor. Updated projections, made before Morris came on board, predicted that the TAD would instead yield around $1.4 billion over its lifetime—less than half of the prerecession estimate. And even that new figure was overly optimistic. The TAD will likely produce only $1 billion or so.

In addition, the TAD contract with the Atlanta Public Schools (APS), which allowed for nonpayment in the initial years, called for the first of many annual fixed payments to begin on January 1, 2013. Lacking sufficient income from the TAD, the city failed to come up with the $1.95 million on time, instead paying it in December, without the $119,000 late interest fee. What's more, the following two years' payments were due to go up to $6.75 million each, and the annual amount was to escalate through the ensuing years, so that the final year's payment in 2025 would be over $16 million. APS was to receive a total of $162.4 million (plus $10 million for a recreation center) over the life of the TAD.

Paul Morris inherited this unfortunate contract. Payment of a percentage of the annual TAD income, instead of fixed amounts, would have been logical, but in the rush to get the TAD authorized by the end of 2005, the city had agreed to these terms. Now Morris had to deal with the result, although, as he pointed out, ABI did not even exist when the agreement was reached, so he and ABI were not official parties to the contract. At least school officials said that they were open to renegotiating the agreement with the city, so there was some hope.

In addition to managing budgetary concerns, Morris quickly had to adjust to the Atlanta way of doing business. When asked for the most important thing he had learned during his first year, he said, "I realized that in Atlanta, personal relationships are enormously important. For all its being one of the top ten cities in the country, it's really a small town. There may be six million people in the metro Atlanta area, but only 450,000 in the city itself. So because Atlanta is a small-scale city, it's been important to build solid relationships with a lot of people."

The other lesson? "The BeltLine isn't about us here at ABI. This is a project that will only happen if the community at large believes it is theirs. Most Atlantans continue to feel a sense of personal ownership and pride in the BeltLine and want it to succeed. Their biggest concern is how long it's going to take."

Show Us the Money

When pressed about how the BeltLine would be funded and completed, given the financial challenges and the fact that the city didn't yet own 40 percent of the corridor, Morris expressed a kind of hedged optimism. "People say, 'The odds are against you.' I say, 'You're right. The odds are against us. We have a pretty simple choice. We could give up, or we can acknowledge that reality and look for a way to make it a success anyway.' We'll find a way."

In September 2013, that way partially materialized when Atlanta learned that it had won a second federal TIGER grant for $18 million to help pay for a three-mile stretch of paved corridor in southwestern Atlanta, to be dubbed the Westside Trail. Running past less affluent, mostly African American neighborhoods such as West End, Adair Park, and Washington Park, it would cost an estimated $43 million, far more than its first cousin, the Eastside Trail. In addition to being streetcar-ready, the Westside Trail would feature lighting and multiple connections to neighborhoods, unlike the Eastside Trail. It remained to be seen where the rest of the money would come from, but with the federal seed grant, it looked as if Morris could now counter critics who claimed that the BeltLine development was inequitable, only helping wealthier neighborhoods.

The long-anticipated *Strategic Implementation Plan* for the BeltLine, which Brian Leary had put in motion, was published in December 2013, providing a dream blueprint for the rest of the TAD's lifetime, until 2030, when the BeltLine would supposedly be complete. It divided the project's remaining execution into three phases: Period 1, 2014–2018; Period 2, 2019–2023; and Period 3, 2024–2030. The 142-page document laid out relatively detailed plans for the first phase, during which four parks would be completed, the remaining corridor secured, the Westside Trail finished, and the Eastside Trail extended a bit further south. In addition, streetcars would run on the east and west BeltLine, connecting to the downtown Atlanta Streetcar loop, which was under construction. During the last two phases, the entire trail and transit would be completed, as would the huge Westside Park, with its water-filled quarry, and all would be well.

The trouble was that these rosy plans were, as the document admitted, "heavily reliant" on large-scale federal funding and other hypothetical revenue sources. Over halfway through Period 1, there was no indication that a streetcar would run any time soon along the BeltLine or even that ABI would gain control of the entire corridor. The total budget in the *Strategic Implementation Plan* called for $4.4 billion, including an unrealistic $1.5 billion from the TAD, $275 million from private donations, a wished-for $1.27 billion from the federal government, and 20 percent "unidentified."

The streetcars were projected to cost $2.3 billion, over half of the total $4.4 billion BeltLine budget. Gadfly Mike Dobbins of Georgia Tech once again complained about the transit plan for the BeltLine. "It has so many technical flaws, cost issues, and obstacles to overcome, and it doesn't serve any existing or foreseeable ridership need," he said. "I'm skeptical it will be built."

Nonetheless, Paul Morris promised advances on all fronts. "We will work on all program components simultaneously, and we will work across all parts of the BeltLine at all times to make sure every community is realizing tangible benefits of the program in an equitable manner."

Growing Pains

In the meantime, the wildly popular Eastside Trail exhibited growing pains. On weekends, 10,000 people hit the fourteen-foot-wide trail. "The BeltLine is the great laboratory where it's starting to come together," observed an ABI spokesman. This human petri dish could get annoying or dangerous, however. Knots of people stopped to talk, blocking the path. Racing bikers swooped and veered, nearly knocking down pedestrians. Litter, public urination, and dog poop defaced the area. Thieves stole purses and cell phones. A runner called someone a faggot and shoved him against a fence.

Fortunately, the city secured a Justice Department grant to pay for the PATH Force, a special eighteen-member police unit composed initially of military veterans, to patrol the BeltLine trails, sometimes by car but most often on bicycles; cops also rode horses to monitor the trail. One day I met Jeff Baxter, a former marine and Atlanta police veteran who headed the PATH Force, at his precinct station in the basement of the Lofts at Reynoldstown Crossing, then toured the Eastside Trail with him. He smiled and waved at joggers and strollers, then stopped to question a somewhat disheveled black man, but in a friendly way. "We've mostly taken care of BeltLine crime," Baxter said. Video cameras monitored the trail. "Kids at the skate park smoke marijuana and drink beer, so we deal with that. Mostly, though, we're like ambassadors, answering questions." He sought to hire sociable officers who enjoyed being outdoors. At a special event, his officers read children's stories to kids along the trail.

ABI also mounted a BeltLine etiquette campaign, with admonitions not to walk three abreast, to keep moving, and for bikers to shout, "On your left!" in a timely manner. An ABI spokesman summarized proper behavior succinctly: "Stay to the right, don't clog the trail, ride slowly on your bicycle, pick up after your dog, and watch out for kids on foot, bikes

The popular, crowded Eastside Trail, with Ponce City Market, the former Sears warehouse

and scooters." That translated into a "Southern Charm" campaign, with volunteers standing along the trail with signs bearing messages such as "Slow down, Sugar," and "We saw that, y'all, pick it up."

One critic, apparently from the suburbs, wrote a letter to the editor calling the BeltLine a "boondoggle" and claiming that etiquette courses would be useless because one day "a pack of wild 'urban youth' thugs will sweep a section of the BeltLine mugging, raping, and beating senseless any who can't escape them." But such racist comments were unusual.

Another growing pain involved neighborhood protests over a proposed development by Fuqua Corporation along an unbuilt eastern portion of the BeltLine, across the street from Glenwood Park, a successful mixed-use community. Early BeltLine proponent Cathy Woolard lived there; I had conducted interviews with her and others at Drip, their community coffeehouse. Fuqua was buying the old LaFarge concrete plant to redevelop it. Woolard and other community activists were incensed that the developer planned an old-fashioned mall, built around an anchor Walmart, featuring acres of parking lots. It violated the spirit of the Belt-Line, they claimed. In the end, Fuqua backed away from a Walmart, instead attracting a large Kroger grocery store as the anchor, but the mall concept and parking lots went forward.

Emergency Millions, the Atlanta Way

In May 2014, the US Department of Transportation unexpectedly imposed a tight deadline on private fund-raising for the $43 million Westside Trail. Unless Atlanta could come up with at least $10 million in private donations by July, the feds threatened to cancel the promised $18 million TIGER grant. Atlanta business movers and shakers scrambled to prove that, when the pressure was on, they could deliver. Charlie Shufeldt, head of the BeltLine Partnership board, John Somerhalder, chair of Atlanta BeltLine, Inc., and Ray Weeks met to strategize. They wanted Mayor Kasim Reed to make a strong personal plea for funds to business leaders on the Atlanta Committee for Progress, an elite mayoral advisory group.

They asked Jim Kennedy of the James M. Cox Foundation to jump-start the campaign, as he had done for the Eastside Trail. He astonished them by pledging $5 million, half of the needed funds. They couldn't go back to the Robert W. Woodruff Foundation, as it had already pledged money to push the Eastside Trail south to Memorial Drive, which remained undone. They needed big philanthropic donors, so they turned to corporate Atlanta. "We got the old gang back together again," Shufeldt said. Weeks pledged $200,000. Phil Kent, recently retired CEO of Turner Broadcasting, and Herman Russell, a self-made African American developer and real estate mogul who died later that year, also agreed to make donations. The BeltLine also received substantial gifts from Kaiser Permanente and Wells Fargo. The biggest surprise came when Richard Anderson, CEO of Delta Air Lines, called out of the blue to say that he and his wife, Susan, would contribute $1 million personally.

"People want to give to successful things," Weeks observed. "It's a matter of getting people to see we're all going to do it." The "we" referred to Atlanta's power brokers, all of whom knew one another, often through the Atlanta Committee for Progress. They rubbed shoulders at the Capital City Club. Most donors were white, contributing to a trail that would go through an overwhelmingly black part of town. Within three months, they raised $12.5 million and saved the Westside Trail. The balance of the money would come from state, regional, and local funding.

The Astra Corporation, which had built the Eastside Trail, won the bid for the Westside Trail, breaking ground in November 2014. The workers soon found that the west side neighborhoods were rougher than those on the east side. One day a car carrying a black man bleeding from a gunshot wound, with guns visible in the backseat, begged to traverse a road block to get to the hospital. The construction workers also ran into unforeseen problems, such as oozing water at the southern end and a huge concrete tunnel MARTA had left underground at the northern end. Originally planned to be completed by the end of 2016, the trail opening would be delayed by at least a year.

Many longtime residents remained skeptical that the Westside Trail would make much difference and had no plans to use it. Young black realtor Nia Knowles, a West End resident, explained, "They heard change is coming but still see the crime and stink of foreclosure and have kind of lost faith." She herself worried that the BeltLine would bring inflated prices. "I may be outpriced in an area that I helped to build."

Kasim Reed's Second Bully Term

In November 2013 Kasim Reed won reelection to a second mayoral term with virtually no opposition, but his supreme self-assurance now began to strike some observers as arrogance, and critics accused him of ignoring the poor in favor of big business. He forced out several well-regarded members of city government, including Renee Glover, head of the Atlanta Housing Authority, who had led the movement to tear down the city's dilapidated public housing projects and replace them with mixed-income developments; George Dusenbury, head of the Parks Department, who had pushed for better funding and maintenance of city parks; and Tom Weyandt, who had served as Reed's transportation advisor. One of those fired told me that Reed discouraged teamwork. The mayor did not take criticism lying down. If you got on his wrong side, you would likely get blasted. "No perceived foe or irritant is too insignificant," wrote a reporter, referring to Reed's "bellicose manner."

Yet Kasim Reed got things done. The city of Atlanta owned a number of aging properties that were drains on the budget but could, like the old Sears building, be redeveloped as tax-paying assets. Over the course of his second term, in a rebounding economy, Reed negotiated the sale of the Civic Center, built in 1967 in the former Buttermilk Bottom and now dated and rarely used, for $30 million to Houston-based Weingarten Realty. Though the deal fell through late in 2016, the mayor still hoped to sell it before the end of his term in 2017.

Underground Atlanta, a moribund set of shops in the heart of downtown next to the Five Points MARTA station, lay under the viaducts that had raised city streets nearly a century before. It was costing the city $8 million a year in bond payments, and Reed wanted to unload it. The city ended up agreeing to sell the site to WRS, Inc., a South Carolina real estate firm, for nearly $26 million. WRS planned to build a mixed-use complex there with housing and retail.

Another redevelopment opportunity came unbidden late in 2013 when the Atlanta Braves shocked the city by announcing that in 2017 the professional baseball team planned to desert downtown's Turner Field in favor of a new stadium in the Cobb County suburbs to the north. Georgia State University (GSU), in conjunction with private developers, proposed buying Turner Field and the surrounding parking lots to build a $300 million mixed-use complex there. GSU, a small commuter school that had grown dramatically in the previous two decades in the downtown area, had long sought a real campus. The university wanted to convert the stadium for its own football, soccer, and track-and-field teams and to build a new baseball park, student housing, shops, restaurants, a grocery store, and other homes and apartments. "The walkable concept would connect neighborhoods cut off from the city core by car-choked freeways and a sea of parking lots," a reporter noted, but the surrounding poor black neighborhoods remained wary.

In the meantime, Home Depot billionaire Arthur Blank wanted to construct a new stadium for his Atlanta Falcons football team to replace the Georgia Dome, built in 1992 as the largest cable-supported dome stadium on earth. But that was not enough for Blank, who wanted to tear it down and build a bigger, better stadium with a retractable roof next door, at a cost of well over $1 billion. The city went along with the idea, partially funding it. In 2014 construction began on the massive Mercedes-Benz Stadium (the car company having purchased the branding rights).

Despite the popularity of sports teams, stadiums usually generate little in the way of regional economic benefit. They bring temporary crowds together to spend money at concessions, but fans generally flee the neighborhoods after games. Indeed, the communities of Vine City and English Avenue, near the Dome, were among the poorest in the city. The Arthur Blank Foundation promised to set aside $15 million to help those local neighborhoods, and the city matched it, but the effect of that relatively small amount of money remained to be seen. These neighborhoods, within a mile of the BeltLine, were representative of the troubled Atlanta west side.

Another huge piece of real estate virtually fell into Reed's lap when the US military decommissioned Fort McPherson in southwestern Atlanta, only a few miles from the planned BeltLine. The city acquired the 488-acre site in 2006. The Great Recession squashed initial plans for a mixed-use science/technology park, and Kasim Reed subsequently worked a privately arranged deal with filmmaker Tyler Perry, who in 2015 bought 331 prime acres for $30 million to build a massive, walled-off movie studio there. Veteran Atlanta journalist Maria Saporta wrote passionately that if the deal with Perry could be stopped, "Fort McPherson can send off ripples of rebirth and redevelopment to communities that have been hungry for new investment for decades." Instead, she predicted that Perry would create a "fort within a fort."

Kasim Reed remained unmoved by such criticism. He took pride in all of his negotiations. "When I finish," Reed boasted, "the city is going to have the strongest spine it's ever had." That might well be the case, along with the BeltLine project surrounding that spine, but Reed's deals had an ad hoc backroom-deal quality. In typical Atlanta fashion, there appeared to be no master plan.

The Bitter Battle over the TAD School Contract

The combative Mayor Reed also became personally involved in negotiations over the TAD contract with the Atlanta Public Schools. After the city failed to pay APS the $6.75 million due on January 1, 2014, school superintendent Erroll Davis suggested various alternatives, such as the city's paying for broadband Internet for the schools, giving the schools a break on water bills or police costs, or donating the underused Civic Center. Reed refused, citing various reasons, but mostly he seemed to relish a good public battle.

The Atlanta school system certainly could have used the money—that is, if it could figure out how to spend it to raise the educational level of its students. The schools were in a shambles, still reeling from a cheating scandal, blamed in large part on Beverly Hall, the previous school superintendent, who had pressured teachers to produce ever-better (allegedly faked) student test results. The poor performance of the Atlanta schools was in part due to the legacy of forced desegregation, when many white parents either fled or put their children in private schools.

In 2011 Reed had brought in Erroll Davis, former chancellor of the University System of Georgia, as the new superintendent to restore morale and credibility. But by the summer of 2014, with negotiations over the TAD payments at a standstill, Davis, who was about to retire, went public with his grievances. He claimed that the city actually owed the schools nearly $19 million, since the TAD contract called not only for annual payments but for donated land plus $10 million to build a recreational facility. Davis threatened a lawsuit if the arrears weren't paid. "Nobody's going to negotiate at the end of a gun," Mayor Reed fired back. "If you're going to take hostages, you'd better be ready to shoot them."

When Davis retired and new superintendent Meria Carstarphen took over in July 2014, Davis continued to represent APS in the now personal dispute. The city's side pointed out that, during the first three years of the TAD, the Woodham lawsuit held up the school's payments, which amounted to $26 million that the BeltLine never received. Ryan Gravel lamented that, with the world watching the BeltLine project, it was unseemly "to bicker about this stuff."

Lawyers for both sides traded barbed memos. City attorneys lambasted the public school system, asserting that expensive litigation would divert APS from more pressing educational needs. "Students would benefit from renewed concentration on a more effective use of a budget that exceeds $600 million. [Yet] APS only produces a 59 percent graduation rate," the lawyers wrote. "APS is attempting to resolve the worst school cheating scandal in the history of Georgia and perhaps the United States." It would be better to address those issues than to engage in intra-urban lawsuits.

The conflict remained unsettled in 2015, when the city once again failed to deliver its annual payment. City council president Ceasar Mitchell, a black politician likely to run for mayor two years later, wrote an editorial calling for a compromise. "Supporters of the BeltLine have been pitted against supporters of our schools," wrote Mitchell, "and parents like myself who believe in the promise of the BeltLine have been put in the untenable position of being forced to choose." It was "high time to put this unfortunate distraction to rest." He suggested setting aside $13.7 million from the city reserve fund to pay APS, on the precondition of a renegotiated contract.

Kasim Reed accused Mitchell of political grandstanding and dismissed the proposal as harmful to the city's bottom line. Further exacerbating ill feelings, the mayor then blocked the sale of a long-abandoned elementary school building in Adair Park for $412,000 to a developer. Superintendent Meria Carstarphen, who had previously kept out of the fray, publicly complained. "I want the very best for our kids," she said. "I need every obstacle moved out of my way." In response, Reed said the school superintendent was "inexperienced in Atlanta and doesn't know what she's talking about."

BeltLine chief Paul Morris, who had kept silent about the dispute, finally cracked. "It has made it virtually, physically and legally impossible for us to get loans, to interact with investors and go to our banks with opportunities," he told his board. The ABI website posted a blunt one-word answer to the question *Can the Atlanta BeltLine continue with the current agreement?* "No." It then reviewed how the Great Recession had dramatically reduced funds. "According to the original projection, TAD revenues in 2014 would be $47 million. But actual TAD revenues in 2014 were only $18 million. All those TAD funds are required to pay bondholders, are committed as local match to capital improvement projects currently underway, and are paying program and project management expenses required to implement the Atlanta BeltLine." It was simply impossible to honor the TAD contract with the school system. "If the $6.75 million annual payment is made to the Atlanta Public Schools, all money for operations will be gone, Atlanta BeltLine, Inc. will be shut down, and there will be no expansion of the Atlanta BeltLine to new neighborhoods."

With the dispute unresolved as 2015 wound to an end, the unpaid debt continued to mount, but the BeltLine project proceeded on the assumption that there would be some resolution.

The Debut of the Atlanta Streetcar

After multiple delays, the Atlanta Streetcar, originally scheduled to begin operations in May 2013, finally made its debut run on December 30, 2014, barely fulfilling Kasim Reed's promise that it would get under way sometime that year. A federal grant funded $47.6 million of the project, which ended up costing $98 million, due in large part to Reed's insistence that the city buy four sleek new Siemens streetcars, only two of which would run at any given time.

I attended the ribbon-cutting event, which was a quintessential over-the-top Atlanta experience. Because the streetcar would run down Auburn Avenue, once the heart of a thriving African American business and religious community, a succession of black ministers came to the microphone to call down God's blessing on the streetcar, which was indeed a kind of Second Coming, since the city once enjoyed extensive trolley service. Along with other speakers, they conveyed the idea that this small transit circle, covering a little over a mile in each direction, would save the city. Before Kasim Reed—no longer a lifelong bachelor, with his new wife and child on the podium—gave his own speech, he took multiple selfie photos, announcing that they were going out to thousands of followers.

The next day, I took MARTA to the Peachtree Center stop, the only such connection to the new streetcar. Maximum headway was supposed to be fifteen minutes, but I had to wait twenty minutes to board, along with other curious Atlantans and a few tourists. At the next stop, the driver briefly opened the door on the street side, a potentially catastrophic mistake should anyone step out into the path of a car. A few months later, I took another ride. Most of the other passengers were there to check out the novelty, not to reach a destination, though a few homeless people were heading to the library or just staying warm. The ride was supposed to cost $1 after the first free three months, but the city decided to extend the gratis trips for an entire year.

City officials, including Paul Morris, made valiant efforts to portray the Atlanta Streetcar as a huge success, with $568 million in private investment developed nearby within the previous four years and more in the pipeline. Over 200,000 people had taken a ride by mid-May. Morris touted a new, comprehensive streetcar plan with fifty miles of track and six lines, including the BeltLine. Kasim Reed applied for a $29.3 million federal grant to extend the streetcar loop east to connect to the Eastside Trail.

But Benita Dodd of the Georgia Public Policy Foundation offered a scathing critique. It took her thirty-five minutes to ride the entire 2.7-mile loop on the streetcar, which she could walk in forty-three minutes. The traffic lights were "painfully unsynchronized," leaving the streetcar stuck with the rest of the traffic. As the trolley rolled along Auburn Avenue, it passed boarded-up buildings, graffiti, and empty beer bottles, although the parallel path down Edgewood Avenue offered new bars and restaurants. Dodd concluded that the streetcar was "uninspiring, uncomfortable and unlikely to succeed."

In October 2015, Atlanta lost its bid for federal funds to extend the loop east to the BeltLine, perhaps because of problems with the new Atlanta Streetcar, which had experienced staff turmoil and negative audits; federal transit authorities expressed "continuing concerns with the safety and operation" of the system.

Kasim Reed appeared undaunted, asserting that the city would pursue public-private partnerships to fund more streetcars. The Georgia legislature had recently passed a bill allowing such partnerships, and perhaps a large national or international corporation would come forward to put streetcars on the BeltLine and elsewhere within its loop. Otherwise, it was difficult to see where funding would come from.

Going in the Right Direction

Yet many trends in Atlanta were clearly headed the right way, moving toward a more sustainable, livable future. The short streetcar loop might not have accomplished much, but if it was really the beginning of a network that would run on the BeltLine and connect to a spiderweb of transit within it, then streetcars, in conjunction with the faster-moving

MARTA system, really might help get people out of their cars. On the other hand, bus rapid transit lanes—that is, buses in their own dedicated lanes—would be cheaper and equally effective.

MARTA itself was undergoing a remarkable transformation under the leadership of new CEO Keith Parker, who had previously turned around the San Antonio rapid transit system. When he took charge of the troubled Atlanta agency in December 2012, Parker inherited a projected annual deficit of $33 million. MARTA, though heavily regulated by the state, received no state funding. "There was a perception that MARTA was only for poor and working-class black people, that it was crime-ridden, poorly run, mismanaged, full of scandal," recalled Parker, who is himself African American. MARTA had raised fares 42 percent over the previous three years while cutting services, increasing the amount of time people had to wait for trains and buses.

In short order, Parker solved the agency's financial problems by bringing its IT functions in house, switching to electronic payments, converting buses to natural gas, and implementing other cost-cutting measures. Within six months, he achieved a $9 million surplus. Service improved; time between trains and buses lessened. Adding more police, Parker instituted a "Ride with Respect" campaign, ejecting annoying panhandlers. He began to plan for free Wi-Fi, first in buses and MARTA stations, then on the trains.

Parker hired Amanda Rhein to negotiate transit-oriented develop-ments on the sea of underused parking lots surrounding many MARTA stations, which would add businesses and residential density (with 20 per-cent affordable housing), swelling the agency's bottom line while increas-ing ridership. For the first time in years MARTA began to get positive press, and many of the mostly white Millennials moving back to the city preferred to use public transit over automobiles. Now a MARTA app for their smart phones indicated when trains and buses would arrive. Major businesses, such as State Farm Insurance, NCR, and Mercedes-Benz, moved their headquarters to be close to MARTA stations. "Transit access has gone from being an afterthought to a priority for companies that don't want their workers and products stuck in traffic," a reporter observed.

At one station, MARTA installed a bike-repair kiosk; at another, a farmers' market. Corporate CEO Mark Toro penned an article bragging that he rode MARTA. "It's a statement often met with a look of pity, or disbelief, or even disdain," he observed. "It apparently surprises—even shocks—most people, that a dignified businessman or businesswoman actually uses metro Atlanta's public transit system."

For the first time in years, MARTA expanded, with Clayton County voters overwhelmingly choosing to pay a penny sales tax to get bus service in 2014 and perhaps someday trains. In 2015 Keith Parker and his colleagues started talking about trying to raise $8 billion to extend heavy rail service—hitherto inconceivable.

On September 14, 2015, I attended a Millennial Advisory Panel on the eighteenth floor of a building in Atlantic Station, with gorgeous views of the downtown skyline, where the Atlanta Regional Commission had assembled a group of 135 bright, diverse, influential young people from the metro Atlanta area. With slick PowerPoints, eight panels presented ideas for improving the city. Some, such as a "Pledge to Win the Future," seemed hopelessly naïve, although the pledge's goals, such as creating healthy, livable communities, were admirable. These Millennials—some of whom worked for MARTA or the BeltLine—were engaged, confident, and thoughtful, focusing on public transit and regional cooperation. They suggested that MARTA hire an art curator. Imagine Music Mondays at transit stations! Imagine pop-up community gardens at bus stops!

Another group wanted mobile food trucks to provide fresh vegetables, fruits, and meats in communities throughout Atlanta, including free cooking classes. Perhaps the Atlanta Food Bank could operate them. A different panel championed an inclusionary zoning ordinance that would require all Atlanta developers to provide a certain percentage of affordable housing. Others suggested educational reform and mentoring programs for underprivileged children.

As 2015 came to an end, Atlanta still faced huge problems, schisms, inequalities, fiscal challenges, and political posturing. But this next generation of leaders seemed poised to move the city in the right direction, even as the BeltLine's Westside Trail was under construction.

Part II

NEIGHBORS

*Part II explores the neighborhoods in the four quad-
rants adjacent to the BeltLine as well as selected
areas outside the Atlanta city limits and downtown.
The final chapter brings the story through most of
2016 and offers my conclusions.*

*To orient themselves, readers should consult eas-
ily available online maps such as Google Maps,
MapQuest, or OpenStreetMap as they read these
chapters, zooming in and out to follow along. Atlanta BeltLine, Inc., also offers helpful maps on its
website.*

CHAPTER 10

EAST BELTLINE: CHIC, WALKABLE NEIGHBORHOODS

....

Prices have skyrocketed in very short order. If you ask why, this part of the city was already in resurgence, but the Beltline Eastside Trail is the big artery pumping life into it.

—Burke Sisco, Old Fourth Ward resident and realtor, December 2014

The BeltLine is under way, with long-term momentum, but who are the people the loop is connecting? What kinds of neighborhoods do they live in, and what impact will the transformative project have on them? All too often (in my opinion), books about urban issues offer high-flown generalizations without delving into the nitty-gritty and getting to know individuals who actually live in the cities. In the next four chapters, I will conduct a personal tour, meeting some of the people in these distinctive, historic neighborhoods. The BeltLine will eventually make them all neighbors, as it attracts other visitors from "outside the Perimeter" or the "hole in the donut" downtown area. I will explore those areas as well, before bringing BeltLine and other Atlanta developments up to date, along with drawing some of my own conclusions.

It's appropriate to start with the east side neighborhoods of the Old Fourth Ward and Inman Park, both impacted hugely by the Eastside Trail, the first major BeltLine corridor trail, completed in late 2012. Then we will travel clockwise, to the southern, western, and northern quadrants.

As people mobbed the Eastside Trail, developers in recovery from the Great Recession rushed to build high-rise apartments around the new Historic Fourth Ward Park, investing more than $400 million within a block of it in the first two years. An additional $775 million worth of residential and retail projects sprang up within a half mile of the Eastside Trail.

The new BeltLine trail intersects the Freedom Park PATH bike trail, which curves east-west through a linear meadow alongside Freedom Parkway, with the Carter Center and Presidential Library as its centerpiece. Peaceful and bucolic, this trail had been there for years, yet it never attracted the crowds that thronged the new Eastside Trail. Why? Maybe in part because it is hilly, whereas the BeltLine trail, following the former railroad, is easier to traverse, with only a subtle slope rising toward the southern end.

A more compelling reason is that the BeltLine trail goes through real neighborhoods, offering differing views and attractions along its length. Like New York's High Line, it shows visitors the big picture, but unlike its shorter, elevated Manhattan cousin, Atlanta's trail runs at ground level in and among the communities, connecting them in a new way.

One Tuesday afternoon in the fall of 2015, I walked the trail south from the intersection of 10th Street and Monroe. On the right I passed the huge old magnolia tree where Babe Ruth planted a home run when he played an exhibition game against the Atlanta Crackers. In the field where bats once slammed balls, there's now a mall with a Whole Foods and Home Depot.

On the left I passed Paris on Ponce, a funky commission shop of thirty-plus boutiques packed with curios, antiques, mirrors, strange taxidermy, vintage clothing, clocks, paintings, sculpture, and other treasures. As I crossed the bridge over Ponce de Leon Avenue, the huge Ponce City Market dominated the right-hand side, with Ford Factory Lofts and a Kroger supermarket on the left (called "Murder Kroger" after several killings in its parking lot, it would be redeveloped a few years later as a 12-story mixed-use project, featuring a new Kroger supermarket at the base).

Jamestown Properties, nearing completion of its massive redevelopment of the old Sears warehouse, had already attracted giant IT-based companies such as Mailchimp, Cardlytics, and athenahealth; the cool Dancing Goats coffeehouse; retail stores such as Anthropologie, J. Crew, Williams-Sonoma, West Elm, and Mountain High Outfitters; and food options ranging from Dub's Fish Camp to Simply Seoul. It included high-end apartments for those wishing to live right on the BeltLine. An amusement park, a miniature golf course, and other delights were planned for its four-acre roof, with incredible views of the Atlanta skyline.

A bike valet took care of the two-wheelers who rode over the old rail bridge directly into the building, and someday the BeltLine may become more the front door of Ponce City Market than the street. Already many of those who work there don't own cars, which is virtually unheard of in other parts of Atlanta. "We ride the elevator every day with a bunch of Millennials in jeans and T-shirts," said Jodi Mansbach of Jamestown Properties. "And a lot of skateboards. They live nearby, and they are walking, boarding, or biking to work."

Continuing south on the BeltLine, I looked down on the Historic Fourth Ward Park on the right. On the trail, a volunteer docent for Trees Atlanta led an environmental tour the other way, explaining which wild grasses and native shrubs had been planted. Two Urban Licks, a trendy restaurant in a former warehouse, abuts the trail on the left. I walked on past the Telephone Factory Lofts on one side, the NuGrape Lofts on the other, crossed Ralph McGill Boulevard, and admired swooping young skateboarders at the skate park. I passed Lee Butler, a retired English teacher and self-appointed BeltLine poet, who recited her weekly offering, gratis. "On your left," a biker called. I smiled at a couple pushing a stroller with twins as I walked under Freedom Parkway. A man scooped up his dog's poop and threw it into a nearby trash can.

At the polished head of a metal rhinoceros, one of the few permanent offerings from Art on the BeltLine, I turned left off the trail, descending into the Inman Park neighborhood, and approached a walk-up window on Bernina Avenue for King of Pops, which offers extraordinary gourmet popsicles with flavors such as chocolate sea salt, coconut latte, and kiwi banana honey.

Back on the trail, I fell in with a young couple. Tom lived in Midtown, not far away, and had frequented the trail often since it opened, but Mindy lived in suburban Alpharetta. This was her first visit. It turned out this was a blind date, a good indication that the Eastside Trail had become a hip destination in and of itself, allowing people to soak in the green walkable urbanity sought by these Millennials.

Many new bars and restaurants had sprung up adjacent or close to the trail. As I neared the end of my two-plus-mile walk on the section completed so far, which dead-ended into Irwin Street, I passed Ladybird

Grove & Mess Hall on the right on John Wesley Dobbs Avenue (named
for the early civil rights leader who lived there) in the Old Fourth Ward.
Opened in 2014, the bar/restaurant was specifically designed to appeal
to BeltLine consumers as a "base camp for the urban explorer."

Further down the Eastside Trail on the left, Kevin Rathbun Steak
opened on nearby Krog Street in 2007. "We never could have predicted
the transformation of the abandoned rail corridor next door," Rathbun
recalled. "It's been a revelation." The chef added a nine-hundred-square-
foot covered patio, featuring a six-foot-wide fireplace, facing the trail,
offering drinks and light snacks.

The New Old Fourth Ward

The name of the Old Fourth Ward, on the inner west side of the Eastside
Trail, south of Ponce de Leon Avenue and north of Auburn Avenue, derives from the pre–Civil War era, before Atlanta's division into city council districts. For most of its history, it was an African American enclave,
encompassing wet, low-lying land, including Buttermilk Bottom, probably named for the sour smell of the sewage that accumulated there. The
area was devastated by the Great Fire of 1917. By the 1960s, many streets
remained unpaved, and the poorest residences had no electricity. As part
of "urban renewal," in 1967 the city razed the homes in Buttermilk Bottom, leveled the land, and built a new Civic Center—now dated and
rarely used. Because various springs provided a convenient water supply,
light industries such as laundries, dairy processors, and paper manufac-
turers had set up there.

Although Ponce de Leon Avenue, its northern border, had once been
home to some of Atlanta's wealthiest families, they had moved north long
ago, leaving a decaying commercial zone and once elegant apartment
buildings going to seed. Ponce became notorious for drugs, panhand-
lers, and prostitutes. Crime reached "absurd levels," according to one
reporter. Crack dealers openly conducted business on sidewalk couches.

The area began to improve, however, as whites moved back to
the city in the late 1990s and early twenty-first century. Kit and Stuart Sutherland were among them. In 1984 they had moved to the traditionally white Virginia-Highland neighborhood, north of Ponce, an
area fraying around the edges, with little old ladies subdividing their
homes into apartments. "During the time we were there," Kit Sutherland

recalled, "the neighborhood took off," with remodeled homes, nanny clubs, park restoration, and upward mobility. Virginia-Highland was one of the BeltLine neighborhoods that had thrown a fit about Wayne Mason's planned towers.

In 2001, the Sutherlands moved south of Ponce to the Glen Iris Lofts in the Old Fourth Ward, across the street from the derelict old Sears building. "I was forty-one. We sold for a handsome profit, came south and invested here, to be urban pioneers. We might not have come if we had children." Her husband's job as a lawyer allowed Sutherland, who had a master's degree in historic preservation, to become active in Old Fourth Ward affairs, and she was delighted to watch the creation of the park and restoration of Ponce City Market outside her window.

Gentrification of the Old Fourth Ward was well under way even before completion of the Eastside Trail. In his 2007 novel, *Them*, African American Atlanta journalist Nathan McCall wrote about the neighborhood, with his black protagonist riding "past the ash-brick factories now being converted into trendy lofts to make way for the chi-chi Yuppies swarming in." McCall portrayed blacks and whites as equally fearful of *them*, the opposite race. "Among blacks, the mounting influx of whites was eventually viewed like the notion of death: a grim inevitability."

Rents and property taxes in the Old Fourth Ward soared, and many longtime black residents sold for a profit or were forced to move to a more affordable neighborhood. But even McCall admitted that there was more to the story. "With all the hemming and hawing about the perils of 'whitey' coming in, there was no denying that the neighborhood was slowly flowering into a more attractive place."

Princess Wilson, an African American woman who grew up in nearby public housing, loves the BeltLine and the blossoming neighborhood, and she welcomes her new friends, including Kit Sutherland. Born in 1948, Wilson was the third of four children. Her father owned a shoe repair shop in Buttermilk Bottom. As a child, she remembers daring to take a drink from the whites-only water fountain at the Municipal Market down on Edgewood Avenue to see if it tasted any different, then dashing away. In 1962, she was one of five black students to integrate St. Joseph's Catholic High School. "It was terrible," she recalls. "There was no blatant racism, but the white students you knew in school would ignore you when they saw you in town. I couldn't be a cheerleader—that was for the long-haired blond girls."

I interviewed Wilson in her small, neat home on East Avenue, just north of Freedom Parkway and a short walk to the Historic Fourth Ward Park and Eastside Trail. She served on the board of the park's conservancy, and when we walked down Ralph McGill Boulevard to the Bantam Pub, a new community gathering place, she greeted many friends in what had become one of the most racially diverse neighborhoods in Atlanta.

Yet Wilson admits that she is in a fortunate situation. A retired travel agent, she inherited her mortgage-free home and was able to refinance improvements. Property taxes have gone up, and new $450,000 homes have sprouted across the street. "Those townhomes they're building on the corner will start at $500,000," Wilson says. "People knock on my door with offers all the time. I tell them it's $2 million, I'm not interested, I like where I am."

The Bedford Pine Problem Corridor

One street only a couple of blocks from the Historic Fourth Ward Park has yet to be rehabilitated: a broad thoroughfare named Boulevard that runs north-south along a high ridge, originally intended to serve the white upper crust of Atlanta. On the stretch running south to Freedom Parkway it hosts Bedford Pine, a bastion of Section 8 housing made affordable by federal vouchers. The blocky red brick buildings are a cash cow for owner Continental Wingate of Massachusetts. With minimal upkeep, for each of nearly seven hundred apartments, Wingate has received about $1,000 a month in Housing and Urban Development subsidies and $72 in rent, which amounts to more than $9 million per year. Yet Atlantans cannot blame Continental Wingate for all the problems in the Boulevard corridor, with adjacent properties in worse shape, many of them crack- and flophouses.

On one of my early research trips to Atlanta late in 2011, I walked around the newly completed Historic Fourth Ward Park, took a tour of the gigantic vacant Sears, and wandered into the funky Masquerade building, an old excelsior factory built in the late nineteenth century to produce wood shavings as packing material. Like most of the businesses once serviced by BeltLine trains, the factory was long defunct; it now served as a grungy rock music venue, featuring three levels called Heaven, Purgatory, and Hell.*

---

* The Masquerade concerts had to relocate from this original location late in 2016.

Then I walked west up North Avenue, crossed Glen Iris, and trudged up the long hill to its crest at Boulevard. I had heard Bedford Pine was a sketchy neighborhood, but it was a sunny afternoon, so I hesitantly turned left at the corner, where I encountered an imposing black woman dressed in a flowing African-style dress. "How are you?" I asked, and she squared herself, eyeballed me up and down, and said, "I'm fine. What you want?" I explained that I was a writer doing research for a book about Atlanta, and I had been told that this might be a dangerous street. I asked if walking down it would be safe for me.

She looked at me incredulously. "A white man with a notepad and a camera? No, it would not be safe. Are you crazy?" Thus began my Bedford Pine education by Felicia Matthews, known as Miss Lisa by everyone in the neighborhood. Born in Chicago, she had kicked a heroin addiction in her twenties. Now forty, she had moved to Atlanta to work for AT&T, lost that job, worked for a laundry that went out of business, then started a day care in her Bedford Pine apartment. But with the Great Recession, the kids' parents lost their jobs and didn't need her services.

Matthews then launched into an eloquent tirade in defense of Bedford Pine residents that, with her permission, I caught on tape:*

> We have mediocre, meaningless jobs to the rest of the world. We're the people that clean the bathrooms, we're the people that serve your breakfast through the window at the drive-through, we're the people that clean your laundry, we're the people that wash your car at the car wash. We are the bottom-of-the-barrel people, but we mean something to each other. We might not mean nothing to the rest of the world, because the rest of the world is flying by us. But we maintain our apartments.

Yes, there were drug dealers, but white people drove there to buy the drugs. "I'm not saying every white person gets high, that's a stereotype. I'm saying you can't just depict one neighborhood, and say, 'Oh, Bedford Pine's a bad place.' White folks move in and they decide they want a neighborhood, they come back and take it from the blacks. They been taking every damn thing every time, everything we got. First we had

---

* You can hear this taped interview, along with others, through links on my website, www.markpendergrast.com or www.cityontheverge.com.

Afros, now they have Afros. We wore our pants halfway to our knees and now they doin' it."

I did not continue down Boulevard that day, but a few months later I arranged to take a walk through Bedford Pine with black city council-man Kwanza Hall, who represents the district and declared 2012 "The Year of Boulevard," focusing on summer camps and internships for kids and arranging for a police precinct to move into the neighborhood. When we encountered a group of loitering men, they were far from threatening, but they had a litany of complaints: The police stopped people randomly and tried to get women's phone numbers. One man had just spent $2,400 to get his teeth fixed because he had no health insurance, and Atlanta Medical Center, just south on Boulevard, treated those from the neigh-borhood "rough." They claimed the neighborhood had gone to hell since Katrina refugees had moved there from Louisiana, with increased gun violence. Hall listened sympathetically but offered few solutions. Start a business to fix cell phones, he suggested. Get an ice cream cart.

Hall, born in 1971 and raised in southwestern Atlanta, held a degree from the Massachusetts Institute of Technology. He slipped easily into colloquial black speech with the men, but he switched to standard En-glish when talking to me alone. The problem, he observed, was the con-centration of poverty. Since 1996, Atlanta's crime-ridden public housing units had been demolished, replaced with high-quality mixed-income developments built by black-owned firms such as Columbia Residential and Integral Group. Those displaced received Section 8 vouchers. But privately owned Bedford Pine remained, with nearly half of its 2,400 res-idents living below the poverty line. Most were single mothers and their children, living on about $3,000 a year.

Fortunately, "The Year of Boulevard" (2012) produced tangible bene-fits, including $1.2 million for infrastructure improvements, such as repair-ing sidewalks, painting crosswalks, and making curb cuts to help people with disabilities. Continental Wingate renovated and painted buildings and, along with three dozen partner organizations, including Coca-Cola, contributed to other enhancements. And the effort continued, stretching into the *years* of Boulevard, with more summer camps and museum visits for kids. In 2014, residents began the Boulevard Food Co-op, where a $5 joining fee and $3 biweekly payments purchased forty pounds of food every two weeks, much of it grown at local urban farms. And in 2015, Wingate broke ground on a four-story "City Lights" building for eighty low-income senior apartments at the corner of Boulevard and Angier, where two apartment buildings had burned in 2005. The city of Atlanta approved $7.5 million in tax-exempt bonds to help fund construction.

Saving Sweet Auburn

Freedom Parkway really divides the Old Fourth Ward into two distinct neighborhoods, with the southern half resting on Auburn Avenue. The eastern part of Auburn held a mix of housing, from cheap "shotgun" homes to more elegant two-story residences, such as the home where Martin Luther King Jr. lived as a child, now preserved as a museum. As a result of desegregation, many middle- and upper-class blacks moved from the neighborhood, and local businesses failed. The area swiftly went downhill, until one determined black newcomer named Mtamanika Youngblood spearheaded an effort to turn it around.

Raised in New York City, where her father was a construction worker, Youngblood moved in 1971 to Albany, Georgia, to help manage New Communities, a large communal black-owned farm that evolved out of the civil rights movement. She eventually attended Atlanta University, earned an MBA, and worked for Bell South. In 1985, she and her husband, with their month-old daughter, moved to Howell Street just off Auburn Avenue, into a big, old disheveled house that they rehabbed. "We thought, *This is the Martin Luther King Historic District. Surely it will be revitalized.*"

But as the older generation died, leaving abandoned homes, things just got worse. The area became rife with crack dealers, prostitutes, shootings, and nightly thefts of building materials. Busloads of tourists would drive east down Auburn Avenue between the Martin Luther King Jr. National Historic Site (run by the National Park Service) and the privately run King Center, go past the King birthplace, then turn left onto Howell Street. "We could see their faces drop, aghast at the vacant, overgrown lots and dilapidated houses," Youngblood recalls.

She turned the nascent Historic District Development Corporation (HDDC) into a dynamic, volunteer-run organization that developed a "block-by-block" strategy, beginning on Howell Street, fixing up contiguous homes so that no one would have to live next to a trash-strewn vacant lot or decaying house. Determined not to displace anyone, with funding from NationsBank and other sources, HDDC built in-fill houses and relocated impoverished residents—mostly elderly black women—on the same block, during the revamping of their original houses. Yet none of them chose to move back into their old homes, preferring to stay in their new digs. "Baby, I done lived there forty years, and that's enough," one woman told Youngblood.

I took a walking tour of the neighborhood with Mtamanika Young-blood, and sure enough, block by block, running north to John Wesley Dobbs Avenue, the homes were restored. She winced at one concrete monstrosity that violated historical preservation codes, but otherwise the dwellings were charming bungalows, shotgun cottages, or more upscale homes. Down Auburn sat Studioplex, another project Youngblood had championed (along with Starling Sutton), combining lofts and artist's spaces.

"No one was forced out of this part of the Old Fourth Ward," Young-blood said proudly. "We sold high-quality housing at good prices. But in the late 1990s, people were selling out to white people who could afford them. It happened in two years, doubling what they had paid. By the time we got a handle on it, we did sales differently, putting protective covenants onto homes, providing a subsidy to make a home affordable, but if you sold it within five years, you had to pay the subsidy back."

As a result of her work, Mtamanika Youngblood was tapped to join the board of the Atlanta BeltLine Partnership, where she pushed for 20 percent of tax allocation district proceeds to go toward an affordable housing fund, though she had to settle for 15 percent.

The Butterflies of Inman Park

Inman Park, Atlanta's first planned suburb, developed in the late nine-teenth century, lies across the BeltLine on its eastern flank, opposite the Old Fourth Ward. The Hurts, Woodruffs, Candlers, and other leading Atlanta families once lived here. But by the 1950s and 1960s, the neigh-borhood had fallen on hard times, with the big mansions subdivided into boardinghouses, often with weekly rentals and predictable neglect.

One day in 1969, young antiques appraiser Robert Griggs looked out a bus window and saw a huge Victorian hulk on Euclid Avenue. He bought it for $22,000, got rid of the thirty-four tenants, and slowly began to restore it, leading a vanguard of energetic young baby boomers who, over the next two decades, restored Inman Park as a beautiful, thriving neighborhood, with a full-winged butterfly as its symbol of rebirth and an annual springtime Inman Park Festival to celebrate the community and its homes.

As I visited neighborhoods around the BeltLine in researching this book, I adopted what I humorously called a "sleeping around" strategy. Rather than just making flash visits, I tried to find somewhere to stay overnight so that I could get to know people and their communities better. I stayed two nights in September 2015 with Rod and Bobbie Paul in their large Inman Park home on Elizabeth Street, a short walk from the Eastside Trail. Bobbie had recently retired as the executive of an anti-nuclear watchdog organization, and Rod, a documentary filmmaker, traveled the world for his job.

They bought their lovely Victorian home for $149,000 in 1984, when the neighborhood was already coming back, but at the time the home still had black mold, rats, and bare wires hanging out of the walls. Having fixed it up and raised two sons there, they now live with their two dogs and remain active in neighborhood affairs.

One night we walked across the street for a wonderful salmon dinner on the back patio at the home of their friends John and Midge Sweet, who were among the neighborhood pioneers. John, a lawyer who later became a city councilman, came to Atlanta in 1968 as a VISTA volunteer. Three years later, he bought his dilapidated Victorian for $23,000. "The former boarders had parked their cars in front yards, so it was hard-packed dirt where no grass could grow," he recalled. "One day a group of us were helping a guy up the street, digging a stump out, sweat pouring off us. A man walking by was amazed when I told him it wasn't even my house. He ended up being inspired to move to Inman Park himself."

Sweet, a community organizer, took part in what everyone called the Road Fight, which spanned an astonishing four decades. In 1964, the Georgia Department of Transportation introduced plans for Interstate 495, a toll road that would rip through Inman Park and other neighborhoods on its way to Stone Mountain and Athens, Georgia. Over two hundred acres of homes were cleared in preparation for the expressway, with the last home, belonging to Judge Durwood Pye in Inman Park, torn down in 1971, the same year John Sweet moved there, as did Cathy Bradshaw, an Atlanta native who became a leader in the fight to stop the road. During a driving tour, Bradshaw gave me an overview of the Road Fight.

When Jimmy Carter was elected as the Georgia governor, he helped put a stop to the road plans, but years later, after his presidency, in 1981

Carter resuscitated the idea of a raised eight-lane Presidential Parkway in the same area as part of his planned Carter Center. It would have destroyed many more homes, with seven bridges ramping over residential streets. Neighborhood activists helped form CAUTION (Citizens Against Unnecessary Thoroughfares in Older Neighborhoods), which mounted legal actions against the road, while the rowdy Road Busters lay down in front of bulldozers and were arrested. In 1989 a court-mediated compromise led to a 1994 groundbreaking for Freedom Parkway, a much smaller, four-lane, nonelevated road that followed the natural curves of the land and included a trail system. Inman Park and other neighborhoods still bear scars from the Road Fight, with steps leading from curbs up to where houses once stood.

I asked Rod and Bobbie Paul what they thought of the BeltLine. They appreciated how it has brought people together and linked their mostly white neighborhood with the traditionally black Old Fourth Ward. Years ago, black and white kids used to throw rocks at one another across the railroad tracks. Now all enjoy the Eastside Trail together. Both of the Pauls' sons rent near the BeltLine in the Old Fourth Ward and off Monroe Drive (the same street as Boulevard, but the name changes north of Ponce de Leon Avenue). So Rod and Bobbie can walk up the Eastside Trail to visit their grandchildren.

"But we don't do that on weekends," Bobbie told me. "It's too crowded!" She prefers the quieter and less congested Freedom Park trail, where we walked on a Saturday morning to a local farmers' market held near the Carter Center. The Pauls despise Inman Quarter, the new multistory development at the bottom of Elizabeth Street, fronting on Highland Avenue, which they watched develop as a six-story concrete parking garage eventually wrapped in 223 luxury apartments. Rod Paul says the "mausoleum" blocks the view of trees, and he calls the BeltLine "a developer's wet dream."

The next day, as I walked out the Pauls' front door to take an early morning walk, a young black man walked down Elizabeth Street, wearing earbuds and reciting rap lyrics. A few upper-class black families live in Inman Park, but this man probably was walking down the hill from the nearby Inman Park–Reynoldstown MARTA station, perhaps heading to work at one of the new restaurants on Highland Avenue.

I walked up the street, took a right on Waverly Way, and came to Springvale Park, with its pond, fountain, and children's playhouse. Ducks

Victorian-era Inman Park home

swam, and a great blue heron stood so still on a rock that I thought it was a statue until it flew away, calmly beating its huge wings. Continuing up Waverly Way, I crossed Euclid, walking along another part of the park, then came to Edgewood Avenue and the restored Trolley Barn, where the old streetcars were once serviced and Inman Park events, meetings, and weddings now take place. I turned left, then left again on Elizabeth Street, where I spotted Callan Castle, built by Coca-Cola magnate Asa Candler, on the corner of Euclid. If I turned right on Euclid, I would reach nearby Little Five Points, with its funky, hip businesses, but I walked back down Elizabeth to complete my circle.

What a gorgeous, peaceful neighborhood, I thought. *Who wouldn't want to live here?* And nowadays, who could afford to? The lovely restored homes would sell for over $1 million.

Moving to Inman Park

But you don't have to buy an old restored Victorian home in order to live in Inman Park. On the Eastside Trail, I ran into a mother and daughter walking their dogs; both had moved recently to the neighborhood and

perfectly illustrated who was moving in-town to be near the BeltLine:
empty nesters and Millennials.

Lynn and David Chandley lived for twenty-five years on a cul-de-sac
in the Gwinnett County suburbs, driving their kids to softball, soccer,
and football games. David had commuted forty-two miles daily to and
from Atlanta in rush-hour traffic. With their kids grown, they moved
to Inman Park. "The home prices here are shockingly high," Lynn observed, but at least they could buy a house on Lake Avenue for six figures. David, the chief meteorologist at *Fox News*, now drives three miles
to work. "We are happy and healthier than we have ever been," he told
me. "It's a badge of pride to say we live along the BeltLine. And we enjoy
showing off our new neighborhood to longtime friends who are still living in suburbia." Lynn added that she likes meeting "the variety of dogs
and proud dog parents" as she walks the BeltLine and loves having her
daughter Lauren so close by.

Lauren Reidy, twenty-seven, and her husband, Kyle, were determined to live in Inman Park near the BeltLine. "So after putting nine offers on seven places, we finally were successful in buying a one-bedroom
condo," she told me, grabbing it in the $200,000-plus range before it was
officially listed. "The BeltLine is part of our everyday life. Whether it is
walking our dog in the evening, my husband running in the morning
before work, or a date night walk down to Ponce City Market, we are so
grateful for the way the BeltLine enhances our life together." They live
on the corner of North Highland in Inman Park Village.

That's the site of a former Mead packaging plant that in 2001 had
helped Ryan Gravel explain his vision to fellow architects. In designing
the Inman Park Village apartment complex, he had to decide whether
to shove the parking garage up against the defunct railroad line, then an
impassable kudzu jungle, or to orient the apartments toward what would,
he hoped, become the BeltLine. He chose the latter strategy.

Now Gravel himself also lives in Inman Park, along with his wife,
Karen (also an architect), and children, Lucia and Jonas. When I first
met them, the Gravels had me to dinner in their big, old home in Capitol
View Manor, near the unfinished BeltLine corridor in southwestern Atlanta. In 2013, they moved to a funky loft on Krog Street in an old refurbished warehouse, near the trendy new Krog Street Market.

Gravel also sometimes walks south through the Krog Street tunnel
(which the future BeltLine trail will use, at least for a while, to pass under

the Hulsey Rail Yard), then turns right into Cabbagetown (left would take him to Reynoldstown), where workers for the Fulton Bag and Cotton Mill once lived—mostly poor whites from the Appalachian Mountains with their own distinct music and culture. Designated a historic district, the cute restored Cabbagetown bungalows look the same, but the neighborhood has largely gentrified, and the mill itself has been converted into lofts. Walking past a wall painted with fantasy murals, Gravel turns left up Carroll Street, where he enjoys lunch at the counter of Little's Food Store and Grill, long a neighborhood hangout.

Late in 2015, the Gravel family invited me for another dinner, after which we all walked along the Eastside Trail for a King of Pops dessert. That year, Gravel quit his job at Perkins + Will to start his own consulting firm, renting an office in Ponce City Market. Now he could commute to work on bike or foot on the BeltLine he himself envisioned as a Georgia Tech grad student.

In summary, the eastern BeltLine is not only happening; it is exploding, apparently proving Gravel's thesis correct: the BeltLine could help to revitalize and transform the city and its neighborhoods.

But not so fast. The east side was already beginning to turn around when the BeltLine arrived, and Inman Park had solid bones, even though its homes had suffered somewhat in the past. What about other neighborhoods around the future BeltLine? What about neighborhoods that have *always* been relatively poor?

CHAPTER 11

SOUTH BELTLINE: A SLOW DANCE TO BETTER COMMUNITIES

It's time to retire the term gentrification *altogether. . . . The media focus on gentrification has obscured problems that actually are serious: the increasing isolation of poor, minority neighborhoods and the startling spread of extreme poverty.*

—John Buntin, "The Myth of Gentrification," *Slate*, 2015

Mary Porter, born in 1947, grew up in the South Atlanta neighborhood, originally known as Brownsville, founded by freed slaves after the Civil War; there black residents turned back white police and vigilantes during the Atlanta Race Riot of 1906. I interviewed Porter in the heart of that community, where Jonesboro Road forks off from McDonough Boulevard. We sat a block away from the future BeltLine in Community Grounds, a coffeehouse that serves as a convivial meeting place and refuge from the abandoned buildings and impounded car lots nearby.

As I spoke to Porter, who had recently moved to a nearby retirement complex, I felt a curious affinity. We were almost mirror images of one another. She is only a year older than I. We both grew up in Atlanta, albeit on opposite sides of the city. Her parents had eight children. I was one of seven. I had known few black people, other than yardmen or maids. She had known hardly any white people, other than a few local store owners.

Porter has warm memories of growing up in the two-bedroom home on Buchanan Lane that her father Robert, a World War II veteran, bought on the GI Bill. He worked for Southern Railway. "I wanted to be a railroad conductor when I grew up," she told me, "but I was female and black." Her mother, Marion, worked as a hairdresser before becoming the housekeeper for Norris Herndon, son of Alonzo Herndon, whose barber-shops and insurance company made him Atlanta's first black millionaire.

South Atlanta was a close-knit community. "People took care of each other's children," Porter recalled. "If we got in a fight, Momma would know it before we got home. We had party line telephones, so everyone would listen in." Church was the center of social activity. There were quite a few local businesses—a variety store, pharmacy with a lunch counter, hardware store, dry cleaner, café, service station, movie theater, two groceries—all catering to and mostly owned by African Americans. There was also a rough street with an apartment complex nicknamed the Titanic. "That was a place you didn't go, with bad people."

Although Mary Porter knew that blacks were treated differently from whites and had to sit in the back of the bus, growing up she had taken segregation for granted. It was just the way things were. For a while, she played with some white children who crossed the trucking company parking lot from the Lakewood community, until one brought a cousin who said, "You're playing with niggers," and they never returned. "I had no clue what 'nigger' meant, so I asked my Momma, and she said it was a bad word."

When she was in elementary school, the Atlanta Board of Education voted to give white children free milk in the cafeteria. When the black parents found out, they protested, and eventually their children got free milk as well. When she was in high school, Porter received hand-me-down textbooks discarded by white schools, until 1965, the year she graduated, when civil rights agitation finally wrangled new books.

After high school, Porter was one of the first blacks hired as a switchboard operator by Southern Bell, at the corner of Auburn Avenue and Ivy Street. "In school, we had been taught how to speak and dress. We knew integration was coming and we would have to interact with white people." One rainy April evening in 1968, Porter reported for work at Southern Bell and found the place in an uproar. She learned that Martin Luther King Jr. had been assassinated, and none of the white operators dared come to work on Auburn Avenue. "Which one of y'all wants to be white tonight?" her supervisor asked. So Porter had put on her best imitation of a white Southern drawl.

As the schools, parks, and communities were forced to integrate, others besides whites fled. African Americans, free to move elsewhere for the first time, could now shop at white establishments as well. In 1972, Porter moved in with her grandmother, who had bought a home off Cascade Avenue vacated by a fleeing white family, although her parents stayed in the family home in South Atlanta.* By the mid-1970s, that community was in decline, with local businesses going bankrupt and more people leaving every year. "Older people passed away," Porter said, "and their children didn't want to live here, so they either left the houses vacant or rented them out. As a child, I don't remember any empty houses or vacant lots. Integration killed this community and others like it."

Although I grew up in Atlanta, I had never realized that the civil rights movement had this indirect, counterintuitive impact, but I heard and observed this same story in other black Atlanta neighborhoods. That's why Auburn Avenue, once the gem of black business and society, fell on hard times. No one would want to go back to those racist Jim Crow days, but Mary Porter's matter-of-fact observations were all too accurate.

By 1976, technology had eliminated the need for switchboard operators, so Porter found office work, and in 1984 she moved back to South Atlanta to care for her ailing father, who died two years later. She stayed, eventually becoming a community activist, doing battle with city hall bureaucrats to get federal Empowerment Zone funding during the Bill Clinton administration. Little of the money ever filtered down to the thirty-three designated Atlanta communities, however.

Then, as the twenty-first century dawned, South Atlanta experienced an inexplicable building boom. "It was crazy to me," Porter recalled. "The banks were lending to people who couldn't afford it. Some was mortgage fraud. Others got balloon payments, then had to pay all at once and couldn't. A lot of brand new homes stayed empty. They were just boarded up."

---

* Her father, Robert Porter, a friendly man who smoked two packs of Camels a day and enjoyed fatty foods, had a massive heart attack at forty-eight but lived another sixteen years. With the coming of the interstate highway and the demolition of Terminal Station in 1972, he could no longer work for the railroad and made a living as a part-time barber and furniture mover.

Porter's brother still lives in the old family home, but in 2012 she moved into Veranda at Auburn Pointe, a senior housing facility in the southern Old Fourth Ward on the site of the former Grady Homes, a razed public housing project. She likes it. "I can walk to the Atlanta Streetcar, the MLK Historical District, MARTA, and the Sweet Auburn Curb Market." She never married because, as she told me, she is "fiercely independent and brutally honest," though she has a son who works as a security guard for Coca-Cola.

Porter returns to South Atlanta every Sunday to attend Community Life Church in the former movie theater at the back of the same building as Community Grounds, where we met. "This building was vacant a long time," she said.

It's fortunate that the building survived at all. "In Atlanta, they will tear down a historic building to build a parking lot." Nearby Leete Hall, now part of a high school complex called the New Schools at Carver, is a magnificent 1922 building designed by local black architect Alexander Hamilton on the former Clark College campus. After the college moved to the Atlanta University campus on the west side, Leete served as a vocational school where Porter's parents learned barbering and hairdressing. The Board of Education had planned to raze it, but Porter and other neighborhood activists got it put on the National Historic Register and saved it.

Focused Community Strategies

New hope came to the South Atlanta community in 2001 when residents, including Mary Porter and other seniors who had remained there, approached Bob Lupton, founder of faith-based Focused Community Strategies (FCS), asking him to bring the project to South Atlanta, and he agreed.

Lupton, a white Ohio native and son of a Methodist minister, had moved to Atlanta in 1972 to work with troubled young men on probation. He soon realized that he had to deal with their families to have any real impact, and eventually he concluded, "If you're going to change a community, you have to do it from the inside out." So in 1981, he moved his family from suburban Stone Mountain to the crime-ridden Grant Park neighborhood in southern Atlanta.

Grant Park, founded in 1882 by Lemuel P. Grant, was the first Atlanta suburb, featuring large Victorian homes and craftsman bungalows around a large park, which also held the Atlanta Zoo and the Cyclo-rama, a circular painting of the Battle of Atlanta. But by the time Lupton moved there, Interstate 20 had sliced off the northern tip of the community. During the 1960s, most whites had fled Grant Park as blacks moved in, and many homes had been subdivided into apartments. Some older white widows held on, but impoverished black residents predominated.

Bill Adams, who owns Adams Realty on Cherokee Avenue, the street that runs along the western side of the 131-acre park, grew up on Cherokee in a house his grandfather built in 1902. He played safely in the park in an Eisenhower America. But when he returned to the neighborhood in 1975, many homes stood abandoned. Out his bathroom window, he saw someone shooting up heroin. As happened with Inman Park, however, white urban pioneers began reclaiming the neighborhood.

In 1983, Adams bought a big, old home on Woodward Avenue featuring turrets and twelve-foot ceilings, badly in need of repair, in the northern section cut off from the park by I-20. It lay just a block south of Memorial Drive, with historic, peaceful Oakland Cemetery across the street, but it was also near two public housing projects. "We could hear automatic weapons." On Martin Luther King Day in 1994, Adams was shot in the leg and hip while jogging through Grant Park. Prostitutes turned tricks in the alley behind his house. In 1996, no longer willing to expose his children to that activity, Adams moved his family to Decatur, but he kept his realty firm on Cherokee Avenue in the old Masonic building.

Bob Lupton moved his FCS project into this turmoil in 1981, beginning his education in community building. He took over an empty church on Georgia Avenue, where FCS offered a free clothes closet and food pantry. When Lupton spent his first Christmas Eve in a local African American home, a well-dressed white family arrived to deliver beautifully wrapped Christmas presents. As the black children joyfully grabbed the gifts, Lupton noticed their father quietly slipping out of the room. He had never before observed "how a father is emasculated in his own home in front of his wife and children for not being able to provide presents for his family."

Lupton's thinking underwent a seismic shift. As he argued in his 2011 book, *Toxic Charity: How Churches and Charities Hurt Those They Help (and How to Reverse It)*, "patronizing pity and unintended superiority" foster feelings of resentment, inferiority, and entitlement. He does not oppose emergency charity, but Lupton concluded that it is better to teach someone to fish than to give him a fish and that people appreciate the dignity of paying for goods. "Never do for others what they can do for themselves" became a commandment. FCS converted its clothes closet into a thrift shop that accepted unwrapped Christmas gift toys and then sold them for a small amount. He established the Georgia Avenue Food Co-op, which leveraged $3 semiweekly dues into $30 worth of groceries, mostly donated by the Atlanta Community Food Bank.*

Today, Grant Park has turned back into a safe, desirable community, as I discovered when I stayed overnight with Sarah Toton and Micah Wedemeyer in their classic three-bedroom bungalow, built in 1907, with hardwood floors, high ceilings, and a huge oak in the backyard on Park Avenue, adjacent to the park's northeastern section. They bought it for $363,000 in 2013, which seemed a bargain to me. The young Iowa couple came reluctantly to Atlanta for Toton to attend grad school at Emory University in 2003. "I never wanted to move to Atlanta. I heard it was a cancer on America with its urban sprawl." Now they love it. In Grant Park there are frequent festivals, bike and running races, and other events, and they are close to everything, including the BeltLine Eastside Trail, where Wedemeyer, a computer programmer, rides his bike. It's a great place to live, with the park and zoo (the Cyclorama is moving to Buckhead to the Atlanta History Center), the Grant Park Coffeehouse, and many nearby restaurants.

Bob Lupton doesn't take much credit for Grant Park's gentrification, though. Too late, he realized that poor people were getting pushed out. "Prices went up very quickly, and we were unable to capture most of the real estate when it was affordable. So in subsequent communities, we try to get ahead of the market, securing affordable land and property." Near Grant Park, on Glenwood Avenue, FCS was able to buy the old At-lanta Stockade, a magnificent old stone and concrete nineteenth-century prison, and convert it into affordable lofts, along with a charter school. Yet that enterprise, renamed Glenwood Castle, was also a learning ex-perience, as drugs and other problems surfaced. Lupton concluded that even with the best intentions, concentrated poverty does not work, and after securing other housing for its occupants, he put the Stockade build-ings up for sale in 2015 to fund other FCS projects.

---

* By 2016, FCS operated six similar Atlanta food cooperatives.

After fifteen years, FCS moved from Grant Park to a series of other troubled southern Atlanta communities—Summerhill, Ormewood Park,* East Lake, and finally South Atlanta. Each community featured its own challenges, successes, and frustrations. By teaming up with wealthy developer Tom Cousins, FCS helped transform East Lake from a violent, poverty-stricken community into a model success story, built around the reclamation of the defunct East Lake Golf Club, where golfing great Bobby Jones had played. The FCS-Cousins turnaround, which began in 1995, was miraculous, featuring mixed-income housing at the Villages of East Lake (the public housing project was razed), sought-after charter schools, an urban garden, and a nine-hole public golf course. Out of the East Lake experience grew Purpose Built Communities, led by former Atlanta mayor Shirley Franklin, which has sought to replicate the neighborhood revitalization in New Orleans, Fort Worth, Indianapolis, and nine other cities thus far.

Homing In on South Atlanta

In December 2013, Bob Lupton semiretired from FCS in order to write, consult, and speak, leaving the South Atlanta FCS project to Jeff and Katie Delp, a young couple with two children, Sam and Maya. Jeff, a Pennsylvania native, had come to Atlanta as an AmeriCorps volunteer, while Katie, who grew up in Texas, had come to work for FCS. In January 2015, I stayed overnight with the Delps in their pleasant five-bedroom Thayer Road home, built in 2006 but boarded up in the mortgage fraud scandal. They bought it for $119,000 and paid only $34 in annual property taxes because of the Georgia Homestead Exemption.

Sam and Maya attended the Wesley International Academy, a charter school on Memorial Drive in northern Grant Park. Like many concerned parents in poor areas of Atlanta, the Delps avoided sending their children to inferior public schools. Charter schools, which receive the same per-student public funding, have more freedom to avoid

---

* I spent a memorable night on Prospect Avenue, a quiet dead-end street in Ormewood Park. Just up the street, quite by chance, I wandered into the monthly meeting of the Robert Burns Club, the oldest social gathering in Atlanta, at the stone Burns Cottage, a replica of the poet's birthplace, built in 1911. Sipping high-quality Scotch, we listened to an author speak about Patrick Henry.

bureaucracy and can use innovative educational methods. Students are chosen by lottery, but then younger siblings are automatically eligible to enroll. The charter schools are generally impressive, but because more aware, better-educated parents tend to seek them out, critics claim that the charters create an unequal system in which regular public schools are the losers.

Katie Delp was FCS's executive director, while Jeff ran the day-to-day operations, including the thrift shop, coffee shop, and bike-repair outlet, all started by the organization in the defunct Carver Theater building, which had become a liquor outlet and crack cocaine hangout before being abandoned altogether. FCS is slowly helping to transform the neighborhood, though it has a long way to go. "We've built about forty affordable homes," Jeff Delp explained, "with zero interest mortgages." Habitat for Humanity has also built homes there. "In the last six years, we rehabbed and flipped houses to bring in market-rate families, to create mixed-income blocks." In 2008, about half of the homes in South Atlanta were vacant. Now the vacancy rate was only 15 percent.

"Yes, we are slowly gentrifying the neighborhood, but in a good way," Delp said. "Young professional African Americans are moving here, finding good prices on homes." Gentrification itself is not necessarily a bad thing, according to Delp, who cited studies showing that the process generally helps residents who have at least graduated from high school. Years from now, when the paved BeltLine finally sweeps past South Atlanta, Delp thinks it will spawn businesses other than the current impoundment lots, junkyards, and trash recyclers. "By the time my son is sixteen [in nine years], I hope I don't have to buy him a car, because he can ride his bike on the BeltLine."

In the meantime, neighborhood kids can work in the South Atlanta Bike Shop, where they learn to show up on time, repair bicycles, and deal politely with customers, while earning points toward their own bikes. In 2015, with another thrift shop opening down the street, Jeff Delp converted his thrift shop into the Carver Neighborhood Market in the space next to Community Grounds. The new store, which sources locally grown produce when possible, was an immediate success. Otherwise, the nearest grocery is 3.5 miles away. Through a grant, the store offers cooking classes by Atlanta chefs. "We do sell a lot of snack-type items, since we are so close to a high school," Delp admitted.

Jeff and Katie Delp enjoy their work and home. "We love South Atlanta because it feels like a small town in a big city," said Jeff. "Neighbors know each other, and we think it's a great place to raise a family. I also like its proximity to everything. And we couldn't afford to live this close to downtown in most cities."

Kinesthetic Learner

Before we leave South Atlanta, I have to tell you about Chris McCord, thirty-seven, whose life changed when he met Bob Lupton's daughter-in-law, Dana, founder of Moving in the Spirit, a youth dance program. McCord grew up in a rough part of nearby Decatur with his wheelchair-bound mother, who became a paraplegic when hit by a drunk driver. Diagnosed as learning disabled, McCord flirted with joining a gang and dealing drugs, but in 1991, when he was twelve, he saw a performance of Moving in the Spirit and was mesmerized. "You gonna be a sissy and dance with girls," his friends mocked. Soon after he joined, Dana Lupton pulled him aside and said, "You know, you're smart. I've never seen anyone pick up dance moves as quickly as you do."

One day McCord, his eyes smarting from rereading a high school assignment, took a break and began to dance the story. He found that he could remember it that way and got one hundred on a test the next day. He told Dana Lupton, who said, "Chris, you are a kinesthetic learner." Quite literally, he remembered what he performed.

"This totally changed my life," he said. He graduated from high school, then Perimeter College and Georgia State University in business management. "And I'm not supposed to be in college, I'm supposed to be a garbage man." In 2003 he raised $68,000 to start Men in Motion, his dance program for inner-city boys, and has continued to fund-raise for it. The next year, with help from FCS, he bought a home in South Atlanta for $16,000 and learned to rehab it. He now owns four homes, three of them in South Atlanta, where he lives.

On May 7, 2015, I attended "Wonder Years," a Moving in the Spirit dance program set to Stevie Wonder songs, performed at the historic Rialto Theater in downtown Atlanta on the Georgia State University campus. Men in Motion performed, and in a solo showstopper, McCord did things with his lithe body that didn't seem possible.

Peoplestown Perseveres

Just north of South Atlanta, on the other side of the future BeltLine, Peoplestown is another impoverished black community where activists have pursued a slow revival, even though half of the adult residents were unemployed in 2013. The populist-sounding name actually derives from the nineteenth-century Peeples family, which owned most of the land lots. I toured the community with William Teasley, forty-six, a black Alabama native who moved to Atlanta with a business degree from Boston University. On Atlanta Avenue, near the neighborhood's northern boundary, Teasley owns one of a string of homes designed in the 1920s by female Atlanta architect Leila Ross Wilburn. People can look down the street at others on their porches, making for an old-fashioned community feeling. Teasley, a workforce development consultant, pressured Atlanta BeltLine, Inc. (ABI) to install solar panels during its renovation of Peoplestown's D. H. Stanton Park, adjacent to the BeltLine, so it requires zero energy.*

In April 2012, when Atlanta public school superintendent Erroll Davis announced plans to close the Stanton Elementary School up the road, the community united, under Teasley's leadership, demanding that it stay open. Within a few weeks, Davis reversed the closure decision, though the school still needed a new roof, and 98 percent of the students qualified for free or reduced lunch.

Meanwhile, Boynton Village, a subsidized Peoplestown complex once notorious for violence and drugs, was being renovated under new management. Nothing is perfect, Teasley admitted. Even though he helped save the local public school, he sent his own kids to a charter. "Poverty is really hard, especially intergenerational poverty," he said, and that makes improving the public schools a struggle. Some middle-income people—mostly white—were moving to the neighborhood, but concentrated poverty remained predominant. Teasley was trying to raise funds for a young local woman to go to college. Her father, a truck driver, had died in a crash, and her depressed mother was homeless for a while. "She is among the top three in her class. Her number one issue is money."

---

* This is the park built over a landfill that was closed in 1999 when a girl going down the sliding board caught on fire.

The Pittsburgh Disaster

For pure devastation, few BeltLine communities can match the Pittsburgh neighborhood, a triangular wedge in southern Atlanta once completely surrounded by railroads, just to the west of Peoplestown. Founded in 1883, it housed black railroad workers in small homes. Smoke from the trains and railroad shops blackened the air, as in the polluted steel city of Pittsburgh, Pennsylvania; hence the name.

I first took a depressing tour of the Pittsburgh streets in 2012. Nearly half of the houses were vacant. On Delevan Street, next to Pittman Park, every house stood empty. One new three-story home had never been occupied. Its windows were broken, all the copper and fixtures stolen from it. A toilet lay on the sidewalk where a thief had abandoned it. Yet even in Pittsburgh, I passed a neighborhood event put on by an after-school youth group, and there were forty-three churches, mostly in homes or storefronts.

It's hard to believe that Pittsburgh, hit harder than any other Atlanta neighborhood by mortgage fraud, was once a stable African American community. Moriba Kelsey, born there in 1925, had such fond childhood memories that, well into his eighties, he published a series of three books titled *Pittsburgh: A Sense of Community*, based on oral histories of those who recalled life in the 1940s and 1950s, when McDaniel Street, which runs north-south through the neighborhood's heart, was a kind of lower-class version of Auburn Avenue, with the Squeeze Inn, Benny Wright Shoe Repair, Hines Grocery, Maggie Friday's Beauty Shop, Mayfield Barber Shop, Jabo Cleaners, Yates and Milton Pharmacy, and other businesses. Trucks, wagons, and pushcarts sold vegetables, fruit, coal, wood, and ice.

Sure, there were illegal activities—numbers men, craps games, prostitutes, moonshiners—and there were bullies and occasional knife fights, but few locked their doors. Everyone knew everyone else. Most people were dirt poor, but they were self-reliant, tended big gardens, raised chickens, and canned, pickled, or dried food. Some worked at the railroad roundhouse; others were porters, postal employees, janitors, or domestic servants. Some professionals—doctors, teachers, pharmacists, musicians, ministers—also lived in the neighborhood. Churches provided emergency help, job training, and child care. Four streetcar lines ran along Pittsburgh streets, but few whites ever crossed the railroad tracks, other than mean-spirited policemen. "In many ways, our neighborhood was a world unto itself," one woman told Moriba Kelsey.

Desegregation destroyed Pittsburgh, as blacks who could afford to leave did, and Interstate 75/85 cut off the southeastern corner of the community. The population fell by more than half from 1970 to 2000. McDaniel Street had become a wasteland, all of its businesses defunct, notorious now only for the "Pink Store," which sold junk food and lottery tickets, where violent drug dealers hung out. Two men were shot to death in front of the store in separate incidents in 2014. The average price of a Pittsburgh home dropped to $13,000.

In May 2015, I stayed overnight with Ashlee and Caleb Starr, a young white couple, originally from Indiana, who moved to Pittsburgh in 2007 and bought their modern four-bedroom home on Mayland Circle in 2012 for $32,000. They had three children: Ava, seven; Jay, four; and Lee, one. Ashlee, a social worker, had worked extensively with the homeless, and Caleb built homes for Habitat for Humanity. I was there for the weekly Wednesday neighborhood potluck hosted by the Starrs, but in the late afternoon, Ashlee took me for a walk through the neighborhood with baby Lee in a stroller.

It was disturbing. Although some houses were well kept, many were boarded up, some so overgrown with kudzu that you couldn't see them from the street. When we walked past the Pink Store on McDaniel Street, Ashlee told me that staring at the men hanging out there might be dangerous.

African American neighbors and children crowded the potluck that night, including ninety-year-old Lula Bailey, who lived next door. She still ran Bailey's Beauty Shop out of her garage. She told me how she had lost five of her six children: one daughter died soon after birth, another daughter had contracted AIDS from drug needles, one son had become a drug addict in the marines and died in a fight, another son had succumbed to high blood pressure, and an overweight son with diabetes had crashed his car into a phone pole. Her remaining son lives nearby and takes care of her. I said it was awful to lose so many children. "You know," she said, "I had to realize that once they came out of my body, I had no control. The Lord gives breath and He can take it. And so far I'm still here."

In the wake of her daughter's death, someone had conned Bailey into taking out an $80,000 loan on her home—otherwise nearly paid off— at 11 percent interest, sticking her with much higher monthly payments than the Starrs made, even though her home was smaller and older.

Toni Morrison-McBride, another memorable neighbor who grew up in the Pittsburgh neighborhood, was the first black child to integrate an elementary school in nearby Adair Park. Not timid about expressing her opinion, she loudly challenged Pierre Gaither, head of the Pittsburgh Community Improvement Association (PCIA), who was attending the potluck for the first time and got an earful. Why did the PCIA, with offices on McDaniel Street, focus on the other side of Pittsburgh? Couldn't he get Atlanta's Housing Code Enforcement Bureau to clean up or knock down nearby vacant homes? Gaither, who lived in the South Atlanta community, listened patiently, but even finding out who owned the homes could be difficult, and Code Enforcement was overwhelmed and underfunded.*

Ironically, BeltLine publicity was partly responsible for the glut of empty homes. Investors were just sitting on them, hoping for development and rising prices. When Gaither tracked down a California woman who had bought a shabby vacant house in Pittsburgh sight unseen, she told him, "I'm waiting for the BeltLine to come through." He said, "Ma'am, this is a twenty-five-year project. Can you cut your grass until then?"

The Annie E. Casey Foundation, funded by UPS with a mission to improve the lives of children, had helped the PCIA buy and renovate about fifty Pittsburgh homes. Their energy-efficient, green-certified "Pittsburgh Now" homes were on the market for $95,000, while other PCIA homes, priced at $80,000, were part of a community land trust, selling the house but not the land it sat on. While they would be good deals in another neighborhood, all of these homes were overpriced in Pittsburgh, and they were scattered throughout the community. The contiguous house-by-house, block-by-block strategy that had worked in the historic Martin Luther King district might work in Pittsburgh, if it were possible to secure ownership. Otherwise, few urban pioneers would buy a nice house surrounded by abandoned homes and crack dens.

"I think Casey and PCIA should lower their prices," Ashlee Starr said. "We just need bodies in those houses to help the neighborhood come back." Caleb Starr was pleased that Habitat for Humanity was building a new home in Pittsburgh for the first time in eight years, with a projected monthly mortgage of $600.

In part because of the potlucks, the Mayland Avenue/Mayland Circle area in Pittsburgh's southwestern corner had a somewhat neighborly

---

* See Chapter 15 for more on code enforcement issues.

feeling, as exemplified by the Mayland Motivators Art Garden, once a vacant concrete slab at the corner of Mayland and Metropolitan Avenue where Jennings Grocery stood long ago. Toni Morrison-McBride and her husband, Eddie, had led the neighborhood drive to remove the trash, weeds, and spindly trees growing between the cracks. They painted every square inch with rainbows, roses, smiling faces, and signs: "Success." "Learn." "Lean." "In Spirit." "Love Your Block." Pansies grew from the loose dirt. Caleb Starr built a bus stop shelter at the corner. They held a grand opening in May 2014, with music, dancing, and kids skipping rope. Not much of a real garden, since only a few flowers grew there, it was nonetheless a relatively clean and well-maintained symbol of community pride and caring.

In September 2015, I spent an afternoon helping a group of men nail pieces of plywood to ties along railroad tracks on the unused (but not legally abandoned) CSX lines near Pittsburgh. The idea was to turn it into a do-it-yourself bike trail even before ABI managed to get control of the corridor. Walking west beyond where we finished laying almost two hundred feet, I looked down the hill to my left and saw what looked like a vast asphalt parking lot. It was a thirty-one-acre wasteland, a former trucking transfer station, bought by the Casey Foundation in 2006. Lying along University Avenue just south of the Pittsburgh neighborhood, it is a tantalizing piece of real estate, abutting the future BeltLine. If only something could go there to provide desperately needed jobs for Pittsburgh residents!

The Casey Foundation chose a development team later that year that tentatively planned to avoid the top-down "one big project" trap that Atlanta has frequently fallen into. Instead, it planned a mix of small retail businesses, including a grocery store in the heart of this food desert. If one business failed, another could hopefully replace it.

I returned to the Starr residence four months after my first visit for another potluck and was pleased that seven-year-old Ava remembered me fondly as the man who wrote *Jack and the Bean Soup*, my fart-joke children's book, which I had given her. I told Ashlee that I really admired what she was doing in Pittsburgh. "When you're in," she said, "you're all in. It would be hard to be part-way. I am no one's savior, but just being present has gone a long way. We have loved our time in Pittsburgh. We wouldn't trade it for anything."

CHAPTER 12
WEST BELTLINE: TROUBLE AND PROMISE

....

Charity can make things worse, especially when well-meaning white people come into Grove Park with giveaways. You have to live here. You have to build relationships and really listen. Otherwise, they'll just milk you.

—LaTonya Gates-Boston, PAWKids program director

The communities near the BeltLine in western Atlanta are, in general, among the most troubled in the city, especially as you travel northward, from Adair Park in the southwest to Grove Park and Bankhead in the northwest. Yet even the bleakest streets evince some hope, as residents, activists, religious leaders, and philanthropists strive to improve health, education, jobs, and safety.

Adair Park on an Upward Trend

When Jeanne Mills, born Jeanne Edison in 1947, was growing up in Adair Park on the southwestern side of Atlanta, it was a stable, quiet neighborhood. Her family lived in a bungalow at the corner of Lexington Avenue and Catherine Street, next to one of two neighborhood parks. Hers featured a clay tennis court, playground, and baseball field. From a small recreation building, Miss Francis distributed baseball bats and gloves, board games, and other toys and equipment. The Edison family and everyone else in the community were white.

In 1960, when Jeanne was in the eighth grade, her father died. Her mother rented out the house and moved the family to Florida, but in 1969 Jeanne and her young husband (they later divorced) returned to Adair Park to the same house. She still lived there when I interviewed her in 2013. The small recreation building sat in the park near her home, locked and unused. There were no signs of a tennis court or baseball field, although picnic tables sheltered under a roofed pavilion.

By the time Mills returned to her Adair Park home, white flight was in full swing, with African Americans buying or renting most of the houses. "Drugs came during the 1970s and 1980s," Mills recalled, "and 80 percent of the houses were owned by absentee investors." She stuck it out, working for twenty years at the switchboard at the Saks Fifth Avenue store in Phipps Plaza on Peachtree Road in North Buckhead, which required an hour's bus commute each way. She then earned a master's in historic preservation and became a freelance researcher.

About the time the BeltLine idea began to percolate, a reverse migration had commenced, as young people began to buy cheap homes to restore in Adair Park. Mills considered the Great Recession a "blessing to this neighborhood," because it forced "bottom-feeder" investors into foreclosure.

Derrick Duckworth, an African American Seattle native, moved to Adair Park in 2001. Later he became a realtor, calling his firm The Belt-Line Team, though he was in fact the entire team. In 2008, he facilitated the sale of a house on Catherine Street to Tim and Becky O'Mara, a white couple, who moved in from the suburbs. Appalled by the litter on the streets and looking for a way to engage neighborhood children, they started the BeltLine Bike Shop in an abandoned warehouse on Murphy Avenue adjacent to the future Westside Trail. There, kids (mostly black) could earn donated, refurbished bicycles in return for filling four tall kitchen bags with junk from the streets. That proved so successful that the kids ran out of trash, after which they earned bikes by helping to repair them.[*]

I visited their shop in 2013, where "Mr. Tim" and "Miss Becky" were much in demand. I was impressed with their caring, no-nonsense

---

[*] The South Atlanta Bike Shop works in similar fashion (see Chapter 11). At WeCycle Atlanta in West End, founded by Shawn Walton, earning a bike includes work on community gardens along with bike repair and education.

Becky O'Mara helping a boy in the Beltline Bike Shop (now Bearings Bike Shop)

approach and the frenetic pace of questions and repairs. Jerell, fifteen, told me he had earned four bikes there. His father lived in Florida and his mother was studying cosmetology. I asked what he planned to do. "I might take over the shop from Mr. Tim," he joked. Just before I left, ten-year-old Darius, who lived in the Pittsburgh neighborhood to the east, received his first bike and got his name engraved on it.

In the two years following my visit, the O'Maras started two more bike shops in west Atlanta, one in the troubled English Avenue area, another in Westview near the original location. Because neither was right on the BeltLine, they renamed the enterprise the Bearings Bike Shop. "We exist to teach kids the value of hard work, goal setting, and respect, by rewarding community service with something tangible and valuable," they observed. They hoped that kids would become empowered adult leaders. "And it all starts with a bike."

In 2011, Angel Poventud—a Miami native of Puerto Rican ancestry, railroad conductor, and BeltLine enthusiast—showed me the derelict house Duckworth helped him find for $14,000. As noted in the prologue, I couldn't imagine that it would ever be livable, but he moved into the renovated home two years later, complete with a mailbox shaped like a caboose, on Lexington Avenue facing the park. His backyard abutted the BeltLine, where the Westside Trail broke ground late in 2014. Just across the corridor was the BeltLine Urban Farm, where Andy Friedberg and Andrea Ness were struggling to renew the soil on the former Harmon Brothers bus repair site.*

Poventud's enthusiasm and multiple contacts helped turn Adair Park into one of the more desirable neighborhoods on the southwestern side of town, as he attracted friends and acquaintances to fix up derelict homes, though 10 percent remained vacant. A certain tension now existed between Adair Park and Pittsburgh, just across Metropolitan Parkway to the east. Many Pittsburgh residents felt that Adair Park people looked down their noses at them.

Idealistic about turning his home into a community meeting place, Poventud initially welcomed Christopher and Brandon, two black kids who lived down the street with their mother, who had eleven children. I met them when I stayed overnight at Poventud's house, soon after he moved in. But when the kids repeatedly stole from his home, he reluctantly banned them. Three years later, as Poventud and one of the boys watched bulldozers making way for the Westside Trail, he explained how great the trail would be when it was finished. After a moment's thought, the boy asked, "Are they building it for the white people or the black people?" Shaken, Poventud answered, "For all of us."

A few months later, that family was evicted. Poventud posted on Facebook, "This boy, his mom and his 10 siblings' stuff was all out in the front yard getting rained on. Such mixed emotions. Those kids, I've worked with most of them the last three years around the house, with their bikes, and on the BeltLine cleaning up, paying them with my time, water, soda, and some extra money here and there. The house was a problem for the street, no question, but those kids. Uprooted once again." Without more progress on affordable housing, such disturbing evictions would likely continue as the Westside Trail progressed.

This Adair Park family's plight was not unusual. Most poor American renters spend over half of their income on housing, and one in eight fear being thrown out. "Fewer and fewer families can afford a roof over their head," wrote Matthew Desmond in his 2016 book, *Evicted: Poverty*

---

* On Earth Day in 2012, I joined community volunteers, who lugged concrete, old tires, wire, and much other junk to huge dumpsters in preparation for a farm that would turn an illegal garbage dump into a source of much-needed fresh produce.

and Profit in the American City. "This is among the most urgent and pressing issues facing America today."[*]

Matt Garbett, a writer and community organizer who had managed to live in Atlanta without a car since 1995, was one of Poventud's friends who had moved to Adair Park when his Old Fourth Ward neighborhood became too expensive and overdeveloped for his taste. He took me for a walk through Adair Park, past the Bearings Bike Shop and over the Belt-Line Westside Trail on Murphy Avenue. Garbett then ducked through a hole in the wire fence and into the old State Farmers Market, abandoned for decades, which had operated there from the 1940s into the 1960s. I followed him into an intriguing world of derelict buildings acquired in 2014 by Atlanta BeltLine, Inc. (ABI).

ABI issued a "request for proposals" for the sixteen-acre site, which might include affordable housing, small shops, businesses, and perhaps (appropriate for its history) a farmers' market. Garbett opposed the typical Atlanta scenario in which one developer took over with a single master plan. "Grow slower, and appropriately scale," he advised. "Mix it up. If one portion fails, someone goes out, someone goes in." Whatever happened would certainly be an improvement, although some of the open pavilions were beautiful and could be preserved.

"THE ODDS ARE _NEVER_ IN OUR FAVOR," a fading red-painted message on one building stated, but that may no longer be true—and besides, it was lettered by the crew of *The Hunger Games*, partially filmed here, part of a movie industry boom in the metro Atlanta area due to state tax credits, inexpensive labor and housing, and (in this case) ready-made postapocalyptic-looking stage sets.

West End

The West End neighborhood, just to the northwest of Adair Park, actually predates the city of Atlanta, having been named the village of Whitehall in 1830. Annexed to Atlanta in 1894, by the turn of the twentieth century, it had become an upper-class white suburb, though a small black community lived in its northern section. West End turned majority

---

[*] Matthew Desmond conducted research for *Evicted* in Milwaukee. With nearly 600,000 people living in 97 square miles, Milwaukee has greater population density than Atlanta, with its 450,000 people in 132 square miles, but the two cities have similar racial/economic segregation.

black during the white-flight era of the 1960s and 1970s, experiencing a concomitant decline in socioeconomic level.

In July 2013, for my West End sojourn, Liz Ragsdale let me stay in the upstairs guest room of her Atwood Street home, filled with books and African sculpture. She had moved there in 1969, just as most whites were fleeing; only two houses on her block were then occupied. (The block now looks pretty good.) Ragsdale told me her life story. Born the fourth of seven children in Atlanta in 1935, she grew up extremely poor in the Summerhill neighborhood. When she was seven, white women from Grant Park brought her to their homes to iron, until she borrowed a white child's comb, and the mother scolded, "Don't let a nigger use your comb." Ragsdale vowed never to work for whites again.

When she was sixteen, she got pregnant with her only child, Tony, but the father moved to California, and she raised Tony alone. She quit school after the tenth grade. At nineteen, she married Jack Ragsdale, whose father owned a limousine service for funeral homes. "I discovered he had nothing either, he just lived off his parents." The marriage lasted three years. For another four years, she became the kept mistress of a black card shark. "I had an apartment, diamond ring, furs, and a car." Then she met Lucius Waters, whose parents both taught at Booker T. Washington High School. Though she and Lucius, nicknamed Jelly, never married, they were a couple, living separately, for fifty years until his death.

Ragsdale worked as a waitress, then in a General Motors factory for nine years. She learned to hustle to make money, buying and reselling cars. "I take care of myself financially and emotionally," she said. "I want to be independent. The less I need, the more I get." At seventy-eight, Ragsdale was taking yoga classes ("I'm the oldest one there and have to pull myself off the floor") and tai chi. She also enjoyed traveling, especially to Jamaica.

Ragsdale didn't know much about the BeltLine's Westside Trail, but she asked me if it would really make much difference. "Will it keep these crackheads out of the neighborhood?" I told her that I hoped it would lead to an improved community, but I didn't know for sure. We walked down Atwood to Ralph David Abernathy Boulevard, renamed for the civil rights leader (formerly Gordon Street, after a Confederate general), and turned left, walking past a dollar store and auto parts shop to reach Q-Time, a soul food buffet, where we ate delicious, greasy barbecued spare ribs.

On another January visit, I returned to Q-Time for breakfast, where I sat with a sixty-one-year-old man, there for a weekly bible study group. He had ridden his bike, having lost his driver's license in 1999. He told me that he had been in and out of jail numerous times, had been an alcoholic and used cocaine and marijuana, and then had become a born-again Christian and gone straight for four years. He made his living as an auto mechanic with his own tools. This was a cold, rainy day, and he said he would do small things like changing wipers but didn't want to crawl under a car unless he could find a dry piece of cardboard.

He usually hung out at O'Reilly's Auto Parts down Abernathy, looking for jobs. He said that Abernathy was "the hood" and not safe at night, all the way west to Cascade Avenue.* He showed me a photo of a grandson and said he had four children "as far as I know," all with different women. He had never married. I found understanding him very difficult—almost as if I were in a foreign country—even when he slowed down, because he spoke black English vernacular. He told me at one point that we were all just "flush," but I couldn't figure out what he meant until he pulled at the skin on his hand: "flesh."

After breakfast, I walked further down Abernathy to the Wren's Nest, the Victorian-style home of Joel Chandler Harris (1848–1908), author of the Brer Rabbit stories. Since his death, the home has served as a Harris museum. In the backyard were a small amphitheater and a path of concrete steps, inscribed with the names of the West End "Queens of Festival," from 1909 to 1983, all of them white. Harris's dialect-laden stories, told by old black Uncle Remus, have come under fire for racist stereotyping, but Harris actually portrayed Remus as a covert trickster. As early as 1878, Harris suggested "mowing down the old prejudices," and in 1905, a year prior to the Atlanta Race Riot, he encouraged "the obliteration of prejudice against the blacks, the demand for a square deal, and the uplifting of both races."

Jeri McWilliams, an African American who grew up in West End, gave me a tour of the Wren's Nest and explained Harris's liberal racial attitude to me. She revealed that in the 1960s, as a teenager, she used to walk by the Wren's Nest, never knowing what it was. One day, she and a

---

* One West End resident said that as long as you were careful at night, it was safe, but he went on to tell me, "One night I was on Peeples Street, turning onto Oglethorpe, and I didn't see a group of five teenagers till I was right on them. They shuffled around behind me and came back and robbed me. They had two guns."

friend saw some animal characters on the lawn, so they rang the doorbell to ask what it was all about. Two elderly white women appeared. "We don't let niggers in here," one said, and slammed the door. The museum was not integrated until 1985, after a lawsuit. Nonetheless, McWilliams applied for a job in 1998 and had been working there ever since.

West End is no food desert, with Kroger and Big Bear grocery stores, several community vegetable gardens, and three vegetarian restaurants. There is also a West End MARTA station. With some elegant homes— including the Hammonds House Museum, featuring African art, much of it collected by the late Otis Hammonds, a black physician who lived there—West End is on the National Registry of Historic Places. Like Adair Park, it is on the way back, but it most certainly has a way to go.

So does the Westview neighborhood just to its west, which includes the pastoral six-hundred-acre Westview Cemetery, established in 1884 for prominent white decedents after the downtown Oakland Cemetery filled up.* I went to Westview partly to find the crypt of my maternal grandfather and other relatives in the castle-like mausoleum there. But near the entrance, on a prominent knoll surrounded by the graves of Confederate veterans, I also found a tall statue of the "Unknown Confederate Soldier," in whose hand a tattered Confederate flag fluttered in the wind. I was amazed that no one had objected, since the surrounding area is now African American.

A few blocks from the cemetery, I visited the KIPP Strive Academy on Lucile Avenue,** adjacent to the BeltLine West End Trail. This charter public school is housed in the former Joel Chandler Harris School, which had been abandoned and condemned before KIPP renovated it and opened in 2009. One of eight KIPP schools in metro Atlanta, it serves about 320 students in grades five through eight, mostly poor black kids from West End, Westview, and other southwestern Atlanta neighborhoods.

---

* The South-View Cemetery, in southern Atlanta on Jonesboro Road, was established in 1886 for African Americans. Martin Luther King Jr. was interred there, along with his father, before the body was moved to the Martin Luther King Jr. National Historic Site on Auburn Avenue.

** KIPP stands for Knowledge Is Power Program, begun by two Teach for America teachers in 1994. It emphasizes call-and-response learning, long school days, and high expectations. Some critics complain about its strict standards and college-bound orientation. In West Atlanta I also visited the Kindezi School, a different charter approach, also with outstanding results.

Confederate statue and tattered flag at Westview Cemetery

I visited on May 13, 2015, with only two days of regular school left. Signs in the halls read, "Attention: Only Positive Attitudes Allowed in This Area" and "We Are All College Bound." In a sixth-grade science class, students filled out forms asking what they had learned about themselves that year. A girl named Jada wrote, "I learned that being good and smart got me places. I didn't know that I fit in & get along with everybody."

Science teacher Joshua Mathews then led a lesson on the phases of the moon. His students enthusiastically waved their hands to answer questions. Mathews would give them thirty timed seconds to complete a task, and if he wanted to verify that they all understood, he would say, "Kapish?" and they would yell back, "Kapish!" Having taught in both high schools and elementary schools, I was impressed. The KIPP results were even more impressive. By the end of sixth grade, all of its enrollees outperformed average Georgia students in reading, science, social studies, and math.

Washington Park

Once completed, the first section of the BeltLine Westside Trail will end at Washington Park. To get there, I drove north from West End on Joseph E. Lowery Boulevard (once Ashby Street, named after another Confederate general, and in the 1960s a hotly contested boundary line between white and black neighborhoods). I drove past the Atlanta University Center complex of historically black campuses on the right and crossed Martin Luther King Jr. Drive.

If I turned right on MLK, I knew I would pass the bankrupt campus of Morris Brown College, including its abandoned, decaying stadium, built in time for the 1996 Olympics, and then I would run into the massive construction site of the new Mercedes-Benz Stadium, funded by billionaire Arthur Blank, which would be home to the Atlanta Falcons football team as well as a new professional soccer team, Atlanta United FC. I pondered how the two stadiums, about a half mile apart, represented a glaring contrast between the two sides of Atlanta—extreme wealth and intense poverty.

But I stayed on Lowery, and just past the Ashby MARTA station, I turned left on Lena Street to reach Washington Park a block away, on the right. It was the first Atlanta park and neighborhood created specifically for African Americans in the 1920s by black developer Heman Perry and once a source of great racial pride. With its indoor swimming pool ("natatorium"), baseball field, and tennis courts, the park is still appealing, but the surrounding neighborhood declined, as middle-class African Americans moved out during the last decades of the twentieth century.

I visited the park one warm Sunday night in September 2015. A tailgate party was in full swing, with television sets showing football games and boom boxes blaring from the backs of pickup trucks. Some folks were grilling chicken for sale. I was the only white person there. I asked around to find someone who lived nearby, but although friendly, everyone had driven some distance to get there. Finally someone pointed me to a man nursing a beer. Yes, he had grown up in Washington Park and still lived here. I explained that I was writing a book about Atlanta, with a focus on the BeltLine and its neighborhoods. He wrote his name in flowing cursive script, Cherine Pierce Carter, but he was called Benny.

We walked through the park and onto the dirt path of the Westside Trail under construction. Carter was scornful, not seeing how it would bring needed jobs to the area. "These are all houses along here," he explained, and the BeltLine would just make it easier for thieves to approach and get away.

I said that the trail would be well lit and patrolled by police and would connect people to other neighborhoods, but he remained unimpressed. At his suggestion, we got off the trail, taking a left onto Harwell, a one-block street just south of the park, where he had grown up, raised by his white grandfather and black grandmother. Ten out of the forty-four homes on the street were empty and boarded up.

Carter, born in 1962, said that Harwell had had no vacant houses when he was a boy. Nearby there had been a theater, flower shop, dry cleaner, grocery, cafeteria, and clubs, now all gone. What had happened to his family home? It had been foreclosed, lost to the bank somehow, and was now rented out. We knocked on the door, and I met Clayton Griffith, a young white man who gave me his contact information.

Benny Carter and I continued down Harwell and turned up Ollie Street, heading back to the park, past a large, vacant YMCA building. I asked how he supported himself. He showed up at 5 a.m. on a particular street corner, where Labor Ready chose temporary laborers for minimum-wage work. I asked why he didn't go to Westside Works, the job program set up by the Blank Foundation, mostly to train locals for construction jobs on the $1.5 billion stadium Arthur Blank was building. "I tried that," he said, "but I couldn't pass the math test." He complained that he had been doing construction work for years, but they didn't care. In his younger years, he had dealt drugs, though he insisted he never took them. He had been in and out of prison several times, but at least then he'd been in a safe place. "Sometimes prison saves your life." For the last eighteen years, he had gone straight, painting houses, laying floors, and doing other odd jobs. "Ain't nothing else I *can* do."

Several months later, I returned to Washington Park, having arranged to see Clayton Griffith on Harwell Street. Born in a northern Atlanta suburb in 1982, Griffith held a bachelor's in ecology from the University of Georgia and a master's in city planning from Georgia Tech. He had studied invasive species in Chile, done desert restoration in California, and worked for an environmental engineering firm in Norcross, Georgia. But he hated that job, which helped build big box stores, so now he drove a mobile food truck for Waffle House and taught tennis part time.* He used to live in the Old Fourth Ward, but it got too expensive, so he rented a room with two other men in this house. It didn't look like the landlord did much maintenance, since water from a recent heavy rain dripped into the kitchen.

---

* Clayton Griffith was a runner. In July 2015, with three dozen other men, he ran clockwise around the entire BeltLine (including active railroad tracks), starting and ending in Washington Park. It took him about five hours.

Griffith said a white policeman lived across the street, but all other Harwell neighbors were African American. He had befriended several black kids on the street, who would play football in the backyard. "I give them drinks and ice cream, keep an eye out on them. We can be good role models, show them to work hard, do their homework, and stay off the streets."

As if on cue, a fifteen-year-old boy named Willy came up on the porch. "Clayton, where you been?" When Griffith said he's been working crazy hours on the food truck, Willy became excited—he would love to find a job on a food truck because he'd heard you got a lot of tips. Griffith cautioned him to stay in school. Willy attended Booker T. Washington High School, where he said there were a lot of serious fights in the halls, which he stayed out of. I asked him if he had considered college. Yes, he wanted to get a football scholarship. A freshman, he was about five-eight and 150 pounds, so I thought this an unlikely possibility. Willy had no real idea what the Westside Trail at the end of his street would be, though he'd heard they were going to put a train on it again. I asked if Willy swam in the local park pool, and he said he couldn't go in the deep end. In other words, though he had grown up within a block of a public pool, he couldn't swim. He did, however, ride an illegal dirt bike in the park and told us, with gleeful motor sound effects, how he had avoided the police.

After I left Harwell, I went up Ollie to the end of the park and turned onto Michigan Avenue to the address Benny Carter had written down, because the cell phone number he had given me didn't work. It turned out to be his mother's house, but just then Carter walked up. He hadn't been able to pay the cell phone bill. Again we discussed how the neighborhood had gone downhill. Even dealing drugs was more deadly now, due to guns and a violent culture he attributed to rap music. As we spoke, a young black man, assisted by an older woman, staggered by. At first I thought he might have cerebral palsy, but he was falling-down drunk. "He be that way every day," Carter said, shaking his head.

Grove Park and Bankhead

Driving another few miles up Lowery would bring me across Joseph E. Boone Boulevard (formerly Simpson Street) to Donald E. Hollowell Boulevard (formerly Bankhead Highway). To the right is the notorious English Avenue neighborhood known as "The Bluff," with its drugs, prostitutes, and empty buildings, and to its south, Vine City, almost as bad, where Martin Luther King Jr. lived at the time he was killed.

On another day I drove west on Hollowell, past empty buildings, junkyards, pawn shops, and a Church's Chicken. I crossed Marietta Boulevard and noticed Maddox Park on the left, a gate barring the entrance. The BeltLine will supposedly run alongside this park someday, although this segment will be the last built because active rails make the northwest the most difficult section.

On the right, a large building behind a parking lot holds the Fulton County Department of Family and Child Services, just before the Bankhead MARTA station. Even from the parking lot, there is no easy walk to or from this end of the branch line—symbolic of a broken promise to extend the line to Perry Homes public housing, now razed and part of the future Westside Park, with its huge quarry, which lies just to the northwest.

I drove a bit further on Hollowell and turned left on Holly Street, searching for the address where I would spend this late December night here in the Grove Park neighborhood. I had wangled an invitation through a friend of a friend to stay with Gary (not his real name), an African American in his late forties. The house next door to his small brick home was empty. Down the street, on a boarded-up apartment complex, a spray-painted message on the bricks read, "REBUILD ME! *IGNORE*NCE DEFEATED."

Empty apartment complex on Holly Street in Grove Park

Gary welcomed me into a living room redolent of cigarette smoke; on the TV a loud cable channel sold hair products. He apologized that the toilet wasn't functional and the heat wasn't working. It turned out to be his mother's house. She had recently moved in with her daughter's family. Gary, who was unemployed, now lived there with two other men.

Gary had lit all the gas stovetop burners to heat the house, which was unsafe, so I drove him five miles to the Walmart on Howell Mill Road and bought a couple of cheap electric space heaters. Without a car, it took him a long time to walk to and from the nearest store, the Super Giant Food, a couple of miles west down Hollowell. We drove around Grove Park for a while as he told me his career history. Mostly, he had restocked grocery store shelves at night, but as the neighborhood declined, he had to drive over twenty miles for a job. Then he reloaded fire extinguishers for a while.

We stopped on Hollowell at Bankhead Seafood, a hole-in-the-wall joint open several afternoons a week, where I stood in line to buy two huge take-out helpings of fresh-fried fish for $5 a plate, plus a $7 sweet potato pie.

We went back and ate by the space heaters. Fried food isn't good for you, but the meal was delicious, melting in our mouths, and much more than we could eat. (As residents complained in a community survey, there are no real restaurants in Grove Park.)

I slept in Gary's mother's room, which was poignant, because most of her belongings were still on the dresser, including childhood photos of Gary and his sister, nicely dressed for Sunday school. His parents had paid for a half page in his high school yearbook, which displayed a picture of Gary wearing his mortarboard with the message "To our son Gary, Congratulations and Much Success in the future." I got up once in the night to pee behind a tree in the backyard. I found later that a housemate had stuffed most of a toilet paper roll down the john and the thermostat was broken.

Gary was talkative and likable. I was surprised to find out later that he was also a drug addict. He entered rehab a few months later, but as this book went to press, he was in jail for petty theft. The house had suffered two fires due to faulty wiring, and awaited repairs.

Edwin Wiley Grove founded Grove Park in 1913 as an upscale white suburb originally called Fortified Hills (a reference to Civil War battles). He had made his fortune with Grove's Tasteless Chill Tonic, a

Inside Maddox Park poolhouse, 2014. It was renovated, along with the pool, in 2016.

patent medicine with quinine. Among other hotels, he built the magnif-icent Grove Park Inn in Asheville, North Carolina, featuring huge stone fireplaces, as well as Atkins Park in Midtown Atlanta. Here in Grove Park, he named the streets for his daughters and granddaughters—Holly, Emily, Charlotte, Eugenia, Evelyn, Elizabeth, Margaret, Hortense—though there is also an Edwin Place. A 1913 ad boasted of the "beautiful stone houses and bungalows." The majority are still standing, though mostly in disrepair. In a now familiar scenario, whites had fled when blacks moved in, and most of the nearby industries failed, taking with them the jobs they had provided.

On another occasion I met Reverend Larry Hill at the day-care center he and his wife ran near the Bankhead MARTA, grandly called Northwest Youth Power Early Learning Center. Every day his vans picked up preschoolers from their homes, where single mothers or grand-mothers cared for most of them. The school overlooks Maddox Park, where Hill, a muscular African American (a former powerlifter), would have liked to take the children on outings, but the park had become the domain of alcoholics and homeless men by day, drug dealers and prosti-tutes by night. No one would bring children there for a picnic. Hill took me to the park, where I saw the cracked, waterless swimming pool and the empty stone gazebo on the knoll.*

At least the tennis court had a net, and so did the basketball hoops. Inside the handsome stone building by the pool were blankets and other evidence of a homeless encampment.

Then Hill drove me on a tour of Bankhead, to the east of Grove Park, and the adjacent English Avenue community, ravaged as badly as the Pittsburgh neighborhood, with block after block of shuttered homes. On Neal Street we passed a small, well-kept brick ranch, a rarity in the neighborhood. In the picture window was a painting of an elderly black woman, Kathryn Johnston, ninety-two, whom Atlanta police shot multiple times in 2006 during a botched drug raid on her home. They'd had the wrong house, and her home now stood empty, a kind of shrine to the tragic incident.

Reverend Hill, who never attended college, was pastor of the Word of God Ministries and held services every other Sunday at his church further west on Hollowell, in a former nightclub called the Bankhead Bounce, immortalized in several rap songs. I attended a service there, with rousing gospel music, enthusiastic call and response, and a sermon during which Hill built from quiet contemplation to shouted exhortation. He focused on the story of Job, saying that even if God took all you owned, you had to stay humble and connected to the Lord. He also observed that gas prices were higher in poor neighborhoods, that single women headed 40 percent of the households in northwestern Atlanta, and that "young people are not only killing themselves but killing others at the drop of a hat."

A 2011 pseudodocumentary called *Snow on Tha Bluff* illustrated Hill's point all too well. Filmed in the English Avenue area, it starred twenty-five-year-old Curtis Snow (his real name), a black crack cocaine dealer who wielded guns, stole, and sold drugs; had been shot, imprisoned, and released; and cared for his infant son while he packaged drugs. In one scene, he visited his grandmother, who told him that death was just a step away and that she hoped he would live to fifty. Only months after the film was released, a box-cutter gash to the neck nearly killed him.

---

* Another day I returned to the park and found two African American men in the gazebo. One had an extremely long fingernail on his left hand, apparently for dividing, then presumably sniffing, cocaine. He told me he owned a food mart on English Avenue.

Hip-hop star T. I. (Clifford Harris Jr.) released a song about Snow. Born in Bankhead in 1980, T. I. was raised by his grandparents and became a drug dealer after dropping out of high school, writing lyrics such as "Westside of the A-Town, nigga you don't know no better nigga, Bankhead! . . . See me ridin' through Atlanta. . . . Make these bitches wonder what he be in so much trouble for." After achieving wealth and fame, T. I. moved from Bankhead to an estate in Buckhead.*

Praying for Life and Renewal

I attended another service on Hollowell at Paradise Missionary Baptist Church, where I had already met and interviewed Pastor Charles A. Harper III. Retired from a career at MARTA, he earned a doctorate in theology from the Interdenominational Theological Center at Morehouse, then in 2004 became the minister at Paradise. The church, originally established in 1870 in the Atlanta Summerhill community as the Pleasant Hill Baptist Church, had moved six years later to a larger building and become the Reed Street Baptist Church. In 1965, the city razed the church to build Atlanta Stadium, so the congregation moved to its current Grove Park location, where fleeing whites had left a vacant church.

Harper, born in 1932, grew up in Atlanta in a middle-class black family that valued education. He attended Morehouse before joining MARTA. In his sermons, he said, "I try to encourage people, to give them hope. People don't come to church to catch hell, but to be affirmed, encouraged, and loved." He practiced some traditional black preaching, waxing alternately loud and soft. "I try to remain relevant and effective, and I will attack social issues." At the service I attended, Harper introduced me by saying that his wife had texted him, "There's a white guy here." I was indeed the only white worshiper. Sundays are the most segregated days in Atlanta.

One of the deacons began the service. "Give praise to the Lord," he said. "God gave you another day. You could have been on your cold slab, but you woke up. You might not have the house or the car you want, but

---

* T. I. also starred in *ATL*, a movie about black buddies graduating from high school. It explores the two worlds of Atlanta, with the main character from the inner city falling in love with a girl whose father has "made it" as a wealthy businessman who lives in Buckhead.

you have the clothes on your back." He mentioned that another neighborhood shooting had taken place the day before. Then a guest pastor held forth, and finally Reverend Harper gave a sermon on Paul's First Letter to the Corinthians, in which he admonished people to pull together. "We can't all be chiefs," Harper said. "Somebody has to take the garbage out. In fact, I was here picking up paper in the sanctuary yesterday." Like many African American services, this one lasted nearly three hours, and I got fidgety,* but the music and atmosphere were inspiring.

In a white church, you often get a few moments to greet those in nearby pews. Here, people took fifteen minutes to circulate, hugging and welcoming one another (and me). I was particularly taken by the little boys with white shirts and bow ties and the elderly women sporting elegant plumed hats. I met ninety-six-year-old Dorothy Spear, who had attended for eighty-seven years, starting back at the Reed Street location.

Charles Harper later introduced me to Chuck Johnston, a white man who had moved to Grove Park with his wife, JoElyn, in the fall of 2011, at age seventy-one. A lifelong English teacher and school administrator, Johnston had retired to an upscale gated golf community in Buckhead, but when his daughter Jane and her husband moved to Grove Park, and they saw the profound needs and possibilities, Chuck and JoElyn moved two doors down on Evelyn Way. "The idea of racial reconciliation was at the forefront of our minds," he told me. They were inspired by Bob Lupton's idea of "intentional neighboring," getting to know the community. "That was our only motivation. We weren't planning to save the neighborhood, we just wanted to be a part of it."

They attended Atlanta Westside Presbyterian Church, whose dynamic young white minister, Walter Henegar, had moved from the suburbs and held services in the nearby Defoor Community Center. Henegar wanted a multiracial, multicultural congregation, but he mostly attracted young middle-class whites who heard about the cool new church.

The day I went to the service, Johnston asked me to drive Mike, one of the few African American churchgoers from Grove Park, to the hardware store and then home. In his early fifties, Mike told me that the Johnstons were great advocates, but he still drank and took drugs. In early 2016, I checked and learned that he had recently dried out at

---

* Near the end, I really had to go to the bathroom, an embarrassing walk to the front of the church. There I met an elderly parishioner who made me feel better by saying, "I like to sprung a leak."

a thirty-day clinic and come back determined to stay straight, but only time would tell.

With funding from a philanthropic former student, Johnston started Grove Park Renewal and bought thirty-nine derelict homes in the neighborhood, gradually getting them fixed up and selling them at cost or tearing down those that were too far gone. I visited the Johnstons in their restored bungalow, with JoElyn's art gracing the walls. Chuck told me, "This is the most enjoyable sense of neighborhood I've had in my life." He had become particularly close to Arian Johnston (no relation), his next-door neighbor, who moved to the community in 1962, in the midst of white flight. She had raised three daughters there, two of whom graduated from Spelman College. He took me next door to meet Mrs. Johnston, eighty-seven, and one of her daughters. They told me that in the fall of 1962, just before the academic year began, disgruntled whites had burned Grove Park Elementary School, so the students had to start school in temporary trailers.

Life in Grove Park had its challenges for Chuck and JoElyn Johnston. "There are obvious prostitutes here. If I acknowledge them in any way, they come to my car. We know which are the drug houses. Around the corner, in a house on Madrona Street, they found the bodies of two murdered prostitutes." The Johnstons' home has been robbed twice (both times while they were at church), and they've had their spare tires and car batteries stolen. Surely, they must have considered leaving? "No, we will stay here," Johnston said. "I think we will not burn out. Our relationship with our immediate neighbors is so sweet, we are helping in our small way, and it's great having our daughter, son-in-law, and three grandchildren two doors away."[*]

Not all do-gooders in Grove Park (or elsewhere) are white. LaTonya Gates-Boston and her husband, Carlos Boston, both African Americans, ran an after-school program called PAWKids[**] on Hollowell, in a former crack house right next door to Bankhead Seafood. Gates-Boston was

---

[*] Jane Gilbert, the Johnston's daughter and neighbor, kept a blog with her thoughts and insights at www.compellinggrace.com. On October 1, 2014, she wrote, "Do not show up in a neighborhood as if you are the doctor and those already there are the perpetually sick! Who are you to be so arrogant? It is so typical of white people to assume the position of power, to come in and take over, to tell others what they need rather than listening and waiting and learning."

[**] PAW stood for Paradise Atlanta Westside, named for the two churches that helped the program: Paradise Missionary Baptist and Atlanta Westside Presbyterian, where Gates-Boston attended church.

born in 1975 in a Georgia prison to a heroin-addicted mother and father. Well-educated aunts had kept her off that path, and Chuck and JoElyn Johnston had encouraged and helped her and her two children. Now she was trying to do the same for twenty-four impoverished children in Grove Park, from 2:30 p.m. to 6 p.m. on school days. She insisted that parents donate time in the program. "I have to earn their trust," she said. "I want to help, but they have to come alongside."

Most of the children had been severely traumatized. Few had ever sat down to a family meal. Several bagged their excrement and put it in the trash because that's what they did at home—either because the water had been shut off for unpaid bills or the toilet was hopelessly plugged. "We are teaching them the most basic things," Gates-Boston said. She and her husband were there every morning as well, maintaining a food pantry and offering counseling and sewing classes for parents (mostly single mothers) or rides to medical care or a grocery store.

One preschool child in particular stuck in Gates-Boston's mind and heart. "She was about three and came with her older siblings to our first Saturday picnic." The child was barefoot, with a shaved head because of lice or impetigo. The teacher got permission to take her home for the evening, where she gave her a big bubble bath, dressed her nicely, and put on a decorative headband. The child looked at herself in a big mirror and said in wonder, "I'm pretty." Since then, the girl's family had been evicted three times. The mother, a prostitute, is stuck in place by intergenerational poverty, and without a miracle, her children will be too.

Proctor Creek Runs Free—and Filthy for Now

One spring day, just after driving west past the Bankhead MARTA station, I turned right off Hollowell and parked in front of a locked gate. I walked past it into the large vacant parking lot and abandoned buildings of Bankhead Enterprises. Around the farthest warehouse, I crawled through a fence and found a footpath following Proctor Creek. As I strolled along, the sun sparkled off water riffling over flat shoals of rock. Little waterfalls. Wildflowers. A kingfisher. I could have been in the north Georgia mountains.

Proctor Creek's watershed is the only one that lies entirely within the Atlanta city limits. Its tributaries begin farther south near the downtown Gulch, Georgia World Congress Center, Georgia Dome, Atlanta

Proctor Creek downstream from Maddox Park, polluted but beautiful

University Center, and Mozley Park, but they are mostly piped, buried, and polluted by runoff and sewer overflows until the creek resurfaces on the west side of Maddox Park, between Parks and Recreation greenhouses and the MARTA tracks. There a concrete-encased sewage line creates an unplanned dam, trapping a fetid, junk-ridden cesspool nicknamed Mosquito Hole, before the stream flows over the top. It's little wonder that in 2015 west side residents protested with signs that read, "Stop Poop in Our Creeks."

Debra Edelson, head of the nonprofit Emerald Corridor Foundation, has big plans for the creek, beginning with a nine-acre park adjacent to Maddox Park, just off Hollowell, south of the Bankhead MARTA station. Edelson, who led redevelopment of the New York City High Line and worked for the Trust for Public Land's Georgia office, helped win a $280,000 grant from the National Park Service for Proctor Park, which will include a nature center, boardwalk paths, and wetland marshes designed to help clean the polluted waters of Proctor Creek. Eventually, a seven-mile trail along the reclaimed creek will provide access to the planned Westside Park and continue onward to the Chattahoochee. The trail will also connect to the BeltLine as it skirts Maddox Park.

Another day I walked through the future Westside Park, where the former quarry, a magnificent hole in the ground, would be filled with water from the nearby Chattahoochee River. I strolled over acres of rolling fields dotted with wildflowers, along wooded paths, and down by Proctor Creek. At one point I walked along a cracked asphalt path lined with vine-covered, rusting streetlights, vestiges of the razed Perry Homes public housing project.

I could easily envision picnic areas by the lake, hiking and mountain bike trails, sports fields, pavilions, and food stands. Within the next decade, the Westside Park would probably become a reality. But what would become of the Bankhead and Grove Park neighborhoods right next to it? Would the impoverished African Americans living there be welcomed and find employment? Or would higher rents and land values push them out? These are the challenges faced by the BeltLine project.

CHAPTER 13
NORTH BELTLINE: EASY STREETS

··

My neighborhood, Brookwood Hills, is where I caught frogs in the creek behind my house. . . . I had Little League practice in the park and hit tennis balls at the community club. And my first job was at the concession stand at the pool, where I eventually worked my way up to lifeguard. . . . Was it a nice place to grow up? Let's just say Norman Rockwell would have had a field day.

—Ed Helms, actor on *The Office* television show, born 1974

The northern arc of the BeltLine offers a startling contrast to the troubled west side neighborhoods. Gracious, affluent communities—extending from Berkeley Park in northwestern Atlanta over to Ansley Park in the northeast—lie only miles away from devastating poverty and abandoned homes.

Berkeley Park

The living may be easier here, but there's no lack of controversy, as I found during my overnight stay with Dwight Glover in his small, neatly appointed Berkeley Park bungalow on Antone Street. Tucked between Howell Mill Road to the west and Northside Drive to the east, with I-75 slicing across to the north, Berkeley Park in fact has no parks of its own. When the neighborhood was first developed from farmland in the 1920s, the Atlanta Waterworks (Hemphill Station) reservoirs—one on each side of Howell Mill Road just to the south—served as recreation areas.

The waterworks, established in 1892, provided good fishing from the grassy banks. A bandstand hosted concerts. In the 1950s, the city built an attractive stone lodge along with a picnic pavilion with barbecue pits. The white residents, many of whom worked at the nearby steel mill (now Atlantic Station) or railroad, enjoyed spending time there—at least they did until the 1996 Atlanta Olympics, when chain-link fences went up, ostensibly for fear that terrorists would poison the waters. Another motivation was shutting out the embarrassing homeless squatters.

An Atlanta native born in 1961, Glover used to run cross-country meets around the waterworks, which the BeltLine should one day pass. In his 2004 *The BeltLine Emerald Necklace* report, Alexander Garvin lamented, "The entire site is restricted from public access," and admonished, "Atlanta must reclaim this magnificent jewel," built on one of the highest points of land between the Chattahoochee and downtown. Glover, who worked for the Newbridge Group, a private equity firm doing mergers and acquisitions, wanted the Atlanta Department of Watershed Management to take down the fences.

So did Chris Palmer, a young English professor at Kennesaw State College who lived in the White Provisions development a bit south on Howell Mill Road, where we met for breakfast at the trendy West Egg Café on the ground floor. In 2010 Palmer started the Atlanta Waterworks Park Facebook page, which depicted families walking and biking by an open reservoir. The Facebook site quickly attracted over 1,500 followers, but the fences remained.

Today Berkeley Park residents are much more diverse than in the past, with some middle-class African Americans and a smattering of Asians and Hispanics. Georgia Tech students skew the ages lower, but there are also longtime residents, such as Ron and Terry Horgan, who got married at the waterworks in 1992, before the fences went up, and raised their children on Antone Street. Terry, an interior designer who moonlit at nearby Ikea in Atlantic Station, enjoyed sharing the small neighborhood with sculptors, artists, and musicians. Ron was an executive chef for years at the Ansley Golf Club.

Anthony Miller, a young black Houston native with a master's degree in educational research, lived with two housemates on Holmes Street in Berkeley Park and tutored affluent white kids in Vinings to the north. "It's a very eclectic neighborhood," Miller observed, with different generations living there and houses of varying architectural styles. "Nothing

Proposed vision, with fences removed, from Waterworks Park Facebook page

is cookie cutter." The community had an antique store, two small independent gyms, a restaurant supply company, a law firm, a glass shop, and two hip-hop recording studios, one owned by Outkast, a pioneering Atlanta rap group. In the early morning hours, residents sometimes heard unmuffled engines, screeching tires, or gunshots near the studio. On the corner of Holmes and Howell Mill sat Sanctuary Village of Power, a small African American church.

Formerly an industrial area near a stockyard, Howell Mill Road near Berkeley Park had in recent years become hip, from the Northside Tavern's grungy blues venue just south of West Egg, up along a corridor of restaurants and retail shops. In May 2015 I walked north up Howell Mill with Sally Flocks of PEDS, as she noted the horrible shape of the sidewalks, the long distances between traffic lights and crossing opportunities, and the way some buildings practically pushed pedestrians out into the street. Supposedly, "Complete Streets" improvements, including bike lanes, will fix these issues in the next few years. Four-lane Northside Drive, running parallel to the east, was even worse, despite multiple improvement plans submitted by Mike Dobbins's Georgia Tech students over the years.

Walking north, just before the fenced waterworks, I could have turned down Huff Road to the left for a block, then taken another left on Foster Street, dead-ending at the Goat Farm, one of those strange historical leftover places that only Atlanta, with its lack of density or planning, could offer. The crumbling brick walls shelter the remains of a cotton machinery factory built in the 1880s and used during World War II to produce ammunition and mortars. Today it serves as a venue for rock concerts and contemporary dance and houses a funky cafe/library, an organic farm (yes, with grazing goats), an education center, and creative artists' studios.

I didn't visit the Goat Farm that day. With Sally Flocks I continued walking up Howell Mill, past the settling ponds for water about to be treated (only feet away—I could have lobbed a Coke or pesticide can over the fence into the ponds). We turned right on 17th Street, which had no sidewalk, followed by a quick left onto Reservoir Drive (the street sign misspelled it Reservior), past trees, to a rural-feeling parking lot. Not far behind the fence stood the unused waterworks stone lodge.

Further up Howell Mill, on the southern edge of Berkeley Park, a right onto Trabert Avenue would have brought us to a dead end at Monday Night Brewing, one of Atlanta's new microbreweries. Its enthusiastic young owners, along with many other local businesses, yearn for the waterworks fences to come down, since the green open space could become a community hub to attract more customers. Monday Night Brewing has hosted several fund-raisers to promote an Atlanta Waterworks Park, which Park Pride also supports.

Collier Hills

Across I-75 to the north lies the bucolic Collier Hills neighborhood in southern Buckhead. The community was named for Andrew Jackson Collier, whose parents, Meredith and Elizabeth Collier, acquired extensive land along Peachtree Creek and its tributaries upon their arrival in 1823, when Creek Indians were their nearest neighbors. The couple's fifteen children became prominent citizens, real estate developers, and business owners. Andrew Jackson Collier owned an antebellum gristmill powered by Tanyard Creek, site of one of the bloodiest skirmishes during the Battle of Peachtree Creek on July 20, 1864. Now the BeltLine Northside Trail, a little over a mile long, winds peacefully along Tanyard Creek in the small neighborhood, established in 1941 and built up after World War II.

The simplest way to find the upscale, white Collier Hills neighborhood is to drive north on Northside Drive. As soon as you cross the interstate, the road's character shifts dramatically, from gritty and industrial (anchored by the Dreams Gentlemen's Club strip joint at the southeastern corner) to the rolling, genteel residential hills of southern Buckhead. Turn right onto Echota Drive, go past Greystone, Colland, and Meredith, and you dead-end into Walthall Drive. Turning left takes you past imposing homes set across from the forested, winding Tanyard Creek Park.

That's where I met Barbara Kennedy, who built her large colonial home on Walthall in 1987 and raised two children there. Divorced, she was a freelance financial manager. She was also a severe critic of the PATH Foundation, which oversaw the trail building for the BeltLine, and had invited a young mother, Katherine Montgomery, to join us on this sunny fall day in 2015. Montgomery, who lived on Evergreen Lane and worked at Georgia Tech, had served as the president of the Collier Hills Civic Association for several years.

Montgomery and Kennedy voiced many concerns, which boiled down to their feeling invaded. They did not believe their neighborhood park should be part of a regional BeltLine plan. It had been a pleasant, little-known forested gem, but now there were 5K running races, yoga classes, and people driving in from other parts of the city. Cars parking on Overbrook Drive turned it into a one-lane hazard on weekends. Irresponsible owners failed to clean up after their dogs. The neighborhood had to provide its own poop-bag stations along the trail. Taggers had defaced the bridge under Collier Road until an art mural solved the problem. Others wrote "nasty sayings about girls" on some of the rocks in the creek.

Crime was another huge concern. Just two weeks before, a thief had broken into a car at the Bitsy Grant Tennis Center, in broad daylight, and run off down the new spur trail to the BeltLine. Someone had once stolen a truck downtown, driven off I-75, abandoned the vehicle on Walthall, then run north on the trail. A few years ago, police questioning a suspicious character on the trail discovered that he was a registered sex offender. I asked if the women were concerned that when the BeltLine was completed, thieves and drug dealers might travel from neighborhoods to the south. "That doesn't concern me much," Montgomery claimed. "I can't believe they would come several miles just to commit crimes here."

That may already have been happening, though. Barbara Kennedy, security chair for the Collier Hills neighborhood, later sent me the

Atlanta police report for a week in September 2015 for Zone 2, which included one incident on Greystone Road: "A neighbor walking heard a window shatter and observed two black males in a black Cadillac STS. A gym bag w/ clothing and a J Bird headset were taken." Like denizens of many other Buckhead neighborhoods, Collier Hills residents paid off-duty police officers to patrol the area.

Then there was the flooding problem. Kennedy showed me where rising waters had come close to her home. The impervious twelve-foot-wide path no doubt added to the problems, she asserted, despite Ed Mc-Brayer's claims that the trail's slant and other design elements would prevent that. She practically spat out the PATH Foundation head's name.

We left the house and walked down the Northside Trail, though Montgomery had to leave shortly. As Kennedy and I continued to walk south, she noted that beavers had gnawed through a tree and pointed to a slope in the woods where someone had found a big circle of rocks— perhaps a sign of devil worship, she thought.

I was skeptical about the satanic cult but did understand that Kennedy and Montgomery might feel proprietary about their neighborhood park, and I didn't doubt that many of their concerns were valid. But as we walked underneath the picturesque wooden trestle over which CSX trains still traveled, I couldn't help thinking that this was a beautiful section of the BeltLine trail, and I only hoped it would connect in a full loop around the city sooner than later. True, the water was still polluted, as signs attested ("WARNING: HEALTH HAZARD"), but it certainly looked lovely as it slid over the flat stones.

I later visited Kakhi Wakefield, who lived on Colland Drive in Collier Hills. The blonde young mother of three girls told me she loved living near the BeltLine Northside Trail, where she often jogged. She and her children could walk down the street, into the park, and right into a children's playground next to the trail. So I did that on my own, turning north this time. I found the informal dog park across a bridge, then skirted the Bobby Jones Golf Course, which ended at Colonial Homes, just south of Peachtree Creek. It would have been a short walk to Peachtree Road, but I turned back and took the spur trail to the tennis center, then back toward my car.

I stopped to chat with several people, including Ken and Rose Rosenberger, empty nesters (an engineer and lawyer) who moved to the

City Park Townhomes off 26th Street in 2013. Twice a day they walked to Ardmore Park to pick up the southern end of the trail with Lucy, their Labrador. At my request, Ken Rosenberg wrote about their experience:

> It's an idyllic little green belt nestled in city neighborhoods. Even on the hottest days, you get a 5 or 10 degree benefit from the shade. Lucy has a plethora of dog friends in the big field. The dogs sniff each other, wag, and run around chasing each other like happy maniacs, and over time the people get to know each other. I usually give Rose and Lucy a head start, since they're in better shape than I am. They'll get all the way down to the end of the golf course and turn around, and I'll meet them 3/4 of the way. Lucy will come running towards me from 50 yards away, smile bright, tongue out.

Brookwood Hills

After passing Collier Hills, the BeltLine streetcar is slotted to follow the CSX railroad tracks just north of Piedmont Hospital, curving to the east before crossing under Peachtree Road, where it will trace the northern boundary of Brookwood Hills, one of the most desirable, well-established neighborhoods in Atlanta. The extension of the Northside Trail, however, will cross Peachtree at grade or on a bridge, probably along Bennett Street to Peachtree Park Drive on the other side of Peachtree, just north of Brookwood Hills.

Subdivided in 1922 on land formerly owned by the Collier family, Brookwood Hills has always featured winding roads, original water oaks planted for shade between the sidewalks and the street, and a variety of large homes in the Tudor, Georgian, Mediterranean, Dutch Colonial, and American Colonial styles. The main roads leading east into the neighborhood off Peachtree are Brighton, Palisades, and Huntington. Until 1952, when Atlanta annexed much of Buckhead, those who lived north of Palisades didn't pay city taxes. This historical anomaly explains why Peachtree Street turns into Peachtree Road as it runs past Palisades. Clear Creek winds around the eastern edge of the community just before merging with Peachtree Creek at its northern boundary.

In the center of Brookwood Hills is a five-acre community recreation center, first created in 1927, where a natural spring was dammed to create a swimming lake, concrete pool, and bathhouse. In 1939, residents formed the Brookwood Hills Community Club, Inc., still the organization that charges dues for use of the pool (no more lake), tennis courts, and park. Especially on hot summer days, this private amenity has always been the center of community life, with popular swimming, diving, and tennis programs.

Brookwood Hills was (and remains) a wonderful place to raise a family or to grow up, which is why three generations of a family have commonly lived there. Kids could ride their bikes on the rolling hills, swing from vines in the woods, or play on the rocks in Clear Creek. They could place pennies to be smashed on the train tracks that ran on two sides of the neighborhood. Their parents could walk to a grocery store (today, a Fresh Market), dry cleaner, hair salon, restaurant, or pharmacy. Or they could jump on a streetcar (until streetcars were stopped) or bus or quickly drive downtown. Brookwood Station (currently the only Amtrak stop in Atlanta) was a short trip across Peachtree. Physicians could walk to their work at Piedmont Hospital. Annual block parties featured a watermelon scavenger hunt, contests, and parades. At Halloween, for over thirty years, resident realtor Sarah Hagood gave away pumpkins to neighborhood families.

After Hurricane Opal knocked down many of the original water oaks in 1995, the neighborhood got together to replant with a variety of oaks, elms, maples, and ginkgoes. In later years, Trees Atlanta helped maintain the urban forest. Residents did battle with Georgia Power to prevent overpruning of the shade trees. In 2012 PEDS awarded the Brookwood Hills Community Club its Golden Shoe Award for a neighborhood effort to fix broken sidewalks and curbs. As Sarah Hagood told me, "We are our own little island here," a safe world unto itself. To keep it safe, off-duty police officers have patrolled the streets since 1979, with Jeff Baxter, head of the police BeltLine patrol, taking the job most recently.

For its first five decades, Brookwood Hills was strictly white, with deeds prohibiting "selling, renting, or otherwise disposing of the property to persons of African descent." Until World War II, however, it was common for African American domestic servants to live in garage or basement apartments. By the late 1940s, black maids arrived for a twelve-hour workday by bus, receiving about $7 a week. In 1971, racial restrictions were finally removed from the bylaws, but there are still few black residents in Brookwood Hills, where renovated homes have sold for

$2 million. The African American couple who had lived there longest worked for IBM and Merrill Lynch.

In the 1970s, to protect their urban oasis, residents (many of them lawyers) fiercely resisted various road or development efforts that would have impinged on the neighborhood. They soundly rejected a proposed extension of Palisades Road over Clear Creek to connect to Armour Drive Industrial Park to the east. To create a protective buffer, they purchased the fifty-five-acre woods along Clear Creek to the east and Peachtree Creek to the north as a nature preserve with a conservation easement. It is therefore not surprising that when Atlanta BeltLine, Inc. (ABI) and the PATH Foundation initially suggested running the Belt-Line trail along Clear Creek, in similar fashion to the peaceful Northside Trail along Tanyard Creek, they ran into a firestorm of opposition from Brookwood Hills residents. The BeltLine planners backed off. Instead, a bike lane from Brookwood Hills up Peachtree may someday connect the neighborhood to the BeltLine.

I visited retired environmental lawyer Jim Stokes twice in his beautiful Palisades Road home, built in 1926, which he has shared with his wife, Esther, a landscape designer, for over three decades. The first time I met him, in April 2012, Stokes was trying to get the T-SPLOST penny transportation tax passed (it failed miserably). Like many liberal, well-educated white Atlantans, he lamented the lack of regional planning in metro Atlanta and was deeply concerned with issues of energy usage, public transit, affordable housing, and inequality. He had served as president of the Georgia Conservancy and on the boards of Sustainable Solutions Georgia, the Livable Communities Council, and other worthy organizations. His wife, Esther, also served on many boards, including the Historic Fourth Ward Park Conservancy and Park Pride.

Jim Stokes was among the leading young lawyers who, in the 1970s, fought to maintain the neighborhood as a protected enclave. In 2015, during my second visit, he was lobbying for a road diet for Peachtree Road that would allow for bike lanes. The issue split the neighborhood, with the younger vanguard favoring the change but most older residents bitterly opposing it. As of 2016, there would be no bike lanes on that section of Peachtree.

From the Stokes home, I walked to the end of Palisades and crossed Huntington to the dirt path winding down to Clear Creek. It was peaceful and green; no one else was there. Then I came back to Huntington Road and walked down to the community park, where happy white children, teens, and adults played tennis, romped in the water, or practiced diving. It reminded me of my own childhood, playing games for hours in the swimming pool.

I couldn't help pondering the stark contrast between this private, thriving Brookwood Hills park and the desolation of Maddox Park in Bankhead, about five miles—just a seventeen-minute drive, according to Google Maps—but a world away.

Yet hip-hop culture and money had already made the jump between those worlds. "Everybody wants to move to Buckhead," observed black singer-songwriter The-Dream (Terius Nash). "And that's not just because it's where the rich white people stay"; it's because "everything [nice] is there." As Nash was growing up, his grandfather used to drive through Buckhead, pointing, "Now *that's* a house." Today Nash lives in one of them, near my childhood home.

In April 2012, after touring Brookwood Hills, I walked up Peachtree past the venerable Darlington apartment building, built in 1951 and featuring the metro Atlanta population sign (nearing 6 million in 2012).* I then crossed Peachtree and walked down short, dead-end Bennett Street, noted for its art galleries but also home to Anytime Cutz, a twenty-four-hour barbershop catering to African American men. There I interviewed master barber William Alonzo Baugh III, then thirty-three, whose clients included rappers Baby D and Alley Boy. Baugh explained cuts such as the Fade, Fair Daddy, and Temple Taper, for which he charged $28 during regular hours, $35 at night. Baugh lived in the barbershop, twenty-four hours a day, catching naps on a cot in the back room. He planned to scale back his hours once he established a loyal clientele. It is no surprise that *Good Hair,* a 2009 documentary about the importance of hair in black culture, featured Atlanta.

Baugh had never heard of the BeltLine trail, which will probably run right by Anytime Cutz. He liked the concept but wished they would hurry up. "In twenty-five years I'll be fifty. I'll be a little too old to walk the whole BeltLine."

---

* The Darlington offered inexpensive rentals, including to people with Section 8 vouchers, and was widely perceived as a local source of crime, drug dealing, and violence.

Armour/Ottley and Piedmont Heights

It isn't entirely clear where the BeltLine trail will head once it skirts north of Brookwood Hills. The BeltLine transit is supposed to take a kind of detour north to the Lindbergh MARTA station, site of a botched transit-oriented development at Lindbergh Center, where Lindbergh crosses Piedmont Road. There are far too many parking garages and not enough amenities close to the station. There's no compelling reason for the trail (or transit) to extend that far north, other than to connect to a rapid transit station. It would make more sense to follow Peachtree Creek east between the Peachtree Hills neighborhood to the north and Brookwood Hills to the south, then turn south and enter the odd little Armour Drive Industrial Park, also known as Armour/Ottley.

It is odd because it has two concrete plants, a lumberyard, and a few other light industries, including the SweetWater Brewing Company, right there in the heart of affluent northeast Atlanta, and additionally odd because there is only one vehicular access point, which runs under multilane I-85, a MARTA line, and the Buford Highway Connector, which is the old I-85, built up on a large, impassable dirt bridge.

Norfolk Southern rail lines run there as well, tunneling under the roads to head south to the abandoned northeastern corridor of land that ABI purchased from Wayne Mason. On that as yet undeveloped stretch, the BeltLine rail and trail could easily run south together into Piedmont Park and then back across Monroe and 10th to meet the already completed Eastside Trail.

But how to get there? As one BeltLine official wrote in 2007, "There is no silver bullet to get from Peachtree Creek to the BeltLine right-of-way on the other side of I-85. The combination of Buford Highway, I-85, MARTA rail, and Norfolk Southern rail amount[s] to a huge challenge for the trail."

Ideally, MARTA would build a new station in Armour/Ottley, since the transit agency's maintenance yards are already there. If Norfolk Southern established an adjacent rail terminal, and the BeltLine streetcar and trail stopped there as well, it would become a multimodal transportation center, obviating the need to go further north to Lindbergh. That would probably cost over $1 billion, however.

Still, the funky Armour/Ottley area has great potential to become a multiuse area that would justify such a transportation hub. The Heights

Armour condos already have 372 residential units. Most evenings, Sweet-Water's is mobbed with happy customers taste-testing beer, and the parallel streets of Armour and Ottley, now named the SweetWater Design District, feature adaptive reuses of old warehouses. For instance, Armour Yards, a loft-office complex with a restaurant and other amenities, offers "a sense of community, blurring the traditional lines between work and play," according to promotional literature that envisions people grabbing a SweetWater brew and strolling the BeltLine.

Armour Drive provides the only entrance to and exit from Armour/Ottley. It dead-ends into Monroe Drive, the western boundary of the next BeltLine neighborhood I visited, Piedmont Heights. Interstate traffic, together with delivery and cement trucks going to and from Armour/Ottley, plagues its residents. The BeltLine trail and transit, once they somehow get through Armour/Ottley and exit through the southern tunnel, will run on the abandoned rail corridor along the western side of this community.

In December 2013 I stayed overnight with Bill and Irene Seay on Rock Springs Road, which runs east-west through the heart of Piedmont Heights. The neighborhood is shaped something like a long isosceles triangle with the narrow end pointing south, where Monroe and Piedmont intersect. Faset J. "Bill" Seay, a retired architect born in 1938 in the North Carolina mountains and an Atlanta resident for nearly five decades, was the perfect host, heavily involved in his community. He and his wife moved to Piedmont Heights in 1999, downsizing from their larger home in nearby Ansley Park.

In the backyard of his Rock Springs Road home, Seay had built himself a small "treehouse" office over the garage, from which he could look out over the treetops and write. As Seay noted in a history of the neighborhood, "Piedmont Heights developed piecemeal over a long period of time," and many commuters pass through it without knowing it is a neighborhood with a name. Yet, settled in 1823, it has a long history by Atlanta standards. A one-room schoolhouse, built beside a spring bubbling out from under a rock, is now the site of Rock Spring Presbyterian Church, a historical landmark at the corner of Piedmont and Rock Springs Road.

In 1925 landscape architect W. L. Monroe bought fifteen acres on what was then called North Boulevard, establishing a plant nursery that thrived for many years. In 1937, the street north of Ponce de Leon was renamed Monroe Drive in his honor (and to distinguish it as a white area as opposed to Boulevard to the south of Ponce). Monroe's former nursery is now the site of Ansley-Monroe Villas, townhomes with a greensward featuring Monroe's old stone fireplaces.

Ansley Mall, Atlanta's third shopping center, was built in 1964 near the intersection of Monroe and Piedmont, just to the east of the BeltLine. I could easily walk from its rear parking lot onto the dirt trail. The mall houses over thirty stores offering a wide variety of shopping. It spawned smaller Ansley II mall across Monroe, and Ansley Square on the other side of Clear Creek.

Up and down either side of Piedmont Drive on the eastern side of Piedmont Heights are more food outlets, ranging from Fat Matt's Rib Shack to Atmosphere, an upscale French restaurant. Small businesses line Piedmont, including a health center, car wash, motor scooter store, bike repair shop, gym, and DUI school.

The area becomes seedier at the top of the Piedmont Heights triangle, where InTown Suites offered cheap rent-by-week rooms for transients.* The area has a number of strip clubs, including the Tattletale Lounge, whose sign proclaims, "Girls Girls Girls, Rockin Atlanta Since 1976." There's also a bowling alley and several auto repair shops.

It's a surprisingly diverse neighborhood. Two-thirds of the residents are white, and a fifth are black, with a smaller number of Hispanics and Asians. The average household income is $81,500, and the median home value just tops $500,000. Yet most residents are renters, and a fifth makes less than $25,000 a year. In the last few years, in anticipation of the Belt-Line, speculation has driven up values, attracting affluent young couples and singles who want to balance work and leisure activities. Old houses are being torn down and replaced by more expensive edifices, including one McMansion of 10,000 square feet.

Bill Seay observed that Piedmont Heights is like a "small town in a big city," offering enough amenities so that it is virtually self-sufficient: "Over 100 businesses include two shopping centers, two major grocery stores . . . and shops providing all manners of goods and services." That includes sixteen restaurants, three banks, two pharmacies, doctors, dentists, veterinarians, two churches, and a private elementary school.

---

* In July 2016, Atlanta developer Paces Properties bought InTown Suites with plans to convert it to a boutique hotel—an indication that Piedmont Heights is becoming a more attractive area.

Piedmont Heights has only one small park, and few streets have sidewalks. Residents, keen for the BeltLine trail to pass nearby, have created a master plan for the neighborhood that includes a road diet for Monroe Drive, roundabout intersections at critical points, and a transformation of Ansley Mall into a town center with small blocks, new streets, and pedestrian plazas interfacing with the BeltLine, which will join long-neglected Clear Creek, where a gristmill stood 175 years ago.

The master plan also calls for removing the dirt bridge under the Buford Highway Connector and bringing the road back down to street level. That would allow several more entrances into Armour/Ottley, better integrating it into the community. The vast dead space under I-85 could house a farmers' market, gathering spaces, and other pedestrian attractions. A neighborhood trail would connect Gotham Way Park to the BeltLine. Now Piedmont Heights only needs the city, Georgia Department of Transportation, and local businesses to make some of it a reality, some day.

Ansley Park

As the BeltLine corridor runs south in a straight line along the former rail track, to its west lies the Ansley Golf Club, created in 1912 by Edwin Ansley, who developed the adjacent Ansley Park neighborhood. After the golf course, the BeltLine continues past the southwestern part of Ansley Park, crosses Piedmont Road, and enters Piedmont Park on its way to the Eastside Trail, thus completing our selective survey of neighborhoods in each Atlanta BeltLine quadrant.

Developer Edwin Ansley, a lawyer, bought the land from heirs of George Washington Collier in 1904. He hired Solon Ruff, a local engineer who had worked with Frederick Law Olmsted, to lay out a spider-web of wide, curvy roads that follow the contours of the rolling hills east of Peachtree (south of Brookwood Hills, developed two decades later), leaving plenty of room for horses and buggies and early automobiles. He laid out five miniparks in low areas.

Ansley promoted his development as the ultimate garden suburb for the upper crust—the "finest, most attractive, most DESIRED residence section in all Atlanta." By 1910 mansions had sprouted along roads called The Prado, Peachtree Circle, Westminster, Yonah, Lafayette, and Maddox Drive, the winners of a pretentious naming contest Ansley sponsored so that, as he put it, "Atlanta will become as cosmopolitan as she is metropolitan." More prosaically, 15th, 16th, and 17th Streets also run off Peachtree Street into the neighborhood. Ansley himself moved into a thirteen-room, five-bath home on The Prado, but failed ventures in Atlanta, New York, and Cuba later forced him to sell the home, and he left the city. His house became the Georgia governor's mansion from 1925 to 1967, but in typical Atlanta fashion, it was razed in 1969.*

Like Brookwood Hills, Ansley Park allowed no black residents. "[Ansley Park] has not and never will have a home belonging to a person of color or occupied by one other than as a servant," an early flier promised, undoubtedly reassuring those shaken by the 1906 race riot. The policy was finally reversed in 1968, when Leon Eplan, a progressive resident and urban planner, circulated a petition opposing racial discrimination against homebuyers, but Ansley Park has remained predominantly white. Although it went through a period when some homes became boarding houses, while hippies, bikers, and drug dealers took over nearby Peachtree Street and Piedmont Park for part of the 1960s and 1970s, the neighborhood today is as popular, attractive, and affluent as it was in 1910. Its homes vary in size and style, many designed by Atlanta's premier architects.

It is hard to believe that druggies and bikers once dominated nearby Peachtree, which has now sprouted skyscrapers in a Midtown renaissance. The High Museum of Art sits just across the street from Ansley Park at the corner of Peachtree and 16th Street, because in 1926 wealthy Harriet Wilson High donated her mansion there for that purpose; it is now part of the Woodruff Arts Center, along with the Alliance Theater, the Atlanta Symphony Orchestra, and an arts school. In 2011, Georgia Tech jumped across the interstate into Midtown with its wildly successful Technology Square development, which attracted corporate innovation centers, including NCR Corporation's world headquarters.

In Ansley Park, I stayed overnight in the hilltop home of Marcia Bansley, who had retired as the longtime head of Trees Atlanta. She was a thoughtful host who told me that my mother had helped her with botanical and political advice early in her tenure. She lives on Montgomery Ferry Road (the only street to cut through the golf course and continue

---

* The current governor's mansion was built in 1967 on West Paces Ferry Road in Buckhead by racist governor Lester Maddox.

into Piedmont Heights), near the 1950s Sherwood Forest development just to the north, with street names like Robin Hood Road, Lady Marion Lane, and Nottingham Way.

Bansley bought her classic four-bedroom brick home, built in 1931 with two dormers and four columns, for $163,000 in 1993 but figured it was worth $600,000 in 2015. She loves Ansley Park, with its cosmopolitan, well-traveled residents. "Many are deeply involved in making Atlanta better," she said. "We have city planners, state legislators, entrepreneurs, lawyers, real estate developers, women business owners, university professors, basketball stars, business leaders, international business people, artists, historians and nonprofit executives."

Bansley also enjoyed bimonthly dinners held in different neighborhood houses. These did not include the home of Al Horford, the six-foot-ten black Dominican basketball player for the Atlanta Hawks (now with the Boston Celtics), who lived next door but kept a low profile, despite his height; Bansley had never seen him. Home prices in the neighborhood can range up to $5 million, but there are also apartments, townhomes, and condos.

I walked along the sidewalks of the quiet streets (patrolled by off-duty police since 1983), shaded by oak, hickory, and tulip poplars, down The Prado, past two of the neighborhood's five small contiguous parks, owned by the city but maintained by the Ansley Park Beautification Foundation. My favorite was Winn Park, with its pond, small waterfall, ball field, playground, and benches. I wondered how welcome BeltLine bikers will be as they venture into this elegant neighborhood. They might get lost, as many do, in the meandering confusion of streets. Residents once wore T-shirts that said, "Lose Yourself in Ansley Park."

I later spoke to Rose Holston, an El Paso native who lived with her husband and daughters, thirteen and ten, in a townhouse on Ansley Walk Terrace on the eastern edge of the neighborhood, quite near the future BeltLine. Holston and her husband, who worked at Georgia Tech, had been incredibly frustrated with the noise level from several bars—particularly Burkhart's and Mixx, both gay nightspots in Ansley Square, just on the other side of the BeltLine. "They have patrons who honk horns, scream, and engage in general craziness between 3 and 4 a.m.," Holston told me. Sleep deprived, the Holstons called the police repeatedly, to no avail.

Hopefully, when the BeltLine trail is actually paved up through Piedmont Park to Armour/Ottley, the bars will close at a reasonable hour, as they do along the Eastside Trail, and Ansley Mall may be redeveloped as a mixed-use community, which would demand quiet.

That completes our selective tour of BeltLine neighborhoods, which offer such racial and socioeconomic contrasts. When the loop trail (and possibly transit) connects them all, the impact will undoubtedly be a mixed blessing. But making Ansley Park residents nearer neighbors of those in Pittsburgh or Grove Park will ultimately help to unify the city.

CHAPTER 14
OUTSIDE AND INSIDE THE BELTLINE

···

[There is an] eternal conflict between OTP and ITP. Cobb,
Gwinnett, downtown, Midtown. It's all Atlanta, right? Sort of
and not really. I-285 represents a sharp division of worlds
in collision, with mutually assured derision.

—Bill Torpy and J. Scott Trubey, *Atlanta Journal-Constitution*, 2013

Outside the Darlington Apartments on Peachtree, the electronic Atlanta population sign had long since broached 6 million human souls as I finished writing this book. Yet the city of Atlanta held only 454,000 people, about 7 percent of that figure. That's because the sign estimated—in fact, overestimated—the number of people in the twenty-nine-county metro Atlanta area, including suburbs and edge cities that mostly lie outside Interstate 285, the multilane Perimeter Expressway, built to relieve traffic congestion by circumventing the city. Instead, the ring road became part of the problem, encouraging external development and sprawl while providing a shorthand designation for those who live "outside the Perimeter": OTP.

This chapter explores representative areas in that vast world where most people who say they live "in Atlanta" actually reside, then dives back to the heart of a troubled downtown, the hole in the BeltLine donut. This book has focused on the BeltLine and its part in helping to remake the city into a more appealing, walkable, connected set of neighborhoods. As with many other American cities, a reverse migration back to the urban core has begun. Yet the suburban dream is far from defunct, and its changing dynamic affects life within the Atlanta city limits, and vice versa.

A map of the central ten counties of the metropolitan Atlanta region. The city boundaries lie mostly within Fulton County, with a bit in DeKalb County to the east. Route I-285 is known as the Perimeter, and the area outside it is often called OTP: Outside the Perimeter.

The Peripheral Center

Some view the Braves' 2017 move to Cobb County as emblematic, asserting that the center of metro Atlanta has shifted from downtown toward the northern suburbs. Over the past few decades, money and skyscrapers traveled north, so that many of metro Atlanta's corporate headquarters (Mercedes USA, Cox Enterprises, UPS, InterContinental Hotels Group, and State Farm Insurance, among others) reside in Perimeter Center, an oxymoronic name that fails to make residents laugh because that's really what they call it. Perimeter Mall opened there in 1971, surrounded by farms. Now it is encompassed by gleaming skyscrapers and hotels, near "Pill Hill," a huge medical complex.

Perimeter Center lies within three new cities—Sandy Springs, Brookhaven, and Dunwoody—that declared independence from Fulton and DeKalb Counties, in part to avoid paying taxes for impoverished black areas in the southern part of the counties. Like other suburban areas, Perimeter Center is striving mightily to reinvent itself as a walkable, bikeable area, and it is fortunate to have several nearby MARTA stations.

Yet it remains reliant on automobiles. After all, that's why it was built there at the conjunction of I-285 and Georgia 400, which cuts north from Buckhead. The traffic there had become so horrendous by 2015 that the Georgia Department of Transportation (GDOT) planned to spend over $1 billion to add new "fly-over" lanes and other improvements that would save each driver an estimated eight hours per year. The winning bid promised to build it for $679 million, though cost overruns may push that toward $1 billion anyway.

GDOT is infamously devoted to automobiles over public transit. In early 2016, the governor announced GDOT plans for $14 billion in new interstate construction projects over the next decade, mostly to add toll lanes and improve interchanges. "The governor's plan assumes you can pave your way out of traffic congestion," the director of the state chapter of the Sierra Club complained. Regardless of conflicting opinions about possible solutions, there is no doubt that metro Atlanta's northern suburbs are choking on traffic, as exemplified by Gwinnett County.

Gwinnett County

OTP growth has mostly gone north, then, to Perimeter Center and beyond, particularly to Cobb and Gwinnett Counties. Gwinnett lies northeast of Atlanta, with I-85 ripping through its heart on the way to South Carolina. During the 1970s and 1980s, Gwinnett was one of the fastest-growing counties in the United States because of its maniacal drive to convert farmland into single-family houses, cul-de-sacs, and malls, with Wayne Mason and other developers leading the charge.

In the spring of 2012, I took a tour of Gwinnett with Chuck Warbington, executive director of the Gwinnett Village Improvement District. Born in 1971, Warbington is a seventh-generation Gwinnett resident. Part of the white establishment that still ran the county, he was quick to point out that Gwinnett, approaching 900,000 people (nearly twice the population of the city of Atlanta), was the most diverse county in Georgia. "When I was born, it was 95 percent white," he said. Now it was "majority minority, a true melting pot of the South," with substantial numbers of African Americans, Hispanics, and Asians. Over a quarter of the residents were not born in the United States.

Vietnamese boat people came in the 1970s; now the second generation is established and generally prosperous. A flood of Mexicans and other Latin American immigrants came (often illegally) for the construction boom of the 1996 Olympics and continued to arrive until the 2008 recession. Wealthy Koreans, Japanese, Chinese, and Indians followed. Upper-class African Americans moved to Gwinnett, often from New York or other points north, attracted by jobs, relatively inexpensive housing, and a warmer climate.

Over five hundred international companies do business in Gwinnett, with over one hundred establishing regional or national headquarters there—four of them Fortune 500 companies. Still, of the 21,500 county businesses, three-quarters have fewer than ten employees. There are also forty-six parks in the county, covering 10,000 acres.

Warbington and I started our tour from the north, so that by late afternoon we would be driving south as the commuter traffic from Atlanta clogged I-85 going north during the after-work rush hour. Gwinnett voters opted out of MARTA transit twice, in 1971 and 1990, and now they are paying the price with gridlock. A toll lane on I-85 allowed paying commuters to travel more quickly with a Peach Pass, but that jammed the nontoll lanes even more. Two new "diverging diamond" interchanges sped traffic off I-85, only to cause backups on Pleasant Hill and Jimmy Carter Boulevard. A large 2015 transportation survey of Gwinnett citizens showed that they yearned for some kind of public transit and felt trapped in car traffic, which was "congested, limiting, and isolating."

Just off I-85, near the town of Buford in northern Gwinnett, we saw the huge Mall of Georgia, built in 1999. With over two hundred stores on three levels, plus a five-hundred-seat amphitheater and restaurants, it is the largest shopping mall in the state and attracts customers from all over north Georgia.

Further south, we drove through the town center of Suwanee, created in 2003 as a mixed-use area of retail shops, restaurants, townhouses, condos, and homes, including the city hall, a ten-acre park with a fountain and surrounding wading pool, and a performance space with a terraced 1,000-seat amphitheater. Built from scratch, it helped make Suwanee "the fair-haired child of Gwinnett County—cool, hip, and rich,"

Warbington observed. The annual Suwanee Fest in late September attracts some 40,000 people to the park.

This "town center" emulation of new urbanism, funded in part by Livable Centers Initiative planning grants from the Atlanta Regional Commission, became popular in many suburban cities of metro Atlanta. The live/work/play ethos, combined with walkability, is the same force driving BeltLine development. Suwanee was among the first and most successful.

Further south, along Sugarloaf Parkway near Duluth, we passed the headquarters of the Georgia Baptist Convention and Gwinnett Center, which featured a performing arts and convention center, along with a sports arena. In Duluth, we visited the sad Gwinnett Place Mall. When it opened in 1984, anchored by Rich's and Davison's department stores and a Sears, it was a regional draw. But the Mall of Georgia and other options sucked away shoppers, and now Gwinnett Place sat mostly vacant, except for the struggling Sears and Mega Mart, a Korean food mart/department store that replaced Macy's (which replaced Davison's). "I took my first date to this mall," Warbington recalled wistfully.

Driving around southern Gwinnett County in Duluth, Norcross, and Lilburn was a surreal experience. What looked outwardly like 1980s American suburbia had been overlaid with a remarkably international reality. Wealthy Koreans had taken over whole neighborhoods, with street signs in Korean. Indians owned and shopped at Global Mall in Norcross. Another entire mall was Vietnamese. To the east, in Lilburn, I later toured the BAPS Shri Swaminarayan Mandir, a gigantic white Hindu temple imported stone by stone from India and built on the site of an old shopping center. The Victory World Church, a multicultural, nondenominational Christian megachurch, attracted over 8,500 people from one hundred countries to its services in Norcross.

There had been some white flight north within Gwinnett County, as more minority groups—especially poor Hispanics—moved into the southern part of the county. Much of Jimmy Carter Boulevard in Norcross, site of some of the first industrial buildings and warehouses, had become run-down and seedy. The huge Optical Fiber Solution factory (formerly Western Electric) at the intersection of Jimmy Carter Boulevard and I-85, owned by a Japanese company, had automated and drastically reduced its footprint and number of employees. Movie studios eventually

Hindu temple in Lilburn, Gwinnett County

moved into the large space to film parts of *Fast and Furious 7* and *8*, *A Walk in the Woods*, and *The Hunger Games 3* and *4*. Television shows would be filmed at the nearby Eagle Rock beer distribution building (vacated by Kraft).

Home foreclosures and evictions escalated after the Great Recession hit, with more homeless, many of them children—in 2012 the average homeless person in Gwinnett County was six years old. Most lived in run-down extended-stay hotels along Jimmy Carter Boulevard or nearby. A middle-class African American couple told an interviewer on the street that they were contemplating a move farther north in the county. "The Hispanics and Asians are taking over our neighborhood," the wife complained.

I visited the Latin American Association office in Norcross, where legal and undocumented Hispanics could seek help with food stamp applications, language classes, transportation, and family services. Domestic violence, teen pregnancy, and a lack of child support were common problems, and the threat of deportation loomed over many. Section 287(g) of the Immigration and Nationality Act authorized local police to detain undocumented immigrants, and longtime Gwinnett sheriff Butch

Conway and District Attorney Danny Porter were eager to do just that. Gwinnett was the only metro Atlanta county to grow its prison inmate population between 2009 and 2013.

Despite the influx of immigrants, the power structure of Gwinnett County remained white, at least for the time being. In 2011, Gwinnett Republican senator Renee Unterman delivered a vitriolic speech in favor of an anti-immigration bill. "When I graduated from high school in 1972, there was one African American person in my school—*one*," she said. "Unfortunately, [now] we're absorbing all these illegal kids. . . . We need to take care of our own people, not Mexico's people." At least she felt good that "if you're under Sheriff Butch Conway, your papers are gonna be checked, and you're gonna be shipped back to where you came from with the federal program."

Surprisingly, the Gwinnett County public school system managed to absorb not only undocumented Hispanic immigrants but children from 168 countries, speaking over one hundred different languages, and 56 percent of all the schoolchildren qualified for free or subsidized lunches. Since 1996, the school system—with 136 public schools and over 175,000 students, the largest in Georgia—had thrived under Superintendent Alvin Wilbanks, with only a 3 percent high school drop-out rate; 83 percent of graduates planned to attend college.

"If kids show up at the schoolhouse door, we have to take them," regardless of their parents' legal status, Wilbanks told me. As of 2016, white children accounted for 25.4 percent of students in Gwinnett County classrooms; African American children made up 31.5 percent; Hispanics, 29 percent; Asians, 10.3 percent; multiracial, 3.6 percent; and Native Americans, 0.2 percent.

The schools routinely provide English-as-a-second-language instruction. For younger children, that isn't too difficult. "But as we started getting lower socioeconomic children from Thailand, Vietnam, and smaller Asian countries, and Mexico, who were illiterate in their own language, it was a challenge," said Wilbanks. "And they came in fairly large numbers, beginning in the late 1990s."

One secret to the schools' success has been voters' willingness to approve a 1 percent local option sales tax to supplement the regular school budget. This E-SPLOST tax provided an extra $140 million (approximately) per year that helped to fund capital improvements, including up-to-date computer technology in every classroom.

Riverdale in Clayton County

The success of the Gwinnett school system stood in stark contrast to many of Atlanta's troubled schools or those of Clayton County outside the Perimeter to the south, which had even greater problems. Due largely to school board infighting, the Clayton schools lost accreditation in 2008, having it fully restored only in 2011.

As the economy tanked, in 2010 the Clayton County commissioners abruptly cancelled C-Tran, the public bus service that had provided 2 million rides a year, leaving impoverished residents without a way to get to jobs, schools, or medical services. Some apartment complexes along the former bus lines were half empty. The county supplied many of the janitors, rental car employees, and other low-paid workers at the nearby Atlanta airport, the world's busiest and the largest employer in Georgia. Private jitney buses, charging relatively high fees, began to ferry Clayton residents to work.

According to 2010 census data, the average per capita income of the 267,000 residents of Clayton County was about $19,000, the lowest of any county near Atlanta. Clayton is shaped something like New Hampshire, long from north to south and broader at the top, with Forest Park, Riverdale, Morrow, and Jonesboro the principal cities nearest Atlanta. Bonanza and Lovejoy lie farther to the south.

I took a driving tour of several towns, including the largest, Forest Park, where African Americans and Hispanics each accounted for over a third of the population, with whites constituting a 19 percent minority. The town is also home to Stately Oaks, a white-columned antebellum mansion, touted as a possible model for the mythical Tara of *Gone with the Wind*. In 1990, Clayton County was mostly white, but in the aftermath of Hurricane Katrina and the destruction of Atlanta's public housing projects, impoverished African Americans with Section 8 vouchers, along with many undocumented Hispanic immigrants and increasing numbers of nonviolent ex-offenders released from prison, moved to Clayton to take advantage of plummeting real estate values.

Crime, drugs, and sporadic violence accompanied the seismic racial and ethnic shift, leading to white flight and racist comments such as those on this 2009 blog: "Clayton County has been taken over by Gangs and Criminals since White residents decided to leave the county. . . . Neighborhoods look like 3rd world countries. . . . Thugs patrol the streets with one hand holding up their pants and the other on their weapon of choice. Young females walk up and down the streets dressed like Hookers." While a few contributors tried to defend the county, the majority agreed with another blogger's conclusion: "Clayton County is broke [*sic*] beyond repair and the whites are NOT coming back."

I focused my research on the small city of Riverdale, on the western side of Clayton County, where my paternal great grandparents once lived. Incorporated as a town in 1908 and named after prominent resident W. S. Rivers, it had been majority white for most of the twentieth century, but now African Americans accounted for 72 percent of the population of 15,000, with only 8 percent white, another 8 percent Asian, and 7 percent Hispanic.

In April 2012, I spent a day in Riverdale. Most cars roared through town on State Route 85, stopping only for fast food—Dairy Queen, Wendy's, Hotlanta Wings, McDonald's, Popeyes, Krispy Kreme, Krystal, Chick-fil-A, Subway, American Deli—or to stop at pawn shops, liquor stores, or auto parts stores. With its hodgepodge of garish billboards, Route 85 was one of the ugliest stretches of road in Georgia, and one of the most dangerous for pedestrians trying to cross the six-lane divided road. Local incomes were even lower than county averages. In 2012 Riverdale High School had only a 43 percent graduation rate.

Yet there was hope in Riverdale, especially since the election of Mayor Evelyn Wynn-Dixon in December 2007. I interviewed her in her office at the new town center on Church Street, a block west off Route 85. The oldest of nine children, Wynn-Dixon, born Evelyn Favors in 1949, had an African American, Cherokee, and Seminole bloodline. She grew up in Atlanta's Peoplestown neighborhood in public housing, still pleasant in the 1950s, with vegetable gardens and neat clotheslines in the back. As a child during the Jim Crow era, she had to sit at the back of the bus, but older women taught her, "Can't nobody ride your back unless you bend it." When Auburn Avenue was at its peak, she heard Ray Charles, Mary Wells, and Sam Cooke singing at the Royal Peacock.

But in her thirties, as an abandoned, divorced, homeless mother of four, Wynn-Dixon found herself without hope, standing on the Pryor Street bridge, about to throw herself onto the interstate below. She couldn't do it, so she took an overdose of aspirin, threw it up, and then slit her wrists. Still, she survived. "God picked me up when I was at my lowest," she said—and sent her back to school to become a nurse. She cleaned houses in the evenings, living on welfare in Section 8 housing, but she eventually earned a master's in gerontology from the University of Georgia, where two of her sons became football stars.

While she was living in Riverdale and working at Grady Hospital in Atlanta, her pastor said that the Lord had told him that she would be the next mayor. After campaigning through every neighborhood and visiting every church in Riverdale, she won election and then went on to repeated reelection, unopposed. "I'm the people's mayor," she told me, "regardless of color." She had an open-door policy, answered all of her e-mails, and had a "magnificent obsession to help others," as she put it. In her spare time, she volunteered for hospice. When I met her, she was a full-bodied, attractive woman in her sixties who radiated goodwill. Still single, she was not eager to remarry. "I'll let the right one find me this time."

When elected mayor, Wynn-Dixon inherited a plan for a new town center complex, a 2007 Livable Centers Initiative funded by the Atlanta Regional Commission. Designed by Atlanta's Sizemore Group, which had also done the Suwanee Town Center in Gwinnett, the project was funded in 2008 by a $25 million bond, just before the Great Recession hit. The 47,000-square-foot Riverdale Center and the adjacent 28,000-square-foot city hall, where I interviewed Wynn-Dixon, opened in October 2010 on twenty-seven acres, the site of the former Travon Wilson Park, an athletic field complex.* It sat across the street from a plaza with a Kroger supermarket and pharmacy, already a community gathering place of sorts.

Michael Syphoe, an African American who worked as a consultant for Riverdale and the Sizemore Group, took me on a tour of the town center. With a master's in planning from Georgia Tech, Syphoe had worked for the Atlanta Bureau of Planning and facilitated the development of Studioplex on Auburn Avenue, among other career accomplishments. He and Mayor Wynn-Dixon worked closely with community members to make sure the town center met their needs. "The seniors told us they wanted a safe place to walk indoors," he said. "Others were tired of going to Atlanta for entertainment."

A gym in the recreation center can serve as a basketball court, while an elevated rectangular track has a resilient cork floor for walkers. A

---

* The park was named after four-year-old Travon Wilson, killed by a stray bullet during a drug deal shoot-out in Riverdale in 2004.

dance studio, art room, fitness room, digital game room, boardroom, and warming kitchen occupy other areas. Parts of the facility can be rented for inexpensive weddings. Every room has a projection and sound system. Citizens can gather to watch a movie or community theater on a portable stage, attend health fairs, or see the Super Bowl on a big screen. The Leadership in Energy & Environmental Design (LEED)–certified building harvests rainwater from the roof to fill three large tanks, while surplus water goes to an attractive detention pond with a little gazebo on its bank. An outdoor amphitheater serves as the site for a summer After Work Cool-Down Music series and a fall Seafood Festival. Nearby, kids cavort in a splash-pad fountain on hot days. Down the street, using $5 million in federal "recovery zone" bonds, Riverdale built a new park with three baseball fields, a football field, an area for a future skateboard park, and a walking trail.

To end the day, Syphoe took me on a more sobering city tour. Few streets had sidewalks. A former Lowe's stood empty, unable to lure a new tenant. Over objections from some business owners, Wynn-Dixon had supported a local ordinance to limit the size and height of billboards along Route 85 and to prevent the addition of more pawn shops, liquor stores, auto parts dealers, and adult sex toy/pornography outlets. With an $800,000 grant from the Atlanta Regional Commission, Riverdale added new sidewalks, street furniture, lighting, and traffic signals along sections of Route 85. Despite such improvements, Syphoe did not live in Riverdale. "I live near the BeltLine in the Old Fourth Ward in Atlanta, where I can walk to twenty restaurants."

Yet some hopeful developments occurred over the next few years after my 2012 visit. By 2015 the Riverdale High School graduation rate had climbed from 43 percent three years earlier to 78 percent, with SAT scores rising from an average 924 to 1264—a big improvement, though Norcross High School in Gwinnett County reached an SAT average of 1465 in 2015, even with its numerous immigrant students.

In 2014 Clayton County, after a lobbying campaign spearheaded by Georgia STAND-UP, voted to join MARTA, paying a 1 percent sales tax to regain bus service and, perhaps someday, hard-rail transit. It thus became the first county added to MARTA since 1971.*

---

* There are positive economic developments in this area surrounding the Atlanta airport, with Porsche opening its US headquarters nearby in 2015. The "Aerotropolis Atlanta Alliance" pushes the area's potential.

Clarkston's Refugees

The small city of Clarkston (1.4 square miles, population 13,000 in 2016) in DeKalb County lies just outside I-285 to the east of Atlanta, between Decatur and Stone Mountain. In 1845, Georgia Railroad completed a rail line connecting Athens to Atlanta (then called Marthasville). Along that line, Clarkston, named for a railroad director, sprouted as an early commuter suburb of sorts. Incorporated in 1882, it developed as a quiet, conservative white town nicknamed "Goatsville" for residents who raised Angora goats, prized for their mohair fleece, which explains why the local high school football players are still called the Angoras.

In the 1970s, developers built two-story brick apartment complexes in Clarkston to provide housing for new workers at the expanding Atlanta airport and other employment venues. A decade later, as black tenants began to arrive, most white renters moved farther out to nicer suburbs. As more African American tenants with Section 8 vouchers came, landlords cut back on maintenance, and the apartment buildings grew shabby.

In the late 1980s, as Vietnamese and Cambodian refugees arrived in the United States, the International Rescue Committee, World Relief, and other agencies identified Clarkston as an ideal resettlement location, with inexpensive apartments within walking distance of the city's main shopping center. East Ponce de Leon, which cuts through the heart of Clarkston parallel to the railroad tracks, carried MARTA buses, as did North Indian Creek Drive, another main artery, and MARTA rapid transit wasn't far away, so refugees seeking low-paying jobs in Atlanta hotels or stores or at the airport had commuting options.

As the 1990s progressed, the trickle of refugees placed in Clarkston became a flood, from Bosnia, Kosovo, Liberia, Congo, Rwanda, Burundi, Sudan, Somalia, Central African Republic, Myanmar, Russia, Bhutan, Nepal, Ethiopia, and Eritrea, countries disrupted by violence. By the time I visited Clarkston in May 2015, whites constituted only 13 percent of the population, and refugees accounted for half of residents. They could not naturalize and vote for at least six years, however, so white and black Americans represented 80 percent of the electorate.

Betsy Eggers drove me on a tour. I knew her from the Quaker Meeting in Decatur, where I sat in silent worship with my parents during Atlanta visits. A retired occupational therapist, Eggers had been involved with refugees since befriending a Rwandan family in 1999. She and her husband, architect/developer Jack Honderd, later provided housing for four orphaned teens from Liberia, and when Burundi refugees began attending Quaker Meeting, she formed a support group for them there.

In 2009, Eggers volunteered at the new Global Village Project school in donated space at the Decatur Presbyterian Church, where we met to begin my tour. I observed a first-year reading class and interviewed some of the staff. The school educates about forty refugee girls, ages eleven to eighteen, for up to three years, with the aim of launching them into a successful public high school experience.

Why the focus on girls? They are often undereducated in African and Asian cultures. Some don't know how to turn the pages of a book when they arrive at Global Village. Their parents are generally more comfortable with single-gender education, and daughters help their parents with bills, phone calls, and other matters. The girls at Global Village quickly gain confidence, learning to speak out and ask questions. On this spring day, I talked to two poised students—a thirteen-year-old from Nepal and an eleven-year-old from the Central African Republic—seated next to one another, working on laptop assignments. After less than a year in school, they were nearly fluent and literate in English.

Then we drove to Clarkston. I had first learned about the influx of refugees there from reading Warren St. John's *Outcasts United: An American Town, a Refugee Team, and One Woman's Quest to Make a Difference*, the remarkable story of how Jordanian immigrant Luma Mufleh formed the Fugees, a soccer team of Clarkston refugee boys, in 2004. The scruffy boys, most of whom had endured unspeakable tragedies in their home countries, bonded as a disciplined team that frequently beat rivals from Atlanta's wealthy suburbs. To educate her players Mufleh eventually launched the Fugee Academy, at first just for boys, though it later admitted girls, and the Clarkston private school graduated its first high school class in 2016.*

Clarkston police once targeted refugees for absurd traffic tickets, arrests, and abuse. The old-line white mayor, Lee Swaney, initially blocked the Fugees' efforts to practice soccer on a little-used field in a public park. Many white residents resented what they saw as a foreign invasion of

---

* Betsy Eggers was a founding board member of Fugees Family, Inc., the umbrella organization, and was board chair of the Global Village Project from 2011 to 2014.

their "sleepy little town by the railroad tracks," as Swaney called it. African American teenage gangs didn't like the refugees either, leading to at least one shooting.

By the time of my 2015 visit, Clarkston residents were getting along much better. A new police chief had reformed the force and encouraged citizens to ride along in patrol cars or have "Coffee with a Cop." The formerly all-white Baptist church had renamed itself the Clarkston International Bible Church, embracing Christians from all cultures and offering services in multiple languages. The local mosque, Masjid Al-Momineen, was planning an expansion. And the progressive young mayor, Ted Terry, expressed pride in the town's diversity and welcomed new refugees. A Somalian and an Eritrean now sit on the city council.

Betsy Eggers and I visited the Somali American Community Center at Campus Plaza, on North Indian Creek Drive, where I met Omar Shekhey, an engineer turned cabby, and others who helped refugees with obtaining food stamps, signing up for Social Security, and other issues. Dubbed "Little Somalia," the shopping mall also featured a store selling gorgeous native clothing and a money-wiring service.

Then we drove north to the Clarkston Village Shopping Center on Montreal Road, where we roamed the aisles of Thriftown, an independent grocery store that had nearly gone bankrupt before adapting to refugee food choices, which included goat, whole lamb and fish, exotic spices, soups, dried beans of unusual sorts, rice flour, mango pickles, tamarind concentrate, and a separate pork section for non-Muslims. Then we walked past the International Driving School to eat a Nepalese lunch at the Kathmandu Kitchen & Grill.

Afterward, we went to The Lakes apartment complex to visit a French-speaking disabled father from the Central African Republic and his three adorable preschool-age children, who were watching *Thomas & Friends* on TV in the dark apartment. Their mother was working in a chicken factory in Rockmart, Georgia, an hour and a half away.

Eggers later told me how she and her husband were trying to help Julie (not her real name), a Clarkston widow with six children, from Congo. Soldiers had killed her husband and stolen his cattle. They lived in African refugee camps for years before arriving in Clarkston, where they were placed in an old, smelly apartment—in the Marquis Apartments, formerly known as Olde Plantation—on Montreal Road close to the shopping center. The mother commuted an hour each way to Bethlehem, Georgia, in Barrow County, to work at Harrison Poultry for $9.50 an hour. Julie was one of nearly 1,000 employees (mostly refugees and undocumented Hispanics) who worked in the cold factory, dismembering eight chickens a minute, liable to injuries and carpal tunnel syndrome. She paid $40 a week to a fellow refugee for a ride to work, leaving Clarkston at 5:30 a.m. and returning exhausted at 8 p.m. The oldest daughter, fourteen, fed and cared for her five siblings.

"We became involved with Julie and her family because they came to Friends Meeting," Eggers said. "Their family is being supported by other economically struggling refugees, all doing their best to keep their heads above water. The children are bright, engaging, happy, and want to learn. We bring them to our house on days off of school so they can have outdoor activities, food, and tutoring. It's all heartbreaking, and typical of the lives of struggling Clarkston families."

Stone Mountain's International Hikers

A few days later, in mid-May of 2015, five miles to the west of Clarkston, I hiked up Stone Mountain, reputedly the world's largest piece of exposed granite, for the first time since I was a kid. Back then, I didn't know that in 1915 white supremacists had revived the Ku Klux Klan atop this mountain.* In his 1963 "I Have a Dream" speech, Martin Luther King Jr. invoked the symbolic mountain, crying out, "Let freedom ring from Stone Mountain in Georgia!" Yet in 1970 the carvings of Confederate heroes Robert E. Lee, Stonewall Jackson, and Jefferson Davis were finally completed on its sheer northern face, where laser shows highlight them dramatically at night. The Stone Mountain Park still includes an Antebellum Plantation Area, and I visited the Confederate Hall Historical Center to get my certificate of achievement for having climbed the mountain.

Only a mile long, up a gradual slope to the top of the 1,700-foot elevation, the hike was fascinating, not only because of the natural beauty or the views of the Atlanta skyline but because of the variety of people I encountered. This symbol of Southern white racism has become a mecca for visitors from around the world—some tourists but a substantial number living nearby, and not just in Clarkston. My walking companion was

* See Chapter 4.

Shannon Byrne, whose website, iamthemountain.org, had brought me
there. For over a year, the Stone Mountain native—who describes herself as half Mexican, a quarter English, and a quarter Irish and as the
unofficial "mayor" of the mountain—had been videotaping impromptu
interviews with people trekking up the granite path.

On Byrne's website you can hear people proclaiming, "I am the
mountain!" in an extraordinary array of languages: Italian, Chinese,
Romanian, Serbian, Malaysian, Lithuanian, Dutch, Filipino, Pakistani,
Somalian, Vietnamese, Nigerian, Nepalese, Indonesian, Japanese, and
on and on—even in English.

You can also see her interviews with natives of Togo, Russia, Hon-
duras, Poland, South Korea, Cambodia, India, and Peru, all of whom
live nearby and feel at home on the mountain. Svetlana, a young Rus-
sian, was a Christian evangelist working with Georgia State students.
Pon, a thirty-eight-year-old Cambodian, was a diesel mechanic who had
lived in America for three decades but had been unable to get citizenship
papers. Karuna, a middle-aged Indian social worker who worked with
addicts, had been climbing Stone Mountain for twelve years on Sunday
afternoons to relieve stress. "The mountain is like my mother," she said.
"The positive energy here nourishes your soul."

The Americans climbing the mountain were equally varied. Father
Greg, a retired Stone Mountain priest, called the mountain "a wonderful
place to meet people from all nations, all religions." As a public service,
Bill and Bob, two brothers from Decatur, carried down plastic bottles
people had thrown as litter. Sakeenah, a recent white convert to Islam
wrapped in a burqa, had just moved from New Jersey to a nearby Islamic
community. Ryan, a young white man in a muscle shirt revealing large
tattoos, had been in prison from ages fifteen to twenty for gang activities
and now worked with young men in Norcross to try to keep them out
of trouble. James, a black retired postal worker, had been raised in racist southern Georgia; his mother had taken him to Connecticut, but he
moved back and built a home nearby because he loved Stone Mountain.[*]

---

[*] Shannon Byrne's videos captured a number of people with disabilities, or self-
imposed handicaps, who clearly fascinated her. One black man, missing both legs,
used his hands to swing his torso up the mountain. Another group crawled up to
encourage a friend who couldn't ascend any other way. Another man carried fifty
pounds of chains as he climbed, while another hauled a heavy tire.

The mountain could not entirely shake its history, however. Just a month before my climb, Byrne had interviewed two white men and a woman carrying Confederate flags to the top. One told her, "This flag stands for a lot of brave men and women who stood up for what they believed in." Byrne asked if those individuals had believed in continued slavery. "They may have," he admitted, but that didn't bother him. The woman said, "I had twenty-five men in my family fight and die against Yankee tyranny." Both interviewees lived in Atlanta. "We don't care if it upsets a lot of black people," the woman exploded, "or white people or purple people."

A month after my hike, a white supremacist killed nine black parishioners during a prayer service at the Emanuel African Methodist Church in Charleston, South Carolina, reigniting calls to remove Confederate flags from public spaces. Stone Mountain's management refused to do so but proposed building a tower atop the mountain with a replica of the Liberty Bell to honor Martin Luther King Jr.'s call to "let freedom ring." On November 14, 2015, a group of gun-toting white protesters with Confederate flags marched up the mountain. One Cobb County participant, who started a group called Rebel Yell, said, "Fuck civil rights, this is a Civil War mountain." The Georgia governor backed off from his support of the monument to King, which was not erected.

Serenbe's Serenity

On the other side of Atlanta, outside the Perimeter to the southwest, is Serenbe, a planned community that offers an alternative to the old suburban model of cul-de-sacs and guarded gates. It was the vision of Steve Nygren, born in 1945 and raised on a farm in Colorado. He became a successful businessman in Atlanta, opening a chain of Pleasant Peasant restaurants in the 1970s and 1980s, then selling them for a substantial profit. Nygren and his wife, Marie, whose mother founded Mary Mac's Tea Room restaurant on Ponce de Leon Avenue (still offering downhome Southern food), and their three young daughters lived in Ansley Park in a classic, beautifully restored 1915 home.

"We loved it," Nygren recalled. "We could walk to the symphony or Piedmont Park. We were totally urban people." In 1991, he bought a sixty-acre farm "on a whim" near Palmetto, Georgia, southwest of

Atlanta. On weekends, he watched his daughters, then three, five, and seven, romp in the woods and play in waterfalls. "They couldn't wait to come out to this old farmhouse where there were no toys." Three years later, they sold their Ansley Park house and moved there for good, opening their home as a bed-and-breakfast in 1996.

In 2000, after encountering a bulldozer while jogging, Nygren panicked and bought adjacent land, so that he owned 1,000 acres. He decided to create an idyllic community that his wife named Serenbe (i.e., be serene), inspired by traditional small-town life and British country footpaths. Homes would sit on small lots close to one another, near the sidewalk, so that people could converse from their front porches. But 70 percent of the land would remain green and undeveloped, with miles of trails. In the center of town, he created the Blue-Eyed Daisy, an informal café and community meeting place. The first homes went up in 2004.

Nygren also spearheaded the creation of Chattahoochee Hill Country in the surrounding 65,000 acres, with zoning that required 70 percent of the land to remain undeveloped. He hoped that other villages like Serenbe would one day dot the countryside. And Nygren helped form Chattahoochee NOW, a consortium of environmentalists and developers who want to reclaim a fifty-three-mile stretch of the Chattahoochee River south of Atlanta as an asset with many public access points. The river runs a few miles to the west of Serenbe.

I first met Nygren, an articulate, strikingly handsome, silver-haired man, in 2012 at the Blue-Eyed Daisy. We toured the new community, which at that point had about 100 homes out of a planned 1,200. The recession had slowed things down a bit, but his vision for a vibrant type of new urbanism in the country was already coming to fruition. As I was leaving, I heard another visitor exclaim, "I feel like I'm in Europe!"

When I returned three years later, there were twice as many homes, with 450 people living in Serenbe, 70 percent of them full time. Children made up over a quarter of the population. In other words, it was a real community, ranging from young families to retirees. Some commuted to Atlanta every day for work, but more worked out of their homes, including consultants who appreciated the twenty-five-minute drive to the airport. The varying houses along the winding streets included craftsman cottages, townhouses, and estate homes with many bedrooms and baths. Some of these EarthCraft-certified and energy-efficient dwellings used solar panels and geothermal heat pumps, requiring no outside energy source.

There were three restaurants—the Daisy, the Farmhouse restaurant at the Inn at Serenbe (the former bed-and-breakfast; the Nygrens had moved to the village), and Hil on the Hill, named for chef Hilary White. The town had a high-end grocery store and a few other retail shops, and daughter Kara Nygren ran a summer camp. I was entranced by an elaborate treehouse I found along a trail in the woods.

Nygren designed Serenbe as four "hamlets." Selborne, with its arts and culture theme, had filled up. The Grange, which includes the twenty-five-acre organic farm and horse stables, was booked. Mado, a health and wellness community, was just breaking ground for a senior living complex along with a Montessori school, so there would be a real age mix. The fourth hamlet would specialize in research and education. Already, there were activities almost every day, whether it be an outdoor theater production, movie, book discussion group, lecture, hayride, culinary class, wine tasting, horseback ride, or farmers' market. Because of the winding streets and straight connecting paths, it was quicker and easier to walk most places than to drive.

I stayed that night with Richard and Dianne Harnell Cohen in their three-bedroom home—at 3,200 square feet, larger than you'd think, with an open floor plan and vaulted ceiling. Richard, a retired orthopedic surgeon, grew up in Philadelphia. Dianne, raised in New York City, had served under Mayor Shirley Franklin as the parks commissioner and was now a realtor for Sotheby's. They had sold their big Buckhead home and bought a Midtown Atlanta condo, but their favorite residence was in Serenbe. That night, we had wine on a community patio to welcome singer Bess McCrary, the new "artist in residence." Then we jammed into the Blue-Eyed Daisy to watch "Shorts at Sundown," nine alternately amusing or moving short films. Afterward, we walked across the street for dinner at Hil on the Hill (featuring locally grown produce) before strolling back to their house. Dianne and I discussed the similarities between their adopted community and the BeltLine. "I think of Serenbe as being an off-shoot of the BeltLine," she said.

I was impressed. Later I discovered video interviews made in 2014 for Serenbe's tenth anniversary,[*] in which residents of various ages spoke glowingly about life there. Parents could let their children play outdoors for hours without concern. There was always something to do. One couple

---

[*] See www.serenberealestate.com/about.

discovered birding and photography. Others spoke of the peace they found along the trails. Mostly, though, they talked about community. People really got to know one another. Friendships blossomed across generations. "We've made more friends here in a year and a half than the previous thirty years elsewhere." Another observed that when someone died in Serenbe, "the outreach and support was overwhelming. I've never seen anything like it." The woman who ran the stables glowed about how wonderful life was there for her five children (the youngest, an African American adoptee). "I didn't even know how lost I was until we moved here."

And yet . . . I couldn't help thinking about the Clarkston mother of six who worked in the chicken factory and came home to a dank apartment. What chance had she—or the people I had met in the Grove Park, Washington Park, or Pittsburgh neighborhoods—to live in Serenbe, where homes ranged from $370,000 for a two-bedroom cottage to $3 million for a large luxury home? The adults I met were all white and well educated. What about affordable housing? What jobs would there be for poorly educated, struggling families?

Since I visited, the Serenbe Institute* has paid a mere $20,000 each for two innovative one-bedroom homes, resembling long shoeboxes with added porches and decks, designed by students at Auburn University's Rural Studio. At Serenbe they will house visiting artists, however, not poverty-stricken families.

Plans call for someday connecting Serenbe via PATH bike trails to the BeltLine near the Bankhead MARTA station, which sits in one of the poorest neighborhoods in Atlanta. I hope that the trails will also connect people in need with those who have so much.

The Downtown Donut Hole

We have explored the world outside the Perimeter. Now let us turn to the once dynamic heart of the city. While the BeltLine seeks to link Atlanta's disparate races and socioeconomic levels, it encircles a troubled downtown area that suffered severely from white and black flight and became a kind of hole in the BeltLine donut. A renaissance is starting there, however, raising hopes for more to come.

---

* Serenbe Institute is funded by a 1 percent "tax" on property purchased in the community.

At downtown's geographical and symbolic heart is Underground Atlanta, the city's original epicenter, where nineteenth-century railroads met. The construction of viaducts over the rail yards in the 1920s buried this original street level. Various attempts to revitalize the space failed. "Please consider ceasing to promote Underground Atlanta as a place to visit," a 2012 tourist wrote. "The whole atmosphere reeks of dereliction and decline. We found nothing that we were remotely inclined to spend a dime on."

Adjacent to Underground Atlanta is the city's visitors' center, where, when I entered that year, a lone woman sat behind a counter in the otherwise deserted building. Nearby were signs for Government Walk, directing tourists past the federal and state buildings, but most of the people loitering nearby were homeless. There were numerous surface parking lots where buildings had been torn down, as owners waited for the land to become valuable again. In the meantime, the asphalt is simply an impermeable heat sink. Ironically, at most times of the day, there's little traffic in downtown Atlanta, a city famed for its traffic congestion.

I spoke to A. J. Robinson, longtime head of Central Atlanta Progress (CAP), who was remarkably candid about his frustrations. "In Atlanta, we outgrew the infrastructure and never bothered to reinvest in it. Then we had a kind of postpartum depression after the 1996 Olympics. From 2001 to now, we've played catch-up on a lot of issues—the transportation piece, public education, water, all the things we had ignored."

Although 130,000 people work in downtown Atlanta—anchored by The Coca-Cola Company, Georgia-Pacific, Georgia Power, and Turner Broadcasting—hardly any of them hang around at night. On the walls of Robinson's CAP office are artistic renderings of possible futures for the downtown area, including the Multi-Modal Passenger Terminal, to incorporate passenger trains, buses, and streetcars with easy pedestrian and bicycle access. The terminal would fill the "Gulch" of vacant land and freight rail north of Forsyth Street. "We draw lots of pretty pictures," Robinson sighed.* A grossly inadequate prefab building on Forsyth houses the current Greyhound station, and Amtrak only stops farther north on Peachtree Street near Brookwood Hills.

---

* Among those pretty pictures are CAP's 2016 plans for "The Stitch," a three-quarter-mile-long platform over the interstate in downtown Atlanta to "stitch" the city together again.

Northern downtown is doing well, especially the area around Centennial Park, the Georgia World Congress Center, and the Fairlie-Poplar district. The offices of Atlanta BeltLine, Inc., occupy a suite in the Equitable Building at 100 Peachtree Street Northeast, a few blocks north of Underground Atlanta, in a relatively healthy group of skyscrapers. But as soon as the street numbers reverse themselves, going south on Peachtree Street Southwest, pawn shops and vacant storefronts line the sidewalks.

Saba Long, a young African American who served on the Atlanta Regional Commission's Millennial Advisory Panel, lives there in the Kessler City Lofts, a former department store at the corner of Peachtree and Martin Luther King (MLK) Jr. Drive. In a column in the *Saporta Report*, she noted that people frequently ask her, "Wow, people live downtown?" They do, but they have to put up with drug dealers operating in broad daylight. "It's not uncommon to hear of a shooting in or around the Underground Atlanta area," she observed.

One fall day in 2015 I took a tour of south downtown with Saba Long and her neighbor Kyle Kessler (no relation to the building's namesake), a young white architect who headed the Atlanta Neighborhood Downtown Association and directed the South Downtown Initiative for the Center for Civic Innovation down the street. We walked south on Broad Street, where we met Richard Miller, whose uncle opened Miller's Rexall Drugs there in 1965. The nephew has been able to keep the store going by specializing in old-fashioned items such as Veterinary Liniment and Grandma's Pure Soap, relying on tourists and a website.

Miller recalled when Rich's Department Store attracted shoppers to the corner of Broad and Hunter (now MLK Drive), just up the street. It closed in 1992. He also remembered Roy's Poultry and Fish, where you could choose a live chicken and have it butchered and dressed right there. Ornate Terminal Station lay down Mitchell Street, which hosted a row of elegant hotels for railroad travelers—all gone now. The Richard B. Russell Federal Building replaced the train station.

We walked west on MLK Drive to the corner of Pryor Street, occupied by the old Rich's Department Store until 1924. Now the large brick building, called the M. Rich Center, with its big central skylight, original maple floors, and open spaces, houses creative start-ups such as the Center for Civic Innovation, C4 Atlanta's Fuse Arts Center, and the Iron Yard, along with a chiropractor, architect, law firm, Internet radio station, baker, and printer. It is also home to *Creative Loafing*, the city's alternative weekly newspaper. I chatted there with reporter Thomas Wheatley, who lives in Westview and has covered many BeltLine issues.

Momentum may be shifting toward a south downtown revival. In the spring of 2016, Wheatley wrote about plans to convert the nearby M. C. Kiser Building, a former shoe manufacturing plant, into forty apartments, the area's first new residential units in over a decade. Kyle Kessler was pushing for a vacant school building on Pryor to become apartments as well. The old city-owned Atlanta Constitution Building at the corner of Alabama and Forsyth, right next to the Five Points MARTA station, vacant for forty years, might be renovated. The innovative Goat Farm owners initiated their "Beacon Project" to encourage artists to move to Broad Street. They helped clean up and restore a vacant building rechristened the Downtown Players Club, where the owners plan a performance space. Richard Miller rented out the upper floor of his drugstore as an artist's studio.

WRS, a South Carolina developer, has contracted to buy Underground Atlanta, with plans for a $400 million mixed-use retail and residential tower there. WRS has also purchased adjoining properties on Peachtree and Broad, including the Downtown Players Club. If Underground becomes a viable redevelopment, it could prove a vital link between northern and south downtown.

But Kyle Kessler isn't pinning his hopes for south downtown on such huge projects. "We can make a lot of little things add up, learning and making adjustments along the way, rather than waiting for an expensive silver bullet."

CHAPTER 15
THE FUTURE OF ATLANTA

I don't think people around this country have any idea about Atlanta. The only impressions of Atlanta are big highways with skyscrapers sticking out of them.

—Tim Keane, Atlanta Planning and Community
Development Commissioner

Atlanta is demonstrating how to achieve better balanced, less congested urbanization and create a park system that will supplant the city's interstate highways as the focus of daily life for hundreds of thousands of Atlantans. Still more important, the BeltLine demonstrates how cities in the 21st century can repurpose neglected, obsolete property, in the process creating a public realm that . . . alters daily life.

—Alexander Garvin, *What Makes a Great City*, 2016

As I first noted in the introduction, Atlanta is a city on the verge of becoming a great place to live and work, with sufficient density, multiuse trails, and public transit. Especially through the BeltLine project, it is in the process of remaking itself, connecting disparate neighborhoods while encouraging development and a booming economy. If it can happen in Atlanta, it can happen anywhere, and the BeltLine could provide a model for the rest of the country.

But Atlanta may also be on the verge of falling once more into over-hyped mediocrity, if city leaders continue to grasp at grand-sounding ad hoc plans that do little to change the city's fundamental inequities and inefficiencies. As I completed this final chapter in late 2016, the fate of Atlanta hung in the balance—along with the fate of the country under the next president—as a vote on crucial transportation taxes loomed. Fortunately, the taxes were approved, which could provide an unprecedented opportunity to complete the BeltLine trail system (with tentative transit), along with meeting other urgent public transportation needs. Or the money could be squandered on ill-advised, politically motivated projects that do not address long-term, balanced needs. Only time will tell.

In 2014, Matt Garbett, the carless community organizer who took me on a tour of the derelict old State Farmers Market in Adair Park,* wrote an irreverent editorial. "We need to stop referring to Atlanta as a 'world-class' city," Garbett admonished. "Atlanta is not in the same league as New York, London, Paris, or others." The city's movers and shakers all too often have pursued mega-projects, he noted, such as the new Mercedes-Benz Stadium, "further disconnecting entire neighborhoods from the rest of the city, and doing nothing to reduce the sea of parking that prevents the neighborhoods from becoming vibrant." He approved of the BeltLine but complained that "parking decks wrapped in a thin veneer of apartments spring up like mushrooms along the East-side Trail."

Instead of building expensive, stand-alone, "iconic" projects, Garbett suggested promoting "more walkable blocks on a human-scale street grid; emphasizing slow, incremental, sustainable growth for vibrant neighborhoods; and actively discouraging automobile use through our street design and building codes."

Still, he added, "I love living here. There is an electricity in so many of the people working to make the city better in small increments." That, too, is characteristic of Atlanta's adolescence—it's a small enough place that anyone with energy, vision, and commitment can make a difference. As Angel Poventud observed, "The bar is set very low for involvement in all aspects of the city if you show up and have a passion."

Garbett's editorial struck a chord with readers. "Atlanta is a city that wants to take the easy way out for everything. It's all facade and no

---

* See Chapter 12.

structure," one reader responded. "Problem is, outsiders can see the emperor has no clothes and no amount of sloganeering about being a World Class or International City can change that. Atlanta has great potential. Most everyone can sense that and feel excited about Atlanta. Unfortunately, too many think potential automatically will become reality."

Back to the City

While the city of Atlanta faces crucial choices, its suburbs also face a daunting task, as Georgia Tech architect and urban design professor Ellen Dunham-Jones observed in her 2009 book, *Retrofitting Suburbia: Urban Design Solutions for Redesigning Suburbs*, which offered examples of how to remodel dying shopping malls, big box stores, and acres of surrounding parking lots.* Despite the dramatic titles of other books, such as Leigh Gallagher's *The End of the Suburbs: Where the American Dream Is Moving* (2013), the suburbs aren't going away; they are, however, scrambling to adjust. Most planners and developers recognize that empty-nest baby boomers and young Millennials disdain cars and want to be able to walk to a restaurant, park, or grocery store. That's why Avalon, the upscale mixed-use development in Alpharetta in North Fulton County, opened in 2014 as an instant success—an example of new urbanism in the suburbs.

But Avalon has a problem, as its developer, Mark Toro of North American Properties, acknowledged. It lies eleven miles from the nearest MARTA station. In the middle of our February 2016 phone conversation, Toro, an advocate and user of public transit, groaned. He had just learned that suburban politicians had killed a proposed regional half-cent tax to support MARTA expansion.** "Unfortunately, you have suburban communities with their heads in the sand that will be eclipsed because they are not going to be able to compete," he said. North American Properties sold Avalon later in 2016.

Toro and his wife, empty nesters, moved from suburban Cobb County to Midtown Atlanta, the area around the thriving Peachtree

---

* Many large businesses are also abandoning suburban corporate campuses in favor of urban locations. For instance, IBM vacated its North Buckhead campus, which now houses North Atlanta High School.

** In March 2016 a surprise compromise bill passed, allowing only Atlanta city residents to vote for a half-cent tax in a November 2016 vote. Over forty-one years, that would provide over $2.5 billion for city transit.

Street corridor between downtown and Buckhead. North American Properties bought, improved, and sold Atlanta's Atlantic Station, then in 2016 purchased Colony Square at 14th Street and Peachtree, planning to refurbish that venerable mixed-use development. Citing Richard Florida's *The Great Reset: How the Post-Crash Economy Will Change the Way We Live and Work* (2011), Toro agreed that in the coming decades, cities will reurbanize dramatically. Home ownership rates will decline as more people seek flexible, convenient living in condos, townhouses, and apartments. "This sea-change is underway," he said. "Out my window I can count ten cranes building high-rise residential housing here in Midtown." Toro frequently walks along the BeltLine's Eastside Trail to see his daughter, who rents next to the Historic Fourth Ward Park.

Atlanta has plenty of room to add density in the coming years, as we have seen. Mayor Kasim Reed, despite criticism of his confrontational style, deserves credit for selling ailing city properties for redevelopment, including Underground Atlanta, Fort McPherson, and Turner Field, abandoned by the Atlanta Braves after the 2016 season, with the baseball team's move to Cobb County. Though much lamented, this may actually be one of the best things to happen in southern Atlanta, as mostly parking lots and impoverished neighborhoods surrounded the stadium. Georgia State University, which has been expanding in the downtown area, will buy sixty-seven acres, including Turner Field, in a joint venture with private real estate developers Carter and Oakwood Development. They have plans for student housing, apartments, retail shops, and a converted stadium for Georgia State football games.

Westside Woes and Plans

There is even hope for Atlanta's impoverished west side, impelled largely by Arthur Blank's guilt about building his enormous $1.5 billion stadium there. The Home Depot cofounder pledged $15 million, to be matched by the city, to help provide jobs, decent housing, safe neighborhoods, and new parks, particularly in Vine City and English Avenue. The Atlanta Committee for Progress, where the city's business elite wields quiet power, created the Westside Future Fund in December 2014 to coordinate improvement efforts. Under the leadership of John Ahmann, the ultimate insider who normally worked in the background, the Fund began a series of community engagement meetings in 2016.

Many residents remained skeptical, for understandable reasons. There was very little to show for over $100 million in grants dumped into the west side since the Olympics. More than 40 percent of the homes were still vacant, and over half the students dropped out of high school.

More effective have been small efforts such as Friends of English Avenue, founded by white Atlanta businessman John Gordon after the police murdered ninety-two-year-old Kathryn Johnston in her English Avenue home in 2006 during a botched drug raid. The group created two community gardens that help feed families in this food desert. In 2011, they recruited two African American Atlanta police officers to live rent-free in a home next to one of the gardens. Over the next five years, the community crime rate has dropped by 45 percent.

The Westside Future Fund is not focusing on Grove Park, the troubled west side BeltLine neighborhood I visited. At the Super Giant Food on Hollowell in Grove Park, Emory students helped plant a raised-bed community garden in the grocery store's parking lot. Yet the well-intentioned grocery manager couldn't make a profit, and the store closed in early 2016, leaving even more of a food desert. Reverend Larry Hill agreed to host the relocated garden at his Bankhead day-care center.

Nonetheless, with support from the Blank Foundation and Dan Cathy, CEO of Chick-fil-A, the Westside Future Fund may well have a vital impact on English Avenue and Vine City. Indian native Dhiru Thadani, a prominent architect-urbanist with headquarters in Washington, DC, will create a Land-Use Action Plan with community input. A draft plan promised to set aside 20 percent of new housing—up to 3,250 units—for people making only $14,000 to $24,000 per year.

Westside Works, the Blank Foundation jobs initiative, has already trained over three hundred residents, mostly for construction work. The City of Refuge, the homeless shelter that hosts the community meetings, is expanding beyond its headquarters, with plans to renovate other nearby buildings. The new Lindsay Street Park opened in 2015, and there are plans to complete long-awaited Historic Mims Park in Vine City.* Add to that the under-construction Westside Trail, ongoing efforts to clean up Proctor Creek along with an eco-park and parallel trail, more subsidized

---

* Rodney Mims Cook Jr. offered to pay $10.5 million to build sixteen monuments in the park to honor civil rights legends such as Martin Luther King Jr. and W. E. B. DuBois. But the park would be named for his forebear, Livingston Mims, who was a major in the Confederacy and an early Atlanta mayor, which has created a controversy.

homes for police officers willing to live in the community, a planned youth diversion center (instead of prison), a $30 million federal housing grant, and a possible new elementary school focusing on science, technology, engineering, and math, and you have impressive positive momentum. John Ahmann hopes to attract a major employer to the area. In June 2016 the Barack Obama administration named Atlanta's west side one of four federal "Promise Zones." While the designation does not guarantee funding, it gives communities an edge in applying for federal grants.

It all sounds hopeful. Yet consider that the city committed far more money to billionaire Blank's new stadium—$200 million in bonds backed by hotel taxes toward its construction, plus an estimated $900 million for maintenance through 2050—than to westside revitalization, and it appears that the Fund is underfunded. In addition, the city plans to build a snakelike, modernistic, translucent-covered pedestrian bridge to cross Northside Drive at an estimated cost of $23 million, claiming that it is doing so for the benefit of the community—even though neighborhood leaders loudly objected that the money would be better spent on affordable housing, local business initiatives, and job training. In reality, the bridge's primary purpose is to bring fans more easily to the new stadium. Deborah Scott, executive director of Georgia STAND-UP, has attended the Westside Future Fund meetings and still hopes for substantial community involvement and change. "Otherwise," she predicts, "there will be an uprising of poor black people in Atlanta. The current conditions are ridiculous, almost like slavery."

Affordable Housing, Slum Lords, and Judicial in Rem

If the Westside Future Fund miraculously transforms these devastated neighborhoods into desirable communities, will that push current inhabitants out? "I've not heard concretely how you have this level of development without displacement," an activist observed at the introductory informational meeting. While gentrification may generally help those with high school diplomas, its benefits won't reach many who are stuck in generational poverty, be it in South Atlanta, Peoplestown, Pittsburgh, Washington Park, Grove Park, Vine City, or English Avenue.

Mandatory inclusionary zoning, which forces developers to create a certain percentage of affordable housing in any new project, is no silver bullet, but it would provide a fundamental foundation for assuring that every development offers decent homes or apartments to low- and middle-income city residents. In his 2016 State of the City address, Kasim Reed, not hitherto noted for his attention to the poor, surprised his audience by citing the need for affordable housing. "I'm committed to an inclusionary zoning effort," he said. "It might be controversial for a city like Atlanta—but it's the right thing to do."* City council member Andre Dickens agreed, noting that luxury rentals constituted 95 percent of units built in Atlanta from 2012 to 2014, with many more in the pipeline. It was essential, he wrote, to require new residential developments "to dedicate affordable units for our workforce—I want our teachers, police, nurses and office admins to have the choice to live in the communities they serve."

But it isn't just middle-class employees who need help. I e-mailed Dickens: "I hope that you will have a sliding scale of affordability that includes people who are really poverty-stricken, such as many of the people who live in Atlanta's most devastated neighborhoods on the south and west side." He answered that it was "extremely tough to incentivize developers" to include truly impoverished residents. But it seems to me that demanding true affordability for all would create a level playing field for developers. They might scream and yell, but they would have to obey the law and could continue to profit by charging higher prices and rental rates for luxury homes and apartments. Otherwise, well-meaning affordability efforts such as those of the BeltLine organizations, Invest Atlanta, the Atlanta Housing Authority, and the Federal Home Loan Bank will only put a dent in the problem.

Atlanta is not alone in trying to cope with rapid growth that threatens to displace low-income residents. In September 2016, the White House issued a "Housing Development Toolkit" that warned of a national crisis in which many could not afford to rent near higher-paying jobs or strong career tracks. "Growing, dynamic cities like Atlanta, Denver, and Nashville used to be able to tout housing affordability as a key asset—but now see rents rising above the reach of many working families," the report stated.

Dickens introduced an affordable housing ordinance, passed in the spring of 2016, that forced city developers receiving public funds to set aside 15 percent of new units for those making 80 percent of the area

---

* Many other US cities have mandatory inclusionary zoning, including Austin, Boston, Seattle, and Washington, DC.

median income (AMI), or 10 percent of new units for those making 60 percent of AMI. Since Fulton County AMI was $67,500, families had to earn at least $40,500 for the most generous subsidy, and the ordinance didn't apply at all to self-funded developments. Dickens and two cosponsors subsequently proposed similar mandatory inclusionary zoning for all new multifamily housing in the area covered by the BeltLine TAD, even if no public money is involved. The bill would also create a housing trust fund used to create, preserve, and prevent displacement of affordable housing along the BeltLine. The legislation was still pending as this book went to press.[*]

Kasim Reed and Andre Dickens are both African Americans, and black politicians have run Atlanta for over four decades now. Yet, as Emory University political science professor Michael Rich pointed out, "the gap between black and white in Atlanta is greater now than it was 30 years ago." The inequity has only worsened since he wrote those words in 2002. A coalition of the business elite and politicians has always ruled Atlanta, as Clarence Stone observed in his classic 1989 book, *Regime Politics: Governing Atlanta, 1946–1988*. The concern has been for "what one actor can do for another," Stone wrote. "Instead of promoting redistribution toward equality, such a system perpetuates inequality." Members of the black middle and upper classes have thrived, but the hapless and often hopeless poor, of any racial or ethnic group, have not.

Although the BeltLine project alone cannot solve Atlanta's affordable housing crisis, it does have a mandate to provide 5,600 affordable units along the loop over the twenty-five-year time span of the tax allocation district (TAD), and after ten years, it had funded only a tenth of those, largely because of the impact of the Great Recession. During my research, I took part in a sparsely attended meeting of the Atlanta BeltLine Affordable Housing Advisory Board (BAHAB), charged with advising BeltLine organizations on affordable housing issues. BAHAB doesn't seem to have been particularly effective in its advocacy, however.

In September 2016 Ryan Gravel and Nathaniel Smith, founder of the Partnership for Southern Equity, resigned from the Atlanta BeltLine Partnership board, mostly to protest its lack of focus on affordable

---

[*] A more effective approach would require a federal policy change to provide housing vouchers for every family living below the poverty line. Currently, only a limited number of such Section 8 vouchers are issued. The family would pay 30 percent of its income toward housing, with the voucher covering the rest.

housing. Atlanta BeltLine, Inc. (ABI) chief Paul Morris acknowledged, "The pace with which affordability is declining is much faster than anything else happening in our economy." He said that Atlanta had reached an "inflection point" that required "overinvestment" in housing for lower socioeconomic levels, which is why he allotted an additional $2.2 million for affordable housing in the fiscal budget year ending June 2017. Soon afterward, ABI announced plans to float the first TAD bond package in five years, including new issues for $79.2 million, of which nearly $12 million (the mandated 15 percent) would go toward affordable housing.

But Gravel and Smith, in their resignation letter, called the amount set aside thus far "a drop in the bucket compared to the need." They pointed out, "If not for the underserved, 'blighted' communities of south and west Atlanta, the Tax Allocation District would not have been allowed under state law." They claimed that the Atlanta BeltLine Partnership had focused too much on fund-raising and not enough on equity issues. "We believe that *who* the Atlanta BeltLine is built for is just as important as *whether* it is built at all."

Another obvious and urgent matter is what to do about all the abandoned homes and vacant lots in Atlanta's worst neighborhoods. The city's overburdened Housing Code Enforcement Bureau has fought a losing battle simply to board up empty houses and keep property trash-free.

The vacant properties cost the city an estimated $5.7 million annually in services, lost property taxes, and neighborhood depreciation. Attempts to use the criminal courts to force slumlords and other absentee owners to fix the homes have been time-consuming, expensive, and ineffective. A web of limited partnership records has often made it difficult just to ascertain who the owners are.

In November 2014, an investigative reporter for the *Atlanta Journal-Constitution* traced ownership of many vacant English Avenue homes to Rick Warren, a white Buckhead slumlord who was waiting for the west side to improve so that he could unload the properties for a huge profit. Kasim Reed subsequently made it his personal mission to punish Warren, even sitting in the front row during a trial over squalid conditions and code violations on his properties that put him in jail briefly. Reed put the brakes on a deal in which the Blank Foundation was set to pay around $25,000 each for two dozen blighted homes owned by Warren, which would have gone to the Fulton County/City of Atlanta Land Bank Authority for resale and development.

While Rick Warren's conviction may have scared other absentee owners into making minimal improvements, it had little other impact. In December 2014, Emory University law professor Frank Alexander and a coauthor published a landmark document with an extraordinarily boring title: "Judicial in Rem Code Enforcement and Judicial in Rem Tax Sales: Optimal Tools to Combat Vacancy and Abandonment in Atlanta." Alexander, founder of the Center for Community Progress, works on vacant property issues around the country. In this report, he noted that Atlanta laws already on the books could expedite the acquisition and resale of derelict properties. Forget the "burdensome and expensive" criminal process. Use the civil courts to force property owners to *"fix it up, pay it up, or give it up."*

In a Judicial in Rem pilot program begun in June 2015, the city did just that with fourteen houses, demolishing them and clearing the land at a cost of $20,000 per property. Three owners paid the city back. For the others, the tax commissioner will eventually send out a "superpriority" Code Enforcement lien for that amount. If owners don't pay, the property will then be offered at auction to recoup the demolition cost and any back taxes, but buyers will have to pay at least as much as all the liens. That means no one will likely purchase the property, and it will go to the Fulton County/City of Atlanta Land Bank Authority, which could transfer it to Habitat for Humanity, affordable housing programs, or the like. In this win-win scenario, properties would go back on the tax rolls, new homes would be built, and people in need would occupy them. But as this book went to press, the demolition bills had yet to go out.

Planning Atlanta?

In May 2015, I attended an Atlanta conference to launch a book of essays called *Planning Atlanta*. At one point, a panelist joked that the book should have been called *Planning Atlanta—Not*, which drew laughs because it was painfully true. At that point, the city didn't even have a planning commissioner, the last ineffectual post holder having been gone for nine months.

But Kasim Reed finally lured Tim Keane from a similar position in Charleston, South Carolina. A North Carolina native, Keane, fifty-one, was confirmed in July 2015 and brought a refreshing candor and perspective to the job, spending his first six months revamping the planning department, especially the horrendous building permit process, and getting to know the city. When I met him in Atlanta at the end of 2015, he told me, "My department has not controlled how Atlanta has grown. In some ways, we are not even in the conversation." He was determined to change that.

In the next fifteen years, Keane predicted, the city could possibly triple its population to 1.5 million, while doubling the number of jobs to 900,000, as more people sought the core urban lifestyle.* He planned to create an ambitious design to accommodate that density while also making Atlanta a better place to live, with more green streets, conservation areas, and creek restoration. Instead of waiting to see what developers would do with Underground Atlanta, Turner Field, or the Civic Center, "we should tell them how we want it done."

Public transit has to be a vital part of that process. "We need to stop building parking lots." Forget the expensive plan to reinvent a streetcar grid. The much-hyped downtown Atlanta Streetcar loop was a disaster, with few riders in 2016 once it started charging $1, mostly because it was stuck in traffic. Instead, Keane suggested bus rapid transit (BRT) or some other form of rapid transit in dedicated one-way lanes carved from current four-lane city streets. Three-lane traffic with a middle turning lane would flow faster anyway and provide room for bike lanes. Ideally, parallel streets for this BRT-bike road diet would accommodate travel in either direction, so that transit riders could travel to most places in Atlanta in priority bus lanes.

"But don't you need streetcars because they are sexier than buses?" I asked. Keane scoffed. Give people a predictable, convenient way to get there faster, and they will choose it. "The only way to accelerate to a city of over a million, is if the lifestyle is preferred to other places. Fundamental to that are urban amenities, walkability, and public transit so that you don't have to drive everywhere," Keane said. "For me, the BeltLine is just one of those things. You need much more than that."

Three weeks after I met Keane, he hired BeltLine visionary Ryan Gravel to guide the just-announced Atlanta City Design Project, which would help the city "grow equitably and sustainably while maintaining its core character," according to the city press release. Gravel called it his "dream job," though it was parttime. Over the next year he would build

---

* The Atlanta Regional Commission forecast that by 2040, Gwinnett County would grow to 1.35 million, while the city of Atlanta would only broach 700,000. But it based those figures on past growth patterns.

a team and hold community meetings. Eventually, the process would lead to an overhaul of the city's zoning ordinances.

Gravel seemed the ideal choice for the position. His book, *Where We Want to Live: Reclaiming Infrastructure for a New Generation of Cities*, was just coming out; in it he discussed not only the Atlanta BeltLine but many other "catalytic infrastructure" projects, among them New York's High Line and prospective East River Blueway, Miami's Underline, Philadelphia's Rail Park, Detroit's Dequindre Cut Greenway, the Los Angeles River restoration, the Iron Horse Trestle in St. Louis, the Harismus Stem Embankment in Jersey City, the Midtown Greenway in Minneapolis, Lafitte Greenway in New Orleans, Buffalo Bayou Park in Houston, S-Line in Salt Lake City, Singapore's Rail Corridor, Vancouver's Arbutus Corridor, Buffalo's BeltLine, and Paris's Promenade Plantee and Petite Ceinture—all projects that are reinventing old infrastructure (mostly abandoned rails).

The Atlanta BeltLine is among the earliest and most ambitious of these projects, which constitute a new movement to help answer Gravel's essential questions: *What kind of place do we want to live in? And how can we start to build that vision?* His book provides inspiring examples.

The Future of the BeltLine

In his book, Gravel calls the BeltLine "emphatically simple and unbearably complex . . . a thing and also a place; a project and also a movement." It is indeed a simple idea: a city loop of trail and transit, linking parks and inspiring development. It is also incredibly challenging to execute, as readers of this volume know in much greater detail than Gravel reveals in his book. The BeltLine visionary made it seem that grassroots efforts magically brought the project into being. Although extremely important, Atlanta residents' enthusiastic support alone was insufficient. Gravel did not acknowledge the importance of Mayor Shirley Franklin's adopting the project and assigning Ray Weeks to create the Atlanta BeltLine Partnership and Atlanta BeltLine, Inc., to implement it.

Gravel laments that Weeks insisted on folding his Friends of the Belt Line into the Partnership, writing, "When ABP [Atlanta BeltLine Partnership] absorbed Friends of the Belt Line back in 2005, the project lost a conduit for the grassroots, sometimes rabble-rousing voice of the people." Yet without the four years that Weeks put into getting the project off the ground, securing passage of the TAD, and dealing with emergencies such as Wayne Mason's controversial tower plans, legal challenges to the TAD, and attempts by the Georgia Department of Transportation and Amtrak to commandeer the Eastside Trail corridor, the BeltLine likely would not exist.* Nor did Gravel write about the vital role of Atlanta's philanthropic community, such as the James M. Cox, Arthur Blank, Annie E. Casey, and Robert W. Woodruff Foundations, Kaiser Permanente and Coca-Cola, and others, including individual wealthy donors such as Weeks or Delta Air Lines CEO Richard Anderson. Because of its low density, Atlanta has an inadequate tax base, and the state contributes little to the city coffers. Without the business elite's support, few big public projects, including the BeltLine, could succeed.

Ray Weeks is himself a late-life convert to walkable city living. Following his divorce and remarriage, he moved from his luxurious semi-rural Garraux Road address in Buckhead to a house near the Eastside Trail, and he has a home in Charleston, South Carolina. He boasts that he can walk virtually everywhere he needs to go in both locations.

Still, Weeks is worried. "There is an illusion that the BeltLine is unstoppable. We played our part in making it appear inevitable. But the looming question is, will it really happen?" Weeks is right. At best, the project is a fifth complete, and the city doesn't even own all of the corridor yet. What if the next mayor doesn't push the project? What if federal funding dries up (unclear under a Trump administration)?

The BeltLine momentum is nonetheless undeniable, at least on the east side. Every $1 spent on the Eastside Trail has attracted $6 in private investment. Several new developments planned on Memorial Drive near the future trail include the purchase of the seventeen-acre Leggett & Platt Masterack industrial site, one of the few still active in the area—bittersweet for me, because my father created the Masterack division before selling it. Now the firm will move to rural Georgia. In the southeastern section of the BeltLine, another developer plans to put three hundred residential units along the future trail, and more growth is sure to follow.

Few would disagree that the BeltLine project is vital to Atlanta's transformation into a more livable, walkable, healthy, attractive, equitable city. Yet what began as a grassroots project has apparently become more bureaucratic and less responsive to public concerns. For instance,

---

* On the other hand, if the city had worked out a reasonable compromise with Wayne Mason, his projects could have provided earlier density along the Eastside Trail, a tax boost for TAD funding, and, perhaps, a streetcar line.

ABI is unreasonably proprietary about the use of the word "BeltLine," ordering other entities to cease using it. In October 2016, it asked Jessie Fream, creator of a Facebook page called "Humans of the Atlanta BeltLine," to rename her site, which features photos and short interviews with people on the trail. "It's just such a shame," Fream said. "The Belt-Line is a place where the community comes together; it's a safe place for everyone. But now we can't call it the BeltLine anymore."

Cathy Woolard, whose advocacy as city council president was vital to the BeltLine's early development, is running for Atlanta mayor in the November 2017 election. She continues to support the massive project but laments the lack of enforceable design standards. "Jamming private swimming pools, big fences and back doors along the BeltLine is not good enough," she observed. Instead, she called for "places for civic interaction, pocket parks and trees, terraces for sitting, public art and connections into the community."

Even the BeltLine's most ardent supporters disagree about details of how it should be built. One of the biggest arguments involves bikes and parks versus transit. Ed McBrayer, who lays down bicycle and walking trails for the PATH Foundation in metro Atlanta, would prefer to slap down his trails in the middle of the BeltLine corridor wherever the city currently has leased or purchased the rights. "Get people onto the Belt-Line, let them see how it connects neighborhoods and parks," he says. "Then when you have sufficient money, rip up the trails and do it right, installing streetcars along with permanent bike paths."

ABI is not proceeding that way. The 2.25-mile Eastside Trail cost $12 million, even without lighting or sufficient access points, and the 3-mile Westside Trail is projected to cost $43 million, mostly due to preparation for a streetcar line, as well as to create fourteen points of entry, eleven of which will be handicapped accessible.[*] Ryan Gravel admits that there isn't enough density along most of the corridor to support a streetcar now, but he believes in the *Field of Dreams* solution: build it, and they will come, adding population and employment opportunities.

If the BeltLine consists solely of trails and parks, Gravel fears that it will become only a yuppie recreational path that does little for the working class, those with disabilities, or those below the poverty line. They

---

[*] BeltLine streetcar preparation was necessary to secure federal dollars. The government would not have given an $18 million TIGER grant for the Westside Trail otherwise.

are the ones who really need public transit to travel more quickly on the BeltLine. In September 2016, when North American Properties and Vantage Realty Partners announced plans for a 4.4-acre development on DeKalb Avenue in southern Inman Park, Gravel realized that the way it was planned would prevent the long-planned BeltLine tunnel from diving under Hulsey Rail Yard in a direct line, and he was alarmed that ABI didn't appear to be concerned. Current plans call for the trail to go through the narrow Krog Street tunnel, but that will be an inadequate and hopefully temporary bottleneck. Unless transit and trail eventually go under the rail yard, Cabbagetown and Reynoldstown residents to the south will be cut off from quick travel access. In last-minute maneuvering, Gravel and community activist Angel Poventud helped negotiate design changes to the development that preserved the potential tunnel path, a block and a half to the west of Krog Street.

The money for that potential tunnel may be forthcoming. Atlanta now faces a choice of how best to spend new transportation tax dollars. On March 24, 2016, the last day of the Georgia legislature's session, a bill passed that would allow city voters to approve a half-cent tax to support MARTA, which would generate at least $2.5 billion (more like $3.5 billion as the tax base grows) over its forty-one-year life span. The legislation also allowed an optional vote on an additional tax, up to another half-cent, for five years—once again called a T-SPLOST tax (an unfortunate designation, in my opinion).

The city council opted for a 0.4-cent T-SPLOST tax proposal, aimed at generating around $380 million over the next five years. The biggest single item on the wish list is $65.9 million to complete the right-of-way acquisition and lighting for the rest of the BeltLine. Both tax options passed when city residents voted on them in November 2016— no surprise, since a city majority opted for the failed regional one-cent T-SPLOST initiative in 2012.

Robbie Ashe, MARTA board chair, opined that "the lion's share" of the long-term MARTA tax would go toward BeltLine streetcars, and Kasim Reed agreed. Gadfly Mike Dobbins, the Georgia Tech planning professor, disagreed with this plan, though he admitted that a streetcar might make some sense on the Eastside Trail to connect the current Atlanta Streetcar loop to Ponce City Market.

I can see valid points on all sides of the debate. Frankly, I have struggled with how the BeltLine should be completed. I agree with McBrayer that completing the trail should be a first priority. Complete the trail loop as quickly as possible, which will be much easier—and much cheaper—than figuring out how to get transit under or around Hulsey Rail Yard, or how to run the tracks alongside active rail in the northwestern segment, or how to link different grade elevations. The trail component by itself has already made an enormous difference on the east side.

Such a temporary trail may not require pavement. I have biked on a section of the Toronto Beltline (three segments totaling five-plus miles on the former Toronto Belt Line Railway, built in 1892), which features a hard, even surface of finely crushed gravel and dirt, and it works perfectly well, though it must be maintained.*

But I also think that eventual transit along the loop is vital for a number of reasons, even if Dobbins is correct about the lack of current density and destinations. Unless streetcars clang along the BeltLine—buses are too wide and are not an option—the density (condos, apartments, businesses) that the project attracts will come along with more cars, parking garages, and gridlock, defeating the original intention of the circular route. It would become primarily a crowded recreational path for the upper class, while impoverished residents (those who managed to remain nearby) would have to find some other way to travel any distance.

As of 2016, there were tentative plans to allow a mixed-use development, with at least 20 percent of the residential units designated as "affordable workforce," along the BeltLine next to Piedmont Park at 10th Street and Monroe, where Wayne Mason wanted to build his ill-fated towers. As ever more people flock to live near the Eastside Trail, some form of convenient public transit will become more urgent there.

The BeltLine streetcar should be linked to the existing east-west Atlanta Streetcar along Auburn and Edgewood, though I see no need for streetcars elsewhere in the city. The current Atlanta Streetcar has been a disaster, with low ridership other than tourists. If traffic were banned from its route, it might succeed. Streetcars elsewhere (other than on the BeltLine) would require ripping up streets to install tracks, and if they run in traffic, they won't attract enough riders. It makes far more sense to create dedicated bus lanes for bus rapid transit that would link with BeltLine streetcars.

---

* My brother John Pendergrast, who lives near Toronto and introduced me to its bike trails, wrote, "Other sections are in fact paved, I prefer the unpaved sections, because they are more natural, more park-like."

Completion of the entire BeltLine trail within the next five years is unlikely, even though voters have approved the new T-SPLOST tax. Paul Morris lobbied for using the entire sum to secure the complete Belt-Line right-of-way and finish building the trail, but he got less than 20 percent, with most of the tax revenue going toward street improvements, bike lanes, and sidewalks.

The list for the forty-one-year MARTA tax funding need not be as specific. In my view, that money could best be used for creating bus rapid transit lanes throughout the city as Tim Keane suggests, putting streetcars on the BeltLine, building a new in-fill MARTA station (and multimodal node) in Armour/Ottley, extending rail along the "Clifton Corridor" to the Centers for Disease Control and Prevention and Emory University (though only a mile of that Clifton Corridor lies inside the city limits), installing more protected bike lanes, putting Wi-Fi on trains, and many other possibilities.

Regardless of the specific implementation plans, I agree with Ryan Gravel that vision and commitment are all-important. "Anything is possible," Gravel told me. "It just requires planning and will. And the BeltLine will have a much greater impact than interstate highway improvements that cost far more."

Fencing Off Reservoirs?

Different players have different agendas. The Atlanta Department of Watershed Management will operate the Bellwood Quarry reservoir as an emergency water supply for the city. Contrary to Alex Garvin's plans for swimmers and sailors to enjoy the lake, Commissioner Jo Ann Macrina told me that she didn't want to let anyone near the water, even for fishing, for fear of bioterrorism or accidents. When I Googled the issue, I found only two articles about deliberate contamination of municipal water supplies, both published shortly after the terrorist attacks on September 11, 2001. "Even the most committed terrorist would struggle to obtain and administer the volume of toxin required to contaminate an entire reservoir or aqueduct," one concluded. "It would take an incredible amount of contaminant to cause any damage to our drinking water supplies," the other author agreed.

Macrina told me that Department of Homeland Security regulations prevented her from opening the quarry reservoir to the public or taking down the fences around the waterworks on Howell Mill Road. Yet when I asked her for a copy of those regulations and sent those two articles to her for comment, she never responded. Planning commissioner Tim Keane, who lives near the waterworks, would love to see the fences come down. "It would utterly change the feel of the city there," he said.

There is some hope for a Waterworks Park and perhaps recreational use of the quarry reservoir, since Mayor Reed fired Jo Ann Macrina in May 2016. Much depends on the attitude of new commissioner Kishia Powell (former public works director in Jackson, Mississippi), and the next Atlanta mayor, to be elected in November 2017. When I spoke to Powell, she, too, cited Homeland Security regulations in bioterrorism legislation passed in 2002 that order each municipal water authority "to conduct an assessment of the vulnerability of its system to a terrorist attack."

Yet she met with a broad coalition of business and neighborhood representatives, including City Council Member Yolanda Adrean, BeltLine chief Paul Morris, and Dwight Glover of the Friends of Atlanta Waterworks, to discuss how the Watershed department might partner with the BeltLine and Atlanta parks. "Watershed will not be a silo," she said. "The best solutions come through collaboration." Glover was encouraged that Powell "indicated a desire to open as much of the green space as possible and make it available for passive recreational activities such as walking/ running trails and picnic areas. I left the meeting very optimistic."

In the meantime, Mayor Reed and the Atlanta Public Schools (APS) board finally hammered out a compromise agreement in January 2016 to modify the unworkable TAD contract, which had held the BeltLine hostage for nearly three years. The city would fork over $14.8 million in past-due payments and pay $83.5 million more over the remaining fifteen years of the contract, instead of the $172 million previously promised.* The city would also give APS the west side property where Bankhead Courts, once a drug-infested public housing project, used to be. In the wake of the agreement, Reed finally agreed to release city deeds to vacant schools, such as the George Adair School in Adair Park, to enable their redevelopment.

Now, with sufficient prospective TAD income, ABI could float another bond and fund more affordable housing. According to the *Integrated*

---

* These figures include the $10 million allocated in the original contract for a school sports complex.

Action Plan issued by ABI in December 2015, however, half the annual TAD income of $21 million anticipated in 2016 must go to debt service, with $4.8 million required for BeltLine project costs. The report concluded that the BeltLine needed to raise an additional $1.5 million annually to buy land in order to take more control of affordable housing, development, and new job creation. But exactly how it would get the money wasn't clear.

In February 2016, ABI CEO Paul Morris predicted completion of the entire BeltLine project, presumably including streetcars, on schedule by 2030, though he admitted they had fallen far behind on some items. He promised to "reaccelerate and double down our efforts to catch up." I doubt that it is possible to complete the project on time, however, even if the new MARTA tax pays for the streetcar component, which still adds hugely to the expense and complexity.

The revised APS TAD agreement also removed a barrier to the BeltLine Partnership's continued philanthropic fund-raising. With the extension of the Eastside Trail south through Reynoldstown getting under way and active negotiations for the rights to the southern corridor linking the Eastside and Westside Trails, the time seemed ripe for again approaching major foundations.

Chuck Meadows, appointed executive director of the Beltline Partnership in November 2014 to replace Valarie Wilson, grew up in Washington Park on Atlanta's west side and earned degrees from Morehouse College and Harvard's John F. Kennedy School of Government before serving as head of Mayor Shirley Franklin's budget office, among other positions. When I spoke to Meadows, he stressed the BeltLine Partnership's role not only in fund-raising but in advocating for affordable housing and other equity issues and engaging community support.

In January 2016, Meadows and Deputy Executive Director Rob Brawner, who had been at the Partnership since its inception, launched "Light the Line," a grassroots crowd-sourced campaign to raise over $1 million to light the Eastside Trail. They were also hoping to convince commercial property owners along the BeltLine to create a "special services district" to pay an additional tax in order to finance a bond that might raise as much as $100 million. They planned to move their offices into the Atlanta Stove Works building adjacent to the BeltLine in the Old Fourth Ward, with exhibits, volunteer sign-up opportunities, and community meeting space.

But Meadows lasted less than two years, in part because he failed to establish close ties to the philanthropic community. In July 2016, the Partnership's executive committee, led by board chair Mike Donnelly, a Wells Fargo executive, voted to oust Meadows in closed session without consulting the entire board—among the reasons that Ryan Gravel and Nathaniel Smith ultimately resigned from the Partnership board two months later.

Without a search process, the executive committee appointed long-time second-in-command Rob Brawner as the new executive director of the Atlanta BeltLine Partnership, ready to kick off a new capital campaign and continue to support affordability and public health initiatives. "As a fifteen-year resident of an Atlanta BeltLine neighborhood, I have a deep personal commitment to the project," he said, "and I experience its positive, transformative impact every day."

Many unanswered BeltLine questions remain. When the Westside Trail is completed, what impact will it have? In 2016 a Texas developer bought several vacant warehouses along that trail, near the old State Farmers Market. The twenty-three-acre parcel will be home to several local food and beverage brands, including an expansion of Monday Night Brewing, Honeysuckle Gelato, cheesemaker Southern Aged, and Doux South Pickled—a hopeful sign for the blighted area. Otherwise, investors have been taking a wait-and-see approach.

When will the ABI managers finally pave the BeltLine trail north along the edge of Piedmont Park? And in the process, how will they cross the dangerous intersection at 10th Street and Monroe, where a teenage biker was killed in 2016? (The city is supposed to improve that intersection as part of a "Complete Streets" program.)

And when will the huge Westside Park be developed, at least for hiking or mountain bike paths? The city bought that land around the quarry back in 2005 but has done nothing with it, other than begin to blast a tunnel to fill the quarry from the Chattahoochee River.

What about the sad state of Maddox Park? In August 2016, the city completed a $1.3 million restoration of the swimming pool, with Mayor Reed presiding over the gala opening. I hope that this signals a rebirth for the entire park and that wholesome activity will return, rather than the predominant drug trade. But without vibrant adjoining neighborhoods to keep watch over it, and with no BeltLine passing by it yet, such optimism may be unwarranted. Only time will tell.

Paul Morris at the BeltLine Lantern Parade

The Lantern Parade

Even without "Light the Line," the Eastside Trail is already incandescent during the annual Lantern Parade, when Atlantans demonstrate their joy in communal celebration. On September 12, 2015, I made my own paper light in a local workshop. As night fell, I marched with 60,000 others who held an astonishing array of inventive lanterns, winding down the Eastside Trail like a multicolored serpent, accompanied by marching bands.

Most of the participants lived in Atlanta, but I was unusual in having been born there. Most Atlanta residents come from elsewhere in the South, other parts of America, or foreign countries.* Metro Atlanta is one of the most diverse regions in the country. Although racial issues remain important, socioeconomic class is a more meaningful divide nowadays.

During the parade, for a while I fell in with Chantelle Rytter, the small, lively woman who created the ever-growing event in 2010. A

---

* The US census collects all kinds of demographic data, but it does not ask where people hail from, so there are no firm statistics. In 2015, a reporter interviewed random people on the Eastside Trail. Only three of twenty he spoke with were Atlanta natives. The rest were from California, Arizona, South Carolina, Minnesota, Jamaica, Michigan, Illinois, and Louisiana.

grinning man wearing a green-lighted black suit and top hat pranced joyously nearby, passing out light sticks to children. "Hi, Mark!" he greeted me. When I looked blank, he said, "You don't know who I am, do you?" It was Paul Morris, in his element.

Stay Tuned

Like any other city, Atlanta remains a work in progress. But it is rawer, newer, and more open to change than most metropolises, with an engaging energy and sense of possibility. A scan of the *Atlanta Business Chronicle* shows that business is booming, particularly in the high-tech, service, start-up, and entertainment sectors. Georgia is the third-largest movie location in the country as well as the third-largest cybersecurity provider. Most of the faces you see in the *Chronicle* are still white, though that is slowly changing. Metro Atlanta has long been known as a black mecca, with African American business giants such as Alonzo Herndon, Herman Russell, Egbert Perry, and Noel Khalil leading the way.* Metro Atlanta has the third-largest black middle class in the country, behind New York and Washington, DC. Though the Atlanta region remains highly segregated—albeit voluntarily—more middle-class blacks are moving to mixed-race suburbs.

Atlanta-area businesses are increasingly global, with branches or headquarters overseas, so that time-zone juggling and international telecommunication conferences are common. For example, Sage, which sells software business products, is based in the United Kingdom but has offices all over the world. Rachel Gervin, the company's African American Atlanta-based lawyer, oversees seventeen attorneys in North America, Brazil, and Australia and coordinates with her European counterpart. To facilitate business, the Atlanta airport provides direct access to most major cities in the world.

---

* Herman Russell (1930–2014) grew up in the Vine City neighborhood, starting as a plasterer and creating a construction–real estate empire, despite a severe speech impediment. He mentored Egbert Perry and Noel Khalil, both of whom went on to head their own Atlanta-based construction firms (Integral Group and Columbia Residential) specializing in affordable housing. Perry, an Antigua native, sought to break the poverty cycle through mixed-income developments. "I saw people who looked like me who were sentenced before coming out of the womb because of race and class to go to worse schools and live in worse communities, and I thought I could change that."

In addition, with great restaurants, festivals, microbreweries, museums, music, and nightlife, Atlanta can be, and often is, a lot of fun. Although much about the BeltLine and Atlanta's future may remain uncertain, one thing is clear: for the foreseeable future, Atlanta will remain a "city on the verge," full of potential, hype, and hope.

EPILOGUE
GEORGIA ON MY MIND

Willie Mae Pughsley came to work for my family as a maid in 1950, when I was almost two years old, and she continued until I was a young adult, shortly before she died. She was about five feet tall, built like a fireplug, with thick glasses. When she walked up the hill every morning from the bus, she changed into her white uniform, which contrasted starkly with her rich, dark skin, in the bathroom off the playroom. It was unspoken that this was her special bathroom, just as Kathryn Stockett would write in *The Help*, her moving novel about the life of African American domestic servants in the South. (Stockett now lives in the Brookwood Hills neighborhood of Atlanta.)

Everyone in the family called her Nee, a nickname she apparently received because I couldn't pronounce "Willie." Nee was wonderful. We teased each other. If I disobeyed her—refusing to nap, stealing a treat from the kitchen—she threatened to take a mythical switch to me. I would say, "Ump, Nee!" And we would both laugh. She was my second mother. I loved her without reserve.

Nee fixed our family's dinner before my mother or someone else drove her to the bus stop around 5 p.m. She was an excellent cook but rather secretive—she didn't want my mother hanging around the kitchen.

I went off to Harvard in 1966. Nee seemed ageless and unchanged, and our mutual affection remained. We teased. We hugged. I was married while still in college and had a daughter. Nee offered to come care for her. I thought she was joking, but in retrospect I am not so sure. By the time Nee retired in 1974, I had two children.

Willie Mae Pughsley, called Nee by my family

She had a stroke the following year. I was busy, hassled, living in Vermont, and I didn't return to Georgia to see her. My parents visited her in the hospital, where the puzzled nurses told my mother that Nee kept saying she had seven children, even though they had no record of them. Of course, she meant me and my six siblings.

After her discharge, my parents and younger sister walked up the front steps to a small, well-kept home on Simpson Street where Nee's brother and sister, who had come from the city of Pittsburgh, were caring for her. She was bedridden. A month later, she had a second stroke that killed her. Again, to my eternal regret, I did not return for the funeral at the Wheat Street Baptist Church. She had willed $2,000, her entire life savings, to the church—an astonishing sum, considering her $10-a-day salary.

After Nee's death, it struck me that, although I loved her deeply, I knew virtually nothing about her. My mother told me that she was from Wrightsville, Georgia. When I was getting divorced, a few months before her first stroke, Nee told me that she'd had a son who died young and that she had lost two husbands: one fled; the other died. These things were "God's will, honey, just God's will," she said. I wrote a poem about her and got on with my life.

But I will never forget her, and a desire to get to know Nee's Atlanta, the other half of the city I grew up in, motivated this book to some degree. I found her death record but no obituary. She died on July 17, 1975, at age sixty-seven. So she was probably born in 1908 and was forty-two years old when she came to work for my family.

I talked to Florine Tuggle, the maid for the Chalmers family up the road for fifty-four years, who still lives in southern Atlanta. She remembered Nee as the social spark plug on the crowded bus, who knew everyone's birthdays and celebrated them. "Willie be telling jokes all the time," Tuggle said, though she couldn't remember any of them. "She'd have everyone just rolling on the bus." I asked if they laughed about their employers. "I'm not saying." She didn't like the movie version of *The Help*, in which a maid served her detested socialite boss a piece of chocolate pie made with excrement: "Nobody would have did nothing like that."

In the 1958 *Atlanta City Directory*, I found a listing for "Willie Pughsley, maid, r704 Simpson NW." In September 2015 I drove to 704 Joseph E. Boone Boulevard (the old Simpson) and found a total wreck of a home with a Code Enforcement condemnation sign. The concrete front steps matched my sister's memory. Probably Nee's rented home for many

The house at 704 Joseph E. Boone Boulevard, since demolished, where Willie Mae Pughsley once lived

years, until her death, it was the only remaining house on this block of the Vine City neighborhood, less than half a mile from the home on Sunset Avenue where Martin Luther King Jr. and his family lived at the time of his assassination.

When I drove by a few months later, Nee's old home had been demolished. That vacant lot lies 7.5 miles from my parents' home on West Paces Ferry Road. Yet I never visited Nee while she lived there, and I knew nothing about her friends and neighbors or her life outside our hilltop home.

This jarring juxtaposition of affluence and poverty has motivated quite a few well-intentioned Atlantans to get involved in efforts to improve conditions in difficult west and south side neighborhoods. John Gordon, founder of Friends of English Avenue, told me that he had brought over 1,000 fellow Buckhead residents on tours. "To a person, they say, 'I cannot believe that these conditions exist five miles from where I live.' A lot of them fly off to Africa to do good work, and I'm saying, 'Don't buy a plane ticket. Drive fifteen minutes, and there's plenty of work to be done right here." That's exactly what Bill McGahan, who lives on Ridgewood Road in Buckhead, discovered. For years, he had been going to Guatemala, before he founded Georgia Works!, the remarkable program that helps homeless men secure jobs and stable lives.

The BeltLine is bringing these two worlds together. Change is in the air in Atlanta, mostly for the good. Perhaps someday racial distinctions will mean nothing in this state. Still, I can't help thinking of my mother's story about the time she invited a prominent black minister to lunch at our house. My mother was a white liberal who served on the board of the Georgia chapter of the National Association for the Advancement of Colored People (NAACP). Yet her maid didn't reveal for years that she too was an NAACP member. My mother was shocked when Nee refused to serve this lunch. She apparently didn't want to appear subservient in front of the minister.

My mother didn't really get it, didn't see that she might appear condescending, even while trying to help. I am afraid that many well-intentioned white people (no doubt including me) often come across the same way. Better to try, though, than continue to live segregated and unequal lives.

ACKNOWLEDGMENTS

Lisa Bankoff, my longtime ICM agent, suggested I consider a book about Atlanta, my city of origin, since I had already written two other books related to the city (about Coca-Cola and the Centers for Disease Control and Prevention). I am grateful for her guidance, which led me on a four-year adventure of rediscovery. My original acquisitions editor at Basic Books, Tim Bartlett, was enthusiastic about the project; after he departed, Benjamin Platt took over to edit the book with skill, care, and patience, and then Lara Heimert guided it to publication. Jen Kelland performed a valuable final copy edit.

Howard Lalli, a former editorial staff member at *Vanity Fair*, the *New Yorker*, and *Atlanta Magazine*, among others, now runs an Atlanta marketing and public relations consultancy with a strong focus on urban redevelopment. An admirer of my previous work, Lalli supported this venture from the start and provided invaluable insights. He also helped to promote the book and encourage further discussion of Atlanta's future.

Several people read parts of the early drafts of the book manuscript and made helpful comments, including Dennis Creech, Michael Halicki, Howard Lalli, Betty Molnar (my ever-supportive wife), my brothers Craig and Scott Pendergrast, my parents Britt and Nan Pendergrast, and Grace Trimble.

Ryan Gravel, the architect and planner whose 1999 master's thesis provided the catalyst for the Atlanta BeltLine, was always helpful and gracious, taking me for a walking tour of the loop and inviting me to his home for dinners. Cathy Woolard, the former Atlanta City Council member who took up the BeltLine cause in its early, crucial phase, was always available and let me photocopy her documents as well.

Ray Weeks, who spent four years of his life organizing and launching the BeltLine effort, spent hours talking to me about his experience and has been supportive of my work.

Jim Langford, the former Georgia state director of the Trust for Public Land, let me spend hours in his office photocopying his BeltLine documents. Terri Montague, Brian Leary, and Paul Morris, the successive heads of Atlanta BeltLine, Inc., were generous with their time and insights, as were Valarie Wilson, Chuck Meadows, and Rob Brawner, the three heads of Atlanta BeltLine Partnership.

Wayne and Keith Mason, whose plans to develop the eastern Belt-Line were thwarted, gave me access to their records and hosted a memorable breakfast at the Gwinnett Chamber of Commerce's 1818 Club.

I ransacked Atlanta media archives and owe a debt to the journalists whose work helped me, most notably Maria Saporta, who has covered the Atlanta scene for decades and whose online *Saporta Report* is so informative; David Pendered, who writes for her; and Thomas Wheatley of *Creative Loafing*.

I am indebted to the nearly four hundred people who talked to me about Atlanta in the course of my research for the book, ranging from mayors to the homeless. I list their names in "Note on Sources," but that acknowledgment does not convey the passion and thought each brought to our discussions. Among them are those who invited me to stay overnight in their homes in BeltLine neighborhoods, though not all feature in the book: Marcia Bansley, Jarrett Bellini and Carolina Guerrero, Richard and Dianne Cohen, Debbie Crochet, Jeff and Katie Delp, Marvin and Pamelle Fleming, "Gary" in Grove Park, Rod and Bobbie Paul, Angel Poventud, Liz Ragsdale, Bill and Irene Seay, Caleb and Ashlee Starr, Sarah Toton and Micah Wedemeyer, and Ryan Walker. Thank you all for your hospitality.

Finally, to my family in Atlanta, I owe a deep debt of gratitude for support and information, including my sister Blair Vickery and brothers Scott and Craig Pendergrast and various cousins, but most especially my extraordinary nonagenarian parents, Britt and Nan Pendergrast, who hosted, fed, encouraged, informed, and loved me during my Atlanta research.

Nan and Britt Pendergrast, March 2016, in their backyard

They richly deserved the award they received in October 2016 from Greenlaw as "Environmental Heroes" for their lifelong dedication to preserving the natural world in Georgia. I only wish that my father had been there to receive the award. He passed away shortly beforehand at the age of ninety-nine and a half. I miss him more than I can tell. The research for this book allowed me to spend unforgettable additional time with him, as he reminisced, sang, recited poems, and listened with interest to the stories of my Atlanta explorations.

GLOSSARY

Below are names, acronyms, and definitions for organizations discussed in this book.

Area median income (AMI): frequently used in reference to affordable housing.

Atlanta BeltLine Affordable Housing Advisory Board (BAHAB): group charged with advising BeltLine organizations on affordable housing issues.

Atlanta BeltLine, Inc. (ABI): city organization charged with implementing the BeltLine.

Atlanta BeltLine Partnership: organization that handles fund-raising, community relations, and affordability advocacy for the BeltLine.

Atlanta Committee for Progress (ACP): an elite mayoral advisory group.

Atlanta Development Authority (ADA): see Invest Atlanta.

Boston Consulting Group (BCG): a global business consulting firm.

Bus rapid transit (BRT): dedicated lanes for buses, so that they avoid automobile traffic.

Center for Hard to Recycle Materials (CHaRM): for metro Atlanta household hazardous waste, bulky trash, and other hard to recycle items.

Centers for Disease Control and Prevention (CDC): based in Atlanta, the nation's premier public health agency.

Central Atlanta Progress (CAP): a nonprofit founded in 1941 to promote and improve the downtown Atlanta area.

E-SPLOST: a one-penny sales tax that may be used by school systems to build new facilities, renovate existing structures, improve school bus fleets, upgrade HVAC systems and pay debt from previous projects.

Georgia Strategic Alliance for New Directions and Unified Policies (Georgia STAND-UP): a nonprofit promoting sustainable growth, economic inclusion, and community benefits.

Inside the Perimeter (ITP): the area, including most of the city of Atlanta, inside I-285, the Perimeter Expressway.

Invest Atlanta: formerly Atlanta Development Authority, the city development agency.

Leadership in Energy & Environmental Design (LEED): a certification offered by the US Green Building Council for resource-efficient buildings.

Metropolitan Atlanta Rapid Transit Authority (MARTA): the city rapid transit system, including buses.

Multi-Modal Passenger Terminal (MMPT): a hoped-for Atlanta terminal serving trains, buses, and other transportation modes.

Outside the Perimeter (OTP): the suburban area outside I-285, the Perimeter Expressway.

PATH Foundation: the Georgia nonprofit that builds multiuse trails.

Perkins + Will: an international architectural firm with an Atlanta office.

Regional Transportation Plan (RTP): a regional plan integral to securing federal funding for projects.

Tax allocation district (TAD): an area in which additional tax revenues over a baseline amount, collected during a defined period, can go to area improvements.

Tax Allocation District Advisory Committee (TADAC): Atlanta group charged with advising the BeltLine organizations on how to spend TAD money.

Transportation Investment Generating Economic Recovery (TIGER grant): a federal grant to support designated regional or city projects.

Transportation Special-Purpose Local-Option Sales Tax (T-SPLOST): a tax, usually time limited, to support specified transportation projects.

Trust for Public Land (TPL): national nonprofit that purchases and resells land to be used for the public good, usually parks.

PHOTO CREDITS

Page vi: Mark Pendergrast

Page vi: Christopher T. Martin

Page viii: Carol MacDonald

Page 4:   Mark Pendergrast

Page 5:   Jim Schroder

Page 19:   Ryan Gravel

Page 39:   Atlanta History Center

Page 40:   Atlanta History Center

Page 43:   Atlanta History Center

Page 51:   Alexander Garvin

Page 68:   John L. Spivak, Harry Ransom Center, University of Texas, Austin

Page 73:   *Le Petit Journal*, October 7, 1906, courtesy Atlanta History Center

Page 113:   Mark Pendergrast

Page 118:   Mark Pendergrast

Page 151:   "SEC Index," "Data and Methods," "Atlanta's Neighborhood Quality of Life and Health Project," Center for Geographic Information Systems, Georgia Tech, http://www.cgis.gatech.edu /NQOLH/SEC_Index.

Page 159:   Christopher T. Martin

Page 185:   Mark Pendergrast

Page 205:   Mark Pendergrast

Page 211:   Mark Pendergrast

Page 215: Mark Pendergrast

Page 217: Mark Pendergrast

Page 223: Mark Pendergrast

Page 227: Courtesy of Sylvatica Studio Landscape Architecture and Ecological
           Planning

Page 244: Atlanta Regional Commission

Page 248: Mark Pendergrast

Page 287: Christopher T. Martin

Page 292: J. B. Pendergrast Jr.

Page 293: Mark Pendergrast

Page 297: Mark Pendergrast

NOTE ON SOURCES

....

To conserve space, I include this summary in lieu of specific citations and the full bibliography. They are available at www.markpendergrast.com and www.cityontheverge.com, along with selected taped interviews and videos.

Books About Atlanta

Frederic Allen, *Atlanta Rising: The Invention of an International City, 1946–1996* (1996); Andy Ambrose, *Atlanta: An Illustrated History* (2003); *Ansley Park: 100 Years of Gracious Living* (2004); Susan Kessler Barnard, *Buckhead: Images of America* (2009); Carlton Wade Basmajian, *Atlanta Unbound: Enabling Sprawl Through Policy and Planning* (2013); Kimberly S. Blass and Michael Rose, *Atlanta Scenes: Photojournalism in the Atlanta History Center Collection* (1998); Russell S. Bonds, *War Like the Thunderbolt: The Battle and Burning of Atlanta* (2009); Elliott E. Brack, *Gwinnett: A Little Above Atlanta* (2008); Rebecca Burns, *Rage in the Gate City: The Story of the 1906 Atlanta Race Riot* (2009); O. E. Carson, *The Trolley Titans: A Mobile History of Atlanta* (1981); Betsy Crosby and Elaine Luxemburger, *Brookwood Hills: Images of America* (2013); Ren and Helen Davis, *Atlanta's Oakland Cemetery: An Illustrated History and Guide* (2012); Harley F. Etienne and Barbara Faga, eds., *Planning Atlanta* (2014); Alexander Garvin et al., *The BeltLine Emerald Necklace: Atlanta's New Public Realm* (2004); Jennifer Goad and Philip M. Cuthbertson, *Historic Grant Park: Images of America* (2011); Ryan Gravel, *Belt Line—Atlanta: Design of Infrastructure as a Reflection of Public Policy* (1999); Floyd Hunter, *Community Power Structure: A Study of Decision Makers* (1953); Sharon Foster Jones, *Atlanta's Ponce de Leon Avenue: A History* (2012); David R. Kaufman, *Peachtree Creek: A Natural and Unnatural History of Atlanta's Watershed* (2007); (Richard) Moriba Kelsey, *Pittsburgh: A Sense of Community: Historic Reflections of an Atlanta Neighborhood* (vols. 1–3, 2012–2014); Clifford M. Kuhn et al., *Living Atlanta: An Oral History of the City, 1914–1948* (1990); H. W. Lochner & Company, *Highway and Transportation Plan for Atlanta, Georgia* (1946); Christine V. Marr and Sharon Foster Jones, *Inman Park: Images of America* (2008); Margaret Mitchell, *Gone with the Wind* (novel, 1936); Nexus Research Group and Davidson Consulting, *An Atlanta BeltLine for All: Equitable Development Assessment* (2013); Mark Pendergrast, *For God, Country, and Coca-Cola: The Definitive History of the Great American Soft Drink and the Company That Makes It* (2013); Michael Rose, *Atlanta Then and Now* (2001); James Michael Russell, *Atlanta 1847–1890: City Building in the Old South and the New* (1988); Charles Rutheiser, *Imagineering Atlanta: The Politics of Place in the City of Dreams* (1996); Norman Shavin and Bruce Galphin, *Atlanta: Triumph of a People* (1982); Marilyn Dorn Staats, *Looking for Atlanta* (novel, 1992); Clarence N. Stone, *Regime Politics: Governing Atlanta, 1946–1988* (1989); Terminus Films, *Better Know a Neighborhood: Inman Park and the Road Fights* (YouTube video, no date); *Up Ahead: A Regional Land Use Plan for Metropolitan Atlanta* (1952); Robert Harvey Whitten, *The Atlanta Zone Plan* (1922); Tom Wolfe, *A Man in Full* (novel, 1998).

Books About Cities

Robert Bruegmann, *Sprawl: A Compact History* (2005); Henry G. Cisneros, ed., *From Despair to Hope: Hope VI and the New Promise of Public Housing in America's Cities* (2009); Andrew L. Dannenberg, ed., *Making Healthy Places: Designing and Building for Health, Well-Being, and Sustainability* (2011); Michael Dobbins, *Urban Design and People* (2009); Andres Duany et al., *Suburban Nation: The Rise of Sprawl and the Decline of the American Dream* (2000); Ellen Dunham-Jones and June Williamson, *Retrofitting Suburbia: Urban Design Solutions for Redesigning Suburbs* (2009); Alan Ehrenhalt, *The Great Inversion and the Future of the American City* (2012); Richard Florida's three books: *The Great Reset: How the Post-crash Economy Will Change the Way We Live and Work* (2011), *The Rise of the Creative Class, Revisited* (2012), and *Who's Your City? How the Creative Economy Is Making Where to Live the Most Important Decision of Your Life* (2008); Leigh Gallagher, *The End of the Suburbs: Where the American Dream Is Moving* (2013); Edward Glaeser, *Triumph of the City: How Our Greatest Invention Makes Us Richer, Smarter, Greener, Healthier, and Happier* (2011); Ryan Gravel, *Where We Want to Live: Reclaiming Infrastructure for a New Generation of Cities* (2016); Richard J. Jackson, *Designing Healthy Communities* (2012); Jane Jacobs, *The Death and Life of Great American Cities* (1961); Alyssa Katz, *Our Lot: How Real Estate Came to Own Us* (2009); Joel Kotkin, *The Next Hundred Million: America in 2050* (2010); John Kromer, *Fixing Broken Cities: The Implementation of Urban Development Strategies* (2010); Christopher B. Leinberger, *The Option of Urbanism: Investing in a New American Dream* (2008); David Owen, *Green Metropolis: Why Living Smaller, Living Closer, and Driving Less Are the Keys to Sustainability* (2009); Witold Rybczynski, *Makeshift Metropolis: Ideas About Cities* (2010).

Books About Racial and Social Issues
(Including Some Specific to Atlanta)

Ronald H. Bayor, *Race and the Shaping of Twentieth-Century Atlanta* (1996); Douglas A. Blackmon, *Slavery by Another Name: The Re-enslavement of Black Americans from the Civil War to World War II* (2009); Tomiko Brown-Nagin, *Courage to Dissent: Atlanta and the Long History of the Civil Rights Movement* (2011); Rufus P. Browning et al., *Racial Politics in American Cities* (2002); Robert D. Bullard, ed., *Sprawl City: Race, Politics, and Planning in Atlanta* (2000); Rebecca Burns, *Atlanta: Yesterday and Today* (2010); Edward Randolph Carter, *The Black Side: A Partial History of the Business, Religious, and Educational Side of the Negro in Atlanta, Ga* (1894); John Emmeus Davis, ed., *The Community Land Trust Reader* (2010); Jeff Deel, *The Garden and the Ghetto: Stories and Reflections from the City of Refuge* (2011); Deloitte Consulting, *A Blueprint to End Homelessness in Atlanta in Ten Years* (2003); Matthew Desmond, *Evicted: Poverty and Profit in the American City* (2016); W. E. B. Du Bois, *The Souls of Black Folk: Essays and Sketches* (1903); Peter R. Gathje, ed., *A Work of Hospitality: The Open Door Reader, 1998–2002* (2002); David Fort Godshalk, *Veiled Visions: The 1906 Atlanta Race Riot and the Reshaping of American Race Relations* (2005); Thornwell Jacobs, *The Law of the White Circle* (novel, 1907); Larry Keating, *Atlanta: Race, Class, and Urban Expansion* (2001); Kevin M. Kruse, *White Flight: Atlanta and the Making of Modern Conservatism* (2005); LeeAnn Lands, *The Culture of Property: Race, Class, and Housing Landscapes in Atlanta, 1880–1950* (2009); William A. Link, *Atlanta, Cradle of the New South: Race and Remembering in the Civil War's Aftermath* (2013); Eduard Loring, *The Cry of the Poor: Cracking White Male Supremacy, an Incendiary and Militant Proposal* (2010); Robert D. Lupton, *Toxic Charity: How Churches and Charities Hurt Those They Help (and How to Reverse It)* (2011); Nathan McCall, *Them: A Novel* (2007); Steve Oney, *And the Dead Shall Rise: The Murder of Mary Phagan and the Lynching of Leo Frank* (2004); Charles F. Palmer, *Adventures of a Slum Fighter* (1955); Mark Pendergrast, *Inside the Outbreaks: The Elite Medical Detectives of the Epidemic Intelligence Service* (2010); Theda Perdue, *Race and the Atlanta Cotton States Exposition of 1895* (2011); Patrick Phillips, *Blood at the Root: A Racial Cleansing in America* (2016); Gary M. Pomerantz, *Where Peachtree Meets Sweet Auburn: A Saga of Race and Family* (1996); Robert D. Putnam, *Our Kids: The American Dream in Crisis* (2015); Kelefa Sanneh and Will Welch, *Atlanta: Hip-Hop and the South* (2010); David L. Sjoquist, ed., *The Atlanta Paradox* (2000); Curtis Snow, *Snow on Tha Bluff* (movie, 2011); Warren St. John, *Outcasts United: An American Town, a Refugee Team, and One Woman's Quest to Make a Difference* (2009); Anne Steffani, *Unlikely Dissenters: White Southern Women in the Fight for Racial Justice, 1920–1970* (2015); Hugh Thomas, *The Slave Trade: The Story of the Atlantic Slave Trade, 1440–1870* (1997); B. Wardlaw, *Coca-Cola Anarchist* (2010); Isabel Wilkerson, *The Warmth of Other Suns: The Epic Story of America's Great Migration* (2010).

Useful Newspapers, Magazines, and Websites

Atlanta BeltLine, Inc. (www.beltline.org); *Atlanta Black Star*; *Atlanta Business Chronicle*; *Atlanta Daily World*; *Atlanta INtown*; *Atlanta Journal-Constitution*; *Atlanta Loop* (www.atlantaloop.com); *Atlanta Magazine*; *Atlanta Progressive News* (www.atlantaprogressivenews.com); *Atlanta Tribune*; *Atlanta Voice*; *Bitter Southerner* (www.bittersoutherner.com); *Creative Loafing*; *Curbed Atlanta* (www.atlanta.curbed.com); *Georgia State Signal*; *Georgia Trends*; *Saporta Report* (www.saportareport.com); *Sustainable Communities*.

Interviews Conducted from 2011 to 2016
(in Person, on the Phone, and by Video and E-mail)

Bill Adams
Joe Agaha
John Ahmann
"Alabama"
Frank Alexander
James Alexander
Mike Alexander
Chamina Allen
Michael Allen
Charla Anderson
Karina Antenucci
Chris Appleton
Tina Arbes
Mark Arnold
Sylvia Attkisson
Clara Axam
Carla Bacon
Allison Bailey
Larry Bailey Sr.
Lula Bailey
Phillip Bailey
Van Baker
Scott Ball
Paul Ballew
Marcia Bansley
Patricia Barmeyer
Karl Barnes
William Alonzo Baugh III
Jeff Baxter
Sophie Beal
Joe Beasley
Anita Beaty
Jarrett Bellini
Don Bender
Stephanie Stuckey
    Benfield
Mona Bennett
Simon Berrebi
Edriyas Beyene
Ken Bleakly
Darin Bohm
Hope Boldon
Bill Bolen

Bill Bolling
Cathy Bradshaw
David Branch
Rob Brawner
Brent Brewer
Bob Bridges
Ernest Bridges
Arletta Brinson
Andre Brooks
Mitch Brown
Joel Buissereth
Rebecca Burns
Bill Butler
V. Butler
Shannon Byrne
Sarah Caldwell
Dean Campbell
Terriyln Cannon
Al Caproni
Cherine Pierce Carter
Kevin "Khao" Cates
Dana Chalmers
Adolphus Chandler
Beth Chandler
Lynn and David Chandley
Michael Chang
Penelope Cheroff
Ray Christman
Andres Ciho
Sarah Clamp
Bill Clarkson
Johnny Coates
Dianne and Richard
    Cohen
Lamar Collier
A. J. Collins
Brennan Collins
Nate Conable
Eugene Cook
Rachel Cook
Calvin and Adrienne
    Couther
Liz Coyle

Jessica Craik
Dennis Creech
Debbie Crochet
Jerell Cromartie
Taco Cullins and family
Giovanni Daou
Anthony Daugherty
Ethan Davidson
Ericka Davis
John Davis
Matt Davis
Murphy Davis
Ren and Helen Davis
Ruth Davis
Nazeera Dawood
Doug Dean
Bruce and Jeff Deel
Jeff and Katie Delp
Andre Dickens
Eli Dickerson
Jeff Dickerson
Clinton Dillard
John Dirga
Charles Disco
Mike Dobbins
Paul Donsky
Hattie Dorsey
"Dubelyoo"
Derrick Duckworth
Richard Dugas
Philip Dunphy
Jim Durrett
George Dusenbury
John Eaves
Debra Edelson
Lynn Eden
Sarah Edgens
David Edwards
Herman Edwards
Jacqueline Edwards
Sarah Eggen
Betsy Eggers
Bill Eisenhauer

Debbie Ellis
Korri Ellis
Elise Eplan
Leon Eplan
Barbara Faga
Hank Farmer
Amir Farokhi
Eric Farrell
Mike Ferguson
Frank Fernandez
Anna Marissa Fetz
Harold Fineroff
Marvin and Pamelle
Fleming
Sally Flocks
Pamela Flores
Cynthia Foncha
Matti Foncha
Anna Foote
Austin Ford
Aaron Fortner
Marianne Fowler
Shirley Franklin
Fredalyn Frasier
Christina Fuller
Stacy Funderburke
Erik Fyfe
Pierre Gaither
Jim Galloway
Matt Garbett
Alexander Garvin
LaTonya Gates-Boston
Sharon Gay
Randy Gibbs
Tracey Gibson
Greg Giornelli
Dwight Glover
Renee Glover
Roy and Faye Godwin
Jerry Gonzalez
Desmond Goosby
John Gordon
Lisa Gordon
Angela Graham
Leslie Grant
Mark Gravel

Ryan Gravel
David Green
Shaun Green
Roby Greenwald
Paul Grether
Bart Griffith
Clayton Griffith
Saru Grover
Carolina Guerrero
Bruce Gunter
Sarah Hagood
Michael Halicki
Daphne Hall
Kwanza Hall
Jack Hardin
Charles Harper III
Lyle Harris
Lee Harrop
Ariel Hart
Grace Hawkins
Mary Ann Hearn
Bakari Height
Walter Henegar
Drew Henley
Nick Hess
Kelly Hill
Larry Hill
LaShawn Hoffman
Mattie Holland
Holly Hollingsworth
Rose Gardea Holston
Terry Horgan
Tom Houck
Matt Hovde
Mattie Howland
Philip Hunter
Bobbie Hurt
Heather Hussey-Coker
Dan Immergluck
Uriah Israel
Danny Iverson
Shermarcus Ivy
Richard Jackson
Bill Jaeger
Sandi James
John and Julie Jamilkowski

Na'Taki Osborne Jelks
Valorie Jerry
Jennifer Jezyk
Derrick John
Richard Johnson
Arian Johnston
Chuck and JoElyn
Johnston
Darien Johnston
Sharon Foster Jones
Jeffrey Kalfret
Becky Katz
David Kaufman
Tim Keane
Kristy Kehely
Katharine Kelley
Richard Moriba Kelsey
Barbara Kennedy
Jim Kennedy
Allison Kessler
Kyle Kessler
Nelia Kimbrough
Deante King
Nia Knowles
Mike Koblentz
Andrew Kohr
Mark Kooyman
Abe Kruger
Kevin Kruse
Cliff Kuhn
Martha Kuhn
Howard Lalli
Jim Langford
Jane Langley
Jesse Latimer
Henry Lawson
Dick Layton
Brian Leary
Dean Leeper
Donovan Lee-Sin
Christopher Leinberger
Loretta Lepore
Greg Levine
Nicole Levine
Jerilyn Lewis
Aaron Lichkay

Ben Limmer
Ian Lindsay
Lexie Linger
Jennifer Lingvall
Milton Little
Saba Long
Ed Loring
Carol Lucas
Michael Lucas
Bob Lupton
Dana Lupton
Jocelyn Lyle
Jerry Lyles
Dan MacDougald
Mandy Mahoney
Pierluigi Mancini
Pedro "Pete" Marin
Kelvin Marks
Patricia Martin
Wayne and Keith Mason
Sam Massell
Joshua Mathews
Gayla Mathis
Felicia Matthews
Ed McBrayer
Toni Morrison McBride
Steven McClendon
Chris McCord
Tarria McCoy
Bill McGahan
Brian McGowan
Billy McMullen
Cameron McWhirter
Jeri McWilliams
Chuck Meadows
Josh Mello
Harrison Merrill
Anthony Miller
Richard Miller
Erin Mills
Jeanne Mills
Eric Mitchell
Jerald Mitchell
Gary Mongeon
Terri Montague
Katharine Montgomery

Charles Moore
Linda Moore
John Moores
Jim and Sally Morgens
Paul Morris
Emory Morseberger
Luma Mufleh
Jennifer Mummert
Wendy Murray
Crystal Nasir
Lucille Neeley
Carl Nes
Michael Anthony Newton
Murray Nicol
Yomi Noibi
Chris Norman
Elaine North
Marshall Norwood
Mary Norwood
Rashid Nuri
Steve Nygren
Tim and Becky O'Mara
Rick Odom
Dianne Olansky
Nolly Pabón
Darie Paige
Chris Palmer
Keith Parker
Carl Patton
Bobbie and Rod Paul
Ross Pead
Jason Pedersen
David Pendered
Britt and Nan Pendergrast
Scott and Craig
  Pendergrast
A. Perez
Patrise Perkins-Hooker
John Perlman
Egbert Perry
Alicia Philipp
Amy Phuong
Tony Pickett
Wendy Pike
Dan Popovic
Mary Porter

Tad Porter
Angel Poventud
Joanna Pritchard
Jeff Rader
Liz Ragsdale
Kasim Reed
Tom and Karen Reed
Lauren Reidy
Ivan Rendon
Richard Respess
Amanda Rhein
Michael Rich
Nancy Rigby
Randy Roark
Elizabeth Roberts
A. J. Robinson
Helen Robinson
John Robinson
Willie Louise Robinson
Will Rogers
Ken Rosenberger
Catherine Ross
Helen Ross
Nina Rubin
Jon Rudick
Kismick Rushin
Michelle Rushing
Susan Rutherford
Chantelle Rytter
Ian Sanson
Maria Saporta
Tetra Savoy
Hugh Saxon
Andy Schneggenburger
Franz Schneider
Jim Schroder
Paul Schumacher
Beverly Scott
Deborah Scott
Bill Seay
Justin Segall
Rebecca Serna
John Sherwood
Charlie Shufeldt
John Sibley
Burke Sisco

Jim Skinner
Cindy Smith
Jasmine and Edward Smith
John Smith
Markham Smith
Paul Smith
Priscilla Smith
Nathan Soldat
John Somerhalder
Dorothy Spear
Nancy Stangle
Adam Stanley
Ashlee and Caleb Starr
Christopher Stephans
John Steward
Jim Stokes
Chase Stowers
Kit Sutherland
Starling Sutton
Katherine Suzman
Patrick Sweeney
John and Midge Sweet
Michael Syphoe
Helen Tapp
Michael Tarver
Damon Tate
William Teasley
Ted Terry

Sheryl Thacker
Kalin Thomas
Robert Thompson
Latron Thorne
Jamie Thornton
Eddie Tigner
Sara Toerig
Paige Tolbert
Mark Toro
Brenda Torpy
Tony Torrence
Sarah Toton
Horace Tribble
Grace Trimble
Florine Tuggle
Connie Veates
Andrew Vernon
J. B. Vick
Kakhi Wakefield
Ryan Walker
Ross Wallace
Shawn Walton
Chuck Warbington
Columbus Ward
Micah Wedemeyer
Ray Weeks
Cindy and Mark
    Weinbaum

Barry Weinstock
Carl Westmoreland
Matt Westmoreland
Tom Weyandt
Charles Whatley
Thomas Wheatley
Alycen Whiddon
LaKeta Whittaker-
    Williams
Sermanu Whitten
Alvin Wilbanks
Deborah Williams
Molly Williams
Cain Williamson
Jim Williamson
Tony Williamson II
Princess Wilson
Valarie Wilson
Tracy Woodard
Cathy Woolard
Alyssa Wright
Evelyn Wynn-Dixon
Fred Yalouris
Ivory Lee Young
Mtamanika Youngblood
Sam Zamarripa
Pamela Zhang

INDEX

Adair, George, 34, 98
Adair Park neighborhood, 7, 48, 80, 157, 165, 201, 203–207
Adams, Bill, 193
Adrean, Yolanda, 284
African Americans
 health inequities, 147–149
 racial divide and, 63–83
 See also racial issues
affordable housing, 10, 21, 23, 26, 61–64, 88, 91–92, 112, 122, 128, 130, 168–169, 182, 206–207, 233, 262, 272–276, 284–285, 288
AGL Resources, 103
Ahmann, John, 270–272
air pollution, 18, 41, 43, 138, 140, 146–147
airport, 9, 24, 41, 250, 253–254, 288
Alexander, Frank, 276
Allen, Ivan, Jr., 81
Alpharetta, 175, 269
Ambrose, Andy, 77
The American City: What Works, What Doesn't (Garvin), 48
Amtrak, 101–103, 232, 263, 279
Anderson, Richard and Susan, 161, 279
Annie E. Casey Foundation, 201–202, 279
Ansley, Edwin, 38, 238–239
Ansley Mall, 9, 109, 237–238, 241

Ansley Park neighborhood, 9, 38, 41, 76, 139, 238–241
anti-semitism, 75–76
Arboretum, BeltLine, 99, 128, 146
Ardmore Park, 231
Armour Drive Industrial Park, 233, 235
Armour/Ottley neighborhood, 9, 235–240, 283
Arnold, Mark, 22–24
Art on the BeltLine, 131, 134, 175
Arthur Blank Foundation, 49, 51–52, 56, 93, 163, 213, 271, 275, 279
Ashe, Robbie, 281
Astra Group, 127–128, 161
Atkinson, Henry, 37, 40
Atlanta
 founding of, 32–33
 future of, 267–289
 image of, 75, 81, 268–269
 map of metropolitan region, 244 (fig.)
 population growth, 42, 88, 243
 post-Civil War, 33–34
 street scenes (1914 and 1924), 39 (photo), 40 (photo)
Atlanta, Cradle of the New South: Race and Remembering in the Civil War's Aftermath (Link), 66
Atlanta & LaGrange Railroad, 32
Atlanta & Richmond Air-Line Railway, 14, 35

Atlanta & West Point Belt Line, 14, 37
Atlanta & Western Railroad, 29
Atlanta BeltLine Inc.
    affordable housing, 61, 130
    Brian Leary and, 121–124, 126,
        128, 134–135, 155, 157
    buyout of Wayne Mason, 97
    etiquette campaign, 159–160
    on funding, 165–166
    homeless encampments and, 6–7,
        14, 23, 25, 29, 108–110, 131
    Integrated Action Plan (2015), 284–285
    Terri Montague hiring, 91–93
    opposition from Brookwood Hills
        residents, 233
    Paul Morris and, 153, 155–158,
        165–166, 275
    public health benefits, 153
    State Farmers Market and, 207
    Strategic Implementation Plan, 135,
        157–158
    use of word "BeltLine," 280
    Wayne Mason and, 93–97
Atlanta BeltLine Partnership, 296
    affordable housing issues, 91, 122,
        182, 274–275, 284–285
    Chuck Meadows and, 285–286
    community adoption of trail
        segments, 131
    community involvement, 131
    conflict with TPL, 89
    formation, 55
    Friends of the Belt Line absorbed
        by, 278
    fund raising, 130, 160–161, 275,
        285–286
    Ray Weeks and, 85–86, 91–93,
        102–103, 160–161, 278–279
    resignations from board, 274–275,
        286
    Rob Brawner and, 285–286
Atlanta Bicycle Coalition, 140–141
Atlanta Board of Education, 61–62,
    190, 192
Atlanta Committee for Progress,
    160–161, 270

Atlanta Community Food Bank, 108,
    152, 169
Atlanta Consolidated Street Railway
    Company, 36
Atlanta Constitution, 33, 69, 72
Atlanta Cycling Festival, 141
Atlanta Daily Intelligencer, 64
Atlanta Department of Watershed
    Management, 87, 90, 143–144,
    226, 283–284
Atlanta Detention Center, 150
Atlanta Development Authority, 29,
    45, 53, 57, 59, 91
    see also Invest Atlanta
Atlanta Georgian, 72
Atlanta Housing Authority, 162
Atlanta Journal-Constitution, 17, 25, 48,
    56, 60, 122, 134, 275
Atlanta Land Trust Collaborative,
    131
Atlanta Medical Center, 180
Atlanta Neighborhood Downtown
    Association, 264
Atlanta News, 73
The Atlanta Paradox (Sjoquist), 63
Atlanta Public Schools, 93, 156,
    164–166, 284–285
Atlanta Race Riot of 1906, 63, 73–75,
    73 (illustration), 78, 189, 239
Atlanta Railway & Power Company,
    37
Atlanta Rapid Transit Company, 37
Atlanta Real Estate Board, 76–77
Atlanta Regional Commission, 24,
    28, 45, 123, 169, 247, 252–253,
    264, 277
Atlanta Street Railway Company,
    34
Atlanta Streetcar, 158, 166–167, 192,
    277, 281
Atlanta Streets Alive, 141
Atlanta Technical College, 109
Atlanta Union Mission (Atlanta
    Mission), 108, 115–116
Atlanta University, 65, 67, 69, 71, 76,
    149, 181, 212

Atlanta Waterworks, 8, 50, 142, 225–228, 284
Atlanta-Fulton Public Library System, 62
Atlantic Station, 8, 26, 121–123, 169, 226, 270
Atlantic Steel, 26, 38, 121–122
Auburn Avenue, 181–182, 191, 251–252
automobiles, 38–42, 45
 see also traffic problems
Avalon, 269
Axam, Clara, 55

Bailey, Lula, 148, 200
Baker, Ray Stannard, 74
bank failures, 97–98
Bankhead neighborhood, 8, 86, 101, 104, 122, 203, 214–224, 234, 262, 271, 284
Bankhead Bounce, 218
Bansley, Marcia, 146, 239–240
BAPS Shri Swaminarayan Mandir, 246, 247 (photo)
Barber, Jesse Max, 63
Barnes, Roy, 45, 95
Barry Real Estate, 95–96
Battle of Peachtree Creek, 228
Baugh, William Alonzo, III, 234
Baxter, Jeff, 159, 232
Bearings Bike Shop, 205, 207
 see also Beltline Bike Shop
Beaty, Anita, 116–119, 118 (photo)
Bedford Pine, 178–180
Beeler, John, 40
Bellwood Quarry, 8, 49, 51, 51 (photo), 61, 85–87, 129, 144, 158, 215, 224, 283–286
BeltLine
 cost of, 54, 158
 early friends, 26–30
 funding (see funding)
 future of, 278–283
 grassroots movement, start of, 22–26
 Gravel's early ideas for, 14–15, 18–22, 19 (fig.)

inevitability, 155–169
 press coverage, early, 25–26
 private/philanthropic donations, 49, 51–52, 56, 279
 spending scandal, 133–136, 155
 years 2006–2009, 85–104
 years 2009–2012, 121–136
 years 2013–2015, 155–169
BeltLine Affordable Housing Advisory Board, 274
BeltLine Bike Shop, 2–5 (photo), 204–205
The BeltLine Emerald Necklace: Atlanta's New Public Realm (Garvin), 49, 85, 89, 226
Beltline Partnership. See Atlanta BeltLine Partnership
BeltLine Urban Farm, 206
Benfield, Stephanie Stuckey, 145
Berkeley Park neighborhood, 8, 225–228
bicycling, 23, 140–142, 159, 196, 204, 280
The Birth of a Nation (film), 76
The Black Side: A Partial History of the Business, Religious, and Educational Side of the Negro in Atlanta (Carter), 69
Blackmon, Douglas, 67–68
Blank, Arthur, 83, 114, 163, 212–213, 270
Blue-Eyed Daisy, 260–261
The Bluff, 86, 114, 214
 see also Bankhead, English Avenue
Bolling, Bill, 152
Borders, William Holmes, 79
Boston, Carlos, 221–222
Boston Consulting Group, 92
Boulevard Avenue corridor, 77, 178–181
Boulevard Crossing Park, 126
Bowen, J. W. E., 69
Bowen, Rudy, 123
Bowens, Eugene, 96, 103
Boynton Village, 198
Bradshaw, Cathy, 183

Brawner, Rob, 129, 285–286
Brewer, Charles, 4, 5, 25
Bright, Richard, 99
Brookhaven, 244
Brookwood Hills neighborhood, 9, 41,
    76, 231–234, 291
Brown v. Board of Education, 80
Brownsville, 71, 74, 189
    see also South Atlanta
Buckhead
    affluence, 61, 80, 105–106, 234
    Atlanta annexation of, 80, 231
    KKK Imperial Palace, 76
    streetcar line to, 38
Buntin, John, 189
buses, 40–42, 45, 168, 250, 277,
    282–283
Butler, Lee, 175
Buttermilk Bottom, 176–177
Byrne, Shannon, 258–259

Cabbagetown neighborhood, 4, 21,
    34, 187, 281
Callan Castle, 36, 185
Candler, Asa, 36, 38, 109, 185
Candler Park neighborhood, 41
Carrie Steele Orphan Home, 66
Carson, O. E., 40
Carstarphen, Meria, 164–165
Carter, Cherine Pierce (Benny),
    212–214
Carter, Edward Randolph, 69
Carter, Jimmy, 183–184
Carter Center and Presidential
    Library, 174, 184
Cascade Heights neighborhood, 124
CAUTION (Citizens Against
    Unnecessary Thoroughfares in
    Older Neighborhoods), 184
Centennial Park, 125, 264
Center for Hard to Recycle Materials
    (CHaRM), 145
Center for Civic Innovation, 264
Centers for Disease Control and
    Prevention (CDC), 137
Central Atlanta Progress, 117, 263

Chandley, Lynn and David, 186
Chang, Michael, 146–147
charter schools, 29, 131, 194–196,
    198, 210
Chattahoochee Brick Company, 34,
    67
Chattahoochee NOW, 260
Chattahoochee River, 7, 31, 51, 100,
    142–144, 223–224, 260, 286
churches, black, 67, 69, 83, 218–220
Circle Line, 16
City Lights building, 180–181
City of Refuge, 114–115, 271
Civic Center, 162, 164, 176, 270, 277
civil rights movement, 63, 83, 130,
    176, 181–182, 190–191, 208, 259,
    272
Civil War, 33–35, 64, 100, 189, 259
*The Clansman: An Historical Romance of
    the Ku Klux Klan* (Dixon), 72, 76
Clark University, 74, 192
Clarkston, 254–257, 262
Clayton County, 250–254
Clean Air Act, 45, 146
Clean Water Act, 28
Clear Creek, 10, 35, 231–234, 238
Cleveland, Grover, 70
C-Loop, 25–26
Coca-Cola
    ads in KKK newspaper, 76
    Boulevard revitalization, 180
    cocaine in, 34, 72
    donations from, 52, 123, 279
    invention of, 34, 66
    Robert Woodruff and, 79, 81
Coca-Cola Anarchist (Wardlaw), 116
Cohen, Richard and Dianne Harnell,
    261
colleges, black, 67
Collier, Andrew Jackson, 228
Collier, George Washington, 238
Collier, Meredith and Elizabeth, 228
Collier Hills neighborhood, 8,
    100–101, 228–231
Columbians, 79
Committe, Tim, 47–48, 52

Community Grounds, 189, 192, 196

Community Power Structure: A Study of Decision Makers (Hunter), 79

commuter rail, 52, 101–103

Complete Streets concept, 140, 227, 286

congestion, 18, 21, 37, 40, 42, 132, 140, 243, 245, 263

Continental Wingate, 178, 180

convict-lease system, 67

Conway, Butch, 249

Cook, Rodney Mims, Jr., 271

Cotton States and International Exposition, 69

Cousins, Tom, 195

Covenant House, 116

Cox Enterprises, 17, 52, 126

Creative Loafing, 117, 264–265

Creech, Dennis, 144–145

Creek Indians, 31, 142, 228

crime, 147–148, 158–159, 161, 176, 181, 193, 229–230, 250

CSA (community-supported agriculture), 151

CSX, 3, 6, 8–9, 11, 14, 50, 230–231

C-Tran, 250

Cultural Ring project, 14–15, 18, 23

Cyclorama, 35, 193–194

D. H. Stanton Park, 6, 29, 48, 126, 198

Darktown, 71, 74, 78

Darlington apartment building, 234, 243

Davis, Erroll, 164, 198

Davis, Murphy, 119

Deal, Nathan, 124

Deel, Bruce, 114–115

Delp, Jeff and Katie, 195–197

desegregation, 80–81, 200

Designing Healthy Communities (Jackson), 137–139

Desmond, Matthew, 206–207

detention pond, 90, 143

Dickens, Andre, 273–274

Dirty Truth Campaign, 98

Dixon, Thomas, 72, 76

Dobbins, Mike, 22, 59–60, 132, 158, 227, 281–282

Dobbs, John Wesley, 79, 82, 176, 182

Dodd, Benita, 167

Donnelly, Mike, 286

Downtown Connector, 41, 43, 147

downtown "donut hole," 173, 243, 262–265

Drip Coffeehouse, 5, 160

Du Bois, W. E. B., 71–72, 74–75

Duckworth, Derrick, 204–205

Dunham-Jones, Ellen, 269

Duluth, 246

Dunwoody, 244

Durham, Janice, 109–110

Durley, Gerald, 55

Dusenbury, George, 162

EarthCraft certification, 144, 260

East Beltline neighborhoods, 173–187

East Lake neighborhood, 29, 36, 195

Eastside Trail, 10–11
  building of, 127–128
  cost, 128, 280
  development around, 174–175
  East Beltline neighborhoods, 173–187
  educational tours, 146, 175
  funding of, 279
  growing pains, 158–160, 159 (photo)
  health benefits, 153
  housing near, 129–130, 268
  Lantern Parade, 287–288, 287 (photo)
  lighting, 285
  linking to Westside, 285
  success of, 156

Edelson, Debra, 223

Edgens, Sarah, 22–24

Eggers, Betsy, 254–257

Eisenhauer, Bill, 90

Elsas, Jacob, 75

Emerald Corridor LLC/Foundation, 144, 223

Emory University, 25, 194
*The End of the Suburbs: Where the
American Dream is Moving*
(Gallagher), 269
energy efficiency, 144–146
English, James, 34, 67
English Avenue neighborhood, 80,
86, 114, 163, 205, 214, 218,
270–272, 275, 294
Enota Park, 7
Environmental Protection Agency, 28
Eplan, Leon, 239
Eriksen, Michael, 152
E-SPLOST, 249
Estep, Jessica, 155
*Evicted: Poverty and Profit in the American
City* (Desmond), 206–207

Felton, Rebecca Latimer, 70
Five Points, 72–73
Flocks, Sally, 139, 227–228
flooding issues, 90, 144, 230
Florida, Richard, 270
Focused Community Strategies
(FCS), 192–197
Fonda, Jane, 28
food bank, 108, 152, 169
food deserts, 7, 150–152, 271
foreclosures, 96, 98, 101, 130, 161,
204, 248
Forest Park, 250
Forrest, Nathan Bedford, 66
Fort McPherson, 65, 163, 270
Forward Atlanta advertising
campaign, 40–41
Fowler, Marianne, 16
Frank, Leo, 75–76
Franklin, Shirley, 27–29, 45
Atlanta BeltLine Partnership, 55,
278
Bellwood Quarry purchase, 85–87
BeltLine funding, 54, 59–60, 91
GDOT MMPT project, 102–103
homelessness issues, 108, 111
Kasim Reed and, 124
March 2004 meeting, 47–48

moratorium on large home
building, 99
Purpose Built Communities, 195
water system, 143
Wayne Mason and, 53, 57, 94
Freedmen's Bureau, 65
Freedom Park Trail, 17, 184
Friedberg, Andy, 206
Friends of English Avenue, 271, 294
Friends of the Belt Line, 28–29, 49,
52, 55, 91, 278
Fulton Bag and Cotton Mill, 34, 75,
187
Fulton County Commission, 54,
59–60, 62
Fulton County Department of Family
and Child Services, 215
Fulton County Jail, 87, 108, 117
funding
Alycen Whiddon and, 26–27, 29, 47
Atlanta Streetcar, 166–167
Boston Consulting Group (BCG)
plan, 92
Eastside Trail, 279
Empowerment Zone, 191
E-SPLOST, 249
MARTA, 44, 281, 283, 285
private/philantropic donations, 49,
51–52, 56, 89, 158, 160–161, 279,
285
Shirley Franklin and, 54, 59–60, 91
in *Strategic Implementation Plan,* 158
streetcars, 132–133, 158, 280–281,
285
TAD (*see* tax allocation district)
TIGER grants, 125, 157, 160, 280
T-SPLOST, 132–134, 233, 281–283
Westside Trail, 157, 160–161, 280
Funtown, 11
Fuqua Corporation, 160

Gaither, Pierre, 201
Gallagher, Leigh, 269
Gammon Theological Seminary, 67,
74
Garbett, Matt, 207, 268

Garvin, Alexander, 47–53, 87
  Bellwood Quarry and, 49, 51, 283
  The BeltLine Emerald Necklace:
    Atlanta's New Public Realm, 49, 85,
    89, 226
  future of Atlanta, 267
  Paul Morris and, 156
  Wayne Mason and, 53
Gates-Boston, LaTonya, 203, 221–222
Gateway Center, 108, 112–113, 116
gentrification
  beneficiaries of, 272
  displacement by, 21, 61, 88, 92, 129
  Grant Park, 194
  myth of, 189
  Old Fourth Ward, 177
  South Atlanta, 196
Georgia Department of
    Transportation (GDOT), 24, 238
  ABI agreement with, 123
  attempt to commandeer Eastside
    Trail corridor, 279
  fly-over lanes, 245
  Interstate 495 plans, 183
  MMPT project, 101–103
  pedestrians and, 139–140
  Road Fight, 183
Georgia Dome, 83, 163
Georgia Electric Light Company, 37
Georgia Power Company, 37, 106,
    135, 146, 232
Georgia Railroad, 32, 34–35, 254
Georgia Railway & Electric
    Company, 37
Georgia Regional Transportation
    Authority (GRTA), 24, 26, 45,
    95, 123
Georgia STAND-UP (Georgia
    Strategic Alliance for New
    Directions and Unified Policies),
    61, 253, 272
Georgia State University, 162–163,
    197, 270–271 Georgia Tech
  Atlanta Neighborhood Quality of
    Life and Health Project, 150, 151
    (fig.)

BeltLine feasibility study, 51, 59
bike-sharing program, 141
Brian Leary and, 121–122
Ryan Gravel and, 13–14, 49,
    121–122
Technology Square development,
    239
Georgia Works!, 112, 113 (photo), 294
Georgians for Community
    Redevelopment, 93
Gervin, Rachel, 288
Gilbert, Jane, 221
Gilded Age, 66–71
Giornelli, Greg, 29, 45, 53–54, 57, 59
Glenn, Luther, 32
Glenwood Castle (old Atlanta
    Stockade), 194
Glenwood Park neighborhood, 4, 25,
    160
Global Village Project school, 255
Glover, Dwight, 225–226, 284
Glover, Renee, 162
Goat Farm, 227–228, 265
Goatsville, 254
Godshalk, David, 75
Gone with the Wind (Mitchell), 78, 106
Good Hair (film), 234
Gordon, John, 294
Gordon, Lisa, 135, 155
Grady, Henry, 33–34, 67–69
Grady Homes, 192
Grady Hospital, 113, 148, 252
Grant, Lemuel, 35, 192
Grant Park neighborhood, 5, 35, 48,
    76, 81, 126, 192–195
grassroots support, 22–26, 278–279
Gravel, Karen, 22, 29, 186
Gravel, Ryan, 4 (photo)
  Atlanta City Design Project,
    277–278
  on bickering, 164
  Friends of the Belt Line, 28–29, 49,
    91
  on future of BeltLine, 283
  Garvin and, 49
  Inman Park and, 186–187

Gravel, Ryan *(continued)*
  master's thesis, 13–15, 18–22, 19
    (fig.)
  in Paris, 13
  presentation of Belt Line concept,
    22
  resignation from BeltLine
    Partnership board, 274–275, 286
  streetcars, desire/plans for, 9, 15,
    18–23, 51, 280
  tunnel path negotiations, 281
  walks with author (2011–2012),
    3–10
  *Where We Want to Live: Reclaiming
    Infrastructure for a New Generation of
    Cities,* 278–279
Great Fire of 1917, 176
Great Recession, 96–99, 108, 156,
    163, 174, 179, 204, 248, 252, 274
*The Great Reset: How the Post-crash
    Economy Will Change the Way We
    Live and Work* (Florida), 270
green building, 144–146
Griffith, Clayton, 213–214
Griffith, D. W., 76
Griggs, Robert, 182
Grove, Edwin Wiley, 216–217
Grove Park neighborhood, 8, 80, 86,
    214–217, 215 (photo), 271
the Gulch, 25, 44, 101, 103, 233
Gwinnett County, 44, 52, 55–56, 65,
    80–81, 138, 186, 245–250, 277,
    296

Habitat for Humanity, 196, 200, 276
Hagood, Sarah, 232
Hall, Beverly, 164
Hall, Kwanza, 86, 129, 180
Hamilton, Alexander, 192
Hammonds, Otis, 210
Hampton, Lionel, 17
Harper, Charles A., III, 219–220
Harris, Clifford, Jr. (T. I.), 219
Harris, Joel Chandler, 209–210
Harris, Madison, 79
Hartsfield, William B., 79–80

HEALing Community Center, 148
health, 137–153
  bicycling, 140–142
  food deserts, 150–152
  green initiatives, 144–147
  health-impact assessment of
    BeltLine, 152
  inequities, 147–149
  water issues, 142–144
Helms, Ed, 225
The Help (Stockett), 291, 293
Henegar, Walter, 220
Herndon, Adrienne, 69
Herndon, Alonzo, 66–67, 69, 190,
    288
Herndon, Norris, 190
Hess, Nick, 110
High, Harriet Wilson, 239
High Museum of Art, 239
highways, 41–43, 147, 245–246
Hill, Larry, 217–218, 271
Historic District Development
    Corporation, 181
Historic Fourth Ward Park, 10,
    88–90, 126–129
  author's visit to newly completed,
    178
  detention ponds, 143
  development around, 174–175
  land purchase for, 88
Historic Mims Park, 271–272
Holston, Rose, 240
Home Depot, 49, 52, 83, 123, 163,
    270
Home Park neighborhood, 41
homelessness, 6–7, 14, 23, 29, 105,
    107–120, 131, 226, 248, 271
Honderd, Jack, 255
HOPE Atlanta, 110
Hopkins, Charles, 75
Horford, Al, 240
Horgan, Ron and Terry, 226
housing
  affordable housing percentage,
    developers and, 168–169,
    272–274

along BeltLine, 4, 10, 21, 23, 88, 129–130, 274, 279, 282, 285
Beltline Partnership and, 91, 122, 182, 274–275, 284–285
for homeless, 112
mortgage fraud, 98
near Eastside Trail, 129–130, 268
post-WWII, 78–80
public, 6, 29, 78, 81–83, 86, 151, 162, 177, 180, 192–195, 215, 224, 250–251, 284
segregation, 71, 76–78
subsidized for police officers, 272
tax allocation district (TAD) funds and, 61–62, 92, 182, 274–275, 284–285
vacant/abandoned, 98–99, 150, 275
Howell, Clark, 72
Hulsey Rail Yard, 3, 10, 21, 50, 187, 281
Hunter, Floyd, 79
Hunter, Phil, 112
Hurt, Joel, 35–37, 67

Immergluck, Dan, 97
immigrants, 248–249, 250
Imperial Palace (KKK), 76
Inman Park neighborhood, 10, 35, 38, 76, 94, 173, 175
history of, 182
revitalization of, 182–187
Road Fight, 183–184
Victorian-era home, 185 (photo)
Inman Quarter, 184
integration, 80–83, 190–191
internal combustion engine, triumph of, 38–41
Invest Atlanta, 29
see also Atlanta Development Authority
ITP (inside the perimeter), 25, 243, 299

Jack and the Bean Soup (Pendergrast), 202

Jackson, Maynard, 28, 82
Jackson, Richard J., 137–139
Jackson Heights, 76
Jackson Hill, 78
James M. Cox Foundation, 56, 160, 279
Jamestown Properties, 174–175
Jews, 75–76
Jim Crow, 69, 71, 78, 87, 191, 251
jitneys, 40, 250
Johnson, Walter Lee, 79
Johnston, Arian, 221
Johnston, Chuck and JoElyn, 220–222
Johnston, Kathryn, 218, 271
Judicial in Rem, 276

Kaiser Permanente, 127, 152, 161
Katz, Becky, 142
Kaufman, David, 142–143
Keane, Tim, 267, 276–277, 283–284
Kelsey, Moriba, 199
Kennedy, Barbara, 229–230
Kennedy, Jim, 17, 126–127, 160
Kennesaw State College, 226
Kent, Phil, 55, 161
Kessler, Kyle, 264–265
Khalil, Noel, 288
King, Martin Luther, Jr., 63, 78, 80–81, 111
assassination, 190
homes of, 10, 181, 215
I Have a Dream speech, 257
King, Martin Luther, Sr., 78
King Plow Arts Center, 8, 15
KIPP school, 210–211
Knowles, Nia, 161
Koolhaas, Rem, 18
Korda, Michael, 126
Kruse, Kevin, 78, 81
Ku Klux Klan (KKK), 65–66, 72, 76–78, 81, 257
kudzu, 5, 5 (photo), 8, 14, 23, 49

labor camps, 67–68, 68 (photo), 86
Land Use Task Force, 58

Langford, Jim, 47–49, 88–89, 95, 99
Langley, Jane, 56
Lantern Parade, 131, 287–288, 287
    (photo)
Leadership in Energy &
    Environmental Design
    certification (LEED), 253
Leary, Brian, 121–136, 155, 157,
    296
    GDOT lease option, 123
    Kasim Reed and, 126
    on Ponce City Market, 128
    promotion efforts for BeltLine
        project, 123–124
    spending scandal, 134–135, 155
    Strategic Implementation Plan, 135,
        157–158
    tax allocation district (TAD) and,
        122–123
    on T-SPLOST, 133–134
Leinberger, Christopher, 31
Levine, Greg, 146
Lewis John, 102
lighting, 128, 145, 157, 253, 280–281
Lilburn, 246
Lindsay Street Park, 271
Link, William, 66
Little Five Points, 109, 185
Livable Centers Initiative, 247, 252
Lochner, H. W., 42
Lofts at Reynoldstown Crossing, 4,
    130, 159
Long, Saba, 264
Long, Stephen Harriman, 31–32
Loring, Ed, 119
Loring Heights neighborhood, 8
Louisville and Nashville Railroad
    Belt Line, 14, 37
Lupton, Bob, 192–195, 220
Lupton, Dana, 197
lynching, 67, 70, 72, 76

Macon & Western railroad, 32
Macrina, Jo Ann, 143, 283–284
Mad Housers, 109–111
Maddox, Lester, 44, 80

Maddox Park, 8, 48, 215, 217–218,
    217 (photo), 223, 286
Mall of Georgia, 246–247
A Man in Full (Wolfe), 58
mandatory inclusionary zoning, 130,
    272–274
Mansbach, Jodi, 175
MARTA (Metropolitan Atlanta
        Rapid Transit Authority), 24, 161
    African American support, 81–82
    Atlanta Streetcar connection, 166
    BeltLine intersections with, 20, 24,
        50, 59
    in Clayton County, 253
    funding, 44, 281, 283, 285
    in Gwinnett County, 246
    initial plans (1960), 15
    inner core study, 54
    in Perimeter Center, 245
    Ride with Respect campaign, 168
    stations, 44, 50, 168, 210, 212
    transformation of, 168–169
Marthasville, 32
Martin Luther King Center, 125
Martin Luther King Jr. National
        Historic Site, 181, 210
Mason, Keith, 53, 56, 94, 97
Mason, Wayne, 52–59, 62, 86, 93–97,
    126, 245, 279, 282
Masquerade building, 178
Mathews, Joshua, 211
Matthews, Felicia, 179
Mayland Motivators Art Garden, 202
McBrayer, Ed, 16–17, 23–24, 47
    Barbara Kennedy criticisms of, 230
    Fred Yalouris, 127
    funding for BeltLine, 48
    on future of the BeltLine, 280, 281
    Wayne Mason and, 54
    West End trail, 99–101
McCall, Nathan, 177
McCord, Chris, 197
McCrary, Bess, 261
McGahan, Bill, 294
McWilliams, Jeri, 209–210
Meadows, Chuck, 285–286

Mercedes-Benz Stadium, 163, 212, 268

Mercy Care, 113

Metro Atlanta Task Force for the Homeless (Peachtree & Pine), 108, 116–119

Metropolitan Street Railroad Company, 35

Miller, Anthony, 226

Miller, Richard, 264–265

Mills, Jeanne, 203–204

Mims, Livingston, 271

Mitchell, Ceasar, 165

Mitchell, Margaret, 78, 106

Mobility 2030, 28

Monday Night Brewing, 228, 286

Monroe, W. L., 236–237

Montague, Terri
  Eastside Trail, 126–127
  GDOT lease option, 123
  GDOT MMPT project and, 101
  hiring, 91–93
  resignation from ABI, 103–104
  Wayne Mason and, 93–97
  West End trail, 100

Montgomery, Katherine, 229–230

Moore, Charles, 148

Morehouse College, 67, 112, 149, 219, 285

Morningside neighborhood, 41

Morris, Paul, 153, 155–158, 284
  on affordable housing, 275
  Atlanta Public Schools contract, 156
  on Atlanta Streetcar, 166
  on funding, 165–166, 283
  on future of BeltLine, 285
  on importance of personal relationships, 157
  Lantern Parade, 287 (photo), 288

Morris Brown College, 67, 76, 212

Morrison-McBride, Toni, 201–202

Morseberger, Emory, 128

mortgage fraud, 98, 191, 195, 199

Moses, Robert, 127

movie studios, 247–248, 288

Mozley Park, 7, 80, 150

Mufleh, Luma, 255

Multi-Modal Passenger Terminal (MMPT), 101–103, 263, 299

Mumford, Lewis, 105

National Association for the Advancement of Colored People (NAACP), 75, 133, 294

neighborhood planning unit (NPU), 60, 82

neighborhoods
  East Beltline, 173–187
  North Beltline, 225–241
  South Beltline, 189–202
  West Beltline, 203–224
  See also specific neighborhoods

Nelms, John, 73

Ness, Andrea, 206

New South, 33–34

Niggertown, 71

NIMBY (not in my back yard), 100

Norcross, 213, 247–248, 253, 258

Norfolk Southern railroad, 9, 17, 52, 101, 235–236

North American Properties, 269–270, 281

North Beltline neighborhoods, 225–241

Northside BeltLine Trail, 8, 126, 228–230

Northside Tavern, 227

Norwood, Mary, 124

Nygren, Steve and family, 259–262

obesity, 137, 139, 151

Office of Sustainability, 144–145

Oglethorpe, James, 64

Old Fourth Ward neighborhood
  Auburn Avenue, 181–182
  Boulevard corridor, 178–181
  derivation of name, 176
  gentrification of, 176–178
  homelessness in, 109, 111
  impact of Eastside trail on, 173
  Martin Luther King Jr. birthplace, 10

Old Fourth Ward neighborhood
     (continued)
   Mary Porter and, 192
   park plans, 48, 90, 129
   racial issues, 76, 94
   urban gardens, 151
old State Farmers Market (Murphy's
     Crossing), 207, 268, 286
Olmsted, Frederick Law, 35–36, 38,
     49, 238
Olympics (1996), 13, 16–17, 83, 116,
     146, 212, 226, 246, 263
O'Mara, Becky, 205 (photo), 204–205
O'Mara, Tim, 204–205
Omni National Bank, 98
Open Door Community, 108, 116,
     119–120
Ormewood Park neighborhood, 5,
     195
OTP (outside the perimeter), 132,
     173
   Clarkston, 254
   Clayton County, 250–254
   Gwinnett County, 245–250
   Perimeter Center, 244–245
   Serenbe, 259–262
   Stone Mountain, 257–259
Our Kids: The American Dream in Cities
     (Putnam), 148–149
Outcasts United: An American Town, a
     Refugee Team, and One Woman's
     Quest to Make a Difference (St.
     John), 255

Palmer, Chris, 226
Palmer, Howard, 76
Park Pride, 131, 144, 228, 233
Parker, Keith, 168–169
parkland, percentage in American
     cities, 50
parks, connected by BeltLine, 48–52
Partnership for Southern Equity, 274
PATH Force, 159
PATH Foundation, 16–18
   Barbara Kennedy criticisms of,
     229–230

Beltline Partnership and, 55
bike trails, 16–18, 23–24, 47–48,
     99–100, 140
   opposition from Brookwood Hills
     residents, 233
   West End trail, 99–100, 126
Paul, Rod and Bobbie, 183–184
PAWKids, 203, 221
Peachtree Creek, 9, 100
   in Brookwood Hills, 231, 233
   in Collier Hills, 228
   pollution, 142, 230
Peachtree Creek: A Natural and Unnatural
     History of Atlanta's Watershed
     (Kaufman), 142
Peachtree Street, 9, 38, 231, 239,
     263–264
   homeless shelter, 108, 116–120
   racial tensions and, 65, 76, 78
   streetcars on, 25, 35, 125
pedestrians, 13, 17, 20, 23, 38, 44,
     138–140, 155, 158, 227, 238, 251,
     263
PEDS (Pedestrians Educating
     Drivers), 139–140, 227, 232
Peers Reaching Out, 112
Pendergrast, John, 282
Pendergrast, Mark
   autobiographical, 105–107,
     291–294
   BeltLine neighborhood tours,
     173–241
   Outside the Perimeter tours,
     245–265
   visits with the homeless, 110–120
   walking the BeltLine, 3–10
Pendergrast, Nan, 80, 291, 294
Peoplestown neighborhood, 6, 126,
     143, 198
Perdue, Sonny, 124
Perimeter Center, 244–245
Perimeter College, 197
Perimeter Expressway (I-285), 9,
     13, 24, 42, 243–245, 244 (map),
     254
Perry, Egbert, 288

Perry, Heman, 77, 212
Perry, Tyler, 107, 163
Perry Homes, 82, 86, 215, 224
Phagan, Mary, 75
Phoenix City, 33
Piedmont Heights neighborhood, 9, 235–238, 240
Piedmont Hospital, 9, 231–232
Piedmont Park, 10–11, 48–49, 53, 56, 69, 93, 95, 102, 239, 282
Pill Hill, 244
Pittman Park, 199
Pittsburgh neighborhood, 6, 36, 71, 98, 199–202, 206
Pittsburgh: A Sense of Community (Kelsey), 199
Planning Atlanta (book), 276
Plessy v. Ferguson, 71
police, 44, 73–79, 109, 116–119, 124, 150, 159, 168, 180, 200, 212, 214, 218, 230, 232, 240, 248, 255–256, 271–273
pollution, 21, 28
   air, 18, 41, 43, 138, 140, 146–147
   Peachtree Creek, 142, 223, 230
Ponce City Market, 10–11, 128–129, 153, 159 (photo), 174–175, 177, 186, 281
Ponce de Leon Springs, 10, 35, 41
Ponder, Prince, 64
Porter, Danny, 249
Porter, Robert, 190–191
Portland, Oregon, 20–21, 23, 58, 141
Poventud, Angel
   Adair Park home, 205–206
   on involvement, 168
   tunnel path negotiations, 281
   walks with author, 6–10
Powell, Kishia, 284
Power (Korda), 126
press coverage, early, 25–26
private/philantropic donations, 49, 51–52, 56, 89, 158, 160–161, 279, 285
Proctor, Henry Hugh, 75

Proctor Creek, 7, 144, 222–224, 223 (photo), 271
Proctor Park, 223
Promise Zones, 272
public health, 26, 117, 127, 136–153, 286
public transit, 14, 20, 38, 48, 57–58, 168–169, 245–246, 267, 269, 277, 281–282
Pughsley, Willie Mae (Nee), 106, 291–294, 292 (photo), 293 (photo)
Purpose Built Communities, 195
Putnam, Robert, 148–149
Pye, Durwood, 183

Q-Time restaurant, 208–209

racial issues, 63–83
   anti-Semitism, 75–76
   health inequities, 147–149
   housing segregation, 71, 76–78
   Jim Crow, 69, 71, 78, 87, 191, 251
   Ku Klux Klan, 65–66, 72, 76–78, 80–81
   late nineteenth century, 66–71
   post-Civil War period, 64–66
   race riot of 1906, 73–75, 189
   school desegregation, 80–81
   slavery, 64
   voting rights, 65, 68, 79, 81, 254
   white flight, 78–82
Ragsdale, Jack, 208
Ragsdale, Liz, 208
railroads
   belt line, 14, 37
   city growth along tracks, 35
   commuter rail, 101–103
   network in Atlanta, 32–34
   stations, 43–44, 43 (photo)
Rails to Trails Conservancy, 15–16, 18
rapid transit, 24, 50, 59, 168, 254, 277, 282–283
   see also buses, MARTA
Rathbun, Kevin, 176
Reconstruction period, 65

recycling, 6, 120, 145, 196
Reed, Kasim, 124–126, 160–167,
    273–276
  Atlanta Streetcar, 166–167
  BeltLine funding, 160
  on bicycling, 142
  firing of Macrina, 284
  on inclusionary zoning, 273
  Maddox Park, 286
  Peachtree Streetcar project, 125
  redevelopment projects, 162–164,
    270
  Rick Warren and, 275
  Sears building sale, 128
  second term as mayor, 161–164
  sidewalks and, 140
  streetcar funding, 281
  style of, 125–126, 161–162, 164,
    270
  sustainability and, 144–145
  TAD and, 93
  Time Keane and, 276
  T-SPLOST, 132–133
refugees, 254–257
*Regime Politics: Governing Atlanta
    1946–1988* (Stone), 274
Reidy, Lauren, 186
*Retrofitting Suburbia: Urban Design
    Solutions for Redesigning Suburbs*
    (Duham-Jones), 269
reverse migration, 88, 204, 243
Reynoldstown neighborhood, 4, 130,
    159, 187, 281, 285
Rhein, Amanda, 168
Rich, Michael, 274
Rich, Richard, 80–81
Riverdale, 250–254
Rivers, W. S., 251
Road Fight, 183–184
Roark, Randal, 14–15, 22
Robert W. Woodruff Foundation, 56,
    93, 160, 279
Robinson, A. J., 263
Rogers, Will, 88
Rosenberger, Ken and Rose,
    230–231

Rothchild, Jacob, 80
Ruff, Solon, 238
Russell, Herman, 161, 288
Rytter, Chantelle, 131, 287

Salvation Army, 108, 116
Sandy Springs, 244
Saporta, Maria, 25, 163
school desegregation, 80–81
school system, Gwinnett County,
    249
Schroder, Jim, 49
Schwab, Otto, 75
Scott, Deborah, 61, 272
Seaboard Air Line Railway, 14,
    37
Sears, Roebuck and Co., 41, 247
Sears building, 10, 15, 41, 48, 90,
    128–129, 162, 174, 177–178
Seay, Bill and Irene, 236
segregation, 44, 63, 71, 76–79, 81,
    149, 190, 207, 288
Serenbe, 259–262
Serna, Rebecca, 140–141
sewage/storm water system, 28,
    89–90, 142–143, 223
Shekhey, Omar, 256
shelters, 105, 108, 114–120, 271
Sherman, William Tecumseh, 33
Shermantown, 71
Sherwood Forest, 9, 240
Shufeldt, Charlie, 103, 160–161
sidewalks, 137–142, 180, 227, 232,
    238, 240, 253, 260, 283
Sierra Club, 133, 245
Silver Comet Trail, 18
Sisco, Burke, 173
Sjoquist, David, 63
skate park, 10, 129, 159, 175, 253
slavery, 64–69, 78, 189, 259, 272
*Slavery by Another Name: The Re-
    enslavement of Black Americans
    from the Civil War to World War II*
    (Blackmon), 67–68
slum lords, 275
Smith, Hoke, 72

Smith, Nathaniel, 274–275, 286
Snow, Curtis, 218–219
Snow on Tha Bluff (film), 218
solar power, 6, 144–146, 198, 260
Somerhalder, John, 103, 160–161
The Souls of Black Folk (Du Bois), 71–72
South Atlanta neighborhood, 189–197
South Beltline neighborhoods, 189–202
Southeast Atlanta Green Infrastructure Initiative, 143
Southern Banking and Trust Company, 37
Southern Belt Line rail line, 35, 37
Southern Spring Bed Company, 75, 106
Southface Energy Institute, 144–145
Speaks, Donald, 149
Spear, Dorothy, 220
Spelman College, 67, 221
Springvale Park, 184–185
St. John, Warren, 255
Stanton Elementary School, 198
Stanton Park
  see D. H. Stanton Park
Starr, Ashlee and Caleb, 200–202
Steele, Carrie, 66
Stockett, Kathryn, 291
Stokes, Jim and Esther, 233–234
Stone, Clarence, 274
Stone Mountain, 17, 76, 78, 183, 192, 254, 257–259
Storrs School, 65
Street Railway Journal, 36–37
streetcar suburbs, 7, 34–42
streetcars, 91, 100, 102, 109
  Atlanta Streetcar, 158, 166–167, 192, 277, 281
  Brian Leary and, 121–122, 127
  C-Loop, 25
  cost projection, 158
  criticism of plans for, 58–59
  downtown loop, 158, 166–167, 192, 277, 282
  Ed McBrayer and, 280

  electricity for, 36–37
  Fred Yalouris and, 127
  funding, 132–133, 158, 280–281, 281, 285
  history in Atlanta, 34–42, 67
  importance to the BeltLine concept, 282–283
  Joel Hurt and, 67
  Kasim Reed and, 125, 132, 166–167, 281
  Northside Trail, 231–232, 235
  racial tensions and, 67, 73, 79–80
  Ryan Gravel and, 9, 15, 18–23, 51, 280
  in *Strategic Implementation Plan,* 158
  streetcar suburbs, 7, 34–42
  Tim Keane and, 277, 283
  Wayne Mason property and, 58, 94
  Westside Trail, 157–158, 280
Street-to-Home program, 112
Studioplex, 15, 182, 252
suburbs
  automobile transport and, 41–43
  new urbanism in, 269
  streetcar, 34–38
  See also specific locations
subway system, 44
Summerhill neighborhood, 71, 195, 208, 219
sustainability, 144–145
Sutherland, Kit and Stuart, 176–177
Sutton, Starling, 14–15, 182
Suwanee, 246–247
Swaney, Lee, 255–256
Sweet, John and Midge, 183
SweetWater Brewing Company, 9, 235–236
SweetWater Design District, 236
Sylvan Hills, 41
Syphoe, Michael, 252–253

Tanyard Creek, 8, 100, 103, 126, 142–143, 228
Tanyard Creek Park, 229
Tapp, Helen, 99

tax allocation district (TAD), 54,
    58–62
  affordable housing and, 61–62, 92,
    182, 274–275, 284–285
  Alycen Whiddon and, 26–27, 29,
    47
  Atlanta Public Schools and, 93,
    156, 164–166, 284–285
  authorization, 85, 89
  poor acceptance of issue, 97, 99,
    122–123
  revenue projections, 156, 165
  tenth anniversary, 155
  voter referendum (2008), 93
  Woodham opposition to TAD
    bonds, 90–93, 156, 164
Tax Allocation District Advisory
  Committee (TADAC), 96, 103
Teasley, William, 198
Terminal Station, 43–44, 43 (photo),
  191, 264
Terminus, 31–32, 64
Terry, Ted, 256
Thadani, Dhiru, 271
Them (McCall), 177
TIGER (Transportation Investment
  Generating Economic Recovery)
  grant, 125, 157, 160, 280
Toro, Mark, 123, 168–169, 269–270
Torpy, Bill, 243
Toton, Sarah, 194
Toxic Charity: How Churches and Charities
  Hurt Those They Help (and How to
  Reverse It) (Lupton), 193
traffic problems, 18, 39–42, 45, 60,
  107, 132, 140–141, 167–168, 236,
  243, 245–246, 277, 282
transit-oriented development (TOD),
  168, 235
Travon Wilson Park, 252
Trees Atlanta, 128, 146, 175, 232,
  239
Trolley Barn, 185
trolleys, 34–41
  see also streetcars
Trubey, J. Scott, 243

Truly Living Well, 151
Trust for Public Land (TPL), 16,
  47–52, 88–89
  Emerald Corridor LLC, 144
  land acquisition strategy, 99
  Proctor Creek and, 223
  Wayne Mason, negotiation with, 95
T-SPLOST, 132–134, 233, 281, 283
Tuggle, Florine, 293
Turner, Henry McNeal, 65, 69, 71
Turner Field, 144, 162, 270, 277
Tuskegee Institute, 70

Underground Atlanta, 44, 162,
  263–265, 270, 277
Union Depot, 43–44, 74
United Way Regional Commission on
  Homelessness, 112, 114
Up Ahead: A Regional Land Use Plan for
  Metropolitan Atlanta, 42–43
Upper Chattahoochee Riverkeeper,
  143
Urban Parks and Open Spaces (Garvin),
  48

Veiled Visions: The 1906 Atlanta Race
  Riot and the Reshaping of American
  Race Relations (Godshalk), 75
Vine City neighborhood, 163, 215,
  270–272, 288, 294
Virginia-Highland neighborhood, 41,
  94, 176–177
voting rights, 65, 68, 79, 81, 254
Vulcan Material Company, 51, 85–87

Wakefield, Kakhi, 230
Walton, Shawn, 204
Warbington, Chuck, 245–247
Wardlaw, B., 116
Warren, Rick, 275–276
Washington, Booker T., 70, 71, 75
Washington Park neighborhood, 7,
  48, 77, 157, 211–214
water system, 142–143, 225–226
Waters, Lucius, 208
watersheds, 35, 142–144, 222

Waterworks Park, 227 (illustration), 228, 284

Wedemeyer, Micah, 194

Weeks, Ray, 55–60, 85–86, 89, 91, 93, 278–279
    Atlanta BeltLine Inc. (ABI) creation, 91
    Bellwood Quarry purchase, 86
    editorial (2008), 93
    funding, 160–161
    on future of the BeltLine, 279
    GDOT MMPT project, 102–103
    importance to BeltLine project, 278–279

West Beltline neighborhoods, 203–224

West End neighborhood, 34, 80, 98, 100–101, 109, 130, 157, 161, 207–211

West End Trail, 101, 126, 201

West Highlands, 86

Western & Atlantic railroad, 32

Westside Future Fund, 270–272

Westside Park, 8, 87–88, 144, 223–224, 286

Westside Trail, 11, 271
    cost, 157, 280
    development along, 286
    funding, 157, 160–161, 280
    groundbreaking, 206
    linking to Eastside, 285
    streetcar preparations, 280
    TIGER grant, 157

Westside Works, 213, 271

Westview neighborhood, 7, 98, 210

Westview Cemetery, 126, 210, 211 (photo)

Weyandt, Tom, 22, 162

Wheatley, Thomas, 265

Where We Want to Live: Reclaiming Infrastructure for a New Generation of Cities (Gravel), 278–279

Whiddon, Alycen, 18, 23, 26–30, 47, 53

White, Hilary, 261

white flight, 78–82, 88, 191, 193, 204, 208, 247

White Flight: Atlanta and the Making of Modern Conservatism (Kruse), 78

Wiggins, Kevin, 98

Wilbanks, Alvin, 249

Wilburn, Leila Ross, 98

Wilson, Princess, 177–178

Wilson, Valarie, 93, 130–131, 285

WIMBY (wanted in my back yard), 101

Winn Park, 240

Wolfe, Tom, 58

Woodard, Tracy, 110–111

Woodham, John, 90–93, 122, 156, 164

Woodruff, Robert, 79, 81

Woodruff Arts Center, 239

Woolard, Cathy, 23–29, 48, 52, 160, 280

Wren's Nest, 209–210

Wright, Richard R., 65, 69

Wynn-Dixon, Evelyn, 251–253

Yalouris, Fred, 127, 131

Young, Andrew, 28, 82–83

Youngblood, Mtamanika, 55, 181–182

Zero Mile Post, 31–32

zoo, 35, 193–194

Betty Molnar

Atlanta native Mark Pendergrast is the author of critically acclaimed nonfiction books, including (among others) *For God, Country and Coca-Cola; Uncommon Grounds; Inside the Outbreaks; Mirror Mirror; Beyond Fair Trade;* and *Victims of Memory.* His work has been translated into a dozen languages. He has traveled the world to research his books, but for *City on the Verge* he came full circle, returning to the city of his birth. He lives in Colchester, Vermont, and welcomes contact through his website, www.markpendergrast.com.